CW01081988

END OF A BERLIN DIARY

END OF A BERLIN DIARY

William L. Shirer

RosettaBooks®

Copyright © 1947 by William L. Shirer

ISBN: 978-0-7953-0091-2

To the memory of my mother, who died in our little Iowa town while I was on my last assignment in Germany

FOREWORD

The notes that made up the book *Berlin Diary* ended in December 1940, when I left Germany to return to my native land. The Third Reich, which Hitler had boasted would last a thousand years, was at that excruciating moment at the zenith of its brutal power. The Master Race had conquered most of Europe and made slaves of its stunned inhabitants. The extermination of the Jews and other peoples was under way. So were plans to turn on Russia, finish gallant Britain, and then go on, with Japan, to conquer the world by bringing the United States to heel.

When I came home from Berlin at Christmas time in 1940, I found most of my fellow countrymen unaware of what Hitler was really up to and somewhat confused as to how he had accomplished his evil designs. Some Americans didn't much care. Since it had been my lot to witness Europe's agony at first hand, I collected some of my notes in a book for the edification of such citizens as cared to read it.

This book of notes is, in a way, a sequel to *Berlin Diary*. It is the end of my own small contribution to the Berlin story. There was a great deal, of course, that a reporter had not been able to learn in the frenzied Nazi capital beyond the Elbe. The sinister plots, the fateful decisions, that had plunged the world into such awful horror and misery had been made in secret. And what had really gone on in Germany after I left? Had defeat and collapse solved the German problem—at least for the rest of our lifetime?

After the war's end I went back to Berlin to try to find out. I prowled the obscene ruins of the once proud capital and talked with the remnants of the *Herrenvolk*. At Nuremberg, amidst the debris of the lovely medieval town, I saw the surviving leaders of the Nazi gangster world, who had wielded such monstrous power so arrogantly when last I beheld them, finally brought to justice. Most important of all, I had access to a good part of the fourteen hundred tons of secret German documents that the Allies had captured intact. You will find the essential portions of many of them in this book. I have been content to let the German authors tell in their own inimitable words the dark and almost unbelievable tale of their savagery and deceit. Had these secret archives of the German government been destroyed, as the Nazis intended them to be, much of the truth about our weird period in history would have been buried forever. Now it is here for those who care to learn it.

I have also tried to include in this book the thread of another story—the story of the beginning of the Peace. Reader, you and I have already forgotten the fleeting moment of glory and man's magnificent sense of dedication the day peace descended on this wretched earth. I know that erring mortals cannot remain on the heights for long. But these notes, scribbled down at the time, may help to remind you that many on our side achieved those heights after the war's bloody struggles had brought out their inhuman courage, their bravery, and their wonderful fortitude. At San Francisco, for a flicker of time when the United Nations was being born, I saw the high hopes, the noble purpose, the patient understanding of the men of our world seeking to find a way to permanent peace.

Where and when and how did their hopes start to turn to stone? In these day-to-day notes, perhaps, you will see how the dark cloud, which presently envelops us, grew.

Finally, this book is a record of the most momentous year any of us have ever lived through. Have you forgotten what it was like—the year of Our Lord 1945—when the Nazi and Jap barbarians were finally destroyed and the terrible carnage ended and peace came, and ingenious men burst the atom and a new age, for better or worse, was suddenly upon us?

New York
May 1947

END OF A BERLIN DIARY

PART I
BEGINNING OF THE PEACE

WLS

New York, *Thursday, July* 20, 1944

Someone threw a bomb at Hitler, but Berlin claims he escaped with only minor injuries. The luck of the man! Still… is it not the beginning of the end?

Lake Placid, *Thursday, July* 25

The mountains and the lake and the clear air and the smell of pines and the wild laughter of the kids and all the comfortable, well-off folk—and the bloody war so far away.… My musician friends came over to the cottage to play chamber music and sip beer. They played Mozart's Quartet in F Major for oboe and strings—one of my great favorites. The oboe-player, a youngster from the St. Louis Symphony Orchestra, who kept telling me that oboe-players usually end up in the lunatic asylum, was magnificent—and quite sane.

New York, *Sunday, August* 20

Tomorrow at Dumbarton Oaks, an old Washington colonial mansion lately used by Harvard for early Christian and medieval research, there will be held the first of the most important international conferences that we shall ever see in my lifetime. Representatives of the United States, Britain, and Russia will sit down and attempt to do what human beings have never been able—in their monumental foolishness—to do in the long and sorry history of the human race: prevent war by collective action.… The time is late. Another war, with its giant rockets and flying bombs—will no doubt finish the human race. This is probably our last chance to save ourselves!

New York, *Wednesday, August* 23

Paris, the glory of France, as Montaigne said, has been liberated!…

New York, *Sunday, August* 27

Berlin is trying to frighten us with tall talk about an atomic bomb. Scientists do say that the explosive force released by splitting the atom is more deadly than any hitherto discovered. But a scientist who knows a great deal about the atom—Theodore Svedberg, a Swede and Nobel prize-winner for his work with atoms—said last week: "Talk about the atom bomb is so much hooey."

New York, *Sunday, September* 10

The Battle of Germany has begun! Today—for the first time in history, I believe—American artillery shells began hitting German soil.

New York, *Monday, September* 18
The Germans at last are facing something all of them—from generals to peasants—have feared above everything else for the last century: an all-out attack on the Fatherland from the east and the west. That they will fight tenaciously and even fanatically cannot now be doubted. But if you study the writings of the great German generals from Clausewitz down to the generals of this war, you will find that they, at least, never believed it possible for Germany to survive the ordeal of a two-front war....

New York, *Friday, September* 29
The Russian phase of the World Security Conference at Dumbarton Oaks has ended.... From what I hear, there has been a wide divergence in the approach of the Soviets and ourselves to the whole problem of the peace structure....

London, *Friday, October* 6
It bucks you up to be back in battered, brave, grimy London even if it is just a stopover place on your way back to Germany, where you saw the war start and where—sooner or later—you will see it end, though not exactly as the Master Race calculated.

London seems as unshakable as ever. There is a stamina in its stout, smoke-covered walls and in its people that is incredible. Bruised though it is, and may be again, no doubt, it will go on until the end of time—one of the great cities of the world.

London, *Sunday, October* 8
Judith phoned at noon and said Wendell Willkie had died. This came as a great shock. I had written him a kidding note about his illness a few days before I left New York. Since returning home, I had come to have a warm affection for him and I liked what he stood for in America.

I wonder if Willkie ever solved his great dilemma: what to do before the election? He often spoke of how Dewey's election would be a "catastrophe." He wanted to remain effective in American political life; he wanted to keep the following of five million or so voters who stood for the things he did. If he came out against Dewey too flatly, he used to argue, they might conclude it was a case of sour grapes at his not having received the nomination. We often discussed it through the night.

London, *Monday, October* 9
Details of Dumbarton Oaks published in today's newspapers. The new League of Nations—man's last chance perhaps?—will be called simply "The United Nations"

and it will have the teeth the League lacked, being empowered to take such air, land, or naval action as will be "necessary to maintain or restore international peace and security."

Paris, *Thursday, October* 19

At last!

And how different *this*Paris from the one I last saw in the tragic June days of 190 (how distant they seem!) when I came in with the German army. The streets and the great boulevards were deserted then, the shutters down, the shops, cafés, and bistros closed. The streets belonged to the strutting Prussians. Today the pest is gone, the streets animated and full of bustling French, free again and drinking in lustily their freedom….

Verdun, *Monday, November* 6

A pouring rain, the mud outside ankle-deep, the barracks bitterly cold and lacking even latrines—why could the French, who built this camp after the last war, not give their soldiers more decent quarters? …This is headquarters of 12th Army Group, comprising the Third, First, and Ninth armies.

Curious, coming back to Verdun, the glory of France in the last war though it was a ghastly graveyard. Do you remember the last time you were here, the June days many years ago, bicycling with Camille?

Already—1926 it was—the grass was beginning to grow where there had been such massive, savage slaughter, and you two had looked on the "sacred trench" where the bayonets of the poilus had stuck out after they had been buried alive by what one shell had done, and on the ruins of Forts Douaumont and Vaux, where courageous Frenchmen had hurled back the flower of the Crown Prince's army—you had looked on them as museum pieces, relics of the last great war of our time.

The last great war! And for you two, you thought, there would be always peace and always June days in the country like this, you idiots, with the wondrous June evenings and a friendship turning to love, maybe, now that summer was come.

Spa, Belgium, *Tuesday, November* 7

Here Hindenburg and Ludendorff on September 9, 1918, came to call on the Kaiser at his quarters in the Hotel Britannica to tell him that the jig was up, the war lost—the very Hotel Britannica that I found this evening, after stumbling through the blacked-out streets, to be the headquarters of General Hodges, commander of the U.S. First Army.

Aachen, Germany, *Wednesday, November* 8

I came back to Germany today for the first time since the end of 190, when I had left Berlin. Then I had said to myself: "I never want to see this city again or this German country or these German people." But fate—and your job—would have it otherwise.

I saw these people again today—a few of them—and a tiny corner of their land and this former Imperial city. There is not much left of the city but a mass of rubble. The people, once so arrogant, once so sure of world mastery, are a sorry specimen to behold. Beaten they are; whipped. And they know it and proclaim it, as they dig in the rubble and, as night comes, crawl down to their holes in the cellars.

My first impressions of this day will go into a dispatch to the *New York Herald Tribune* syndicate, which must be written first, since my deadline is tonight:

Here in the city of Charlemagne, where your correspondent once heard Adolf Hitler boast that his Third Reich would last a thousand years, if not longer, one can see Nazism dead amongst the ruins.

Bent and broken Germans of all ages, but mostly old, dig in the debris which is all there is left of this once proud city of 160,000 inhabitants. American artillery thunders from behind the town and shells explode in the German lines not far away. Occasionally a German shell comes over, adding its might to the utter destruction of this German town. Civilians, a little shell-shocked still from the bombardment and bombings and shocked, too, that the war which Hitler waged so long in distant lands should return to lay waste to their German homes, pause in their digging to curse "the brown pest," meaning the Nazis. They dig and curse, and as night falls they crawl down to their cellar holes, dark and cold and damp, to prepare a sparse evening meal.

Pitiful specimens of humanity, you think. And yet I saw them in this same historic town exactly four years ago. They were not bent or broken or shell-shocked then. They did not curse the "brown pest" then. They cheered it. For it had, they thought—and some of them admitted it to me today—won them a great war. Swastika flags flew from their windows and the citizens greeted one another with a resounding "Heil Hitler!"

Today when Hitler is mentioned it is with a curse. And for a very simple reason. He has brought ruin to Germany—ruin they never dreamed was possible four years ago....

Paris, *Saturday, November* 11

This has been a memorable day—and, for once, a happy one—in my life!

In my younger days I had often gone over to the Champs-Élysées on Armistice Day, walked up the broad avenue to the Arc de Triomphe, glimpsed the eternal flame burning over the Tomb of the Unknown Soldier under the arch, and watched the French troops parade past the great crowds. Usually it would be a raw, dark, drizzly autumn day, and as the years went by and memories faded, the event was not so memorable as it once had been. One forgot so much: the dead in the war and why they died.

My own generation, nurturing its cynicism, did not believe in war. It was pretty sure the dead of 191-18 had died in vain. If that unknown fellow under the great tomb were alive, he would agree, we thought. It was all for nothing, his sacrifice. Look at our slimy, selfish, quarreling, crooked, putrid world. Was it any better for all the dead men in the war? The unknown one—if you were honest about it—hadn't had a choice anyway. Probably he had not had the slightest wish to make the sacrifice of himself. Maybe he had even found life worth living. He had been drafted away, like everyone else in France, given a gun, and ordered to the front. Then a bullet or a shell splinter had stopped him, toppling him over into the mud. A great accident had made him a hero, albeit an unidentified one. And homage to him had become a cult—especially on the Eleventh of November each year.

But each year, I seemed to notice, less people turned out on the Champs-Élysées on Armistice Day. They stayed at home and got caught up on their sleep, or played with their kids or maybe went out to a bistro or a café or a bar and got drunk and picked up a girl. It got to be more and more like that. Finally I stopped turning out altogether. The hell with these war holidays....

But today the true glory of the day was restored. Standing in the crowd of a million Parisians who lined the Champs-Élysées from the Arc de Triomphe to the Place de la Concorde, an American could *feel* the resurrection of a great nation and of the people who belonged to it. It is difficult to describe with any accuracy the emotions of a great mass of human beings assembled in the street. But if you remembered what they had been through, the betrayal by their own leaders, the four years of slavery under the German savages, and then suddenly the liberation by their friends, you could begin to understand.

At first, during the early morning when they were gathering on the avenue, they struck me as being in a subdued state of excitement. They had to pinch themselves to believe that what they were doing and seeing this day, what they *were*—free again—was all true. They chatted quietly or not at all—and stood and waited.

Then suddenly something happened. All the pent-up feelings of years exploded. I don't think I had ever seen this before. It was just before the traditional hour of eleven a.m. Down toward the Place de la Concorde we heard the cheers break out. But it wasn't ordinary cheering. It was a mighty roar—even in the distance. Where I was, nobody knew why. Some snooty-looking limousines were slowly making their way up the avenue. De Gaulle would be in the first one, standing stiffly and saluting. He was popular because of what he had done. But he was not the sort of man to set crowds afire.

And then we knew. The cars approached. De Gaulle was in the first one all right, standing stiffly and saluting. It was what was at his side that set the sparks off. Standing at his side was Winston Churchill, his cherubic face lit up as I have never seen it before, his hands waving majestically to right and left. At this moment he became, for the moment, a great symbol to these people, the symbol of France's liberators. And because not a single one of the million people had expected to see him at this instant, the complete surprise and the lightning-sure recognition of the man they knew as the one who, above all others, had saved them, touched off the explosive materials that had lain long and deep in all of them. For security reasons—so that the Germans would not try to sneak through a fighter bomber or two—the public had not been told that Churchill was in Paris or even in France.

At the sight of him there was bedlam. Now you could really see human beings mad with joy. They shouted wildly, gripped by a wonderful hysteria. They shouted and stamped and gesticulated and crawled on one another so that their eyes would not lose view of the man. After he passed, there was a reaction. Several around me were in tears.... Gratitude is not very plentiful in this world; but today the French, who are not noted for it, had it. Probably it would not last. Woodrow Wilson had been received like this in Milan and Rome after the last war; less than a year later the Italians were cursing him as a dirty betrayer. Churchill's fate might be similar. Today it did not seem to matter. The present was too overwhelming.

In the afternoon Sonia and I motored out to Compiègne Forest. There was to be a little ceremony there I wanted very much to see. I had seen the last one in this forest. I had been present that black day of June 22, 190, when the Germans had dictated their armistice to France. Through the car windows of the little old French *wagon-lit*coach where the first armistice had been signed at five a.m. on November 11, 1918, I had watched the sickening ceremony. The Germans had been very arrogant, some of the French had cried, and I had very nearly lost all hope. But not all. Maybe I shall yet live to see the day, I permitted myself recklessly to think, when the Germans and French will again be back in this rickety old Pullman coach. And the third time will be like the first. It did not seem probable, but it could happen. History was so full of fantastic reverses. And Europeans, when they were on top, were so short-sighted.

On the late afternoon of June 22, four years ago, it had been my lot to be the first to broadcast to the world the news that France had signed the armistice and was, for the time being anyway, finished. It had begun to sprinkle soon after the broadcast. I had walked out to the clearing to glimpse the sky. An army of German engineers, shouting lustily, had already started to move the armistice car.

"Where to?" I had asked.

"To Berlin," they had said.

It had indeed been moved to Berlin and shown to all the gawking *Herrenvolk* as a symbol of their great revenge and their high triumph. Then an Allied bomb had destroyed it. Perhaps—I always liked to think—the superstitious Teutons had seen an evil omen in its destruction. Already the victory that seemed so certain in 190 had begun to slip away.

It was nearly dusk when Sonia and I arrived at the little clearing of Rethondes in the Compiègne Forest. Some three thousand people, mostly from the neighboring villages, had gathered there. There was a platoon of French and another of American troops and a scattering of officials. I recognized the bearded face of old Jules Jeanneney, who had been president of the Senate and who had refused to go along with the perfidies of Pétain and Laval.

The clearing itself looked bare except for the statue of Foch in one corner. For some reason the Huns had spared it. All the other monuments they had dynamited and removed. Grass grew over the spot where the French monument to Alsace-Lorraine had been. It was in front of this one that I had watched Hitler step out of his car on the first afternoon of the June armistice negotiations. He had had it covered with German war flags so that he and his gang would not have to gaze upon the Allied sword sticking into a large, limp eagle that represented Imperial Germany in 1918. He did not want to see that nor read the lettering, which said: "To the Heroic Soldiers of France—Defenders of the Country and of Right—Glorious Liberators of Alsace-Lorraine."

But there was another monument that I was chiefly interested in. I saw at once—and to my joy—that it had been restored, hastily and temporarily, to be sure, in wood and canvas. When I had last seen it, it was a great granite block standing some three feet above ground in the center of the clearing. The day of Hitler's greatest triumph he had scrambled up on it with his short little legs and stared defiantly and in anger at the eloquent words:

"HERE ON THE ELEVENTH OF NOVEMBER 1918 SUCCUMBED THE CRIMINAL PRIDE OF THE GERMAN EMPIRE—VANQUISHED BY THE FREE PEOPLES WHICH IT TRIED TO ENSLAVE."

"Hitler reads it…" I had noted in my diary that day, "standing there in the June sun and the silence. I look for the expression on his face…. I have seen that face many times at the great moments of his life. But today! It is afire with scorn, anger, hate, revenge, triumph. He steps off the monument and contrives to make even this gesture a masterpiece of contempt. He glances back at it, contemptuous, angry—angry, you almost feel, because he cannot wipe out the awful, provoking lettering with one sweep of his high Prussian boot…."

He had had it dynamited a few days later. But there, in the crisp autumn dusk of this evening, four and a half years later, it stood again! Though an officious American M.P. tried to wave me aside, I went over to reread the wonderful words. How could you explain to an empty-headed M.P. what they meant?

The sun had gone down behind the trees and it was getting dark. Suddenly into the clearing scampered nine youth of the Resistance in white shorts and shirts. They bore a flaming torch. It had been lit at eleven this morning from the flame over the Tomb of the Unknown Soldier and carried by relays of runners the sixty miles from Paris. Now it was applied to nine pyres that had been set up around the little monument before which I stood. I had scarcely been able to read the lettering because of the darkness. Now the words showed plainly in the crackling light of the burning pyres. The little clearing in the dark forest was aglow. For a time no one spoke. The silence was eloquent. In a way, this was atonement, a purification. Everyone seemed to feel it. Words, however noble, would be superfluous. Yet there would have to be some. I could see old Jeanneney, his white hair and beard looking silvery in the flickering light, begin to stir and clear his voice. André Diethelm, Minister of War, was beside him. He would have to orate too.

"Let's go," I whispered to Sonia.

I took her arm and led her out. We stumbled through the trees in the darkness, found our car, and headed back to Paris.

Paris, *Wednesday, November* 22

Over to the Assembly in the Luxembourg Palace today to see what it was like. De Gaulle made the principal speech. He is a pretty fair speaker, but as a man very formal and stiff. And he talks too much about *"la grandeur de la France,"* about France being once again "a great world power," about "the glorious victory of La France."

France had grandeur and will have it again; and it will again be a world power. France is not only a nation; it's an idea, a civilization, a way of life. In our semibarbaric world we need it badly. But you do not make a nation a great power by *saying* it is one, nor do you restore its grandeur by talking. One cannot tell one's French friends this; they are too sensitive just now. All except a young writer, Camus, who in the most lucid editorials I have ever read in any newspaper in any language tries in his newspaper *Combat* to bring Frenchmen down to earth.

Paris, *Thursday, November* 23

Thanksgiving, and I celebrated it at an all-British party that Tedder (Air Chief Marshal Sir Arthur William), Deputy Supreme Allied Commander, invited me to at his villa at Versailles this evening. A mere youth as top generals go, he turned out to be a very interesting and intelligent fellow.... I learned much....

U.S. First Army Front, Western Germany, *Tuesday, November* 28

The skies were clearing as Lee [Stowe] and I set off for the front line this morning. You could see swarms of medium bombers and fighters racing over and unloading on the German lines just ahead. Our scout planes—Piper cubs—cruised up and down, sometimes five at a time, spotting for our artillery and looking for signs of enemy movement. Our artillery was making a hell of a noise, especially some big mortars firing from near by. We found First Division headquarters considerably farther forward than when I had last visited it. The division was fighting for the town of Langerwehe and we set off to find it, but never did. German mortar fire on our roads was getting very accurate and it was slow going, unless you were in a hurry to get killed. We finally got up to a company headquarters in the cellar of a farmhouse in a ruined hamlet. Some infantry fighting was going on just ahead, but the youthful officers, wiser and more experienced than we, I suppose, would not let us budge farther. Strange how little you saw of actual infantry fighting even when you got up to a company in the line.

We were sent back to battalion headquarters in a village school. In the courtyard a platoon was setting up light mortars. Someone had somehow plotted where the enemy was and soon the tiny little guns were sounding off. It was very impersonal, this part of the fighting. The Germans seemed a long way off. You could not see them. You could not even see where your shells were landing. They went over a wooded hill—probably several wooded hills. Where they hit was just a place on a grimy map. Someone on the other end of a field telephone corrected your aim. Probably even he didn't see much. He had someone up in an observation plane seeing for him and telling over the radio what he saw.

That day about noon the company up ahead had taken forty-two prisoners. They were standing in front of the school looking very beaten and dilapidated—mostly old or very young men. One youngster said he was fifteen; another thirteen. There were also two women prisoners.

Late that afternoon, when the prisoners had been marched farther back to get them out of range of German mortar fire, our people asked Lee and me to help in the interrogation since we spoke German. It was an enlightening but not a very happy experience. Most of the Germans merely repeated Goebbels's stock propaganda phrases, like parrots. This made Lee boil and at one juncture, when one bespectacled, middle-aged kraut told of how cruel the Russian troops were and how beautifully the German army had behaved in Russia and asked why we didn't stop fighting the Germans and help the Germans fight Russians, Lee, who had been with the Russian Army in '2 and seen what the Nazi barbarians had perpetrated in Russia, shouted angrily at the miserable little man. Lee was plenty mad, but I could not share his anger. The guy merely depressed me and made me sad. Nothing, apparently, would ever change a squarehead. These Germans believed they were fighting a righteous war and that, what was more, they would win it.

"How in hell can you win it?" I said to the bespectacled one. He had been a bookkeeper at I.G. Farben, he had said.

"Secret weapons," he rejoined. You could see he actually believed it. "The Führer has promised them," he said smugly.

I was interested in the two girl prisoners and we took them into a separate room in the farmhouse to question them. They turned out to be Russians. Nineteen years old they said they were. Their names were Zoya and Dusya and they came from the village of Zumy near Kharkov, they said. When the Germans had come to the Ukraine they were sixteen. Like millions of other Russians, they had been carted off to Germany to be slaves.

Zoya spoke fairly fluent German. She had learned it in school in Russia, she said, and had had considerable practice the last three years in Germany. She had a frightful tale to tell—the tale of the twentieth-century slave under the Hun. It is too long to tell here, but I must get in a word or two.

At first, she said, the Germans had put them to work on a farm. The work was hard, the hours long, the food hardly enough to keep them on their feet. And always the German farmer, she said, was either trying to beat them or rape them—usually both. In the end they ran away. Picked up in a near-by city, they were put to work in a textile factory.

Wages? Two dollars a month. Food? A daily diet of spinach. On Sundays, potatoes. Never meat. Shelter? Five hundred Russian waifs jammed into an abandoned warehouse. If they were lucky, it might be a schoolhouse. But the years in the mill were the best, Zoya explained. As British and American troops approached Germany from the west, the Russian girls were taken from the textile works and shipped in cattle cars toward the front. In the towns behind the German lines they were literally treated as slaves on the auction block. I asked her what she meant.

They would be herded into a schoolhouse or the town hall, she explained. German farmers, local manufacturers, and army officers would come and state their needs to the overseer: "I need ten girls for the harvest," a farmer would say. "If I am to keep my factory going, I must have thirty of these Russian wenches immediately," the little manufacturer would say. An army captain would demand fifty girls to shovel debris in a town under American artillery fire. And the girls would be given to them, turned over like slaves. Zoya and Dusya had been given to the captain of a company that held the town we took today. When most of the company had cleared out as the Americans started to surround it, the two girls had hidden in a cellar. They had nearly been killed when a squad of GI's, mindful of German treachery, had flushed it out with a couple of hand-grenades.

But now they were alive and they wanted to go back to Russia, they said. The American officer in charge was a little embarrassed.

"This one isn't in the books," he grunted. Outside, a battery of mortars was firing away, raising an awful rumpus and shaking the floor. "It doesn't say here what to do with dames you capture. But damned if I'll put them back with the krauts."

Paris, *Friday, December* 1

December here already, 1944 gone in a month, time racing by, but the war (almost) at a standstill in the west; my life at a standstill (almost)—like everybody else's....

Paris, *Monday, December* 4

Lunch with Yvonne, an old sweetheart of eighteen years ago. Time had changed her looks remarkably little, but it had done a lot otherwise to us both, I felt....

Paris, *Tuesday, December* 5

Ran into Erika Mann, back from both Alsace and Aachen. She is convinced, she says, that the Germans today are all schizophrenics. I agree. But what must her feeling be, and that of her father, one of the world's great writers, since they too are German and those people are theirs? Gorky, in exile, hated the Czarist regime, but he loved the Russian people and believed in them. But Thomas Mann? He detests what the German people have become under Nazism. A strange and tragic situation.

A half hour's talk this morning with General Eisenhower out at SHAEF at Versailles. He did not seem so jaunty as when he briefed us two or three weeks ago. Nevertheless, he was full of confidence. The Germans, he admitted, had had time to regroup and re-form their army in the west, strengthen their fortifications in the Siegfried Line and behind it, and were resisting stubbornly. But we were wearing them down with our preponderance of artillery and air power.

We had a long discussion, which became almost philosophical at times, as to the limit of German endurance, but agreed that no man could calculate that limit. The Germans might crack tomorrow, or not for months. He himself, he said, did not see any signs of crack-up on the German home front or in the army....

Eisenhower is really the head of a titanic organism that makes the largest corporations in the world seem small potatoes. He seems to have a great deal of executive ability, is cool, and of course has done wonders in making the British and Americans work as a team. This is a truly great accomplishment, for our people do not take naturally to the British. You feel this throughout our army, though Eisenhower will not stand for its becoming troublesome.

I doubt, though, whether our people at home or the British realize that this Allied army of the west is largely American. The British did a fine job in getting Antwerp (fine, but slow; Montgomery, contrary to the myth, is most cautious). Most of our officers at the front feel the British are tired and that the offensive drive must come, and does come, from us.

This has been a most busy day for me. At four went to Mme Bradley's to talk over who would publish *Berlin Diary* in France. Later some of the writers of the Resistance came in. First, Vercors, author of *Le Silence de la mer,* a tense, dark-haired, slightly built fellow in his middle thirties. He told some wonderful stories of the hazards of publishing clandestinely under the Nazis. Some of them were funny and we laughed. But the events themselves, I kept thinking, were not so funny when they had occurred. These writers had risked their necks, not to mention hideous torture, in order to publish the things—poems, essays, short stories, novelettes, reportages—that would maintain the integrity and self-respect of French letters and, more important, of French men and women under the German heel.

Far too many French authors had made their peace with Hitler's New Order and were writing what the new masters found pleasing. Unless the voice of the real France were heard, the real France would die and pass out of the world's experience forever. The voice was heard, and many a French writer or artist was tortured because he spoke out, and some were murdered by the Teutonic barbarians and their French stooges. Jacques Decour, co-founder of *Les Lettres françaises*, a heroic underground magazine of French letters in which some of the greatest spirits of France poured out their poetry and their prose and defied the Germans to suppress them, was caught by the Huns and shot. Saint-Paul Roux, the symbolist, and Max Jacob, poet, painter, and Jew, were snuffed out by the Gestapo. Jean Giraudoux, one of France's most eminent writers, was probably poisoned by the Germans. At least, his friends think he was.

In our time in France, then, an incorruptible writer had to have guts unless he remained silent. It was an experience that our writers in America had never had. And though you were glad they had been spared it, still you could not help thinking that to have had more of a test of courage and integrity than their experience of the war in America gave them might have had certain salutary effects, at that. The itch for big money might not have been so strong, the call of Hollywood not quite so alluring. Going to the war was a test, of course, and many went; but many did not. Some of the Broadway dramatic critics, for example, whose personal knowledge of the excruciatingly brutal life of our times was confined, geographically, to the Fifty-second Street bars and the dimmed White Way of New York City and who panned the war plays inanely, for the most part, because war and what war did to people, especially this savage Nazi-Jap war, was wholly outside their peaceful and limited experience....

We talked until seven fifteen and then I raced away to keep a dinner engagement with the Bonnets at the Hotel Bristol, Henri having just been named French Ambassador to the United States. Vincent-Auriol,[1] the Socialist leader, came in for dinner with his wife, and there was much good talk.... Auriol was reassuring on the French attitude toward Germany—reassuring because most Socialists, especially in London but also here, are a little woolly-eyed on the subject. They refuse to learn from history or experience and already are talking about "rebuilding Germany by encouraging the German workers," as though this was not done after the last war—and with such disastrous results. An intelligent man who has done a lot of thinking about foreign affairs, on which he is a recognized expert in France, Auriol was, I thought, like Léon Blum and not a few other French Socialists, a little academic and inclined to make a speech in answering a question, but since I am here to learn, that was all right.

Home on foot, at midnight, in the rain. And tired, pleasantly.

Paris, *Friday, December* 8

With Mme Bradley to Hachette, the publisher, on the boulevard Saint-Germain this morning to sign a contract for the publication here in French of *Berlin Diary*.

I had a bit of *Katzenjammer*, I fear, and felt raw from the lack of sleep, and the Hachette office was so cold everyone sat around in overcoats. The contract signed, Mme B. took me over to a café on the boulevard Saint-Michel—a familiar one much frequented by students, where, I remembered, I had sat for hours during my first year back in 1925, trading English conversation for French with a ballet dancer at the Opéra. I believe she was in love with an American scientist at the time and thought that a smattering of English would help matters.

I was not only interested in learning French but interested in dancing, having just met Isadora Duncan, who used to invite me to her studio back of the Café Dôme and, between drinks, hold forth on the wonders of the dance. She was writing her book of memoirs then and somehow had got the quaint idea that I could help her. She would read a few pages, I remember, and then, before I could comment on the style, which she had asked me to do, a reference to something in the book would set her off to reminiscing and drinking. Finally she would stop.

"God," she would say, "I'm up to page one hundred and I'm still a virgin."

Toward midnight her studio would fill with all sorts of people, from French politicians to poets, and if she were in good form and had had enough to drink, she would do her magnificent Carmagnole dance, accompanied on the piano by a thin little Russian youth with whom, I believe, she was living at the time. She danced it with a scarlet scarf—the very one that strangled her to death not long afterward when it got caught in the wheels of her car on the Riviera.

Paris, *Sunday, December* 10

Did my last broadcast tonight from Europe on this assignment. CBS has ordered me home…. Makes you feel a bit of a louse, flying home for Christmas when so many other Americans are out there dying in the mud and snow….

Paris, *Monday, December* 11

This morning Jacques Maritain, the distinguished French Catholic philosopher, dropped around to see me. I do not pretend to understand his philosophy, though I have never tried very hard, but I admire the man, his *esprit*, and the fight he put up for the real, the great France, at a time when so many French intellectual lights were capitulating before the swashbuckling of Nazism or selling their faded minds to the puerile nit-wits of Vichy…. For a conservative and a Catholic, Maritain has a remarkable tolerance for those farther to the left, including the Communists….

An American airfield somewhere in the Azores, *Tuesday, December* 12

A pleasant surprise: Dorothy turned up among the passengers. Being beautiful, blonde, tall, blue-eyed, and good-natured, she had been so sought after by the

Americani in Paris that I had not seen much of her. But I knew her story. An American girl, she had been on the stage at home and in the films in Hollywood. Her second husband, a French film director, had been killed in Syria fighting for the Free French against the bastard French. She had remained in France throughout the German occupation, had been arrested and interned by the Nazis, and on her release had taken an active part in sheltering Allied fliers and relaying them along the underground route to freedom. She had thus literally risked her neck to do her part in this war, which is more than most of us did.

We do not get off at midnight because of the weather, and our eleven German war prisoners some brass hat in Washington has insisted on flying home are locked up. All day long from Paris they have sat opposite us on the bucket seats, as arrogant in captivity as any German officers I have ever met.

After dinner at the resthouse, D. and I stroll along the cliffs above the sea. It is a beautiful tropical night and she confides that she is going to marry my old friend J. when she returns to Paris in the spring. She is a little afraid of what America will be like, as are we all who have been away too long. The softness of the night is incredible. Can it be that the obscenities of war, the mud, the snow, the awful fatigue, the stink of corpses along the road, the mangled remains that come into the dressing stations, are only twelve hours away by plane from this balmy, heavenly isle?

Bronxville, N.Y., *Thursday, December* 14

Home and Tess and the kids (who stayed up), and the cold outside and this wonderfully clear December night in this blessed U.S.A.!

And the war, its snow, mud, smell of the dead—so far away from this warm hearth that one feels one has flown from some other planet. This is almost too good to deserve. Why, I keep asking, should I have it, and not all those other men of my land, lonely in the strange towns and shivering in the foxholes of western Europe.

To bed, beautifully tired from the flight, tingling with happiness, with thankfulness, and yet—almost ashamed at my personal good fortune.

New York, *Thursday, December* 21

The Germans have broken through our First Army front in Belgium and have been slowed but not stopped. To listen to a lot of comfortable people around here, the war is practically lost....

Bronxville, N.Y., *Sunday, December* 24

Many depressed this Christmas Eve. The surprise German success against our armies in the Belgian Bulge has been too much for them. My own feelings this Christmas Eve are mixed. Depressed I am about the grimness of the sacred night for others—for the ones fighting the war in the snow or in the jungles.

The irony of the date, the contrast of symbol and fact, is ugly. "Peace on earth, good will toward men!" When? How? Ever?

Late tonight we decorated the tree and piled the children's presents under it. Upstairs they are asleep—fitfully. The morning will be something so tremendous for them, or so they think, I find their feelings, childish though they are, contagious.

New York, *Wednesday, December* 27

The Third Army has relieved our heroic garrison at Bastogne. For the first time since the Battle of the Bulge began, the Berlin radio tonight was less confident….

Bronxville, N.Y., *Sunday, December* 31

Another New Year's Eve, our fourth in this war, and the end not yet in sight.

New York, *Sunday, January* 28, 1945

Forty-three days after Rundstedt unleashed his surprise counter-offensive in the west, the Germans are back where they started, minus a hundred thousand troops and a considerable quantity of tanks and guns. Their great gamble has failed. Ludendorff took a similar gamble in the summer of 1918 and almost got to Paris. Yet two months after his break-through he was suing for peace….

New York, *Monday, February* 12

A London newspaper tonight summed up pretty well the reaction of all of us to the Crimea conference of the Big Three, which ended yesterday. It described it as a "landmark in human history" and the communiqué as "the most hopeful document produced in the present century."

For here is a plan to end the greatest of all wars as quickly as possible and then—to make a peace such as until now we have only dreamed of. It will not be a perfect peace, since man is not perfect. But it is doubtful if in modern history, at least, the *sights* of men have been raised so high as they were at Yalta by the three men to whom fate has entrusted so much responsibility for the future of mankind. Even Herbert Hoover believes the Yalta agreement "comprises a strong foundation on which to rebuild the world."

The general terms for Germany are laid down and they are excellent. The Allies are determined to make sure *this* time that, as the communiqué puts it, "Germany will never again be able to disturb the peace of the world."

"We are determined," it goes on, "to disarm and disband all German armed forces; break up for all time the German General Staff that has repeatedly contrived the resurgence of German militarism; remove or destroy all German military equipment; eliminate or control all German industry that could be used for military production; bring all war criminals to just and swift punishment and

19

exact reparation in kind for the destruction wrought by the Germans; wipe out the Nazi party, Nazi laws, organizations and institutions.... It is not our purpose to destroy the people of Germany, but only when Nazism and militarism have been extirpated will there be hope for a decent life for Germans and a place for them in the comity of nations."

In short, we shall do most of the things we failed to do in 1919.

New York, *Friday, March* 2

American troops have reached the Rhine! Today the U.S. Ninth Army took Neuss on the great river opposite Düsseldorf.

New York, *Thursday, March* 8

The First Army is across the Rhine! Historians say it's the first crossing by an invading army since 1805. We got across at Remagen, though just how is not revealed.

New York, *Friday, March* 9

We got across, it's now revealed, on the Ludendorff railroad bridge at Remagen on Wednesday afternoon, a few minutes before the Germans had planned to blow it up.

New York, *Monday, April* 2

The war correspondents are saying today there will be no more big battles in the west. The Germans are finished....

New York, *Sunday, April* 8

The U.S. Ninth Army is only 128 miles from Berlin today. The U.S. Third and Seventh Armies are nearing Leipzig, Nuremberg, and Munich. The Russians began storming Königsberg and virtually completed the encirclement of Vienna. It won't be long now.

Chicago, *Monday, April* 9

En route to see my mother in Cedar Rapids, Iowa, and to deliver a lecture Wednesday evening in Omaha.

God! This place is my birthplace. Once it was my home. And yet I know the city not. And tomorrow in Cedar Rapids, which was also your home? Home? What is it? And where? And how?

Must put down here some notes I wrote the other day on how it felt coming home from Europe and the war that Christmas of 1940. (That was where *Berlin Diary* ended.) Notes for a novel, I think they were—one of those bad auto-biographical things that I hope I'll have the sense *not* to write. They belong here, if any place.

THE NOTES

Another Christmas had come around, and if the ship plowing westward from Lisbon did not founder, I would spend it at home. At home? Ah, yes. But after fifteen years—your entire adult life—in Europe, what was home and where, you wondered.

In Paris, Rome, Berlin, Vienna—even in London—you had come to feel at home, knowing the flavor of each, the personality, the color, the light, the smell, feeling at some time or other that each had been like a mother, taking you in and making you feel at ease when you came back from a long wandering. Here in these great cities of Europe was where your life had been since coming of age. In each of them, maybe, you had loved and struggled and suffered. In all of them you had taken something that added, for good or bad, to what you were becoming. In time you had got to know them and love them or, perhaps, hate them, as one does a home.

New York, to be sure, thrilled you each time you came home on brief leave and stood at the rail of your ship coming up the river and gazed, with high excitement, through the haze of a dawn at the outline of the great buildings on Manhattan Island. But to most of us permanently assigned abroad, New York was a strange city, and in time America, on these hasty visits, seemed to become a strange land even though you had been born and brought up in it, as I had been. I had come back three times in fifteen years for a few weeks or a few days and there had come that sinking feeling in the stomach when you realized you were only a visitor. Here, though it was your native land, your time was fleeting. Here you did not quite belong.

But where, then? Paris and Vienna you might love until you could weep for them. I did. But in them you were always a foreigner, awkward in the language, never quite attuned to the inner rhythm of the people, peering always from the outside and with roots no deeper than those of the weeds that grew between the paving stones.

Yes, where then? In Chicago, where you had been born? In the little Iowa town where you had grown up after your father died? I had been back to them a couple of times and had found myself an utter stranger in both. I did not recognize the Chicago of my boyhood nor like the one I found, with its enormous frustrations, its terrifying dedication to making money, its sickening unconcern with its ugly, degrading poverty; its dead soul. In my boyhood, to be sure, Chicago had been a city of sprawling stockyards, converging railroads, and the great steel and cement mills stretching along the south side of the lake past Gary. It worked and produced and transported for the growing nation and it did it with a raw and wonderful gusto that appealed to the poets and the novelists who at that time were honored in the city. In fact, the Chicago of that generation gave the country most of its important writers, but in time nearly all of them, except Carl Sandburg, drifted to New York, where, I suppose, they found what Chicago was beginning to lack or deny.

In my youthful days the city was alive with vigorous newspapers. But when you came back between the wars the newspapers seemed either dead or dying. People bought them for their comics or their sports pages, for there was little else of interest in them. The livest newspaper and the only one left in the morning field had become a mere mouthpiece for a decadent, opinionated old man who poisoned even its news columns with his ridiculous prejudices, which formerly had been restricted to the cartoons and the editorial page. This caricature of a newspaper was corrupting the entire upper Mississippi Valley—or so it seemed to me.

And where was the grand opera of the days of Mary Garden, which had thrilled one's youth? And the fine symphony orchestra of Frederick Stock? Gaudy movie palaces had all but replaced the theaters. Perhaps four or five legitimate playhouses kept open, peddling the latest New York hits. Could not one of the world's largest and wealthiest cities have its own theater, its own opera? Could it not *originate* something in the arts? I wandered around the milling streets and put the question to a few old acquaintances. But they were in a hurry—everybody was in a hurry in Chicago—and they were not interested. Only up on Michigan Boulevard, beyond the world's largest and ugliest electric signboard, the Art Institute was the same or even better. Here you could still find a great treasure of the world's best paintings, bought and paid for by Chicago's wealthy burghers and beautifully hung by paid professionals in superbly lit galleries bearing the names of the merchant donors. The Art Institute was an oasis in a vast desert, but few of the citizens seemed thirsty.

Perhaps if I could have stayed longer and delved deeper beneath the surface I might have got a different impression of my native city. Tom Wolfe told me once in Berlin that he had to go to Chicago from time to time to get the feeling of America. He was, he said, fascinated by its enormous restlessness, a feeling Wolfe had as an artist; and sometimes when he was in New York, he said, he would amble down to Grand Central and hop a day coach all the way to Chicago, spending a week or two there, roaming the streets and absorbing their raw vitality.

But I seemed to absorb only deadness. In a way it was the same with the little Iowa town two hundred miles to the west of Chicago on the main Northwestern line. In Cedar Rapids I had spent the so-called formative years, through most of grade school and then high school and college. But when you returned it was difficult to recollect this. It was as though you came back in a trance, and people said this was where you grew up, but you could not remember growing up there; and this was the house you lived in, and that was the newspaper office you got your first professional experience in, and those streets where in summer the trees on both sides form a leafy archway block after block in front of the well-spaced modest houses were the ones you used to pedal up and down on your bicycle delivering newspapers in the sultry afternoon summer heat and in the icy darkness of the early Iowa winter mornings. Were they? Are you sure? Was it I?

Oh, yes, and over there at Greene's Square across from the Union Depot was a sprawling pseudo-Gothic—or maybe it was pseudo-Norman—graystone building, its arched windows boarded up. Remember? That was your high school, where you remember getting your first blows and disappointments in life and where, maybe, the first spark was fired that was to lead you on to reading and study and the kind of writing you do for the newspapers and radio. That's right, and across the square the First Presbyterian church, in the style of the high school but not yet boarded up, where your family since time immemorial had a rented pew in which you sat many a weary Sabbath thinking perhaps of the fun—God, was it fun?—of the Sunday-school picnics and of the night in the chapel after a Christian Endeavor meeting when you got your first frightened kiss from that blonde little Bohemian girl whose family lived down by the tracks and who was considered a bad influence by the pillars of the church who did not know life by the tracks very well.

Yes, Greene's Square. Of course. The lawn on which the veterans of the Rainbow Division sprawled that day they came home from the war waiting for the civic reception. You kids played hookey that day, and lounged around on the grass with them, your eyes popping out listening to their tales of the Boche and "beaucoup cognac" and the French girls—French girls?—and the Argonne, and asking them if you could just hold their German helmet for a second.

Remember? Remember the war? The summers working in the Quaker Oats mill to help the nation out on food, and the first acquaintance with the mill girls, who were not like the girls in school or at church, but swore like troopers and at night took you to the park, maybe, to initiate you into the most wonderful thing that had ever happened, maybe. And the day the war ended, on November 11, 1918, when you were fourteen, dancing in the streets in front of Rainey's cigar store and sneaking in for a game of pool and getting your first drink.

Remember? Well, yes and no. And if you did, did that make it home? Was it home to Carl Van Vechten, whose father's house was up the street from ours and who had gone a long way from Cedar Rapids?

It was home still, I knew, to Grant Wood. As a boy I had played across the street in the barn of the family that had run the Packing House. Their mansion was now an undertaker's place, a funeral home, I believe they called it. The undertaker, who was more interested in men's lives than in their deaths, despite his profession, had set Wood up in the barn. Hearses had become motor-driven; horses were no longer needed even to haul a man's body to the grave. The stables had been cleaned out and Wood had rigged himself up a very pleasant studio in the barn.

I did not see him when I came back for a fleeting week or two. He belonged to the war generation, the one ahead of me, and I did not know him very well. People said he was very happy there and I could believe it, for here in his native Iowa he had found himself as a painter—one of the few truly great ones the nation had.

Grant Wood had not found himself in Paris, where I had known him best. In 1926 after a conventional tour through the French countryside he had returned to Paris with a trunk full of his paintings and I had helped him organize an exhibition of them there. They already showed a fine craftsmanship. But, as I remember them, they were all rather conventional—pretty and pleasant little landscapes of Brittany and Provence without originality or guts. I got Elliot Paul to write about them in the Paris *Tribune*, and though he was slightly condescending in tone, as one is liable to be toward unknown artists, he did find much to praise. So did some of the French critics. But Wood, I could see, was not pleased inwardly. Like all great artists in their youth, he was still groping in the wilderness, and like most American painters he was too obsessed with Europe, with France, with the French impressionists. I think that fall before he left he began to see that he would have to free himself from Europe. It was a sounder discovery than I realized at the time and it went for American writers as well as painters, though Hemingway was the only major writer in Paris who knew it.

Wood went back to Iowa and found the inspiration there that made him great. But could it be the same with those of infinitely lesser talents and no trace of his genius? To be honest, I was not coming back to Iowa to seek inspiration, for I was merely an ordinary working journalist, not a literary man, not an artist, and in the Europe that had baffled Wood and made him uneasy, I had been wonderfully happy and free.

Cedar Rapids, Iowa, *Tuesday, April* 10
A nice visit with my mother. She looked ailing, though.

Omaha, *Wednesday, April* 11
Got through the lecture with no mishaps. How I hate it, though! Bill Jeffers, the Union Pacific head, whose daughter had arranged the talk for the benefit of her school, met me at the station, though the train got in at the crack of dawn. A blunt individualist of the old school, he kept telling bitter, amusing stories of Washington during the time he was rubber czar.

Cedar Rapids, *Thursday, April* 12
Along about six p.m. this day I got into a bus at the corner of First Avenue and Third Street. I was going out to Fourteenth Street to have a quiet dinner with my mother and two old college friends, Dave and Helen Bleakley.

The bus was filled—mostly with farmers and workers in overalls, and I found a seat among them in the back. The usual freight train halted us for a few minutes at the tracks. Nobody was saying anything. Probably they were tired. I noticed the caboose of the freight train go by. The signal man waved us across the tracks, and the bus chugged up the hill beyond.

"I wonder what will happen to the country now," a man said. He must have been a factory worker in one of the new war plants. His face was grimy and wet with sweat.

"Yeah," the man next to him said.

There must be some bad war news or something, I thought. At Fourteenth Street I got off the bus.

At the door of her apartment, Mother was in tears.

"He's dead," she said.

"Who?"

"The President."

She was sobbing. Inside, Dave and Helen filled me in with the awful news. Roosevelt had died of a cerebral hemorrhage at Warm Springs, Georgia, an hour or so ago, they said. I felt limp. I sat down on the couch. I couldn't speak. I couldn't think. No one in the room could. We went down to the dining-room and ate our dinner in silence. When we came back to the apartment we turned on the radio. Bill Henry in Washington was telling how Steve Early broke the news to Mrs. Roosevelt. "I am more sorry for the people of the world and of the United States than for us," her first words had been.

There were pickups from all over the world, telling of the sorrow. Andrei Gromyko, the Soviet Ambassador, came on from Washington. "The Soviet people," he said, "share this great national grief which has befallen the American people." Henri Bonnet, the Ambassador of France, in his rich accent but with a voice ringing with sincerity, was saying: "You, citizens of the United States, as well as we, citizens of France, and of other Allied nations, we owe it to the memory of President Roosevelt to remain united after victory, in order to build up the enduring peace which he has prepared and in order to work together for the welfare of mankind, to which he devoted his life."

Most moving of all was Raymond Massey's voice, the voice that portrayed Lincoln in Bob Sherwood's *Abe Lincoln in Illinois*, reading Stephen Vincent Benét's *Prayer for United Nations*,[2] which the President himself had once recited on Flag Day:

> "God of the Free, we pledge our lives and hearts today to the cause of all free mankind.... Grant us brotherhood in hope and union, not only for the space of this bitter war, but for the days to come which shall and must unite all the children of earth.

> "Our earth is but a small star in the great universe. Yet, of it we can make, if we choose, a planet unvexed by war, untroubled by hunger or fear, undivided by senseless distinctions of race, color or theory. Grant

us that courage and foreseeing to begin this task today that our children and our children's children may be proud of the name of Man…. Grant us the wisdom and the vision to comprehend the greatness of man's spirit, that suffers and endures so hugely for a goal beyond his own brief span.

"Grant us patience with the deluded and pity for the betrayed. And grant us the skill and valor that shall cleanse the world of oppression and the old base doctrine that the strong must eat the weak because they are strong.

"Yet most of all grant us brotherhood, not only for this day but for all our years—a brotherhood not of words but of acts and deeds. We are all of us children of earth—grant us that simple knowledge. If our brothers are oppressed, then we are oppressed. If they hunger, we hunger. If their freedom is taken away, our freedom is not secure.

"Grant us a common faith that man shall know bread and peace—that he shall know justice and righteousness, freedom and security, an equal opportunity and an equal chance to do his best, not only in our own lands but throughout the world. And in that faith let us march toward the clean world our hands can make. AMEN."

The phone rang. It was the local radio station, a CBS affiliate. New York wanted me to go on the air in an hour. Dave rushed me down to the station in his car. I sat before a typewriter. But the words came painfully and slowly. I was only half finished when my air time came. I told of how the news had come to this Midwest farming community. I spoke of how the Fascist dictators had lost their greatest enemy.[3] Just words. Well meant, as were everyone's this night. But unimportant.

Toward midnight I went back to say good-by to Mother. She was exhausted, but was still sitting up.

"What'll we do now?" she kept saying. The loss was so personal, though I do not think she had voted for Mr. Roosevelt in the last two elections. She was very tired and there was no time for family talk.

"We'll save it for next time," I said. We said good-by.[4] I phoned for a taxi and caught the night train to Chicago.

Chicago, *Friday, April* 13

Devoured the morning papers over breakfast in the station.

The *Chicago Daily Tribune* headline:

ROOSEVELT IS DEAD!

Truman Sworn in, Pledges War Success

The *Chicago Sun*:

PRESIDENT DEAD: TRUMAN SWORN

All the newspapers, even Hearst's *Herald-American,* whose banner front-page headline reads: "THE WORLD MOURNS," carry moving editorials, except the *Tribune,* whose vicious attacks on the President in his lifetime were no credit to American journalism. The *Tribune* merely ran at the top of its editorial page in a black mourning box four brief paragraphs entitled: "A Nation Mourns."

The best editorial in the Chicago press is, I think, in the *News.* It is called "The Fruitful Journey."

It would be the most natural and characteristic thing on earth or in heaven if Franklin D. Roosevelt were to be saying today at the Bar of Judgment, exactly what he said in beginning the very last speech he made to the American people, the time he returned from Yalta last month and began his report—

"It is good to be home.

"It has been a long journey. I hope you will agree that it was a fruitful one."...

A fruitful journey?

Yes, yes, a most fruitful journey, indeed....

There will be regret in some quarters that now at the journey's end, the late President's body will not lie in state at the capital.

But to Mr. Roosevelt's people in the factories, the villages, the ware-houses across the country, this will be all right, for they know, without ever putting it into words, that his gallant body won't really be on that lonely train today pushing north across a mourning land. They know where it is. They know it's on every camion driving deep into Naziland today. It's riding the quarterdeck of every ship that sweeps treachery from oriental seas.

New York, *Sunday, April* 15

My broadcast this afternoon is my diary for this day:

President Roosevelt was buried this morning in the garden of his old family home on the banks of the Hudson where he was born sixty-three years ago.

The sky was cloudless, and spring was in the air as Mrs. Roosevelt and the other members of the family stood in a little gathering which included President and Mrs. Truman, the heads of the armed forces, members of the Supreme Court, of the cabinet, of the Congress, and also the neighbors from the countryside, and watched the body of the departed President lowered to its last resting place. The funeral rites took but ten minutes. There were no words of eulogy—only the word of God. A detail of cadets from West Point fired a volley of three farewell salutes. A bugler played taps—its sad notes echoing through the wooded land. Then the little group walked out of the garden.

Some minutes later Mrs. Roosevelt, in dry-eyed sorrow, returned to the garden alone. Workmen were shoveling the soil on her husband's grave. She gazed at his final resting place for a minute or so, then turned and walked away. In an hour she boarded Mr. Truman's presidential train for Washington. So ended the great President's days on this earth.

So much has been written and said about Mr. Roosevelt by men more wise and experienced than I that there is little I can contribute.

Traveling across nearly half of this country—from Iowa to New York—between the time the terrible news came Thursday afternoon and the simple funeral in the White House yesterday, I saw the grief of a considerable part of the nation; saw how *personal* was the sense of loss among the citizens of this Republic, whether they were farmers, workers, doctors, lawyers, businessmen, or any other; whether they had agreed with the President or not. Despite his background, he had something—call it his humanity—which made him closer to the mass of the people than any other President of our time. You felt it as men mourned, as if for a friend, in the towns and cities across the land.

My own work had kept me out of this country during most of Mr. Roosevelt's long tenure of office. I was never able to be at home for any of the elections. Perhaps that helped you appraise the man. You were not affected by the bitterness, by the angry mud-throwing of the campaigns. And a certain distance, perhaps, gave you perspective.

It did not seem difficult to see where, with all his faults, his greatness lay. Was it not in the courage and vision he showed in meeting the great crises that confronted the nation? Of these, two imperiled the very life of the country—the panic of 1933 and the war of the fascist barbarians against the Western world. The first—as we see it now—was fairly easily met. It was met when—at the call of the President—we conquered our stupid fears.

The second will no doubt go down in our history as the supreme crisis of our times. And the way Mr. Roosevelt saw it, sized it up, and acted to meet it will also go down in history and be remembered by a grateful people. At first we were not a very grateful people because—in our ostrich-like isolation—we did not understand the danger. Mr. Roosevelt was the first to see it. But when he tried to take the people into his confidence in his "Quarantine" speech at Chicago, the people held back. Like Mr. Neville Chamberlain in London, we were naïve about the fascist dictators and their evil designs. We continued to be naïve for a long time, until long after the war in Europe started. We did not yet realize—as a people—that with our disastrous do-nothing attitude, we were letting our friends go under and that, when they were gone, we would be alone in a corner facing the military strength of a Europe mobilized by Germany and an Asia mobilized by Japan, against which we could not in the end hold out and—that being true—could not remain a free nation and a free people.

The President realized it. And it was his genius that he had the patience, the tact, and also the Dutch stubbornness to gradually convince the people and their representatives in Congress that there was only one possible path to follow which could save the land. That path developed into the foreign policy of the United States. It was to prepare to meet the attack by arming ourselves, to save our friends, principally Russia and Great Britain, by sending them all the help we could and then to forge a grand coalition with them against the Axis, which could ensure Allied victory.

These three things seem so logical, almost so simple to us now. But history will record—even if we forget—the great fight the President had to make to achieve them. It will record how our growing army was saved from dissolution by one single vote in Congress. It will note by what a narrow margin Lend-Lease, which kept Britain and Russia in the fight until they could regain their strength to hit back, passed the Congress.

It will credit the President, too, with a mastery of strategy in this global war that his fellow countrymen even today but dimly perceive. His was the decision—which so many Americans didn't like or understand—to concentrate on Germany first, to weaken it before it could destroy Russia and join up with Japan. For had Germany conquered Russia, it is scarcely conceivable that our enemies ever could have been defeated. It was largely his perseverance and skill that built up the Grand Alliance not only into a military force which brought victory but which, before the war was ended, began to shape a decent and hopeful peace.

Indeed, the greatest tragedy of his untimely passing is, as my friend Anne McCormick pointed out in the *Times*, not that he died on the eve of victory, but that he did not live to make the peace. It was the peace that claimed most of his heart and mind in the past few months. And he was preparing to make the same fight for a decent peace—not perfect, but at least decent—that he had made to win the war, preparing to work with the people and the Congress and our Allies to attain it, with the same ardor and skill as in the awful military struggle.

But fate did not spare him for this momentous task. It will now have to be carried out by a man who did not seek the job, a farmer's son from the Missouri countryside, a simple humble man, whom the same fate has thrust into what he himself Friday called "the most terribly responsible job a man ever had."

What can the country expect from Mr. Truman? How will he perform just about the most important job on this earth?

New York, *Wednesday, April* 18

I'm going to San Francisco after all. Tomorrow. It was a choice between there and Germany....

We are living so close to events it is difficult to realize the importance of the San Francisco conference. Someone calls it "the most important gathering since the Last Supper"—a rather lyrical, hysterical exaggeration. But it is terribly important, nevertheless.

Ernie Pyle has been killed at the front in the Pacific. After the first shock I felt resentful. All the decent guys going, and the heels surviving. Ray Clapper, another swell guy, was killed in the Pacific too. Strange that Pyle had a premonition of his end. He felt he had used up most of his chances to survive.

San Francisco, *Friday, April* 20

What a wondrous, beautiful city this is! And what a wonderful land is ours, as you see it sprawling from coast to coast in all its exciting variety, on an eighteen-hour flight. By train or car, the impression must be even more magnificent. I'm glad they are bringing most of the foreign delegates by train across our continent. Four days of it will give them a better picture of America than they could have got from a mountain of books.

One is astounded by the great waste spaces in our land—the hundreds of miles of desert and mountains in which few human beings can dwell. And yet much of this "wasteland" is of such beauty, such grandeur, that it takes your breath away. Even the Alps, which I know so well, even the Himalayas, which I knew the summer in Simla, pale a little when you view the snowy, rugged peaks of the Rockies. I wonder if they will ever be as peopled as are the Alps. Probably not. Probably you couldn't make a living from them. But as playgrounds for a restless, too hard-working people they are magnificent—if we ever have the sense in this country to relax and learn how enriching leisure can be. And our West! You smelt the fine, free air of the West at Cheyenne. The air was different, and the people.

San Francisco, *Saturday, April* 21

In the lobby of the Palace Hotel, where a thousand correspondents are installed, one bumps into almost every newspaperman—American and European—one has known in twenty years of covering the peace and the war over the world. First it was the peace and then the war, and now the peace again, and these were the plodding fellows who reported each frightening phase and whose words—millions of them—were so little heeded by the peoples and their statesmen, so called. Many of them I knew in Geneva when the League of Nations, even without the U.S.A. and Russia, seemed like such a decent hope. They are all older now, worn a little, stouter, but, considering what they've gone through, not as cynical as you might suppose. Most of them think we will succeed this time.

San Francisco, *Sunday, April* 22

The Russians are within three miles of Unter den Linden in the heart of Berlin. The city is in flames.... Somewhere south of Berlin a junction between the American and Russian armies is imminent....

Such was the war news this week-end as the delegates of the United Nations began gathering here to commence the difficult job of setting up the machinery of peace....

I believe the big news of the San Francisco conference can be given now—on the eve of its opening. It's this: it will succeed! Not that there won't be a lot of argument here. There will be weeks of it. But in the end there will be a charter.... Few responsible people here are as worried about the voting problem as some sections of our press. The great issues of peace and war will never be decided by majority vote, or any vote. We Americans have got to get that through our heads. That, and the fact that Russia, Great Britain and the United States, after due discussion, will largely determine the kind of world organization we are going to have.

One of the wisest of the statesmen here is Jan Christiaan Smuts, the Prime Minister of South Africa. He's the sole survivor of those who played a leading part in shaping the League of Nations at Versailles after the last war. He helped to shape it. Then he saw it slowly fail. He thinks the proposed new league is better than the old. He also believes this is our last chance.

San Francisco, *Monday, April* **23**

The newspapers, particularly the Hearst and Roy Howard press, are kicking up an unholy fuss over the deadlock on Poland. Anything for a headline. And strife makes headlines. And attacks on Russia make headlines. The question is: which Polish delegation shall be seated, the London government-in-exile or the "provisional government" in Poland? We and the British recognize the first; Russia the second. The sensation-mongers are predicting the conference may break up over Poland, but I do not believe it. The delegates are here to draw up plans for a world organization, not to deal with the numerous headaches arising from the present state of the war and the world. But an irresponsible press could wreck this meeting.

After the broadcast tonight I went over to the Bohemian Club for dinner. Some local worthies were entertaining some of the Eastern newspaper editors and publishers. Much good talk, but one felt a certain gulf between *our*East and West. Very late we adjourned to the bar—an immense establishment—and one of the local members sitting at our table played, of all things, a fiddle. You could scarcely imagine an august member in a New York club grabbing a fiddle to play. But here, in this civilized, informal atmosphere, it seemed perfectly natural and I, for one, enjoyed it immensely.

San Francisco, *Wednesday, April* **25**

As Berlin lay dying today in the flames and blood of the war that started there nearly six years ago, we saw in this splendid city today the first step taken on the long road toward an organized peace.

The conference of forty-six United Nations got off to a good start. The opening ceremony was simple, but, like the simple things often, very moving. Here in a resplendent Opera House, built as a *War* Memorial, were expressed all the hopes we have of peace. In Berlin, a maniac's hopes of world conquest were being buried in the debris of a once great city. Here in this beautiful community along the ocean we call Pacific, more decent hopes were being born.

Everyone seemed to feel it. I have never seen diplomats—fellows who usually are rather proud of their cynicism—so solemn as they were today. They all knew—you seemed to feel—that they dared not fail this time in the job of getting an enduring peace.

There was one very symbolic little touch at today's formal opening. Along the great stage, behind the speaker's rostrum, a group of GI's, men and women representing all of our armed services, stood at attention under the flags of the forty-six United Nations. They were youngsters. They had seen war at first hand. Some had been wounded. There were no officers. They were just average Americans—average American citizens—in uniform. It is these Americans, who have fought the war, who now insist on building for the peace so that they and their children won't have to go through this mess of war ever again.

The President of the United States was not here in person. But his words, broadcast to the assembled delegates, created a deep impression. "In your hands," he told them, "rests our future. Make certain that another war is impossible."

Ed Stettinius, our Secretary of State, a rather handsome fellow with his white hair, ruddy complexion, and shiny white teeth, presided. He has a good voice, but does not know how to use it. And he means well; he has, in fact, almost a ferocious sincerity. But he does not impress me as knowing much about world affairs or the fine arts of subtle, cynical diplomacy, of which we, no doubt, will have a great deal here. Certainly he is not in the same class as Eden and Molotov, nor even in that of the representatives of some of the smaller powers, men like Smuts, Spaak, and Jan Masaryk. As a matter of fact, our American delegation is weak—Stassen seems to be the most intelligent man on it—but it is the best we have. And we shall miss, I think, the fine guiding hand of Roosevelt. There is really no one in Washington or here who has any brilliance in foreign policy.

The color and the ceremonies are now over. Tomorrow the representatives of the forty-six United Nations—and soon, everyone hopes, of the forty-seventh, Poland, the first of the United Nations to be attacked by the Nazi monster in this war—will settle down to the detailed job of writing the charter of organized peace.

San Francisco, *Thursday, April 26*

Under the Klieg lights of the world's photographers, who scampered all over the place, the statesmen of the big powers spoke their pieces today in the first plenary session of the conference. Their words were solemn and conciliatory, but behind the scenes some hard feelings were caused at the refusal of Molotov to agree to Stettinius being made permanent chairman of the conference, which most delegates considered to be a mere act of courtesy to the country that was host. We shall have to learn, I suppose, that the proletarian state attaches great importance to these seemingly unimportant questions of procedure and protocol. Apparently Eden finally got a compromise by which the foreign ministers of the four big powers (France is out because it declined, stupidly, to be an "inviting" power) will preside over the conference in rotation.

Some of our people appear to have been a little shocked by Molotov's abrupt and tough manner during the argument. Padilla, the Mexican Foreign Minister, who I gather is pretty much an American stooge, at one juncture took it upon himself. I'm told, to tell Molotov that it was only "simple courtesy" to elect Stettinius as permanent chairman. The Russian, with savage irony, "thanked" the Mexican Foreign Minister for his "lesson in courtesy and diplomatic procedure" and then proceeded to stick to his point.

In his formal speech, which he delivered in Russian, at the first plenary session this afternoon, Molotov, however, was conciliatory and full of hope. To those critics, especially in the Hearst and Howard press, who have been saying that the Russians don't want agreement here, the Russian Foreign Commissar had some pretty convincing words: "The Soviet government is a sincere and firm champion of the establishment of a strong international organization of security. Whatever may depend on it and its efforts in the common cause of the creation of such a postwar organization of peace and security of nations will be readily done by the Soviet government. We will fully co-operate in the solution of this great problem with all the other governments.... An international organization must be created having certain powers to safeguard the interests of the general peace. This organization must have the necessary means for military protection of the security of nations.... As far as the Soviet Union is concerned, I should like to assure the conference that in our country the whole people are brought up in the spirit of faith and devotion to the cause of setting up a solid organization of international security. I should like to assure the conference also that the Soviet people will readily listen to the voice, wishes, and suggestions of all the sincere friends of this great cause...."

What more could you want—if he means what he says?

I was due to speak at five thirty p.m. on America's Town Meeting of the Air with Senator Connally, Commander Stassen, Raymond Swing, and Hans Kaltenborn at the Civic Auditorium, a few blocks down the street from the Opera House. I had to leave the first plenary session in the middle of Eden's speech. (He was saying: "The work on which we are making a start here may be the world's last chance." And, despite his age and long experience as Foreign Minister, he still had such an air of the schoolboy.)

It was nearly five thirty, and radio waits for no one. But when I got to the auditorium, an immense hall that must seat fifteen thousand people, a great crowd was milling around the entrances, which were locked, and I could not get in. Finally I found a stage door and a policeman let me in. The program was just going on the air as I climbed, out of breath, onto the platform. It was a wonderfully sympathetic audience, one of the best I've ever spoken to, though I was a little frightened by the *size*. Stassen proved to be a very effective speaker. Senator Connally puts on the volume, but he is a little old-fashioned for the times—a quality that the radio emphasizes.

San Francisco, *Saturday, April 28*

Great excitement in this country from coast to coast tonight following a phony A.P. report from San Francisco, quoting "a high United States official," that Germany had surrendered unconditionally and that an announcement was expected officially. The official was Senator Tom Connally and it seems he did tell an A.P. reporter that he expected "momentarily" a statement that Germany had surrendered. But if the Associated Press had a greater sense of responsibility, it would at least check such a momentous piece of news in Washington, where it would have been received before transmission to San Francisco. Anything for a headline....

Late this evening President Truman issued an official denial that Germany had surrendered. But it can only be a matter of days or even hours. What seems to be a fact is that Himmler offered through Sweden a German surrender to Great Britain and the United States, but was told the offer would have to be made to Russia too. Thank God we didn't let the Nazis split the victorious Allied coalition this early in the game!

Cocktails this evening with Henri Bonnet, the French Ambassador, and Hélène Bonnet in their suite at the St. Francis, where the French and Russian delegations are staying. It was pleasant seeing them again and I had a chance of meeting the French Foreign Minister, Bidault. He was hard to see in Paris, and I had not seen him there. Here you can guzzle cocktails with them all—all except the Americans (and of course the Russians), who do not yet understand proper press relations and think that if you call a mass press conference you are doing your duty to the press. A good reporter needs much more than press conferences. He wants to talk with the men who are making the peace. He doesn't want "interviews," unless he's an amateur. He wants background and inside dope that he will know how to use discreetly, and that his informants know he will use discreetly.

Spoke with Bidault only a few minutes. A short, slight Frenchman, a little nervous still in his job, he struck me as being shrewd and intelligent.

After the eight-ten p.m. broadcast, joined a score of other correspondents, editors, and publishers whom Anthony Eden had invited for dinner. Stettinius would not know enough about his job to do this, but the British Foreign Secretary is more experienced. A newspaperman, being human, naturally feels all right at being asked to dinner by the British Foreign Minister. The latter, in his turn, not only has a chance to feel the pulse of those who make the opinions of our leading newspapers, but at such an intimate affair has a golden opportunity of getting over his government's ideas. (Radio chains are not supposed to have any political opinions, nor are the news agencies, but their chief representatives, who certainly do have opinions, were invited also.)

Eden, of course, made the most of his opportunities, as did we. For a busy man who had on his mind not only the conference but the imminent end of the war, he was extremely patient, and sat and talked with us for several hours after dinner had been finished. He gave us a pretty good idea, in adult terms (none of the rhetorical flourishes of the press conference), of what the British government was up to, or what he wanted us to think it was up to. He was extremely interesting on the Russians, with whom he has had a good deal to do during the war. I didn't particularly like, though, his references to the "Russians now being members of the club." The world which the Russians, along with the Americans, largely dominate is a much harsher thing.

I came away from the dinner realizing more clearly than before that here, for the first time in history, the two great non-European nations whose military strength had decided the issue in Europe did, in fact, hold the future not only of Europe but of the world in their hands. Great Britain was still a factor, and it would know how to utilize to the utmost that fact. But it had not been strong enough to decide the issue in Europe alone against the German might, even with its traditional Continental allies. France had gone down in six weeks. Italy was finished. And Germany would be shortly. Russia and America were emerging from the war as the planet's two giants. It was they who in the long run, in their relation to each other and to the planet's general situation, would decide mankind's future.

San Francisco, *Sunday, April 29*

A week-end for you!

American troops have entered Munich and Milan, birthplaces, respectively, of Nazism and Fascism. The British Eighth Army has liberated Venice. Nine tenths of Berlin is now in Russian hands.

But the greatest news of all comes from Milan.

Benito Mussolini, the swaggering little sawdust Cæsar, is *dead*. He was executed by Italian patriots at four twenty p.m. yesterday in a little mountain village near Como. Today his body is hanging in the Piazza Loreto in Milan beside the bodies of seventeen of his Fascist henchmen who were also done to death by infuriated Italian patriots…. According to the Milan Free Radio, the Duce's mistress, Clara Petacci, was also executed, and the tyrant's bloody body, after it was cut down, lay on hers in the Milan gutter for all to see this day.

After Il Duce, Der Führer?

Dispatches say he is holding out in the Berlin zoo—a fitting place. Today the Russians were fighting in a half-dozen familiar spots in Berlin: Alexanderplatz, Belle-Alliance Platz, the Potsdamerstrasse, and the Bellevue Castle near the Tiergarten.

Judging by the A.P. and U.P. news tickers, these United States presented quite a spectacle last night. From coast to coast the nation went on a peace jag—and all because of the A.P.'s phony report from here that Germany had surrendered. It appears that there were few cities and towns throughout the land that did not go wild with excitement at the false news.

The realization that the war against Germany is all but over has had a wonderful effect on the conference here. It has made the delegates even more conscious than before that they must get an agreement here on the machinery of the future World Organization to keep the peace. A few days ago, when minor disputes threatened to bog down the whole proceedings, there was talk that the conference might adjourn before writing a definitive charter—adjourn to try again in the fall. Today you hear no more talk of that kind.

Much loose talk here by the professional Russian-haters that the Bolsheviks don't care much whether the conference succeeds in writing a charter or not. My own dope is completely to the contrary. The Russians are certainly difficult to deal with, but they want here what we want.

To dinner tonight at the home of Tom and Harle, she being one of the most beautiful women in America. Harry Bridges, boss of the Pacific Longshoremen's Union, was there. In the East, especially in conservative circles, he has been depicted as an awful monster, a dangerous revolutionary, and so on. He turned out to be a very human fellow, much younger than I had expected, intelligent and well informed. Perhaps his talk is a little too slick, but maybe you get that way talking to a lot of tough men—not only along the docks but in the slick offices of the employers. Afterward MacDonald of the London *Times*(very unlike a *Times* man in manner), Bridges, an attractive Czech girl, and I walked home. We must have walked up and down most of San Francisco's seven (?) steep hills, but we sang a lot, especially MacDonald, who is good at it, and the time passed pleasantly and the hills did not seem steep at all.

San Francisco, *Monday, April* 30

The Russians are in the heart of Berlin. They've taken the gutted old Reichstag building. They've captured the Kroll Opera, where the Reichstag met after the Nazis set fire to its building and where Hitler announced to the world, that gray morning of September 1, 1939, the opening shots in his war.

Berlin is finished, and Germany, and Nazism! The war is just about over. But we learned here in San Francisco today how difficult it is going to be for the nations that won the war, at such a terrible cost, to work together for the peace. For the first time the unity of the big powers, which did almost all the fighting, was publicly broken. And over a strange issue.

We, whose late President and former Secretary of State had been so critical of the fascist pro-Axis military clique in Buenos Aires, insisted that Argentina be admitted to the United Nations. The Russians, flaunting in our faces every bitter word Mr. Roosevelt and Mr. Hull had uttered about Argentina, asked for "a few days' delay" to enable the conference to think it over. We insisted on a vote—today; as if you could run the peace any more than you ran the war with "majority votes"; as if the Russians and everyone else didn't know that we could always garner the twenty or so votes of the South Americans (who did not fight in this war), and the British the votes of the Commonwealth nations (as well as India, which is not even an independent state, though it is a member of the United Nations).

Ed Stettinius demanded his vote, and got it—a thumping majority for America's insistence that fascist Argentina be made a member of the United Nations it had done everything it could to wreck.

Home in a bus with Walter Lippmann, both of us too depressed to speak.

San Francisco, *Tuesday, May* 1

I was lunching with Tom Finletter at the Fairmont when a bellboy summoned me to the telephone. It was our local CBS office. Come quick, they said. Hitler's dead.

So Adolf Hitler—that evil genius—is dead, destroyed like his country, which he tried to make master of the world and ended only by destroying. I must say it never seemed to me possible that a man who incarnated all that was evil and bestial and degrading in our human life, who sent to their deaths so many millions of decent men, women, and children of this world, who broke the spirits and the bodies of so many millions more, who spread so much ruin over this planet—no, it never seemed to me possible that he would get away with it in the end, annihilating all the good, free men of this world or making them slaves to his vile concepts.

Alas, the dead cannot be brought back to life, the broken bodies and spirits restored, or even the ruined places made whole overnight. Nor will the world he poisoned be purified for a long time. But at least he is dead. He can do no more evil on this earth.

The news of his end came from the Hamburg radio. Early in the evening—German time—it had told the German people that an important announcement would be broadcast. Let us record this event in history:

ANNOUNCER: "Achtung! Achtung! The German Broadcasting Company has a serious, important message for the German people." (Three rolls of the drums are heard.)

ANNOUNCER: "It is reported from the Führer's headquarters that our Führer, Adolf Hitler, fighting to the last breath against Bolshevism, fell for Germany this afternoon in his operational headquarters in the Reich Chancellery. On April 30 the Führer appointed Grand Admiral Doenitz his successor. The Grand Admiral and successor of the Führer now speaks to the German people."

DOENITZ: "German men and women, soldiers of the armed forces!

"Our Führer, Adolf Hitler, has fallen. In the deepest sorrow and respect the German people bow.

"At an early date he had recognized the frightful danger of Bolshevism and dedicated his existence to this struggle. At the end of his struggle, of his unswerving straight road of life, stands his hero's death in the capital of the German Empire. His life has been one single service for Germany. His activity in the fight against the Bolshevik storm flood concerned not only Europe but the entire civilized world.

"The Führer has appointed me to be his successor. Fully conscious of the responsibility, I take over the leadership of the German people at this fateful hour.

"It is my first task to save Germany from destruction by the advancing Bolshevist enemy. For this aim alone the military struggle continues. As far and for as long as the achievement of this aim is impeded by the British and the Americans, we shall be forced to carry on our defensive fight against them as well. Under such conditions, however, the Anglo-Americans will continue the war not for their own peoples but solely for the spreading of Bolshevism in Europe.

"What the German people has achieved in battle and borne in the homeland during the struggle of this war is unique in history. In the coming time of need and crisis of our people I shall endeavor to establish tolerable living-conditions for our women, men, and children so far as this lies in my power.

"For all this I need your help. Give me your confidence because your road is mine as well. Maintain order and discipline in town and country. Let everybody do his duty at his own post. Only thus shall we mitigate the sufferings that the coming time will bring to each of us; only thus shall we be able to prevent a collapse. If we do all that is in our power, God will not forsake us after so much suffering and sacrifice." (National anthems.)

By God! The Germans will delude themselves to the end. But their attempt to delude us is childish. Yet Doenitz's proclamation is a fitting end. The whole Hitler regime, the whole Hitler legend, were built on lies. Now lies surround him in death. His successor, like him, wallows in them. And the German people will swallow them up, as they always have.

They are told that Hitler fought to the last breath against Bolshevism. They will believe it. It will become a modern German legend. The German people will never be capable of remembering the simple truths: that Hitler unleashed this World War not against Bolshevism, not against Russia, with whom he was indeed allied by the Ribbentrop-Molotov pact, but against a reactionary, capitalist Poland and a conservative—but also democratic—capitalist Britain and France. Later he voluntarily added Russia to his long list of enemies and finally capitalist America. But the new German legend will be that he tried to destroy not the West, but only the East. And that the West double-crossed him in this noble effort.

Now Doenitz carries on with this immense lie. The British and American armies, which only last December the Germans sought to destroy in the Battle of the Bulge, are now only "impeding" Germany's war on Bolshevism. In doing so they fight not for their countries but "solely" for Bolshevism. Only a German could so argue and really believe his argument. Only a German, with his complete ignorance of the character and mentality of the other peoples who share this globe with him, could fail to see the utter ridiculousness of such patter. Only a German could believe that the rest of the world would fall for such nonsense.

Doenitz claims Hitler died a "hero's death"—the sublimest achievement of all for a German. The Grand Admiral and the announcer say he has "fallen" in battle. Maybe so. But I doubt it. He could also have committed suicide. In fact, I have always been certain myself that that was what he would do in the end.

Konrad Heiden has noted that Hitler had suicidal tendencies in his early days in Munich before he came to power. Certainly he would not relish being executed by the Allies, as he almost surely would have been had he lived. But suicide would be more than just the easiest way out of his impasse, now that he has brought his Fatherland down in flames and ruins in a true Wagnerian setting. To be captured, tried, exposed, and executed would mean the end of the Hitler legend. It would not do at all. But to die at his post in the capital of the Reich at the end of a desperate war and a desperate battle against the Bolshevist horror from the east—that would be the way to perpetuate the Hitler legend. And the German people would be too stupid to remember the suicide. They would remember only the death, the battle. They would come easily to believe that he had "fallen" in battle as became the Reich's first warrior. That was the way a hero died in battle. He did not kill himself. He got killed.

And if he brought down the Fatherland in flame and ruin? You worship the memory of such a man? Make him a legend in your land? Can any people, even Germans, be such fools? Ah, you do not know of the lust for self-destruction in the German soul! ...You have not read the Siegfried saga? The *Nibelungenlied*? Of Hagen of Tronje? Of Wotan? Of Wotan, too, bringing down his world, Valhalla, in flame and ruin to the utter fascination (and approval) of the twisted Teutonic soul?

To write some time: A summing-up of the demon-man, Hitler. Your personal impressions of the fiend. For it was your personal fate to see him in the flesh at many of his greatest and most diabolical moments. Remember the first time you saw him, in Nuremberg in September 1934, when he did not personally impress you so much? When was the last time you actually saw him? I think it was in the Reichstag on July 18, 1940, after he had overrun the Lowlands and France and was making what he thought was a peace bid to Britain.

How important in the understanding of peoples to note that the Italians at least did *their* dictator to death!

San Francisco, *Wednesday, May 2*

The Germans in Italy have surrendered…. Moscow says Berlin fell at three p.m. today…. Acting Secretary of State Joseph C. Grew confirms that Hangman Himmler has been trying to negotiate a surrender, which rather surprises me. Himmler was a great killer and a fanatical Nazi, and I thought he would stick to Hitler to the death. Curiously enough, apparently only Goebbels, of the big Nazi fry, did this. Count Folke Bernadotte of Sweden, it is now learned, met Himmler, at the German's request, in Lübeck, Germany, on April 24. The Gestapo chief asked the Swede to arrange a meeting with Eisenhower at which he would agree to surrender in the west and in Denmark and Norway. He insisted on carrying on the war with Russia, however. Churchill and Truman, to their credit, would have nothing to do with such an offer and so informed Stalin. Our answer was sent to Sweden on April 26 and Bernadotte delivered it to the Germans at Flensburg the next day. Grew reveals that Himmler told Bernadotte that Hitler was suffering from a brain hemorrhage and "might already be dead but could not live more than two days at best."[5]

In the excitement yesterday I forgot to note the eloquent speech to the plenary session by Jan Christiaan Smuts, the elder statesman of this conference. One of the principal architects of the old League of Nations, he told the delegates why it had failed and what they must do to avoid a second and similar failure. I hope our American businessmen get a copy of the speech of this wise old man, for too many of them will not get it through their heads how much the world abroad has changed in the last two decades. Smuts pleaded with the new World Organization to "recognize the far-reaching economic revolution that has taken place since 1919." Our business class may not like this revolution—it doesn't—but since when have all the facts of life been pleasant to everyone? And since when has it been intelligent to be blind to the facts of life?

Smuts is not a good speaker. His manner is too mild and dry, his voice too thin. But he knows how to write eloquently. And he has a sense of history—which no one on our American delegation has. Moreover, he is sensitive to the great moments in history. Certainly yesterday was one.

The war, which had destroyed so much and which had almost been lost, was ending in total victory. Mussolini was hanging by his heels in a square in Milan. Hitler was dead, undoubtedly by his own hand, in the ruins of his Wilhelmstrasse Chancellery, from where he had plotted his evil designs to conquer and degrade the world. Fascism, which had almost overwhelmed our world, which had almost ruined it, and which had caused more obscene misery to more human beings than any other movement in recorded time, was being buried with the men who had made it and led it.

Surely this was a moment in history for the leaders of the nations that had saved us from extinction to show greatness, if they could. Surely it was not the moment for the statesmen of the most powerful nation on earth, whose ideals have stirred men in all countries since the days of Washington and Jefferson, to muff the occasion and to fritter away their time in petty intrigues to get fascist Argentina into a meeting of the nations that had fought and won the war.

Smuts, you could see, sensed the great moment. A wiry little man exuding the wisdom of those rare souls who have not only seen much in their long lives but learned much, he stood on the rostrum in his neat field marshal's uniform, winced at the Klieg lights, cleared his throat, and gave utterance to the greatness of the hour.

"For the human race the hour has struck! Mankind has arrived at the crisis of its fate, the fate of its future as a civilized world… a third world war may well prove beyond the limits of what civilized society can endure… two world wars have been fought; until now the ancient homelands and continent of our Western civilization are a desolation and a ruin unparalleled in history…. Let us see to it that so far as in us lies we shall call a halt to this pilgrimage of death, this march to suicide of our race."

These were great and eloquent words spoken in a quiet but solemn voice and they must have gone ringing around the world. They were followed by sober advice that cleared the minds of lesser men in regard to such controversial matters as the proposed super-rights of the big nations and their power of veto. Such provisions, he said, were not idealistic, not perfect.

"But who with knowledge of the divisions of the last quarter of a century and with thought of the possibilities of mischief in the years immediately before us will venture to say that such drastic provision for unity is not necessary today… is too heavy a price to pay for the new attempt to eliminate international war from our human affairs?"

It is typical of this conference, I think, that this wise old man will not be allowed to play an important role in writing the Charter. As a sop to him, the delegates are going to let him write the preamble to it.[6]

San Francisco, *Thursday, May* 3

Hans Fritsche, Goebbels's deputy (his voice on the radio sounds exactly like his master's), confirms in Berlin that Hitler committed suicide, as did Goebbels.

In Washington the President says he personally believes Hitler is dead. Laval, the treacherous, slimy Frenchman, has escaped to Barcelona from Germany. A proper pal for Franco.

San Francisco, *Friday, May* 4

Drew Middleton begins his *Times* dispatch from SHAEF in Paris today: "This is the hour of victory, complete and overwhelming." All German forces in Holland, Denmark, and northwest Germany—some 500,000—surrendered today to Montgomery. The U.S. Seventh Army has taken Innsbruck, Salzburg—and Hitler's mountain home, Berchtesgaden!

Here the speech-making has ended, and today the conference got down to its real job of drafting a charter. Dr. Herbert V. Evatt, Australia's Foreign Minister, a tough, rough, intelligent fellow, dropped in to see me today. I think he will prove helpful to a little committee I head which hopes to keep Franco Spain out of the United Nations. We certainly haven't had any encouragement from Stettinius or the other Americans. Even Padilla, the Mexican Foreign Minister, in whom I had high hopes, has been lukewarm to us. I think he is afraid of bucking the State Department, which is largely pro-Franco.

San Francisco, *Saturday, May* 5

The success of this conference (which I personally have never doubted) was definitely assured today when the Big Four agreed to sponsor jointly twenty-two amendments to the Dumbarton Oaks proposals. An agreement on twenty-two subjects has confounded those who have been snarling that the Big Four could never get together on anything and that the terrible Bolsheviks would agree to absolutely nothing.

To be sure, the amendments do little to take away the power of the big nations to dominate the new league. But they do liberalize the Dumbarton Oaks proposals in a great many ways, leaving the charter open to change, emphasizing justice and fundamental human rights as its basis, encouraging the development of international law, and tackling the problem of removing conditions that lead to war.

Some problems remain, but the conference is over the hump. And we shall have a charter and a new League of Nations within a month!

San Francisco, *Sunday, May* 6

It's just about over. The whole Allied world waited breathlessly today for V-E Day. It didn't come. But, according to London, it looks like tomorrow.

What a week this has been!

It was the week, of all our lives, we've been waiting for. When it came, and unfolded, one breathless hour after another, it was too much for our poor human minds really to grasp. You could not find words—or at least I couldn't—to express it. For here in one short week—a flicker of time—an evil world crumbled into dust and ruin and we saw, for once at least, that decent things, decent people, or, if you like, justice and right, *do*triumph in our world over evil and injustice and tyranny....

Can we grasp what has happened in Germany? Here lies a once great nation, with an ancient culture, in shambles, its political, economic, and social framework destroyed as completely as its great cities. I do not think man has ever witnessed such a debacle on this planet—at least on such a scale. The Thirty Years' War laid waste much of Germany—but not like this....

One thing only bothers me about Hitler's death. I was sure that just before he killed himself he would issue a grandiose proclamation, a final testament in which he would recapitulate all the Nazi nonsense in which most Germans believed. And in time, I thought he would calculate, this final testament would become a sort of Bible to Germans if they should ever recover from their present catastrophe and begin again on the job that first the Kaiser and then Hitler failed to finish.

But Hitler died without leaving a word, which is most unlike him.[7]

San Francisco, *Monday, May 7*

So it's finally over—the long and bloody war in Europe—the German war that almost destroyed our world!

Over after five years, eight months, and six days—in our puny, absurd lives.

Officially—for some reason—the end will not be announced and duly celebrated until tomorrow. But the Germans themselves announced this morning over the Flensburg radio their unconditional surrender. And the A.P. carries under Ed Kennedy's by-line a factual story from Reims describing the actual ceremony of surrender in a little schoolhouse there which serves as General Eisenhower's headquarters.

Quite a scoop, and the Associated Press has been boasting about it all day. But it seems to have been achieved by Kennedy's breaking his word, and one wonders about the ethics of our greatest news-gathering organization. But this is secondary. The important thing is that the war is over, Germany is beaten, and we can continue to be free men and not have to fear an awful slavery under the outlandish German barbarians.

All day I have had to rub my eyes to believe it; to realize that this is really the end of the nightmare that began for me personally (to be shamefully egotistic about it) on that gray morning in Berlin of September 1, 1939, five and a half years ago. It seems a long time—ages—and some twenty-five million human beings who were alive on that day and relatively happy have perished, slaughtered on the battlefield, wiped out by bombs, tortured to death in the Nazi horror camps.

I have had to rub my eyes too this memorable day to try to get it through my head that Nazism at last lies in ruin and that this monstrous thing that I have had to live with rather closely for most of my adult life is no more and that—what is really important, since one's own life is not—it will never again degrade man, such as he is, on this sorry planet. No doubt there will be other things to degrade him—injustice, intolerance, greed, poverty, and other evils that we shall always have with us—but at least not Nazism, which was a fouler thing than most Americans, who never got close to it, will ever know.

I really feel like offering a prayer, something I have not done for too long.

The CBS office woke me out of a sound sleep early this morning. Someone on the telephone said: "This is it. The Germans have surrendered." I hurried to the office, which was in a great state of commotion. Someone handed me the first bulletins. They said:

A.P.
FLASH
Reims, France—Allies officially announce Germany surrendered unconditionally

FD935AEW

That was six thirty-five a.m. our time in San Francisco.
A minute later a second bulletin had come.

A113
BULLETIN
BY EDWARD KENNEDY
Reims, France, May 7—(AP)—Germany surrendered unconditionally to the Western Allies and Russia at 2.41 a.m. French time today.

FD936AEW

Yes, this was it. This was the end.
For the record, this is Kennedy's story of the German surrender:

BY EDWARD KENNEDY (Associated Press Correspondent)

REIMS, France, May 7—Germany surrendered unconditionally to the Western Allies and the Soviet Union at 2:41 A.M. French time today. (This was at 8:41 P.M. Eastern Wartime Sunday).

The surrender took place at a little red schoolhouse that is the head-quarters of Gen. Dwight D. Eisenhower.

The surrender which brought the war in Europe to a formal end after five years, eight months and six days of bloodshed and destruction, was signed for Germany by Col. Gen. Gustav Jodl. General Jodl is the new Chief of Staff of the German Army.

The surrender was signed for the Supreme Allied Command by Lieut. Gen. Walter Bedell Smith, Chief of Staff for General Eisenhower.

It was also signed by Gen. Ivan Susloparov for the Soviet Union and by Gen. François Sevez for France.

General Eisenhower was not present at the signing, but immediately afterward General Jodl and his fellow delegate, Admiral Hans Friedeburg, were received by the Supreme Commander.

They were asked sternly if they understood the surrender terms imposed upon Germany and if they would be carried out. They said yes.

Germany, which began the war with a ruthless attack upon Poland, followed by successive aggressions and brutality in internment camps, surrendered with an appeal to the victors for mercy toward the German people and armed forces.

After having signed the full surrender General Jodl said he wanted to speak and received leave to do so.

"With this signature," he said in soft-spoken German, "the German people and armed forces are for better or worse delivered into the victors' hands.

"In this war, which has lasted more than five years, both have achieved and suffered more than perhaps any other people in the world."

San Francisco, I must say, has taken the tremendous news with great restraint, befitting its civilized character. I have not seen any wild outbursts of celebrating and revelry such as marked Armistice Day the last time. It has been a gray day with low overhanging clouds, much like that day we had in Berlin when Hitler went off to war on September 1, 1939.

Perhaps emotions were restrained because today's news was anticlimactic. Everyone has known for a week that the German war was as good as over. But I think the main reason for the general soberness with which the news has been received is the realization here—stronger than in the East—that our war is only half over. There is still Japan to lick. The local mayor summed it up: "To recognize the German surrender by a widespread celebration at a time when there is still a job to do against Japan would be an affront to our Allied fighters in the Pacific. Keep on the job!"

There was of course rejoicing among the delegates of the United Nations, though they continued their labors as usual and Molotov actually held a press conference to state that the unanimity of the Big Four was so complete that the success of the conference was assured. The surrender news, if anything, goaded the peacemakers on with their job. Now that we have peace, we must quickly get machinery to keep it.

To record some of the headlines on this historic day:

The *San Francisco Examiner*, in type that covers half the front page:

It's Official:
WAR IS OVER
IN EUROPE!

The *San Francisco Call Bulletin*:

Associated Press Says:
UNCONDITIONAL
SURRENDER!

The San Francisco edition of the *New York Post*:

V-E
DAY
Germany Signs Full Surrender

Tired from the excitement and the many broadcasts of this day, but not sleepy. And a feeling inside that is good. What a pity that Franklin Roosevelt could not have lived just a month longer to see this day! As he lay dying, though, he must have known it was coming soon.

San Francisco, *Tuesday, May* 8
And so this Day too has come, V-E Day—Victory in Europe Day—final and official, and with the heads of state (let us not be cynical about the great today) sounding off in purple proclamations, and the free peoples happy, relieved, glad to be alive, to have survived, but restrained and sober in their joy.

A thought too, a thought of sadness, for those who did not survive. One newspaper today says there were forty million of them. Our own battle casualties in the war against Germany are given by the War Department today as three quarters of a million, of whom 150,000 are dead. The population of a good-sized American city—all dead. Will we remember that—and what for?—when we go back to making money in this land? We will...?

The headlines this day:

New York Times(San Francisco edition):

THE WAR IN EUROPE IS ENDED!
SURRENDER IS UNCONDITIONAL;

V-E WILL BE PROCLAIMED TODAY;
LAST FIGHTING IN CZECH POCKET

San Francisco Chronicle:

TRUMAN CHURCHILL ANNOUNCE
THE SURRENDER OF GERMANY
PRESIDENT CALLS ON US
TO PRESS WAR ON NIPS

Sunday Set As Day Of Thanksgiving
All Guns Stop Firing This Afternoon

Because of a second ceremony of German surrender to the Russians which took place in Berlin tonight, the war will not be officially over until twelve one a.m. tomorrow (May 9, 1945, for the record), Berlin time, which was three one p.m., Pacific war time today, May 8.

But President Truman proclaimed the war over so far as we are concerned at nine a.m., Eastern war time, today, when he issued a formal proclamation and went on the air with a brief speech. It being six a.m. here, I missed it, but perhaps it should go in here:

This is a solemn but a glorious hour. General Eisenhower informs me that the forces of Germany have surrendered to the United Nations. The flags of reason fly over all Europe.

I only wish that Franklin D. Roosevelt had lived to witness this day.

For this victory we join in offering our thanks to the Providence which has guided and sustained us through the dark days of adversity.

Our rejoicing is sobered and subdued by a supreme consciousness of the terrible price we have paid to rid the world of Hitler and his evil band.

Let us not forget, my fellow Americans, the sorrow and heartbreak which today abide in the homes of so many of our neighbors—neighbors whose most priceless possession has been rendered as a sacrifice to redeem our liberty.

We can repay the debt which we owe to our God, to our dead and to our children only by work—by ceaseless devotion to the responsibilities which lie ahead of us. If I could give you a single watchword for the coming months, that word is—work, work, work.

We must work to finish the war. Our victory is but half-won. The West is free, but the East is still in bondage to the treacherous tyranny of the Japanese. When the last Japanese division has surrendered unconditionally, then only will our fighting job be done.

We must work to bind up the wounds of a suffering world—to build an abiding peace, a peace rooted in justice and in law. We can build such a peace only by hard, toilsome painstaking work—by understanding and working with our Allies in peace as we have in war.

The job ahead is no less important, no less urgent, no less difficult than the task which now happily is done.

I call upon every American to stick to his post until the last battle is won. Until that day, let no man abandon his post or slacken his efforts.

PROCLAMATION—

The Allied Armies through sacrifice and devotion and with God's help, have wrung from Germany a final and unconditional surrender. The western world has been freed of the evil forces which for five years and longer have imprisoned the bodies and broken the lives of millions upon millions of free-born men. They have violated their churches, destroyed their homes, corrupted their children, and murdered their loved ones. Our armies of liberation have restored freedom to these suffering peoples whose spirit and will the oppressors could never enslave.

Much remains to be done. The victory won in the West must now be won in the East. The whole world must be cleansed of the evil from which half the world has been freed. United, the peaceloving nations have demonstrated in the West that their arms are stronger by far than the might of dictators or the tyranny of military cliques that once called us soft and weak.

The power of our peoples to defend themselves against all enemies will be proved in the Pacific war as it has been proved in Europe.

For the triumph of spirit and of arms which we have won and for its promise to people everywhere who join us in the love of freedom, it is fitting that we as a nation give thanks to Almighty God, who has strengthened us and given us the victory.

Now, therefore, I, Harry S. Truman, President of the United States of America, do hereby appoint Sunday, May 13, 1945, to be a day of prayer.

I call upon the people of the United States, whatever their faith, to unite in offering joyful thanks to God for the victory we have won and to pray that He will support us to the end of our present struggle and guide us into the way of peace.

I also call upon my countrymen to dedicate this day of prayer to the memory of those who have given their lives to make possible our victory.

In witness whereof, I have hereunto set my hand and caused the seal of the United States of America to be affixed.

Done at the city of Washington this eighth day of May in the year of our Lord Nineteen Hundred and Forty-five, and of the independence of the United States, the one hundred and sixty-ninth.

Harry S. Truman

Churchill, as might have been expected, was perhaps the most eloquent Allied statesman today, not so much in his formal V-E Day message, which lacked his usual fire, but in a second speech he made in London. After recalling to Britons that "we from this island maintained the struggle single-handed for a whole year," he said:

"But every man and woman and child in this country had no thought of quitting. So we came back after long months from the jaws of death, out of the mouth of hell, while all the world wondered. I say that in the long years to come not only the people of this island but of the world, wherever the bird of freedom chirps in the human hearth, will look back to what we have done and they will say: Do not yield to violence and tyranny. March straight forward and die, if need be, to remain unconquered."

His formal message ended: "Advance Britannia! Long live the cause of freedom! God save the King!"

To the soldiers of the Allied Expeditionary Force, who will come out of the war alive now, General Eisenhower issued his final Order of the Day:

"The crusade on which we embarked in the early summer of 1944 has reached its glorious conclusion. It is my special privilege in the name of all the nations represented in this theater of war to commend each of you for valiant performance of duty. Though these words are feeble, they come from the bottom of a heart overflowing with pride in your loyal service and admiration for you as warriors.

"Your accomplishments at sea, in the air, on the ground and in the field of supply have astonished the world…. The blood of many nations—American, British, Canadian, French, Polish and others—has helped to gain the victory. Each of the fallen died as a member of a team…. As we celebrate victory in Europe let us remind ourselves that our common problems of the immediate and distant future can best be solved in the same conceptions of cooperation and devotion to the cause of human freedom as have made this Expeditionary Force such a mighty engine of righteous destruction.

"Let us have no part in the profitless quarrels in which other men will inevitably engage as to what country, what service won the European war.

"Every man, every woman, of every nation here represented has served according to his or her ability…. This we shall remember…."

The text of the document of Germany's unconditional surrender was signed by General Gustav Jodl, chief of staff of the German army, by General Walter

49

Bedell Smith, chief of staff of the Supreme Allied Command, by General Ivan Susloparov for Russia, and General François Sevez for France:

> We, the undersigned, acting by authority of the German High Command, hereby surrender unconditionally to the Supreme Commander, Allied Expeditionary Force, and simultaneously to the Soviet High Command, all forces on land, sea and in the air who are at this date under German control.
>
> The German High Command will at once issue orders to all German military, naval and air authorities and to all forces under German control to cease active operations at 2301 hours Central European time on Eighth May and to remain in the positions occupied at the time. No ship, vessel or aircraft is to be scuttled, or any damage done to their hull, machinery and equipment.
>
> The German High Command will at once issue to the appropriate commanders, and insure the carrying out of any further order issued by the Supreme Commander, Allied Expeditionary Force, and by the Soviet High Command.
>
> This Act of Military Surrender is without prejudice to, and will be superseded by, any general instrument of surrender imposed by, or on behalf of the United Nations and applicable to Germany and the German Armed Forces as a whole.
>
> In the event of the German High Command or any of the forces under their control failing to act in accordance with this act of surrender, the Supreme Commander, Allied Expeditionary Force, and the Soviet High Command will take such punitive or other action as they deem appropriate.

The last official word we are liable to hear from the Master Race for a long time came over the Flensburg radio today. It was the surrender statement of Admiral Doenitz:

> German men and women: When I addressed the German nation on May 1 telling it that the Führer had appointed me his successor, I said that the foremost task was to save the lives of the German people. In order to achieve this goal, I ordered the German High Command during the night of May 6-7 to sign the unconditional surrender for all fronts.
>
> On May 8 at 2300 (11 p.m.) the arms will be silent.
>
> German soldiers, veterans of countless battles, are now treading the bitter path to captivity, and thereby making the last sacrifice for the life of our women and children, and for the future of our nation.
>
> We bow to all who have fallen. I have pledged myself to the German people that in the coming times of want I will help courageous women and

children, as far as I humanly can, to alleviate their conditions. Whether this will be possible I do not know.

We must face facts squarely. The unity of state and party does not exist any more. The party has left the scene of its activities.

With the occupation of Germany, the power has been transferred to the occupying authorities. It is up to them to confirm me in my function and the government I have appointed or decide whether to appoint a different one. Should I be required to help our fatherland, I will remain at my post.

Should the will of the German people express itself in the appointment of a head of state, or should the powers of occupation make it impossible for me to continue in my office remains to be seen.

Duty keeps me at my difficult post for the sake of Germany. I will not remain one hour more than can be reconciled with the dignity of the Reich. I will disregard my person in this matter.

All of us have to face a difficult path. We have to walk it with dignity, courage and discipline which those demand of us, who sacrificed their all for us. We must walk it by making the greatest efforts to create a firm basis for our future lives.

We will walk it unitedly. Without this unity we will not be able to overcome the misery of the times to come. We will walk it in the hope that one day our children may lead a free and secure existence in a peaceful Europe.

On this thorny path, which we all will have to tread, I will try to help you as much as is possible, should I remain at my post.

Should we succeed in going this way together, this step will be a service to the nation and the Reich.

Such was this day in history.

The stink about the A.P.'s scoop is growing. Fifty-three Allied correspondents at SHAEF today signed a bitter letter to General Eisenhower charging that Ed Kennedy's beating the gun on the surrender story is "the most disgraceful, deliberate and unethical double-cross in the history of journalism."

Yet the A.P. for reasons that I cannot comprehend, continues to boast of its "great beat" yesterday, and Mr. Kent Cooper, executive director, protests about the suspension of Kennedy and the A.P. by SHAEF though General Eisenhower himself has informed him that Kennedy's suspension is "due to a self-admitted deliberate violation of SHAEF regulations and breach of confidence." As for Paul Mickelson, general news editor of A.P., he laughs off the whole unsavory mess by exulting: "The suspension is like being thrown out of Wahoo, Neb., after the whole thing is over." It seems pretty clear from the other correspondents in Paris that sixteen of them actually were taken by SHAEF to witness the surrender at Reims and that Kennedy's scoop about which the A.P.—along with too many

American newspapers—boasts, consisted in his flagrantly violating a pledge demanded from all sixteen correspondents, including Kennedy, on their honor, by General Allen, PRO director, not to release the story until permitted to do so by the Allied governments. Boyd Lewis, European news manager of the United Press, who made the trip to Reims, says Kennedy admits violating General Allen's pledge, but maintains the general had no right to impose such a pledge.

A poor scoop to boast about, it seems to me.

Lunched with Jeff Parson, editor of the *Herald Tribune*, at the Bohemian Club, a most civilized place. We decided to take time off to collect our thoughts, but I, at least, was not very successful. At six p.m. to the CBS studio to speak a few lines portraying myself at the Compiègne Armistice in Norman Corwin's V-E Day broadcast. It turned out to be the most moving show I have ever heard on the air. I felt limp afterward.

San Francisco, *Wednesday, May* 9

For the first time in many a moon the headlines today do not scream out the news of war. They are still big, perhaps from habit. But they tell of such things as the curfew being lifted, or horse-racing starting up again. You read them and rub your eyes. Peace in Europe has come so suddenly it is difficult to make the adjustment overnight. And we really can't make it—since there is more to life than night-clubs and races—until the *other* war, the Jap war is finished.

The Japs are not going to quit. Today an official statement from the Tokyo cabinet, specifically sanctioned by the Emperor and therefore, we are told, a "divine command," expresses "deep regret" at Germany's surrender, but declares that the "sudden change of the war situation in Europe will not bring the slightest change in the war objective of the Imperial Government." That objective, according to the cabinet? "The complete destruction of the unjust ambition of the United States and Britain."

A heartening dispatch from Oslo. Quisling, the puppet "premier" of Norway whose name has become a synonym for treason, was locked up in the Oslo jail today.

Allied headquarters today sheds more light on Ed Kennedy's scoop for the A.P. Kennedy's excuse that no military security was involved and that he could not "accept" the view of the Allied Command that the story should be held up until General Eisenhower released it turns out to be pretty preposterous.

It is now clear that General Eisenhower was not joking when he said that the lives of American soldiers were involved in holding up release of the surrender news. In obtaining authority from the Russian Command to negotiate also for the Soviet Army, it was absolutely essential, the American commander-in-chief explains, for no news to get out until it was established "that the surrender was genuine on all fronts and did not represent merely an additional attempt by the Germans to gain advantages at the expense of the Russians."

Mr. Kennedy in Paris and Mr. Kent Cooper in New York could not, of course, have known this on Monday, but their ignorance of the situation was hardly an excuse for thinking their own judgment in such a vital military matter superior to that of General Eisenhower.

So the A.P. scoop, as the SHAEF statement today puts it, placed General Eisenhower "in a position of having broken an understanding with our Russian allies." Because of this he feared that the entire intricate "chain of negotiations might break down and therefore prolong the war."

Was this risk worth taking so that the Associated Press might get "one of the greatest beats in history"?

Apparently some of our newspapers think so. One says: "The A.P. lived up to the highest traditions of the American Press." Another says: "Mr. Kennedy's now historic twenty-four hours news 'beat' is no stigma: it is a distinction." A third says: "Mr. Kennedy can afford to laugh."

Not all our American newspapers are so shockingly irresponsible. One of them writes it "cannot condone Kennedy's broken faith nor the Associated Press's acceptance of and distribution of a story sent under broken faith…. The newspaper profession cannot exist unless it has the confidence of the people with whom it deals. Confidence is not built upon broken faith."

When the press of America thinks a headline and a scoop more important than its word of honor, then its hard-won freedom will have become an awful mockery and sooner or later the people will know it.

Took Del Vayo, the Spanish Republican Foreign Minister, and Freda Kirchwey, editor of the *Nation*, to lunch with Dr. Evatt. The doctor was in great form, his blunt language at first shocking and then charming Freda. He promises to help us in our fight to keep Franco Spain out of the United Nations and especially out of this conference. This morning Evatt (who is Australian Minister for External Affairs) led the fight of the small and middle-sized nations to whittle down the veto power of the Big Four. Even though Molotov took off for Moscow today, I do not think Evatt will get very far, doughty warrior though he is. We do not publicize it, but the United States is as insistent on the big-power veto as is Russia. Without the veto our delegation does not think two thirds of the Senate will ratify the Charter.

San Francisco, *Thursday, May* 10

Presided at a luncheon given in honor of Del Vayo. I do not much like committees, of which we have too many, but Freda bludgeoned me into becoming chairman of the Friends of the Spanish Republic. We have one purpose here only: to keep Franco out. It was the committee that gave the luncheon to further that purpose, and some hundred of the best correspondents here turned out. Del Vayo made the finest speech I've ever heard him make.

But we did not get much help from Ed Stettinius, who, after all, is American Secretary of State and head of the American delegation of the conference. Freda made public a letter to us from him which was wishy-washy even for a State

Department man. He said his delegation "does not expect to be called upon to take cognizance of the request for the admission of Spain at this conference," and then gave us a nice cold shower by adding that such a request "might properly be entertained by the international organization after its formation."

"Properly entertained!"

An amusing and quite lavish cocktail party at the Palace this afternoon given by none other than Harry Bridges and his Long-Shoremen's Union. It was a sight to see Bridges, under sentence of deportation as a Communist, which he has appealed to the Supreme Court, conversing in the most friendly and serious way with Roy Howard and other bigwigs of our capitalist world. The union was not sparing of either food or drink and everyone seemed to have a good time. Afterward to the Robin Kinkaids' for dinner. They are a lovable pair, and from their studio one could look down upon one of the great sights of this world, the bay and the hills beyond.

San Francisco, *Friday, May* 11

Disturbed by a dispatch from Drew Middleton in yesterday's *Times*. He says: "The gravest concern is felt by senior intelligence officers at Gen. Eisenhower's headquarters over the manner in which the German High Command has survived defeat of the Wehrmacht, retaining the respect and admiration of the German people and attaining a position as the only stable element in an otherwise disorganized nation.

"The onus of defeat rests on Adolf Hitler and the Nazi party as far as the average German is concerned... and the tightly bound military priesthood that has been the real ruler of the Reich since 1871 is credited with fighting a brilliant patriotic war that was lost only because of the interference and inefficiency of the party."

Though Kent Cooper, executive director of A.P., was quoted only yesterday as saying he refused to "prejudge" Kennedy for his "alleged violation" of the release on the Reims surrender, Robert McLean, president of the A.P., comes clean in a statement published today: "The Associated Press profoundly regrets the distribution on Monday of the report of the total surrender in Europe which investigation now clearly shows was distributed in advance of authorization by Supreme Allied Headquarters...."

President Beneš is back in Prague today! There is a man whose courage, integrity, and view of history have been vindicated.... Learn that Judge Samuel Rosenmann has been quietly working here to get the British, Russians, and French to join in setting up an international military tribunal to try Axis war criminals.

San Francisco, *Saturday, May* 12

Secretary of War Stimson says that in our zone of occupied Germany we will be both "tough" in our administration and "ruthless" in our denazification. Fine. But will we?

Göring yesterday was interviewed by fifty Allied correspondents and did his best to disassociate himself from Hitler. It is a swindle all the big Nazi thugs will try to put over on us. He does reveal, what is probably true, that by "the middle of 1944" the German generals had become convinced that the war was irrevocably lost and that they tried to convince Hitler it was.

"Hitler," he says, "refused to accept this point of view. He ordered that it never be referred to again."

Cocktails and dinner with the Walter Lippmanns and much good talk about the state of the world. Afterward we peeped in on a dance.

The conference, though no longer getting the headlines, is getting an immense amount of hard work done. The Charter is taking shape.

San Francisco, *Sunday, May* 13

The President this day led the nation in prayers of humble thanks for the victory over Germany.

Later, while writing my broadcast, listened to Churchill's. It was not one of his greatest speeches, but he spoke it with his usual vigor and eloquence. The German war has been over only a week, but we can already see that it is going to be almost as big a job to wage peace as it was to wage war. San Francisco, with its daily bickerings, has been a good place to realize this. And Churchill plainly demonstrated it today. It seemed to me as I listened to him that he was already taking, not without some reason, a stand against Russia in the peace. (That has certainly been Eden's policy here and the Americans have blindly supported it.)

"We have to make sure," Churchill thundered, no doubt with his mind on Poland, though he did not say so specifically, "that in Europe the words freedom, democracy and liberation are not distorted from their true meaning.... There would be little use in punishing the Hitlerites for their crimes, if law and justice did not rule and if totalitarian or police governments were to take the place of the German invaders.... We must make sure that those causes which we fought for, find recognition at the peace table in facts as well as words. And above all, we must labor that the world organization which the United Nations are creating at San Francisco does not become an idle name, does not become a shield for the strong and a mockery for the weak."

Churchill was very bitter about Mr. de Valera and Ireland, as he has every reason to be, though some of our stubborn American Irish have closed minds on the subject. But you cannot dispute Churchill's case that at a moment when the fate of Britain hung in the balance, de Valera's government made it possible for the Germans to block the southern approaches to the British Isles by his refusal to grant Britain bases to fight the German U-boats.

Took some time in my broadcast this afternoon to emphasize that the most important development here outside the work of drafting the Charter has been the loss of our American position as mediator between Russia and Britain. We have been maneuvered—partly by the British, partly by our own ineptness—into a role that some day could be as disastrous as it would be nonsensical. This role places America as the great antagonist of Russia.

This is no position, in my humble opinion, for the United States and Russia to get themselves into. It is true that we shall be the two most powerful nations from now on. But it is also true that the United States and Russia have no great historical conflicting interests. They never have had. One more thing is true. If we don't get along together, Russia and ourselves, there will not be a peace for very long. But we must face the blunt truth: relations between us and the Russians have deteriorated since this conference opened. There has been too much feeling on our side that we have been winning what one of our delegates calls "victories" over the Russians here. On the Russian side there has been an exaggerated feeling that we were working against them, or at least that we intended to co-operate with them as little as possible after the war. They have been unduly suspicious of us.

After the broadcast, which out here is over at three p.m., went for a drive over the Golden Gate Bridge into the hills. The bridge itself has a beauty that I find no words to describe adequately, and the hills beyond, set between the ocean and the bay, remind me of Spain, Sicily, Italy, and the Khyber Pass. We stopped at the water front of Sausalito, as picturesque as any little fishing village on the Mediterranean. Returned in time to take part in a repeat performance of Corwin's great V-E Day broadcast "On a Note of Triumph." There is a great deal that is trashy and wrong with radio in America, but Norman's show indicates what radio can do when it grows up.

San Francisco, *Friday, May* 18

Lunch with the Mexican Foreign Minister, Señor Padilla. Eric Sevareid had told me he was one of the great men of this hemisphere, but he was quite a disappointment to me. His ideas seemed timid, his will weak; and he had a tendency to lecture in somewhat flowery language that meant little. He will not be much help in our efforts to keep Franco out.

Only two main problems remain to be disposed of here: agreement on the veto power of the Big Five; and a plan for trusteeship of the colonial peoples. We are being pretty hypocritical on both issues. Our main interest in trusteeship is to see that it gives us all the military bases we think we need in the Pacific. As to the veto, the American delegation opposes any further modification. Yet several correspondents blame the Russians for insisting on big-power veto rights.

Two good items of news yesterday to record. It's reported from London that the United Nations War Crimes Commission has completed its indictments against all top-ranking Nazis. One of the worst Nazi gangsters of them all was captured Wednesday—Dr. Robert Ley, a drunk, a beast, a degenerate, head of the Nazi Labor Front, from which he made millions, and once a favorite thug of Hitler.

San Francisco, *Sunday, May 20*

Did my last broadcast from here today. Began with a report on the bloody fighting on Okinawa, now in its eighth week. Our own losses on that island already are 4,000 dead, 18,000 wounded.

Last night I sat in the CBS studio and listened to Jan Christiaan Smuts's broadcast. Our executives almost were out of their minds because there was no trace of the old field marshal two minutes before the broadcast was supposed to go on. However, he showed up just in the nick of time.

He had some proper words for the world-improvers who infest San Francisco and worry themselves and everyone else over their impractical schemes. "Some people," he said, "are not satisfied with wrestling with the almost insoluble problem of world security against the dreadful scourge of war. They have a passion for reforming the world in general, and are prepared to push forward at full blast along all fronts.... San Francisco is full of good causes and of pressure groups behind them.... The Conference works under constant stresses and strains which confuse its attention, raise irrelevant matters and slow down the progress of the real major issue before it."

Afterward we had a long chat. From what I had heard of the South African Dutch, I had imagined Smuts to be rather prim and puritan. Actually he is a salty old fellow despite his background and his great learning. We talked of pretty girls (there was one present, from our news room), which led us to talk of the temptations of letting down on Saturday nights and of the dullness of Sundays in puritan lands. (One remembered the bleak Sabbaths in Scotland.)

To sum up this wonderful and exciting month in San Francisco:

Certainly it is the major problems of the peace stemming from the German collapse that have hung over this conference and confused it.

The actual job of the conference, writing the Charter of a new League of Nations, has gone all right. We shall have our Charter before the middle of June. And it will give us a better world organization than was the old League at Geneva. It will have teeth in it whereas the League was pretty much of a toothless old woman. The core of the new league will be the Security Council, which will be mainly responsible for the maintenance of peace and security. And it will be dominated by the five big powers. There will be a General Assembly of all the powers, large and small, but it will be largely a debating society. It may make recommendations, but it is the Council that will make the decisions.

The old League never dared to apply armed force to restrain aggressors against the peace. The new league will specifically call for such application and will have a Military Staff committee to aid it.

There will be, I believe, a much stronger Economic and Social Council than was contemplated at Dumbarton Oaks—one of the unheadlined successes of this conference. Since some of the main causes of war in our time are economic and social in their nature, this council will have great opportunities.

Finally, there is to be an International Court of Justice, functioning as the judicial organ of the United Nations.

Such is the picture today as the delegates of forty-nine nations (or is it fifty, with Argentina?) perspire to establish the machinery of world peace.

But most of the peacemakers—and this is especially true of the Russians, the British, and ourselves—seem to have forgotten all too often here in San Francisco that the success of this new World Security Organization, particularly during its first ten years, depends not so much on the wisdom of the various paragraphs that they are now drafting as on the ability of the Big Five nations and a few of the smaller ones that were also Axis victims in the war to work together....

It may well be that the present deterioration in Allied relations is only temporary, and perhaps more apparent than real. There was bound to be confusion when Germany, which had held and devastated most of Europe, suddenly crumbled. But that at the supreme moment of Allied victory there should be such a spectacle as we now witness in the Allied lands is not heartening. It is stupid. As the *New York Herald Tribune* said yesterday: "There is no discernible difference in interest, policy, purpose or attitude between Russia, Britain and the United States which is worth a candle by comparison with the enormous sacrifices and sufferings through which the respective peoples have fought their way to the threshold of a better world."

That is true. But you would scarcely guess it from the headlines the past week. Mr. Eden hurries back to London from San Francisco to explain to Parliament that the reason for his haste was "a number of serious and disquieting issues." Mr. Churchill, who was a great and inspiring war leader but whose talents for the peace remain to be shown, expresses concern about the possibility of the victors getting together. The Russians complain about the slowness in trying the Nazi war criminals and yet refuse—as they have refused for two years—to sit on the Allied War Crimes Commission. It is the mutual suspicion among the Allies that is our main trouble.

To bed almost at dawn.... The plane leaving in an hour or two.

New York, *Wednesday, May 23*

Churchill has resigned—a temptation, I suppose, he could not resist. At the supreme moment in his career, in the great hour of victory, which his indomitable spirit did so much to snatch from defeat, he cannot lose the general election set for July 5.

An interesting day in Germany. You might say that the Third Reich, which Hitler boasted would last a thousand years, came to its end officially today. The rump government of Grand Admiral Karl Doenitz at Flensburg has been dissolved by the Allies, and its members—Doenitz, Count Schwerin-Krosigk, Speer, General Jodl, and so on—arrested.... Julius Streicher, the notorious Jew-baiter of Nuremberg, was captured today in Germany—by a New York Jew, a U.S. army major.

New York, *Thursday, May* **24**

Himmler, next to Hitler the most evil of the Nazi barbarians, has escaped the justice of this world. The British reveal he was picked up Monday at a bridge at Bremervoerde, northeast of Bremen, but was not immediately recognized, having shaved off his mustache, donned civilian clothes and tied a black patch over his right eye. Recognized as the killer Gestapo chief during a check-up at a prisoner-of-war camp yesterday, he bit a small vial of poison concealed in his mouth as he was being stripped. He was a dead Nazi fifteen minutes later, at eleven four p.m. yesterday. Wonder if the British are just as satisfied to be rid of him this way? The Foreign Office, at least, does not appear enthusiastic about the prospect of trying the Nazi war criminals.

New York, *Tuesday, May* **29**

Lord Haw-Haw has been captured by the British. The greatest of the radio traitors, will he meet a traitor's end? Will our American radio traitors?

Lunch at the Plaza with [Juan] Negrín, Prime Minister of the Spanish Republican government, one of the truly great men I know. (Gandhi is another.) He was as sparkling and brilliant as ever. I often think he is too intelligent for politics. Del Vayo joined us.

New York, *Wednesday, May* **30**

Memorial Day, and more war dead to mourn than ever before and more shabby speeches by the politicos promising there shall be no more dead in wars because there shall be peace. General Truscott, commander of the Fifth Army, who came up, I believe, from the ranks, was one of the few speech-makers today to drop the oratory and make sense. At the Anzio beachhead, where eight thousand of our men were killed, he said: "We pray that when the soldiers' last job is done, the statesmen of the world will make sure of that lasting peace for which their soldier comrades died."

I remember those wounded American soldiers who hobbled into a plenary session at San Francisco one afternoon. They seemed to be saying to the talkative statesmen there: "We did our part. Now you do yours."

But—in San Francisco the statesmen wrangle over paragraphs… in half a dozen spots across the Atlantic there is tension and even bloodshed, despite the peace. In Syria, for example. Strange that the British are insisting the French get out of Syria and Lebanon while they stay on in Egypt, Palestine, and Transjordania.

Washington, *Thursday, May* **31**

General Hap Arnold came to lunch with some of us ignorant broadcasters. He showed us his secret (?) charts calling for two million tons (!) of bombs to be dropped on Japan this coming year. Arnold, youthful in his enormous enthusiasm, thinks the B-29 plane just about the greatest development of the human race to date.

Our university researchers today calculate that World War II has cost this planet more than a *trillion*dollars. What more proof that man is, at bottom, a lunatic! Far worse than the dollar cost, of course, is the cost in human lives.

Learn here that Truman, Churchill, and Stalin will meet soon, probably in Berlin—a most suitable place....

New York, *Sunday, June* 3

This has been a puzzling and disappointing week in Europe and the Near East. Fighting and bloodshed in Syria and harsh words between the British and French over it. Uneasiness about Trieste and Austria and conflicts already among the Allies over Germany. Everywhere bitter undercurrents and a scramble for power, influence, even territory. Is *this*what we fought for?

New York, *Wednesday, June* 6

Pastor Niemöller, whom our troops released from a Nazi concentration camp recently, must have surprised quite a few good citizens in this country who have been urging that we restore democracy in Germany day after tomorrow, or week after next at the latest. Niemöller told our correspondents yesterday that the German people are incapable of democracy and would not like it if they had it. "The Germans," he said, "like to be governed." Incidentally, Niemöller expresses not one single word of regret for what Germany has done to the world. He doesn't even regret having begged Hitler to let him serve in the German Navy during the war. In fact, he stresses that his opposition to the Nazis was religious only; not political.

New York, *Thursday, June* 7

Lunch with Bob Sherwood at the Century. He inveigled me into talking at a dinner for Thomas Mann on the seventieth birthday of this truly great German writer. Justice Frankfurter, Secretary Ickes, and, of course, Mann are to speak and Bob will preside. I pleaded with him to get a more representative American writer.

SHAEF, now at Frankfurt, discloses our American casualties in the campaign that began with the invasion of Normandy and ended with V-E Day amounted to 514,534—killed: 89,477; wounded: 367,180; missing: 57,877. A frightful figure, and it does not include air-force casualties, which were not light. Combined losses of other Allies in the campaign were about half ours, British-Canadian casualties being 39,599 killed, 126,545 wounded, and 18,368 missing. The French lost more than I suspected: 11,080 killed, 49,566 wounded, 4,201 missing. But who, in a year, will remember these grievous figures?

The political news this day is encouraging. The House today approved by a vote of 345 to 18 the Bretton Woods agreement, a great step forward in putting some sense into international relations.... In Moscow Harry Hopkins has succeeded in getting Stalin to instruct the Soviet delegation in San Francisco to drop its insistence on a Big Five veto of even discussion of international disputes and to be more conciliatory, which it certainly has not been. The new League of Nations is to be known simply as "The United Nations," the happy phrase coined by Roosevelt one day in the White House, so the story goes, while waiting for Churchill to finish his bath.

New York, *Friday, June* 8

A great historical document, in my humble opinion, is published today—Justice Robert H. Jackson's report to the President on the contemplated prosecution of the Axis war criminals.

"It has cost unmeasured thousands of American lives," he reminds one, "to beat and find these men. To free them without trial would mock the dead and make cynics of the living.... We could execute or otherwise punish them without a hearing... but [this] would not set easily on the American conscience or be remembered by our children with pride. The only other course is to determine the innocence or guilt of the accused after a hearing as dispassionate as the times and the horrors we deal with will permit and upon a record that will leave our reasons and motives clear.... We propose to punish acts which have been regarded as criminal since the time of Cain and have been so written in every civilized code.... Through these trials we should be able to establish that a process of retribution by law awaits those who in the future similarly attack civilization."

Eloquent words and true.

Justice Jackson revealed that his case would be nothing less than "that a war of aggression is a crime, and that modern international law has abolished the defense that those who incite or wage it are engaged in legitimate business.

"Now we stand at one of those rare moments when the thought and institutions and habits of the world have been shaken by the impact of world war on the lives of countless millions. Such occasions rarely come and quickly pass."

One can only hope that we seize it. We didn't after the last war, when we made an unholy farce of the trial of the German war criminals. But Justice Jackson seems to be a determined man.

New York, *Wednesday, June* 13

The President confirms that a place and date have been set for the next meeting of the Big Three. Germany would be an appropriate place.... At San Francisco today they finally agreed by a vote of 30 to 2 to adopt the Yalta formula for voting in the Security Council. There will be no big-power veto on procedural matters, but there will be on all others.

Buffalo, *Thursday, June* 14

Saw Niagara Falls today at last—in my forty-first year! I found the sight and the sound overpowering even after all I had read. Came here to debate on Town Hall of the Air the question: "Are the German People responsible for Nazi crimes?" On the affirmative side with me was Stanley High, an editor of *Reader's Digest.* Our opponents were Dr. Schuster, president of Hunter College and one of the leading Catholic lay intellectuals in this country, and Gerhardt Seger, editor of the German-language weekly *Volkszeitung* and himself a former deputy in the German Reichstag. The debate, I fear, got pretty hot and personal toward the end.

New York, *Friday, June* 15

Joachim von Ribbentrop, that arrogant, ignorant, insipid flop of a German Foreign Minister, has been caught. The British picked him up as he slept in a bed shared with a thirty-five-year-old divorcee in a Hamburg rooming-house. I should like to be present at his trial.

The Big Three will meet in Berlin or in its "vicinity." …King George VI today dissolved the British Parliament after its longest session since 1679, there having been no elections during the war.

New York, *Tuesday, June* 19

Eisenhower got a memorable reception when he came back here from the war today. There was some deep emotion in the citizens of this polyglot city that made them turn out in the streets in numbers never before seen (the police put the figure at four million) and that led them to give the most spontaneous demonstration of affection and esteem that I have ever seen anywhere in the world for a public figure.

I went down to City Hall Square where the general was scheduled to halt briefly on his thirty-seven-mile drive through the metropolis and make a short speech after receiving the keys to the city. His words came out informally but deliberately and with no little eloquence. He had been deeply impressed, he said, as he rode through the city to see so many children.

"Can you, the parents and relatives of these children," he asked amid the utter stillness of the vast crowd, "look ten years ahead and be satisfied with anything less than your best to keep them away from the horrors of the battle-field? It has got to be done."

New York, *Wednesday, June* 20

Good news from San Francisco. The statesmen there settled their last big controversy today by agreeing to let the General Assembly of the United Nations discuss anything on earth that comes within the scope of the Charter. Curiously enough—or maybe not so curiously—the Russians had held out for severely restricting even what the Assembly could discuss. (In the Assembly, of course, the Russians will be heavily outvoted; in the Security Council they will have a veto.) Also the delegates at San Francisco decided today there was no place in the new league for Spain as long as Franco remained in power in Madrid, which is something of a victory for our little committee, which has worked tirelessly for this result. The Mexicans, the Australians, the French, and the Russians provided the main support against Franco, and the British and the Americans the least. I should have loved to be present at San Francisco today to hear Assistant Secretary of State Jimmy Dunn, who has not been sympathetic or helpful at all to the Spanish Republicans, jump up, as he did, better late than never, to announce that the United States associated itself with the Mexican statement blocking Franco.

New York, *Friday, June 22*

The bloody battle for Okinawa is at last over after eighty-two days of the toughest fighting we have ever had against the Japs. Our own losses to conquer this tiny island, one third the size of little Long Island, have been frightful: 11,260 killed, 33,769 wounded. Through May 20, according to Guam headquarters, the Japs lost 90,401 killed.

New York, *Sunday, June 24*

Day after tomorrow, in San Francisco, the President of the United States will address a group of tired delegates from fifty nations. By then they will have signed the Charter of the United Nations, over which they worked with such patience for two months. Two months must have seemed like a long time to those who day after day and night after night sweated it out in smoky committee rooms, wrangling over legal terms and paragraphs. It seemed a long time to the timid who thought San Francisco might fail. But what is two months in time if it results in machinery that may keep the peace for generations, perhaps for centuries? What is it when we reach, as the wise old Field Marshal Smuts said, "a great milestone along the path of human progress"? He said himself today that the Charter is a great improvement over the old Covenant of the League of Nations.

But shall we remember that the Charter provides only the machinery and that it will be up to the good sense of the peoples of the United Nations—and of their governments—to see that it works?

Intrigued all day by a dispatch from a CBS correspondent in Washington. He quotes Senator Capehart of Indiana as having said last night: "The American people should be told at once of certain Japanese peace offers that I have learned from reliable sources have been made."

New York, *Tuesday, June 26*

This is a day in history! The Charter of the new World Security Organization— it will be known simply as "The United Nations"—was signed today at San Francisco. It gives us an institution, at least, to preserve world peace. Whether we will use it is another matter. If we don't, the human race is finished. Another war like this one, and we're through.

President Truman made an excellent speech at the closing ceremony in S.F. Disregarding his prepared speech, he voiced the emotion of most of the poor souls on this planet when he exclaimed—they were his first words—"Oh, what a great day this can be in history!"

He also said: "That we have this charter at all is a great wonder!" For it was not an easy thing for fifty nations to agree; not even for the Big Five nations, which were largely responsible for the Charter.

The President announced he would send the Charter to the Senate "at once" and that he was sure "that the overwhelming sentiment of the people of my country and of their representatives in the Senate is in favor of immediate ratification."

Will he succeed this time where a greater man—Wilson—failed? I am certain of it. Much credit must go to Roosevelt and Hull for avoiding Wilson's mistakes. They made the issue non-partisan. They invited in Republican as well as Democrat senators to discuss it months ago. Wilson, as I recall, refused to take any prominent Republicans with him to Paris. Roosevelt sent three to San Francisco: Vandenberg, Stassen, and Representative Eaton.

Stassen, incidentally, emerges from the conference with greatly enhanced stature. I thought he was our outstanding man there, a person who grasps fundamental issues, knows how to negotiate with the toughest and cleverest foreign statesmen and not lose his pants, and has a facility for getting things done. On the issue of a narrow regionalism against a World concept, he saved the conference at one juncture by insisting on the World concept. First he had to convince his own delegation, which had been led astray on the question, and then the whole conference, especially the Latin Americans.

A day in history, then! This is what the men who have been fighting this war have looked forward to. But not only they. All of us, all of mankind, which has had enough of the blood and suffering of war. I even think the majority of citizens of this world are now willing to *work* and even *sacrifice* for peace!

New York, *Friday, June 29*

In the Senate, Tom Connally, the Democrat, yesterday and Arthur Vandenberg, the Republican, today spoke their pieces in favor of the new world Charter of the United Nations. They were not without eloquence in what some of the reporters describe as the prelude to the most momentous debate on foreign affairs in the Senate since that body turned down our membership in the League after the last war.

Senator Vandenberg, like Connally yesterday, got a standing ovation when he had finished.

"I shall support the ratification of this Charter," he said, "with all the resources at my command. I shall do this in the deep conviction that the alternative is physical and moral chaos in many weary places of the earth.... I shall do it because this plan, regardless of infirmities, holds great promise that the United Nations may collaborate for peace as effectively as they have made common cause for war. I shall do it because peace must not be cheated out of its only collective chance."

He had a good quotation from Ben Franklin, uttered as that wise old man signed the American Constitution in 1787. Said Franklin: "I consent, Sir, to this Constitution because I expect no better, and because I am not sure it is not the best. The opinions I have had of its errors I sacrifice to the public good. On the whole, Sir, I cannot help expressing a wish that every member of the Convention who may still have objections to it would, with me, on this occasion doubt a little of his own infallibility.... I doubt whether any other convention we can obtain may be able to make a better constitution; for, when you assemble a number of men to have the advantage of their joint wisdom, you inevitably assemble with those men all their prejudices, their passions, their errors of opinion, their local interests and their selfish views. From such an assembly can a perfect production be expected? It therefore astonishes me, Sir, to find this system approaching so near to perfection as it does."

All of which led Mr. Vandenberg to say: "Mr. President, if that was true in a limited area among our relatively close-knit colonial States, how much more true is it when we contemplate the San Francisco Conference where fifty nations, gathered from opposite poles and from the seven seas, separated from each other by race, language and tradition, and dealing with a problem which spans the globe, sought a meeting of minds and found a common denominator to express their common purpose.

"Only those who have engaged in such a universal congress—veritably the parliament of man—can wholly understand the complications and the difficulties.... It is no wonder that none of us can say that he wholly approves the net result. The wonder is that we can all approve so much. Within the framework of the Charter, through its refinement in the light of experience, the future can overtake our errors. But there will be no 'future' for it unless we make this start. I doubt if there could ever be another or a better start."

To those strange people who have been shouting against the big-power veto because the Russians demanded it, the Senator from Michigan said: "Let it never for an instant be forgotten that this veto granted to the five great powers includes a veto for our own United States. It is our protection against our involvement in any use of our forces against our will. It is our defense against what I venture to believe would be bitterly condemned in many quarters as our 'involuntary servitude' if our veto power did not exist. It is the complete answer to any rational fears that we may be subordinating our destiny to alien commands.... It guarantees our perpetuated independence of international dictation.... We sacrifice none of our essential American sovereignty and none of our essential American rights…. In a word, we have not created a super-state. We have not organized a 'world government.' We have not hauled down the Stars and Stripes from the dome of the Capitol…."

New York, *Monday, July* 2

Truman personally presented the United Nations Charter to the Senate today. No fireworks. His speech lasted only five minutes, and it was not broadcast…. The worst heat-spell over this week-end that I remember.

New York, *Wednesday, July* 4

The Stars and Stripes were hoisted over Berlin on this greatest of American anniversaries, as our army of occupation took over its zone in the former German capital. *This* the arrogant Germans really never expected to see…. Despite a bad strike in the rubber works at Akron and one here which has tied up all N.Y. newspaper deliveries, the labor situation is much better than the newspapers indicate. Today, for instance, the nation's workers, by sticking on the job, more than made up for all time lost by strikes since Pearl Harbor!

New York, *Thursday, July* 5

The British voted today, but we won't know the results for three weeks. Everybody agrees the Conservatives won, but with a greatly reduced majority.

New York, *Monday, July* 9

President Truman is en route by ship for Germany. For the sake of the peace, I wish it were Roosevelt. But we shall have to get along with what we have. I am concerned not so much with Truman's lack of experience and knowledge concerning foreign affairs as his apparent lack of feeling for them. You've got to be born with it, I guess.

Has Truman, one wonders, the slightest inkling of the German problem that must be solved if we are to have peace for long? Does he—do any Americans— understand the significance of what Henry H. Fowler, director of the Enemy Branch of the Foreign Economic Administration, told the Kilgore Committee the other day? That if we leave Germany to her own devices and do not disarm her industrially, she will be far better prepared for war within five years than she was in 1939?

New York, *Tuesday, July* 10

To ponder today over some cold, hard figures. It's announced that our losses since the beginning of this war have now passed the million mark—1,049,104, to be exact. British Empire losses are even a little larger; 1,427,634, of whom 532,233 are dead, or, as the British Ministry of Information puts it, are believed to be dead. U.S. Army losses through July 7 are given as 193,508 killed, 567,674 wounded,

37,323 missing, and 117,213 prisoners. Navy losses are by far the greatest in our history: 49,457 killed, 68,165 wounded, 11,454 missing, and 4,110 prisoners.

New York, *Wednesday, July* **11**

Where, one wonders, is the lead, the hope, the inspiration that this great Republic was expected by so many to give to a war-torn world we spilled so much blood to liberate from the Nazi tyranny? Where also is the ringing voice of England, the oldest surviving democracy, as Mr. Churchill not so long ago reminded us?

Is her voice, and ours, to be a dry squeak betraying an oldmaidish annoyance at inevitable change and a hysteric fear of the future? Are we going to throw the weight of the world's two most powerful democracies behind progress or reaction? Are we going to try to go back to 1939 or have we the guts and the imagination still to try to rebuild something better in 1946 and 1950 and 1960?

One wonders about these questions as one recalls the course of Anglo-American policy since the tide of war changed in our favor, remembering our support of Darlan, Mr. Churchill's stout defense of Franco, the Anglo-American insistence on trying to salvage the tottering house of Savoy, the opposition in the White House to the Free French, the high British hand with the resistance forces in Belgium and Greece, and our own silly determination to bring fascist Argentina into the conference at San Francisco.

One wonders, uneasily at times, and often with amazement. A world-famous general buttonholes you after dinner at Allied headquarters and, with deadly seriousness, says: "Well, sir, how soon do you think we're going to have to fight the Russians?" Eminent citizens, entrusted with the most important missions of state, hurry back from Europe to argue that we must rebuild German industry. Why? Why, as a "bulwark against Bolshevism."

In the corridors of the State Department or at cocktail parties at San Francisco our well-groomed foreign-service officers (whom the late Ray Clapper once described as "a rather sorry, moth-eaten crew") fret about "the Russians" or "that de Gaulle." In Italy we break our necks to prop up Umberto, who is a bad joke to almost all Italians, but when a venerable Italian political leader who never trafficked with Mussolini makes a harmless speech in a village square, we promptly have him arrested.

In Austria an excellent government is formed, dominated by Christian (Catholic) conservatives and Social Democrats who do not like Moscow and never have. But London and Washington are so incensed at Russia's admittedly bad manners in not waiting until they had their say as to that government that they fume about it and withhold recognition.

No wonder that Drew Middleton, one of the most thoughtful of our younger war correspondents, journeys through western Europe and finds that the masses, with whom our diplomats and high military officers have scant contact, are turning more and more toward Moscow. Alas, they will continue to do so, and in increasing numbers, until the western democracies show them that the democratic forces which mobilized such a great strength to beat Hitler can mobilize equal strength to make a decent democratic world now that peace has come.

It may be that we shall realize this in time. There is no good reason why this country, which owes its birth and its greatness to one of the most fundamental revolutions in world history, should now ally itself with the forces of stark reaction abroad. We have no particular love for, or interest in, kings, whether they be in Italy, Greece, Belgium, Yugoslavia, or elsewhere. If the Italian or the Greek or the Yugoslav people want a republic, should that offend the citizens of our own Republic?

If the people of Europe want to swing to the left, as most correspondents report they want to do, is there any good reason for us to fear it unduly or to try to prevent it? This nation and the French nation swung left toward the close of the eighteenth century. But the process did not bring the world to an end. It made the world a much better place to live in.

And since in this country we have made a pretty good success of democracy, why should an unholy fear of Communism grip us every time we look across the seas—or even under our beds? It is this baseless fear, it seems to me, that is at the root of much of our trouble at the moment.

New York, *Sunday, July* **15**

President Truman this Sunday afternoon is in Potsdam. So is Mr. Churchill. Marshal Stalin is due this evening. Tomorrow these three human beings, whom fate has made masters of this sorry planet for the time being, will begin their conference. Though not particularly religious, I feel like praying for them on this day of prayer.

Certainly Churchill, who has a sense of history, and perhaps even Truman must have had strange feelings landing in Potsdam. For Potsdam is where German history broke off on its disastrous tangent. Here the modern Hohenzollern rulers had their favorite seat. Here Prussian militarism was hatched and nurtured. Here the German wars were plotted. And it was at Potsdam where Hitler took over power twelve years ago. For three centuries Potsdam, with its ugly royal palace, its grim barracks and parade grounds, its goosestepping grenadiers, its maniacal rulers and field marshals, has been an evil name to the rest of the world—though it is true that the great Voltaire, a Frenchman, also lived there for a time. It was the spirit of Potsdam that glorified war and preached the gospel of tramping down the rights of other nations and peoples if only it served the German Fatherland. Now where the Germans plotted for so long their wars of conquest, the non-German leaders will meet to plot the peace. How fitting! Perhaps even the German people—though one cannot be sure—will grasp the symbolic significance.

All the other Big Three meetings took place in war time. The three Allied leaders had to stick together so that their nations could survive. With the peace, there is no such compulsion. Can we hope, though, that the compulsion of peace will prove as great in keeping them together as did that of war?

New York, *Monday, July* 16

Can it be that the Japanese war is moving to an end more imminent than seemed possible the day Germany was defeated? The United States Third Fleet, reinforced by some British ships, is standing off Tokyo. Lyle Wilson of U.P. reports that President Truman has canceled plans for a tour of Europe after the Potsdam meeting because of the possibility that Japan might be nearer unconditional surrender than has been assumed.

New York, *Wednesday, July* 18

The State Department reiterates today that no official or unofficial peace offers have come from the Japanese government. Senator Capehart, however, again told the Senate today that the enemy has made what he called "peace feelers of a very definite nature. Peace is sought," he said, "on our terms with a view to just punishment and future security, but without enslavement."

New York, *Thursday, July* 19

The Senate today approved the Bretton Woods bill 61 to 16, a good sign that America has decided *not*to stick its head in the sand. Curious that Senator Taft was so adamant against it. Are the Republicans still isolationist at heart, or merely stupid?

New York, *Monday, July* 23

The debate in the Senate over the United Nations Charter began today. It was such an anticlimax as to be almost sensational. Everyone seemed to be for it. Truly, we are growing up as a nation. Why, only a quarter of a century ago there was a life-and-death struggle in this same Senate over whether this nation should join the League of Nations.

More peace rumors today, Senator Wherry being the latest source.

New York, *Thursday, July* 26

What a day! Lunch with Ham at the Century, and plenty to talk about.

Labor has won the election in Britain by a landslide, confounding all the prophets and surprising even the Socialists themselves, who do not seem to have had even a suspicion that they had won. Churchill is out. Attlee is in. For the first time in history Great Britain will have a pure Labour government. It will be governed by an orthodox socialist party. Interesting that most Americans are stunned. It couldn't happen here. It certainly couldn't.

Another big development today. At Potsdam Churchill and Truman (the old British gladiator will not presumably bow out of the conference to be replaced by Attlee) have made public surrender terms for Japan, demanding that the Japs accept them "or face prompt and utter destruction." The question of the Emperor is not mentioned, but Japan will be stripped of her Empire, occupied indefinitely, and deprived of her power to make war. She will "not be enslaved as a race nor destroyed as a nation," however, and enough economy will be left to enable her to live.

New York, *Saturday, July* 28

A fitting end to an exciting week in history. The Senate this day ratified the United Nations Charter by the overwhelming vote of 89 to 2. Only two isolationist Republicans, Senator William Langer of North Dakota and Senator Henrik Shipstead of Minnesota, voted against. Senator Hiram Johnson, who helped defeat our entry into the old League after the last war, would have voted no, he says. But he was ill in hospital.

The Communist Party at its national convention here today ousted Earl Browder and chose William Z. Foster as its new head. It also changed its name, which during the war had been "The Communist Political Association," back to "The Communist Party." And once more it changed its line: it will now return to "a more aggressive role in combating fascism and reaction." You would think it difficult for a comrade to twist and turn every time Moscow changes the party line, but most of the Communists here perform these painful acrobatics without batting an eye or cracking a smile. As I recall, the present attack on Browder originated not in America (very little in the party line originates at home), but in France, where Jacques Duclos, the very able secretary of the French Communist Party, savagely turned on Browder for his tactics of co-operation with American capitalism, which was the war-time line of American Communists—that is, after Russia got into the war, though not before. (When I returned from Germany at the end of 1940, the Commie line then was that this was an "imperialist war" and they were very much against America's getting into it to help defeat Hitler—a line they reversed with stunning suddenness the morning the Führer sicked his troops on the Red Army. Overnight the "imperialist" war became a "War of Freedom." To me it was the same war from the beginning.)

Duclos, of course, got the signal for a new switch from Moscow and for reasons not yet clear was used by the Russian government to pass on the signal to the brothers in the U.S.A.

Interesting that in the world's two greatest industrial states, the United States and Great Britain, the Communists have made no headway in two decades. Though the British people overwhelmingly have just chosen a socialist government, they sent only two communists to the House of Commons. Here they haven't even been able to elect a congressman, though we have the largest population of industrial workers in the world. Doesn't the weakness of the Communist Party lie in the fact that it takes its orders from a foreign government? Though Communists deny this, it is certainly a fact. It will be disproved only when American Communists can show that on any issue they have ever dared to differ with Moscow.

New York, *Sunday, July 29*

The Japanese Premier, Kantaro Suzuki, has rejected our demand to surrender or see Japan destroyed. He said today the Japanese government attaches no importance to the Potsdam declaration. "There is no change whatsoever," he emphasized, "in the fundamental policy of the Japanese government in regard to the prosecution of the war."

We finally learned today what German casualties were in this war. The figures aren't final because the German documents we've captured do not include the period from last December 1 to the end of the war. But even up to that time German casualties in killed, missing, and severely wounded amounted to just over four million men (four times ours), of whom approximately two million were killed—a million and a half of them on the Russian front.

Two million German war dead. Hitler never dared to make public the figure, but we shall now do it. One wonders whether the German people have recovered their senses sufficiently to reflect on what such a terrible blood sacrifice got them.

New York, *Wednesday, August 1*

The Big Three conference came to an end today. A communiqué on what it accomplished, if anything, will be published Friday. Annoying, this secret diplomacy.

New York, *Thursday, August 2*

The communiqué on the Potsdam conference, signed by Truman, Attlee, and Stalin, was made public this afternoon. On first reading, it is a very remarkable document and, on the whole, a good one. Above all, it promises to settle the German problem in a much more thorough manner than was done by the peace-makers at Versailles, though Potsdam was not a peace conference but merely a first step toward a peace settlement.

The main job of the men at Potsdam was to decide on what to do with Germany. Most of the communiqué is taken up with decisions on that matter, which strike me as uncommonly wise. Since they are of historical importance, let us note them briefly.

The purpose of the Potsdam agreement is "to carry out the Crimea Declaration on Germany. German militarism and Nazism will be extirpated and the Allies will take in agreement together, now and in the future, the other measures necessary to assure that Germany never again will threaten her neighbors or the peace of the world.

"It is not the intention of the Allies," the communiqué continues, "to destroy or enslave the German people. It is the intention of the Allies that the German people be given the opportunity to prepare for the eventual reconstruction of their life on a democratic and peaceful basis. If their own efforts are steadily directed to this end, it will be possible for them in due course to take their place among the free and peaceful peoples of the world."

Is this not an eminently reasonable and decent attitude toward a foe who until beaten down was a foul and barbarous creature? We promise to the Germans, despite the enormity of their crimes against humanity, what they were not decent enough to give to those they overran.

Let's wade a little deeper into this great document. On Germany, it lays down, among others, the following points:

Point Three. "The purposes of the occupation of Germany... are:

"I. The complete disarmament and demilitarization of Germany, and the elimination or control of German industry that could be used for military production." (Listed for abolition are all military and Nazi Party forces and organizations, "including the general staff, the officers' corps, reserve corps, military schools, war veterans' organizations, and all other military and quasi-military organizations together with all clubs and associations which serve to keep alive the military tradition in Germany.")

"II. To convince the German people that they have suffered a total military defeat, and that they cannot escape responsibility for what they have brought upon themselves, since their own ruthless warfare and the fanatical Nazi resistance have destroyed German economy and made chaos and suffering inevitable.

"III. To destroy the National Socialist Party and its affiliated and supervised organizations... to insure that they are not revived in any form, and to prevent all Nazi and militarist activity or propaganda.

"IV. To prepare for the eventual reconstruction of German political life on a democratic basis and for eventual peaceful cooperation in international life by Germany."

Point Four. "All Nazi laws which provided the basis of the Hitler regime or established discrimination on grounds of race, creed or political opinion shall be abolished...."

Point Five. "War criminals... shall be brought to judgment."

Point Six. "All members of the Nazi Party who have been more than nominal participants in its activities... shall be removed from public and semi-public office and from positions of responsibility in important private undertakings...."

Point Seven. "German education shall be so controlled as completely to eliminate Nazi and militarist doctrines and to make possible the successful development of democratic ideas."

Point Eight. "The judicial system will be reorganized in accordance with the principles of democracy, of justice under law, and of equal rights for all citizens without distinction of race, nationality or religion."

Point Nine. "The administration of affairs in Germany should be directed toward the decentralization of the political structure....

"II. All democratic political parties with rights of assembly and of public discussions shall be allowed and encouraged throughout Germany....

"IV. For the time being no central Government shall be established.... However certain essential central German administrative departments, headed by state secretaries, shall be established, particularly in the fields of finance, transport, communications, foreign trade and industry."

Point Ten. "Subject to the necessity of maintaining military security, freedom of speech, press and religion shall be permitted, and religious institutions shall be respected.... The formation of free trade unions shall be permitted."

Those are the "political principles." Are they not excellent? Then come the "economic principles." The chief ones are:

Point Eleven. "In order to eliminate Germany's war potential, the production of arms, ammunition... aircraft and seagoing ships shall be prohibited...."

Point Twelve. "...German economy shall be decentralized for the purpose of eliminating the present excessive concentration of economic power as exemplified in particular by cartels, syndicates, trusts and other monopolistic arrangements."

Point Thirteen. "In organizing the German economy, primary emphasis shall be given to the development of agriculture and peaceful domestic industries."

Point Fourteen. "During the period of occupation, Germany shall be treated as a single economic unit."

Under Section B of Point Fifteen, the Allied objective is "to maintain in Germany average living standards not exceeding the average of the standards of living of European countries."

Point Nineteen. "Payment of reparations should leave enough resources to enable the German people to subsist without external assistance."

The agreement on reparations takes up a special section of the Potsdam agreement. The Allies this time make no mention of reparations in money as was demanded at Versailles. Reparations from Germany instead will be taken *in kind*.

Such is the result of Potsdam. Considering human limitations and the tenor of the times following this most savage German war, it seems to me to be an excellent agreement.

New York, *Sunday, August 5*

Second thoughts on Potsdam: It is a milestone in history. In regard to Germany it has attempted something for which there are few precedents since empires and nations first resorted to national wars. For the Germany as we have known it, the Germany that three times in the last three generations has provoked war, was sentenced to death at Potsdam, its very birthplace.

It is difficult to grasp what this means. Formerly, however disastrous a war, or a defeat, a major nation somehow usually managed to survive as a nation, with a government of its own. It could conclude a peace treaty as a sovereign nation, as did the German government after the last war. But now we see a once great and powerful state without the shadow of a government. It has lost, for the time being, all the organisms that constitute a state.

How remarkable it is that the Allies have learned from bitter experience, since nations, like persons, usually don't! The Versailles Treaty failed primarily because it neglected to eliminate the well-springs of German aggression. Instead, it left them intact, partly because in 1919 the west wanted a buffer against Communist Russia. At Potsdam they decided to destroy once and for all those well-springs, the sources of German military power and aggression. And yet high hopes are held out for the German people should they ever want to be free men in a civilized, peaceful, democratic community.

Flying to Cape Cod tomorrow for three weeks of loafing. It looks as though it will be reasonably quiet for the rest of August—pending the final onslaught on Japan. God, three weeks lying on the sands… no listening to radio, no poring through countless newspapers and reports, just basking in the sun, frolicking with the kids, and biting into some good books. Ah, the books. Now at last, for the first time since long before the war, to reread Shakespeare's sonnets and some of his plays, and some of Chekhov's and Ibsen's, and to read another volume of Proust (if my French is not too rusty) and Tom Wolfe's *Time and the River*, which I missed, and some of the English philosophers whom I have neglected—Francis Bacon, Hobbes, Locke, Bentham, Berkeley, Hume, and one of Thomas Mann's Biblical tetralogy and Schiller's essays and two plays of his, *Maria Stuart* and *Don Carlos* (if my German comes back to memory). I've shipped them all, and a few others, to Truro, and what does it matter if I know now I'll not get through half of them? …

Truro, Cape Cod, *Monday, August* 6

A pouring rain all day and the plane could not get off. I finally caught a train to Providence and there a bus to Hyannis, where Tess met me with the car. While waiting, she says, she picked up the tail end of a broadcast about some atom bomb being dropped by us on Japan. I suppose it's important, but am too tired to care this night. The light thunder of the surf near by is the most wondrous rhythmical and restful thing I have heard in years.

Truro, Cape Cod, *Tuesday, August* 7

I caught on very slowly, I can see, now that this day is done.

This morning a lady on the beach, who struck me as being a bit hysterical, accosted me almost belligerently.

"What do you think of the terrific news?" she bellowed.

"What news?" I said.

"Why, the atom bomb!" she screamed. "What do you think of it? Isn't it terrific?"

"I don't know anything about it," I said. "I'm on vacation...."

"What!" She seemed speechless, and I went back to building silly tunnels in the sand with Eileen and Linda.

But after lunch I suggested to Tess that we drive into Wellfleet and buy the Boston and New York newspapers. "Let's find out what there is in that atom story," I said. I can see now, this evening, that I was a bit smug, a bit complacent. It was a pleasant drive over a winding road past the dunes to Wellfleet and we didn't hurry.

"We can't do this often," Tess said. "Not until they unration gas."

We bought some fish in the market and then walked on a few doors to where they sold the newspapers. There were only two newspapers left on the counter.

"Had quite a run on them today," the old lady behind the counter said.

I bought them and picked one of them up to glance at the headline. I will never forget it. It was screaming all over the front page of the Boston paper: "THE ATOMIC AGE HAS ARRIVED!"

I guess I just stared. I could not really get it. Some time later, back in the car, I flopped over the front page of the *New York Times*:

FIRST ATOMIC BOMB DROPPED ON JAPAN;
MISSILE IS EQUAL TO 20,000 TONS OF TNT;
TRUMAN WARNS FOE OF A "RAIN OF RUIN"

So that was it....

There was a subhead over the main story. It said:

NEW AGE USHERED

Day of Atomic Energy Hailed by President Revealing Weapon

HIROSHIMA IS TARGET

"Impenetrable" Cloud of Dust Hides City After Single Bomb Strikes

I think I was frightened. I read on to Tess, who was driving:

"Washington, August 6—The White House and War Department announced today that an atomic bomb, possessing more power than 20,000 tons of TNT, a destructive force equal to the load of 2,000 B-29's and more than 2,000 times the blast power of what previously was the world's most devastating bomb, had been dropped on Japan.

"The announcement, first given to the world in utmost solemnity by President Truman, made it plain that one of the scientific landmarks of the century had been passed, and that the 'age of atomic energy,' which can be a tremendous force for the advancement of civilization as well as for destruction, was at hand....

"What happened at Hiroshima is not yet known. The War Department said... 'an impenetrable cloud of dust and smoke' masked the target area from reconnaissance planes."

So.... So this—since yesterday—is a new age. And how do you feel in a new age? Suddenly, like that? ...The very first day? ...And how long will it last? ... How powerful did they say that bomb was? ...And the old-fashioned ones you dodged in Berlin and London and Liege? Mere toys?...

I took the youngsters for a swim. It would be difficult to explain what an atom bomb was, and why it was—why it was necessary in our world of grown-ups—and I didn't try. We played in the breakers for a while, and when the sun went down we went back to the cottage. There was much more to read in this day's *Times*. What our great men had to say, for example....

The President: "Sixteen hours ago an American airplane dropped one bomb on Hiroshima, an important Japanese army base. That bomb had more power than 20,000 tons of TNT....

"The Japanese began the war from the air at Pearl Harbor. They have been repaid manyfold. And the end is not yet....

"It is an atomic bomb. It is a harnessing of the basic power of the universe. The force from which the sun draws its powers has been loosed against those who brought war to the Far East.

"...We are now prepared to obliterate more rapidly and completely.... Let there be no mistake. We shall completely destroy.... If they [the Japanese leaders] do not now accept our terms they may expect a rain of ruin from the air, the like of which has never been seen on this earth....

"The fact that we can release atomic energy ushers in a new era in man's understanding of nature's forces. Atomic energy may, in the future, supplement the power that now comes from coal, oil and falling water.... I shall give further consideration as to how atomic power can become a powerful and forceful influence toward the maintenance of world peace."

Churchill, it seems to me, is more thoughtful and certainly more eloquent. "By God's mercy, British and American science outpaced all German efforts.... This revelation of the secrets of nature long mercifully withheld from man should arouse the most solemn reflections in the mind and conscience of every human being capable of comprehension. We must indeed pray that these awful agencies will be made to conduce to peace among the nations and that instead of wreaking measureless havoc upon the entire globe they may become a perennial foundation of world prosperity."

Hanson Baldwin, the military correspondent of the *Times*, with whom I often disagree, is also restrained and thoughtful. Says he: "The date, August 6, 1945, and the name, Hiroshima, Japan, will long live in the sanguinary history of war.

"Yesterday man unleashed the atom to destroy man, and another chapter in human history opened, a chapter in which the weird, the strange, the horrible becomes the trite and the obvious. Yesterday we clinched victory in the Pacific, but we sowed the whirlwind....

"We have been the first to introduce a new weapon of unknowable effects which may bring us victory quickly but which will sow the seeds of hate more widely than ever. We may yet reap the whirlwind.

"Certainly with such God-like power under man's imperfect control we face a frightful responsibility. Atomic energy may well lead to a bright new world in which man shares a common brotherhood, or we shall become—beneath the bombs and rockets—a world of troglodytes."

The *Times* (for once) in an editorial poses *the* problem and asks *the* fundamental question: "A revolution in science and a revolution in warfare have occurred on the same day.... Civilization and humanity can now survive only if there is a revolution in mankind's political thinking. But can mankind grow up quickly enough to win the race between civilization and disaster?"

Cowering almost with fright, we mutter yes... yes... desperately. But doubts rise up... deep ones from the belly....

What was it that Sir Oliver Lodge once opined? The *Times* recalls it: "When radioactivity was discovered and physicists first began to dream of atomic energy the late Sir Oliver Lodge was moved to write that 'if ever the human race gets hold of a means of tapping even a small fraction of the energy contained in the atoms of their own planet the consequences will be beneficent or destructive, according to the state of civilization.' He doubted if mankind of his generation was civilized enough to use such a discovery rationally."

And so, with that biting little thought, to bed at the end of this exciting day, the first—no, the second—of our new atomic age.

Truro, Cape Cod, *Wednesday, August 8*

Howard Smith in the first two eleven-ten p.m. broadcasts he has done for me during this vacation has not lacked for something to talk about. Monday he had the atom bomb to juggle with. Tonight he had Russia's declaration of war on Japan. A bit difficult to relax on this vacation, so far.

Truro, Cape Cod, *Friday, August 10*

Paul White got me on a neighbor's phone tonight to say that Japan has offered to accept the unconditional surrender terms of the Potsdam Declaration, subject only to the Emperor retaining his throne as a sovereign ruler. He suggested I get back to work in New York no later than tomorrow.

Will try to catch that rickety little plane that plies between the Cape and New York. My "vacations" have ever been such.

New York, *Saturday, August* **11**
The United States has lost no time in replying to Japan. Our note dispatched today says, in effect, the Emperor may remain on the throne, for the present at least (until the Japanese people have an opportunity to decide their ultimate form of government), but that his authority to "rule the state" will be subject to the Supreme Commander of the Allied Powers. This must be a bitter pill to a people who worship their Emperor as a god.

New York, *Sunday, August* **12**
No word from Tokyo yet. No hint has come of the fateful decision…. In the White House President Truman has stood by all day, waiting like everyone else….

New York, *Monday, August* **13**
Still no news. Washington experts speculate that a deadly fight in the Japanese cabinet and High Command is holding up Japan's decision. Some want to quit; the others want to fight on until Japan is completely destroyed….
Guam headquarters says our carrier planes began attacks on the Tokyo area at dawn today.

New York, *Tuesday, August* **14**
World War II is over!
Pearl Harbor and the treachery of Japan had been revenged. The guys in all the armies who are still alive will die normally and peacefully now. The cities and towns not laid to dust and ashes by the bombs will again stand unafraid tonight—and perhaps forever. The terrible paroxysm, the obscene convulsion, that has shaken our world for six years and nearly ruined it came to an end at seven o'clock tonight, our time.
In the CBS news room we had stood by all day, waiting. A few seconds after seven p.m. one of the half-dozen telephones in the news room tinkled. You could hardly hear it in the bedlam of noise from the teleprinter machines, the typewriters, the loudspeaker, and the rasping voices of tired, nerve-racked men and women.
Paul White grabbed the phone in a flash. I did not know until later that it was connected directly with the White House. For about five seconds he listened intently, as though he were holding his breath. Then he pivoted violently and signaled Bob Trout, who had been standing in the far corner holding a portable mike. Bob flicked a gadget. He was on the air and talking. "JAPAN HAS SURRENDERED UNCONDITIONALLY!" he said calmly. It was the first word, I believe, to an impatient world.

Then the bells of the teleprinter machines carrying A.P., U.P., and I.N.S. started to jangle wildly. "FLASH!" they were hacking out "Japan surrenders…."

I cannot remember exactly what happened in the next moments except that Bob, bending over the machines as they began to unfold the story, kept on talking. He did not talk long. Suddenly there was a switch in the control room. The thin, soft voice of the President came through our loudspeaker:

"I have just received this afternoon a message from the Japanese government in reply to the message forwarded to that government on August 11. I deem this reply a full acceptance of the Potsdam declaration, which specifies the unconditional surrender of Japan. In the reply there is no qualification.

"Arrangements are now being made for the formal signing of surrender terms at the earliest possible moment.

"Gen. Douglas MacArthur has been appointed the Supreme Allied commander to receive the Japanese surrender. Great Britain, Russia and China will be represented by high-ranking officers.

"Meantime, the Allied armed forces have been ordered to suspend offensive action.

"The proclamation of V-J Day must wait upon the formal signing of the surrender terms by Japan."

That was all. That was it.

Outside on this warm night you could already hear the ships and tugs in the Hudson and East rivers screaming and roaring with their whistles and horns. From our seventeenth-floor window you could see the people dashing out into the street in a great state of excitement, moving toward Radio City and Times Square. Cars and taxis were raising an awful din with their horns. But we went back to work.

There was the Japanese note to give:

"1. His Majesty the Emperor has issued an imperial rescript regarding Japan's acceptance of the provisions of the Potsdam declaration.

"2. His Majesty the Emperor is prepared to authorize and insure the signature by his government and the Imperial General Headquarters of the necessary terms for carrying out the provisions of the Potsdam declaration. His Majesty is also prepared to issue his commands to all the military, naval and air authorities of Japan and all the forces under their control wherever located to cease active operations, to surrender arms and to issue such other orders as may be required by the supreme commander of the Allied forces for the execution of the above mentioned terms."

Unconditional surrender indeed. And the end of Japan as we have known it in our time.

At eleven p.m. CBS picked up a broadcast of the Emperor, the first of his life. When the translation came in, the message struck one as a curious concoction of Oriental double-talk, though none the less an extremely interesting document:

"To our good and loyal subjects:

"After pondering deeply the general trends of the world and the actual conditions obtaining in our empire today, we have decided to effect a settlement of the present situation by resorting to an extraordinary measure.

"We have ordered our government to communicate to the governments of the United States, Great Britain, China and the Soviet Union that our empire accepts the provisions of their joint declaration.

"To strive for the common prosperity and happiness of all nations as well as the security and well-being of our subjects in the solemn obligation which has been handed down by our imperial ancestors and which we lay close to the heart.

"Indeed we declared war on America and Britain out of our sincere desire to insure Japan's self-preservation and the stabilization of East Asia, it being far from our thought either to infringe upon the sovereignty of other nations or to embark upon territorial aggrandizement.

"But now the war has lasted for nearly four years. Despite the best that has been done by everyone... the war situation has developed not necessarily to Japan's advantage, while the general trends of the world have all turned against her interest.

"Moreover, the enemy has begun to employ a new and most cruel bomb, the power of which to do damage is, indeed, incalculable, taking the toll of many innocent lives. Should we continue to fight, it would not only result in an ultimate collapse of the Japanese nation, but also it would lead to the total extinction of human civilization.

"Such being the case, how are we to save the millions of our subjects, or to atone ourselves before the hallowed spirits of our imperial ancestors? This is the reason why we have ordered the acceptance of the provisions of the joint declaration of the powers.

"...The hardships and sufferings to which our nation is to be subjected hereafter will be certainly great.

"We are keenly aware of the innermost feelings of all of you, our subjects. However it is according to the dictates of time and fate that we have resolved to pave the way for a grand peace for all generations to come by enduring the unendurable and suffering what is unsufferable....

"...Cultivate the ways of rectitude, nobility of spirit and work with resolution so that you may enhance the innate glory of the Imperial State and keep pace with the progress of the world."

The Emperor spoke in a high, squeaky, singsong voice. He did not mention surrender.

In between the news all of us—Quincy Howe, Major Eliot, Larry Lesueur, Bob Trout, and others—kept broadcasting, though my personal feeling was that there was little we could say and that the listeners over the land on this momentous night were not interested in it.

I did venture to remind any who cared to stay tuned in how hopeless the struggle had seemed for so long on our side. The enemy had won so easily at first, in Ethiopia, in Spain, in Austria, at Munich, in Czechoslovakia, even before the main war started. And when the Big War had come, it had been the same story, in Poland, Scandinavia, the west, Russia. For a long time the Jap war had had the same pattern as the German war: Pearl Harbor and then month after month of one defeat after another as the forces of Japan spread over the Pacific, southwest to Singapore and Burma, eastward over the islands toward Hawaii, northeastward in the Aleutians toward Alaska and our Pacific coast.

In the excitement of our victory tonight, in the joy and relief, it was difficult to remember the dark days when defeat stared us in the face and catastrophe was staved off by only the narrowest of margins. It was utterly impossible for more than a handful this night to recall, as I had done a time or two in Germany when the triumph of the Nazi barbarians seemed so certain, what the awful consequences would have been for us had victory not come in the end. Is there not something magnificent in the fact that it never occurred to the peoples on our side, even in the blackest days (for the British after Dunkirk and when London was nearly destroyed; for the Russians when the Germans swept almost to Moscow and later to the Volga and Stalingrad; for ourselves after Pearl Harbor), that we would ever be finally beaten and therefore enslaved?

Now the desperate and the heroic days are over. Peace will be sweet, yes; but the adjustment to it will take some time, and no doubt it will bring much disillusionment as imperfect little men try to repair the unspeakable damage— physical, moral, spiritual. There will have to be adjustment too for those of us who have lived little else the last ten years but the tense fight against the barbarism of the Nazi and Fascist world. The tensions of that epic struggle have been in my blood for so long, conditioning whatever I did or thought or was, that it will take time and effort and great relaxation to get them out of my system so that I can begin anew, on a different plane, in another world, what- ever life there is to be for the likes of me. One could fail to make the transition satisfactorily. It could be that the imprint of this violent, immoral decade is there to stay on a little man, being too strong, too indelible to be erased. One can only try to master it, to let it sink into the limbo of other impressions that make a man's life and character, and, having conquered it and subjugated it, pass on to whatever new trials await.

We kept on broadcasting until about two thirty a.m., weary and exhausted and yet, deep down, exhilarated by this immense day. Afterward there were drinks and food in the back room of the little pub below with those who had toiled both here and in the war's midst to bring to our fellow men the facts and the background and the smell and the sound and the fury of this gruesome holocaust which had come to its bloody end this night. God, how long and wretched and inhuman it has been!

When I stumbled down Fifty-first Street toward home, the summer's sun was coming up beyond the East River, rising on this first day of peace.

Boston, *Wednesday, August* 15

I felt a sudden urge to get away from New York. There was a plane leaving for Boston at five p.m. and I got it. Tomorrow I shall take the boat to Provincetown and resume my vacation with the family at Truro. Tonight the crowds, mostly sailors with their girls, are dancing in the streets of this sedate old town.

On the plane coming up, read the New York morning papers. To record the headlines:

The Times:

> JAPAN SURRENDERS, END OF WAR!
> EMPEROR ACCEPTS ALLIED RULE;
> M'ARTHUR SUPREME COMMANDER;
> OUR MANPOWER CURBS VOIDED

The Herald Tribune:

> JAPANESE WAR ENDS

> Truman Announces Unconditional Surrender;
> MacArthur Named Supreme Allied Commander

Buried in the front-page news was an item that in Paris Pétain had been found guilty of treason and sentenced to death. It was like reading of a ghost. Dim already were those petty little figures who in the hour of trial had surrendered what was decent in human life in order to lick the boots of the Nazi slave-driver. The doom of all of them was sealed yesterday.

To write down here a few lines from the *Herald Tribune* editorial this morning, for this hour is a fleeting one and all too soon, no doubt, its loftiness, its magnificence, its very meaning, will be forgotten by us all. Men, with their inhuman courage and bravery and fortitude and dedication, cannot remain on the heights for long. I want to remember that they were there, for a brief moment in my time, and hence record these lines:

> VICTORY OF MANKIND

"Through something like ten years of blood and agony and privation, this, the vastest and most destructive paroxysm of human history, has declined to its solemn end. Mushrooming through the fabric of our world society, like the detonations of the terrible weapons which it employed, it swallowed the earth. From that distant moment in October of 1935, when Benito Mussolini launched his braggart 'little war' for the conquest of Ethiopia, the explosive forces latent in our international system burst and spread—through the insurrection of the Spanish reactionaries in 1936, the beginning of the immolation of China in 1937, the rape of Austria and the disgraceful surrender at Munich in 1938, the engulfing of western Europe in 1939, the devastation of Soviet Russia in 1941, the assault upon the United States and the ravishing of Malaya and the Indies down to the titanic battles by land, sea and air which shook all the continents and in which the great issues were decided. Now at last it has died away, died away in a stupendous victory for the Allied peoples, won by a greater exertion of courage, unity, toil and ingenuity than they believed themselves capable of, but won finally and completely.

"They stand, in their hour of victory, upon a vast and somber ruin. It is a ruin of countless lives, of innumerable factories and farms and homes and all the other painfully accumulated apparatus of civilized existence, of institutions and ideas and those intangible values which cemented the old structure of human society. To rebuild a peaceful and prosperous order out of this chaos presents them with a task no less difficult in its own way than that which they have just achieved. But they do not come to it empty-minded. Their war was not simply a war of aimless destruction and their victory was not merely a victory for one set of national flags over another. It was a war of basic concepts as to the nature and end of mankind; and it was a victory of a broad system of ideas—the ideas of freedom, of man's inherent dignity, of the reality of humanitarian and democratic values, of ordered and legal process as against the domination of brute force, of the possibility of peaceful progress by rational analysis and co-operative action—which have survived as great, creative instruments in their hands.

"These ideas take on many different and often conflicting colorations among the various peoples and social systems making up the great alliance, but the same common threads run through all. It is by no mere accident of geography or power or scientific skill that the United States stands today on the common pinnacle of victory. It is because we shared in the fundamental concepts of which alone a new world society can be created; just as the Germans and the Japanese went down to utter ruin because they were dedicated to a brutal and barbarically anachronistic past. The old international society was shattered, by the long-accumulated strains within it, into this cataclysmic ruin; what remains, however, are the elements of thought and purpose and conviction out of which a new one can now be created.

"If the devastation is appalling, the hope is brilliant—as blinding as that first flash from the atomic bomb, which itself symbolizes how great are the creative, no less than the destructive, powers which we now command. We may stand, in this awesome moment, at the end of the last great war in human history; we certainly stand upon the thresholds of immense change and immense promise. To all the millions whose blood and suffering brought us to this end we can only return our gratitude; to all who have survived we can only pledge our highest effort."

Truro, Cape Cod, *Monday, August27*

The last week, already, of this glorious vacation—a rather memorable one considering some of the things that happened in its short span: the end of the war, the beginning of the atomic age. We loll all day on the beach, gazing lazily at the clouds drifting in the sky, arousing ourselves occasionally to make sand pies and tunnels with the youngsters or to venture into the breakers when the sun gets too hot. People drift pleasantly by, sometimes flopping lazily down in the sand for an idle chat. All sorts of people: Larry Lesueur, in from the war and a little tense still; Dorothy Paley, concerned about the political future of the world; Duffy, concerned with that too and putting his concern in his daily cartoons he airmails to the *Baltimore Sun*; Annabella, subdued under the sun, discussing her return to pictures; Waldo Frank relaxing from a novel in progress; Mrs. H., relaxing for the first time in years because the war is over and her husband did not get killed; Mary McCarthy ("The Man in the Brooks Bros. Shirt") too full of drive and energy and perhaps the problems of writing to relax; Jerry Farnsworth and Helen Sawyer, talking of everything else except their art; the psychiatrist, Dr. X., weighed down a little with the awful mental ills of our nerve-shocked, sexually maladjusted generation, but sure, like Freud, that he can cure a few.

Truro, Cape Cod, *Wednesday, August 29*

On the sand shore here looking out across the ocean toward the Old World, one has as good a place as any (and better than most, for there is nothing to distract you for the moment but the rhythmic thunder of the waves) in which to contemplate man's sudden change-over from the old war world to the new world of peace—and atomic energy.

For those not immediately struggling with the staggering task of reconversion, for those, that is, who had a fleeting moment to stop and think, it seemed during the last few days as though we all had made a fateful plunge to a new planet where human life could not possibly ever be the same again and would have to be, therefore, started anew with different precepts. It was not only that the most savage war in history had destroyed so much of the old world beyond recognition and beyond hopes of restoration on familiar old lines. It was that the last searing week of the global war had also rocked man's puny imagination with the prospect, for better or worse, of what the scientists told us was bound to be a new era in the history of mankind based on the fantastic power inside the tiny atom.

It was magnificent, of course, to be confronted abruptly with peace, especially if you had seen a little of this war's slaughter at first hand, especially if you had been a soldier or a sailor or an air man, or a civilian in the hell of the bombed towns, or a woman with your man coming home now whole and alive.

It was magnificent, all right, and good, and provocative of high hope. Even the little world on the Cape Cod sands—writers, painters, businessmen, fishermen, grocerymen and the rest—felt it as did all the other citizens from this coast to the other, preoccupied though many undoubtedly were by the immediate, material little gains: the end of gasoline rationing and a hundred other controls that had loomed larger in their peaceful lives than many a soldier at the front had quite appreciated.

But feeling it did not bring exactly the relief that ordinarily would have come to them with the end of the epic war. It was easy to see, in fact, if you sat in on their little groups, their deadly concern with the new and frightening thing that had been unleashed on a far-away Japanese city. For it was plain to the most naïve citizen that our world henceforth would be dominated not only by the manifold headaches of the problems of the peace, which were bad enough, but by a terrifying little thing which words could not accurately describe, but which, we were told by the medicine men we know as scientists, resulted from the bursting of the atom, a particle itself so small we could not even see it, but holding a power sufficient to blow our world into bits.

Here on the sands of an American beach was a curiously appropriate place to get the news about the effective use of the splitting of an atom. If one remembered a little history and physics it was easy to recall that it was while lolling on a beach that the Greek philosophers, long before Christ, began to ponder over the atom. Was it the water of the ocean or the sand of the seashore, they asked, that gave the truest picture of the ultimate structure of the substance of the universe? Democritus, Lucretius, and others came to believe in the ultimate discontinuity of matter. A mass of sand divided into its grains seemed to them the best illustration of the fact that all substance, including water, could be broken down to basic particles or molecules or atoms.

But from their time until our own the atom, which they believed solid and indivisible, had been regarded as the indestructible brick upon which our world was built. There was change, of course, but only because of the rearranging of the indestructible atom. Then in our time suddenly it was found that the atom was not indestructible at all. It could be broken up. When it was broken up, it released a power that frightened the wits of man.

That is where we stand in this fateful autumn of 1945 and it may be that what we do with atomic power will determine in one way or another the outcome of our life on this planet. Certainly war itself is revolutionized and, if it is not finally outlawed this time, will destroy us all the next time.

But certain it is, too, that in the immediate future, regardless of atomic developments, we must get along with the enormous job of rebuilding a world that was shattered not by the atomic bomb but by the lesser explosives that man, in his inventiveness, developed during the long years of the war that has now ended. They were powerful enough. They were sufficient to destroy the Old World. And how quickly!

When last I lolled on these Cape Cod sands, for a few days in 1941, only four years ago, Germany was still the master of Europe, and Japan was all-dominant in Asia. France was down, Russia was given but a few months of life by all the experts, and Britain was in deadly peril. We ourselves were so blind that we did not realize that should the Axis win, our own destruction, or at least degradation as a nation, was almost a certainty. We awoke in time and Russia and Britain proved tougher than we dreamed and Germany and Japan somewhat softer, and France, we learned, was down but not out. China refused even to go down.

The result, in terms of politics, is that the world of six years ago, which was dominated by seven great powers, has been supplanted by one in which the three powers that won the war, Britain, Russia and the United States, are now all-supreme.

How will they use their gigantic power and their immense resources in the new world? How in Asia and in Europe and in Africa and in our own hemisphere? Europe, the cradle of our own civilization, will be dominated for long by three essentially non-European powers, just as Asia will be run by the three, none of which is Asiatic.

And how will the three dominate and run the vast continents, seeing that one of the three nations is under a Communist dictatorship, the second under a social democracy, and the third the last refuge of a democratic capitalism? How will they agree? How will they hold together in their great task?

On the sands here a puny human being can feel a swelling headache at the mere formulation of a few of the questions. Yet why should man shrink from the answers, you ask, man who has conquered the vast ocean and unlocked the secret of the stars overhead and of the atoms of the sand at your feet?

PART II
END OF A BERLIN DIARY

WLS

Aboard Queen Mary, *Monday, October* 1

New York out of sight now, and one's spirits sink a little. You would think it's the first time, instead of the hundredth…. Eileen and Linda came down to the dock with Tess. I held the youngsters by the water's edge while they gazed up at the giant liner. Very impressed they were. Linda kept calling it "The Big Canoe." She said it reached to the sun. We said our farewells and they went off to school. Both seemed resentful at the separation. You'd think they would be used to them by now. Ed [Murrow] arrived, in uniform. For the first time since Lisbon in December '40, we shall have much time for much talk. A last walk up and down with Tess (our millionth farewell, certainly, but always sad) and then they began to pull the gangplank up.

At sea, *Tuesday, October* 2

Ran into Biddle, who is to be the American judge at the German War Criminal Trial at Nuremberg, and Judge Parker, the alternate American judge. Tried to remember why the Senate refused once to confirm Parker's nomination to the Supreme Court. No trace of bitterness or disappointment in him, though.

At sea, *Wednesday, October* 3

Studied papers on the trial most of the day and read Prof. Glueck's book on the subject. Also started reading Joan Bennet's book on Virginia Woolf, a most fascinating critique of one of our great, though limited, writers in English of this generation…. Eisenhower has kicked Patton out as commander of the Third Army. Patton was great in war, but a flop in peace. He had no understanding of politics or even of the significance of Nazism. General X. said tonight that our American generals simply were not fitted for the job of occupation, though I think he is one who is. He hopes civilians will take over actual control.

At sea, *Thursday, October* 4

Tea and a long talk with Mackenzie King, the Prime Minister of Canada. He seemed greatly concerned with the atomic bomb…. Up most of the night with Ed and Gen. X. discussing the future of broadcasting, if any. So far radio has missed most of its chances, chiefly, I suppose, because too many executives regard it as a business just like any other and have been more concerned with making huge profits than with making broadcasting a public service. State ownership is not the answer either, at least in the U.S.A. No ideal solution, I guess. But even if it is a profit-making business, couldn't radio in our land grow up?

At sea, *Friday, October* 5

Linda wasn't even born when last I left Berlin. When was it, exactly? Must look it up....

At sea, *Saturday, October* 6

Southampton tomorrow, then London and Paris, and finally Berlin! It's hard to be honest with oneself about returning to Berlin. I am not thrilled. Is there a smug feeling of the fine revenge you will experience? I don't think so. My hatred of the Nazis is more complex. I remember the day I left Berlin. I said to myself: "I don't care if I ever see this town, this people, again."

London, *Monday, October* 8

Tried to do my Sunday broadcast from the pantry between the kitchen and the dining-room of a little hotel in Southampton last night. Waiters kept hurrying by and there was much merry talk in the kitchen so that I could scarcely hear my own tired voice. No matter; the broadcast did not get through.

We set off by car for London about midnight, driving through a thick ground fog that lay over the rolling land and made the night a thing of incredible beauty. It was wondrous to see the lights in the streets of London for the first time since the war began.... A stroll down Regent Street to Piccadilly this evening. It looked strange in the lamplight, after you had stumbled up and down it in the years of the black-out.

Tomorrow Parliament convenes and Britain's first real socialist government in history will settle down to work. If there is any panic among the Conservatives, their press does not show it. I think British conservatives are more tolerant than ours.

London, *Tuesday, October* 9

Drinks at five with Norman Douglas, whom I had never met before. Despite his age—he must be in his seventies—he turned out to be a very vigorous fellow.... He says he is through writing, but I doubt it. Still, it's a long time since *South Wind*, one of the great novels of our time.

A vital race—the English. Ed and I were struck by it as we walked down Oxford Street yesterday. Something in their walk; determination. They are tired after six years of war, the bombings, and short rations. But you can sense in the people in the streets a magnificent staying power.

London, *Wednesday, October* 10

The great, grimy city in the Indian summer of the last few days strikes a returning traveler, at first glance, as being almost as gay as it used to be in the peace days when June came. Perhaps it's the fine weather—so unusual for London at this time of year. Certainly it's partly the lights at night in the city streets that were so dark so long. Maybe it's the excitement in everyone's breast over the reconvening of the new Parliament, dominated for the first time by a clear socialist majority. And, of course, it's because the war is over and the killing and the bombing have stopped.

Yet underneath there is little gaiety. Underneath, the people of London share the gloom that has settled over Europe with the approach of winter. They are deeply concerned over the failure of the London conference of foreign ministers. They are depressed at the mere contemplation of the atomic age, and they put the two—the atomic age and the conference fiasco—together. How on earth, they say, are we going to save ourselves from being liquefied by the atom when the foreign ministers of the victorious Allies cannot even agree on the procedure for drawing up a peace treaty with Bulgaria?

In their new mood the people here want an end to cant. They do not like the word "procedure," and they do not believe the London conference broke down merely because of differences of procedure.

"If that were so," the *Sunday Observer* remarked, "we could indeed exclaim that the peoples had not suffered so long and endured so much for diplomats to quarrel over procedure."

Indeed, they know that whatever the quarrel over how to proceed, the real reason for the failure of the foreign ministers' conference was the inability of the western democracies and Russia to find a common ground on which to build a peace settlement....

It would be idle to get the idea that Russia is the only country that provides the British with misgivings. They have plenty in regard to the United States, too. These apprehensions seem to be stronger on the left, which is in the saddle now, than on the right. I myself, like most Americans, doubt their validity. But it might be useful to enumerate them.

First, there is criticism of what many Labour people privately call our "unilateral and imperialist policy in the Pacific." Said the *New Statesman and Nation* the other day: "Russia is not the only power which regards America's seizure of strategic islands and her policy in Japan as the creation of a vast area of exclusive military aggrandizement."

An American soon discovers here the fear, especially among Labourites, that capitalist America will necessarily be antagonistic to socialist Britain. One of the first questions you are asked is whether Washington did not hasten to cut off lend-lease to embarrass the Labour government as soon as it took office....

There is another remarkable suspicion, voiced the other day in the *New Statesman*. It was argued that the formation of a western European bloc—a project as dear to Labour as to the Conservatives—was not really based on any desire to offset Russian influence in Europe. The main object, it said, "is an economic defence against American capitalism, which is busily trying to reduce Britain to the status of a satellite."

Not everyone here, of course, goes that far. But no Britisher is enthusiastic about the state of the world in which he sees the American colossus getting a head start in the race for markets and control of air and sea transportation.

I have been trying to find out this week whether the Conservatives—the people with the money and property, who have, in the main, run this heart of the Empire for so long—were frightened at the spectacle of socialist rule.... I must say I haven't found the slightest sign of it. The conservative business people know the country is in for a fair measure of nationalization. They know that in a year or two the mines and the Bank of England will be nationalized. So far as I can ascertain, no businessman has lost a night of sleep over it.

London, *Thursday, October* 11

Dinner, and long into the night with Kingsley Martin, editor of the *New Statesman and Nation*, and Dick Crossman. D. is a new Labour member of Parliament. He was brilliant, as usual, but almost completely cockeyed on Germany and on America.... Labour circles here see a Gargantuan United States crowding them out of the world markets at a moment when Britain must increase its exports fifty per cent over the prewar level in order to exist. They think we have gone imperialist in Asia and they are not impressed by my argument that whatever imperialist touch we once had we have lost. Much wild and silly talk in the same circles that America is on the verge of war with Russia. I tell them that the *people* at home don't want a war and, in fact, do not even think about it. Back of all these ideas, I gather, is the Labour feeling, which probably has some—but not much—justification, that capitalist America will not be very co-operative with socialist Britain.

On Germany I find my Labour Party friends definitely bad. They want to build up western Germany, especially the Ruhr, they say, "in the interests of European economic prosperity." That this *may* mean building up Germany again as a military power (since military power is based on economic strength) is a consequence they refuse to face. Just as after the last war, these nice Liberal-Labour people feel that Germany is too thoroughly beaten to come back. Depressing that such intelligent folk want to be wrong twice.

London, *Friday, October* 12

Lunch with K., a German and a Communist, who is about to return to Germany. Somewhat ruefully he admitted that the German Communists had received a terrible setback as the result of the excesses of Red Army troops and the policy of the Russians to cart away everything they can lay their hands on. Fred [Oechsner], just back from Berlin, tells some lurid stories of how the Russians raped the German women, stopping at no age. Fred says one stout German lady of fifty-one became pregnant!

Drinks with Geoffrey Crowther, editor of the *Economist*, the most intelligent economic weekly in the world. He is not unduly alarmed at the prospects of five years of socialist rule in Britain. He is more alarmed, he says, at what the Russians and the Americans may do. We argued about Germany, his journal being much too strong for restoring Germany's economic strength.

A long evening with Laski at Ed's. He was his usual sparkling self, citing historical antecedents at every turn, and quoting Burke, Disraeli, Lenin, Churchill, Roosevelt, and a hundred others with great relish and frequency.... He says the bill to nationalize the Bank of England will be very kind to the stockholders. British socialism is a curious thing....

London, *Saturday, October* 13

Lunch with J., and afterward we walked through Hyde Park, lovely on this afternoon of Indian summer, to her home. Part of the way led through the streets where the great houses of the rich and the aristocracy still stand—empty. Belgrave Square, for example, gracious with its sense of space and serenity in the midst of the turmoil of the grimy city. Many of the houses had signs: *For Sale.* Tonight shall ask Ny Bevan, who is Minister of Health and Housing, why these houses are empty when hundreds of thousands of poor people are looking for shelter in London.

LATER.—Dinner at the Ss'. Ny and Jennie there, and after dinner others came in, including a Labour fellow who obviously knew a lot about movies and spoke bitterly of the Hollywood trash hogging the market in Britain. I suggested the solution lay in the British making better pictures, which they seem to be doing, but apparently the problem is more complicated than that. The British people, like our own, go for these Hollywood pictures, however inane. Ny explained that the great houses in Belgrave Square and elsewhere were empty because it cost too much in money and materials to make them over into small apartments. A mighty argument with him, as usual, over almost everything under the sun, it being something of a continuation of one that has been going on between us for years. If I got the worst of it, as I did, I reflected that for years he had been a formidable debater in the House of Commons (a schooling I would never have) and that as a special antagonist of Churchill on the floor he had always more than held his own with that doughty combatant.

London, *Tuesday, October* 16

Foggy today, and raw, and the army plane to Paris could not get off. Tomorrow, maybe. On Sunday the French people, in an election and referendum, will decide their fate, so to speak, and I want to watch them.

One leaves this island for the bleak Continent full of exciting yet confused impressions, but pretty certain of one thing: there will be no revolution here, or anything slightly resembling it, as long as the present socialist government is at the helm. There will be an evolution toward a state-controlled private economy, with government ownership of a few key industries and the Bank of England.

The nationalization of the Bank of England has not provoked the heart palpitations among the solid men of property that many Americans expected. Indeed, the stock of the bank rose ten points during the week before the socialist bill to nationalize it was introduced. Since August 2 it had risen forty points. And why not, since the lucky stockholders will continue to get from their holdings for the next twenty years a government-guaranteed return of twelve per cent interest on their stock. If this is revolution or socialism, I hope our Wall Street banks will go in for some.

British business and Labour circles are convinced that the United States, with its fanatical confidence in the "free enterprise system," is headed for a bad depression in five years. By planning their own economy they hope to insulate themselves from the shock of our bust. Wonder if we are in for *that*.

Paris, *Thursday, October* 18

The wonderful, magic city again! In the autumn light loitering on the bridge and looking up the Seine toward the misty outlines of Notre-Dame, one tingles with a high inner contentment, shedding for the moment life's complications, the impress of ugliness, the corroding worry over things done or not done or to be done. Here, on the old stone bridge, a man, for a moment, feels utterly free, unchained in his spirit at last, the slavery to time, to motion, to obligation, to all the human ties, forgotten. Over the river's quiet water a great loneliness can come upon you, but it is serene, sweet, very deep, engulfing you like the gentle mist, blunting all the sharp edges that have hurt the soul, tortured the mind, wearied the body, seared the nerves. I have felt a great loneliness this day, one of the freest and happiest of my life.

Paris, *Saturday, October* 20

To lunch at the little bistro in Levallois with Eve and Philippe after they had put *Paris Presse*, their afternoon newspaper, to bed. The food even better than before and the wine still good, and much, much talk through the afternoon, mostly about tomorrow's plebiscite and election.

The French people tomorrow will decide, by their votes, the destiny of France. It is rather inspiring to think that such a fateful thing will be decided by the democratic process. For five years ago democracy in France failed. I happened to see it go to pieces. It had become too corrupt, too feeble, too unworkable to function. Across the border, totalitarianism, seemingly, had made Germany strong. A lot of Frenchmen—especially those with large bank accounts—were attracted by this totalitarianism. They did not mind so much its coming, nor Hitler's coming, as both did in 1940.

France tomorrow—unless I am greatly mistaken—will not vote to go back to the old ways that brought disaster in 1940, though even Édouard Herriot and his Radical-Socialist Party, the largest in France before the war, have pleaded with them to do so. They will bury the old Third Republic and elect a Constituent

Assembly to write the constitution for the Fourth French Republic. That is what tomorrow's voting is about.

Paris, *Monday, October* 22

Though Frenchmen had not voted for nine years, and Frenchwomen never until yesterday, it was a pleasure to see democracy functioning so quietly and thoughtfully. The people have decided overwhelmingly not to go back to the Third Republic. They have elected a Constituent Assembly to organize a Fourth Republic. For the first time in French history the Communists emerge as the largest party. They have 152 seats in the Assembly against 142 each for the Socialists and Popular Republicans. The mushroom growth overnight of the Popular Republicans, known as the M.R.P., is a bigger surprise even than the victory of the Communists, for no one expected it to become a major power, equal in voting strength to each of the two Marxist parties, in its very first electoral bid. Though it is predominantly Catholic, its domestic program is leftish, about the same as that of the Socialists. The reactionary parties and even the old middle-of-the-road Radicals, who controlled the French government through most of the Third Republic, have been snowed under.

Borrowed the dilapidated CBS Cadillac today to haul Dos Passos, Marguerite, Jeff [Parsons, Jr.], and Madame X. out to Barbizon, where Jeff and his bride have a quaint charming country place. (She hid Allied fliers in it during the war.) The Cadillac was of ancient vintage and seemed about to fall apart. It puffed and snorted and frequently stopped and one steered it by luck and instinct. Madame X. turned out to be a charming old French lady and, I judged, once a great beauty, but I did not relish her perfume, which rapidly pervaded the car and made me almost swoon from its overpowering, sharp, evil odor.

Paris, *Thursday, October* 25

Yvonne dropped by today and insisted on our lunching at Knam, a little Russian place in the Latin Quarter where we had often gone in our great days many years ago. We had, I fear, a very sentimental time. The proprietor, a man of about thirty, claimed to remember us and insisted on celebrating with a bottle of vodka. The last time we had seen him, he had been a little shaver in knee pants who came in after school to help his parents, Russian émigrés, run the place. Now he was thirty, had been in the war, had fought for France, had spent years in German prison camps. I wish I had Yvonne's blithe unconcern with time and the passing thereof. It is wonderful.

The newspapers say Vidkun Quisling, whose name added a sinister word to every modern language, was done to death night before last by a Norwegian firing squad in Oslo.

Forgot to note: in the Scribe bar Monday evening when we got back from Barbizon, Hadley, the first Mrs. Hemingway, and Martha, the third (just in from Berlin), having a wonderful time over their apéritifs discussing the fourth….

Paris, *Friday, October* **26**

At dinner at the British Embassy tonight, much droll talk with Lady Diana and John Strachey apropos of the latter's having been held on Ellis Island a few years back as a dangerous Red. John, now Minister for Air in His Majesty's government, thinks it is very funny in retrospect.

Paris, *Monday, October* **29**

It has been a striking and encouraging experience—this brief stop-over in Britain and France on my way back to Germany. Britain is not the nation we knew in 1939 nor apparently will it ever be again. France stumbles out of the nightmare of four years under the barbarian conquest and, after a year of trying, suddenly finds its feet. But they are not the feet we knew in 1939. The old ones, apparently, are gone forever....

The structure of society in western Europe is being completely over-hauled—economically, socially, politically. The war swamped the old one, and few regret its disappearance. It spelled misery for too many people. In western Europe the common people have taken over political power. They intend to use it to obtain economic and social power as well.... Thus it is that Paris and London—once the centers of wealth and fashion in the Western world—have taken on aspects of great proletarian cities. The clothes of the rich are as shabby as those of the poor.... That old law of supply and demand (so sacred at home) has lost all meaning over here. You can flutter a whole fistful of banknotes and shout to the housetops for something you want to buy. It will do no good. What the nation produces is allocated by the state to those it considers most in need. Priorities and ration coupons are worth more than any amount of cash.

What the great majority of people in western Europe want is democratic socialism. They intend to get it this time, gradually, to be sure, and orderly, preserving always their democratic freedoms and their respect for the individual and his dignity as a human being.

With luck and decent flying weather, I shall be back in Berlin tomorrow. Nearly five years since I left. December 5, 1940, it was.

By God, our side did not lose—despite the odds, despite the Nazi terror and the obscene Germanic brutality and all the Nazi-German lies and deceits and hideous massacres!

Yet do you remember how hopeless it seemed that raw, dark December day of 1940 when you drove down the Wilhelmstrasse past the Chancellery, where Hitler, who seemed to have Europe at his feet, was, and then out to get your plane at Tempelhof, bristling with Göring's deadly planes? Remember that? And how they scoffed at home when you made it for Christmas that year—Senator Wheeler and the others that night in Washington when you sounded off about what Hitler was really up to? And the night in Milwaukee nearly a year later—just before Pearl Harbor and Hitler's declaration of war on us—with the auditorium full of police because they were afraid my remarks about Germany's criminal purposes might cause a riot?

Don't feel like sleeping tonight. How will it be in Berlin tomorrow—amidst the ruins these arrogant people brought down on themselves?

Berlin, *Saturday, November* 3

So this is the end of Hitler's thousand-year Reich!

The end of the awful tyranny, the bloody war, the whole long nightmare of a storm that some of us American correspondents began covering a decade ago from this once proud capital.

It is something to see—here where it ended. And it is indescribable.

How can you find words to convey truthfully and accurately the picture of a great capital destroyed almost beyond recognition; of a once mighty nation that has ceased to exist; of a conquering people who were so brutally arrogant and so blindly sure of their mission as the master race when I departed from here five years ago, and whom you now see poking about their ruins, broken, dazed, shivering, hungry human beings without will or purpose or direction, reduced like animals to foraging for food and seeking shelter in order to cling to life for another day?

Ah, you say, this is not a pretty thing to observe, but at least these people have learned one thing—that war does not pay. Surely they are now sorry they started this one and are determined never to do it again. Alas, one cannot report for certain that this is so.

What the German people regret, you soon find, is not that they made this war, but that they lost it. If only Hitler had listened to his generals during the Russian campaign; if only he hadn't declared war on the United States; if only the whole world hadn't ganged up on poor Germany, they whimper, Germany would have won and been spared the present sufferings. There is no sense of guilt or even remorse. Most Germans you talk to merely think they have been unlucky....

Berlin, *Sunday, November* 4

"This is Berlin!"

It seemed a little strange to say those words on the air again today. It has been some time since I began a broadcast to America like that. The last time, in fact, I see by my notes, was December 3, 1940—almost five years ago. Things have changed a lot around Berlin since that winter day.

I kept thinking of that tonight as I did the first broadcast since my return, in an improvised studio in a little room in the garret of some magnate's former villa in fashionable Dahlem. Yesterday I drove past the place on Adolf Hitler Platz (as it was then called) where we used to broadcast. It was just another pile of rubble. Were my former Nazi censors buried beneath it? At least they were not present today to try to scratch the truth out of my copy nor to stand over my shoulder to see that I did not, as I had often tried to do at the microphone, cheat, for the sake of truth.

Gone they were, and all they stood for. One could broadcast the truth once more.

Berlin, *Monday, November 5*

To go back to my mountain of notes on the first memorable days in Berlin:

Tuesday, October 30

That first view of Berlin from the air this afternoon! The great city demolished almost beyond recognition.

The center of the capital around the Leipzigerstrasse and the Friedrichstrasse a vast acreage of rubble. Most of the little streets I knew, gone, erased as off a map. The railway stations—Potsdamerbahnhof, Anhalterbahnhof, Lehrterbahnhof—gaunt shells. The Imperial Palace of the kaisers roofless, some of its wings pulverized, and here and there the outer walls battered in. The Tiergarten like any other battlefield from the air, pockmarked with shell holes; the old spreading trees that I had known, bare stumps. And as far as you can see in all directions, from a plane above the city, a great wilderness of debris, dotted with roofless, burnt-out buildings that look like little mousetraps with the low autumn sun shining through the spaces where windows had been.

When we flew over Tempelhof the ground officer would not let us land. Ground fog, he said, though we could see the field perfectly.

"How about a little tour of your old stamping-ground?" the pilot asked. When we ran out of gas in half an hour, the stubborn officer would have to let us land, he said. I crawled into the co-pilot's seat. Around and around the sprawling city we circled. But I could not take it all in so quickly. My brain became blurred. Soon I was lost staring down at the awful wasteland.

Our gas was about gone. The pilot was arguing with Tempelhof field on his radio. The ground officer kept ordering him back to Wiesbaden, two hundred miles away. Ground fog, he kept saying, though visibility was so good we could see from two thousand feet the faces of German prisoners of war repairing the field.

The pilot began to perspire.

"Why not land at Gatow?" I said. "It's the RAF field and I know it well. I used to sail on the Wannsee near by when Gatow was a Luftwaffe base."

"Give me the Berlin map," the pilot said to his co-pilot. But there was none to be found.

"I'll guide you in," I said. There was really ground fog at Gatow, but we made it on the second try.

Toward sundown we got permission to come into Tempelhof. In this district around the airfield I had had my home for three years, but I could not make it out. Then from the canal and the S.-Bahn tracks I got my bearings. As we banked toward the field I saw our old house. It was still standing, and with a roof—the only intact building in the entire neighborhood. Had Frau K., who owned it, survived, then? She had not liked the Nazis, who had hounded her husband to the grave; he had been a famous flying ace of the first World War who had refused to knuckle down to Göring. But like all Germans she had pitched in to help win the war for Nazi Germany. The last night I had seen her she had talked for hours about her patriotic duty as a German. And Germany would win, she had said. Well, at least her roof was still standing.

It was dark this night before I got billeted in an atrociously furnished middle-class villa of a German washing-machine manufacturer in Zehlendorf-West. Before I could set my gear down, he was bowing and scraping and protesting in loud guttural tones that he had always been the staunchest of Hitler-haters.

Will have to wait until tomorrow to prowl through the remains.

Wednesday, October 31

A foggy, chilly morning, my first in Berlin. Very much like the last one on December 5, 1940, when I drove to Tempelhof to get away. I remember it was snowing then.

But, ah, Berlin this morning! The utter wasteland where once stood the proud capital of the regime that Hitler said would last a thousand years!

As we drove block after block past the ruins, I was reminded a little of the Babylon I had seen in 1930 on my way home from India. I was working on the *Chicago Tribune* then, and Colonel McCormick—the eccentric—had cabled me: "Return via Babylon."

I had not had a very clear idea as to where Babylon was, or indeed if any trace of it still remained. But in Delhi, when I had recovered from malaria fever, I had gone to good old Thos. Cook & Son and had said to the Hindu clerk: "I would like you to book me from here to Vienna via Babylon." An imperturbable fellow, like most Hindu scribes, he had done so without any questions or fuss or even interest, and a month later, after journeying up the Persian Gulf, I had got off the train that plied the little narrow-gauge railway between Basra and Bagdad, and had found Babylon and wandered through the excavated ruins of the once great city.

Howard Smith remarked: *"Das ist einmalig in der Geschichte!"* ("That happens once in history!"), a favorite Nazi expression to describe one of Hitler's triumphs.

It had happened before, of course. Babylon and Carthage. And had not Rome been sacked by the Germanic barbarians? But I don't think there has ever been such destruction on such a scale as this.

We drove in through the Kurfürstendamm from the American sector in south-west Berlin. Someone had told me this equivalent of New York's Fifth Avenue had escaped the heavy bombing. But hardly a house was intact. On both sides of the wide street you could see, through the fog, that the houses were mere façades, the buildings but gaunt skeletons. Through the window spaces or through gaping holes torn by bombs and shells you could see the debris.

We came to the Gedächtniskirche—the Kaiser Wilhelm Memorial Church—where the Kurfürstendamm turns half-right into the Tauentzienstrasse. One remembered what a hideous edifice it had been. In the fog it loomed up suddenly and strange—the contours of its battered remains so softened by the gray light that it looked almost a thing of beauty.

We got out of the car and strolled around the neighborhood, a familiar one to me, for I had lived up the street in the Tauentzienstrasse at one time and, like everyone else in Berlin, had always patronized the restaurants, cafés and movie palaces of the quarter. Now I could scarcely recognize it. The Romanisches Café, where the Berlin bohemians used to forgather, was largely rubble. The Eden Hotel, down the Budapesterstrasse, where the racy girls of the town hung out, was entirely rubble. How had these light-hearted damsels, I wondered, taken the horrors of the bombing and the bombardment? All the buildings across from the church on the south side of the zoo were smashed in. One of them, a gaudy place where we had occasionally dined and danced, was no more.

But the zoo? What was that I read in the local newspapers this morning? Something about the director of the zoo assuring the population that the animals would be fed as usual this winter. The Berliners, who are hungry themselves, will not resent that. Curious—man's (or at least, the German's) tenderness toward animals, even the wild, vicious ones, in contrast to the way he treats his fellow men—in a concentration camp, for instance.

Opposite the façade of the church the Gloria Palast, a popular movie house, was just a mound of broken bricks and stone. German women, some of whom looked—from their fur jackets—as though they had once been staunch, if smug, members of the middle class (Hitler's most fanatical supporters), formed a chain gang, passing broken brick to one another with their dainty hands.

A Russian motor convoy rounded the church, a long file of Chevrolet trucks filled with loot. The pickings must be getting slim. Aside from a few bicycles, there seemed to be only junk—piping, wheels, broken machinery.

We walked up the Kurfürstendamm. The beer-halls on the right, in which one had spent many an evening trying to forget the Nazis, were all smashed in. Kranzler's caférestaurant, where in the crisp autumn you used to go for *Rebhuhn* (partridge) and red kraut, washed down with a dry Rhine wine, was just another ruin. And so it went. Life had been gaudy on this broad avenue between the wars. It had glittered like tinsel and had been about as deep and meaningful. The Kurfürstendamm had expressed, in a way, the vulgarity, the cheapness, the showy pretentiousness, the dreadful emptiness of life for the middle classes during the uneasy peace. Was its destruction such a loss? I wondered.

We left it and hit down the East-West Axis—the triumphal boulevard that Hitler had widened from the old Charlottenburger Chaussée into a sort of Via

Triumphale down which his goosestepping supermen used to parade in the brief hours of the Nazi glory. As a reporter, before the war, I had often stood in the reviewing stand and watched them, a feeling of despair and disgust gnawing at my stomach. Up this broad, flag-bedecked avenue Hitler's new tanks and huge self-propelled guns had lumbered by, sending the German people massed along the curbs into wonderful ecstasy, and the rest of the world's people, when they read our dispatches or listened to our broadcasts, into hysterical fear.

This boulevard, which cut a wide ribbon through the wooded Tiergarten, had come to stand, for me, as an ugly symbol of Nazi Germany's military might, as the near-by Sieges-Allee, with its ugly statues of all the Prussian *Fürsts, Kurfürsts,* and kings had stood for the cruel, pompous, vain glory of Prussia. But before I left Berlin, the great street's symbolism—at least for me—became diluted. The spacious boulevard through the Tiergarten turned out to be a great landmark for RAF pilots in the night and I used to watch them fly up and down it as if they owned it. Somehow their regular visits helped to wipe out one's memory of this great highway as the parade ground of the strutting German Army. Hitler, enraged, had had the avenue covered at great expense with wire netting to camouflage it from the British bombers, but one night a fierce wind from the east had blown the covering down, and even the Berliners had chuckled. Yes, the mighty symbol was fading, even then.

Now a gang of German prisoners of war were at work on the once proud avenue, filling the holes made by the bombs and shells. Beyond the curbs, on both sides, the Tiergarten, which for so many years had been the scene of my walks and my meditations and whose wonderful rose garden in June had been a special delight, looked like a dozen other battlefields I had seen. Here the Nazi die-hards had made their last stand after the Reich Chancellery had fallen and Hitler and his mistress and Goebbels and his wife and children had liquidated themselves. Half of the great trees had been shot away, and the ground was criss-crossed with trenches and fox-holes and scattered with the rusty things you see on any battlefield—parts of tanks, armored cars, half-trucks, guns, helmets, and so on.

Curiously enough, that ugly abortion the Siegessäule—the Victory Column— was still standing in the middle of the Grosser Stern. Neither British and American bombs nor Russian shells had toppled it over. But high in the gray sky—the fog was clearing a little now—you could make out a French flag floating atop it, atop this Germanic monument to Prussia's victory over France in 1871.

It recalled to one how fickle in Europe the fates were, and how shortsighted, if natural, it has been for Europeans to conclude that their latest victory over the enemy was final for all time. (But good God! I should like to close an eye to history and think now that this time, certainly this time, the Germans either are down for good or will never rise again in the detestable form they have shown the last seventy-five years.)

One got another reminder of how often in history—as in our personal lives—the tables are turned. Two thirds of the way down the Axis toward the Brandenburger Gate, on the left side, hundreds of workmen were laboring like beavers behind an enormous scaffolding. Howard said it was to be a mammoth monument to the Red Soldier to commemorate the Russian troops killed in the Battle of Berlin. It was to be unveiled, he said, on November 7, the anniversary of the Bolshevik Revolution—in just a week now.

God, I thought, if Hitler is dead, as the British and Americans believe (the Russians are not quite certain), he must be turning over in his grave, wherever it is! For neither he nor the German people, for that matter, ever dreamed the day would come when a monument to the Red Army would rise in the midst of the German capital—indeed, on a spot within sight of the Reichstag, where Hitler had so often fulminated against Russia and its Bolshevism—yes, on the very spot past which, in the high time of the Nazis, Hitler's arrogant hirelings had done some of their fanciest goosestepping!

We drove on through the Brandenburger Gate, which was still standing though a horse or two in the statuary atop it had been badly wounded and the Grecian columns were nicked with shrapnel. The Pariserplatz, just beyond the gate, which had been pretty much the geographical center of my life in Berlin during the war years (for I lived at the Adlon and went much to the American Embassy near by) was scarcely recognizable. The Adlon was a shell; the Embassy completely destroyed, as was the French Embassy across the little square. There was a sign on the battered front door of the Adlon, through which I had passed so often in my Berlin years. It announced bravely that "Five O'Clock Tea" was being served.

"But where?" I asked Howard. Through the broken walls of the once famous hostelry you could see nothing but debris.

"In the cellar," Howard said. "And some of the old waiters are still around in their long, formal coats and starched collars just as if nothing had changed."

We turned into the Wilhelmstrasse, that famous little street from whose ugly ministerial buildings and palaces first Prussia and then Germany has been ruled with an iron hand that brought little good to the world.

Ah! There was a sight for you!

As far as you could see down the street, not a single building stood intact. Debris was piled up on the sidewalks and spilled over on to most of the street. After six months of work clearing up the ruins, a path only wide enough for two cars to pass had been cleared.

On the right-hand side Hindenburg's old palace, which Ribbentrop had taken over and had remodeled the first year of the war (despite the shortage of labor and materials), was just a part of the catacomb of rubble that stretched down the Wilhelmstrasse until your eyes lost it. Some of the walls still stood. The interior was completely destroyed.

The Foreign Office farther down, where we had been convoked so often by the insufferable Ribbentrop every time Germany broke another treaty or attacked a new neighbor, was similarly gutted, though its staunch front walls, blackened from fire, remained. Back there on the left-hand side of the street the shell of a building where Rudolf Hess, who as the Nuremberg trials approach is now feigning madness, used to have his office. Next to it another shell where the clown Putzi Hanfstängel used to receive us before he fell out of favor with his Führer.

Farther down on the left, the few remains of the Propaganda Ministry. I could only recognize it by its position at the end of the street before you came into the square. Most of its walls were gone, and the interior—those palatial rooms where the little worm Goebbels had so often strutted in (despite his limp) to lecture us and lie to us, and where, after the war began, we had assembled each afternoon for a press conference presided over by the cocky Dr. Boehmer and his gang of liars—was simply a mess of twisted girders and pulverized brick and plaster.

Finally, across the street from the Propaganda Ministry, the remains of the place where the war had been plotted—Hitler's Chancellery. The Russians, you could see, had pretty well cleaned it up though, Howard said, it had been in an awful mess when the Russians stormed it the day after an orgy of suicides and murders in the bunker underneath had at last removed Hitler, his mistress Eva Braun, Goebbels and his wife and children, and a few other bitter-enders from this world.

A rather bedraggled Russian sentry stood guard over the doorway. He seemed chilly and bored. Would he have been bored, though, I thought, if he had had my memories of that particular building?

How many times had I stood opposite on the curb and watched the comings and goings of the great! They would drive up in their black super-Mercédès cars, the fat bemedaled Göring, the snake-like little Goebbels, though he lived just across the street, the arrogant, stupid Ribbentrop, though he lived a mere hundred yards down the street—these and Hess and the drunkard Ley and the debauched-looking little Funk with the small eyes of a pig and the sadist Himmler (though he looked like a mild schoolmaster) and the other swashbuckling party hacks and then the generals, their necks stiff even when they dismounted from a car, one eye inevitably squeezing a monocle, their uniforms immaculately pressed. They would come, be saluted by the guard of honor, and pass within this building to plot their wars and their conquests.

Today, I reflected standing there in front of the Chancellery's ruins, they are all dead or in jail. This building too, in whose stately rooms they worked out so confidently and cold-bloodedly their obscene designs, is like them, smashed forever. Germany, their land, which they wanted to rule the world, is smashed too. It will not for a long time recover, and perhaps never.

And yet what suffering they caused on this planet, these German men, before an aroused world turned them back and smashed through to hunt them out and kill them or capture them! How many millions dead, killed and murdered? How many maimed and broken? How many homes in ashes? And yes—how the lives of even those who survive? For even though the fighting has stopped, the peoples of Europe this winter are hungry and cold, and a million or so of them probably will die. All because of what these evil, stupid little men—in this building before it was smashed—did.

And do not forget either that these criminal men with their brutal inhuman designs were—when I last stood before this building, less than five years ago—the heroes of this weird and tragic land. Crowds cheered them in the streets. The workers cheered them in the factories. The whole German nation followed them not only obediently but with enthusiasm. And the German people toiled like beavers so that these men might succeed in their plans to destroy or enslave the rest of the world. So many of our own people forget this as they pity the dazed and broken Germans hauling wood on their backs through the rubble of the German cities today.

We went on from the Chancellery, turned left past the Kaiserhof, the hotel that had been Hitler's headquarters before he came to power and where, during the war years, I had often snatched an evening meal before the broadcasts. On many a dark night I had swallowed down my food and watched the Nazis in another corner toasting their early victories as if they already owned the earth. About all that is left of this little Nazi citadel is the charred front wall, on which you can make out the blurred word: "Kaiserhof."

Beyond the hotel the street was blocked by a mountain of debris. This part of town, stretching out from the corner of the Friedrichstrasse and Leipzigerstrasse, was so pulverized by Anglo-American bombing that we soon became lost. All the familiar little old streets leading into it and through it have been erased. We finally found the Friedrichstrasse, through which bulldozers had driven a path, and drove up it to the Unter den Linden. The broad avenue, once lined with stately linden trees, which had been so familiar to American tourists and such a pride of the Berliners, was unrecognizable. It was piled with rubble, and all of the buildings on both sides were gutted or smashed in.

We turned right on the Linden toward the Schloss. Kranzler's, on the corner, where one used to go for tea or chocolate in the dim days when one had the time and the taste for such things, was gone. A direct hit, probably. Up the Linden a few doors, I looked for Habel's wine house, a pleasant inn where I had had, on occasion, much good wine and food and talk. It too had shared the fate of the district. The University Library on the left of the avenue was a mess, as were, in fact, all the university buildings near by. The Zeughaus—the War Museum—where samples of all the lethal weapons of all the German wars were kept and honored, was badly smashed in. If the Allies have any sense they will blow the remains of it up to help the Germans forget it. On the right, the main part of the State Opera, to which I had often repaired when one could still listen to music, was in ruins, though the front part looked as though it could be salvaged.

The Lustgarten, where one had listened to Göring and Goebbels haranguing the delirious German masses, showed signs of having been fought over during the Battle of Berlin. Bizarre: two battered British tanks from the *first* World War were piled up on the square. The Kaiser's former Imperial Palace we found badly wrecked—past repair, I should say. The university quarter, down toward the river Spree, had received an awful shellacking from bombs and shells. Most of its buildings were gone, though the statue of Hegel, I noticed, stood there in the very midst of the ruins, practically unnicked.

With difficulty we made our way through blocks of rubble to the Alexanderplatz. For the first time we began to see numbers of Russian soldiers, for we were now in the Soviet sector, having passed through the British sector in the Kurfürstendamm and Tiergarten areas. Most of the Russian troops appeared poorly clad, their uniforms dirty and shoddy. Perhaps that was because they had done so much magnificent fighting in them. About one Russian in four, officer or man, carried a slung carbine. Almost all of them carted ordinary civilian suitcases, looted no doubt from Germans, and filled, no doubt, with black-market purchases. The Russians, Howard said, had recently received two or three years' back pay in paper marks, and our GI's had not been slow to take advantage of it. Our troops had had cigarettes and cheap watches shipped posthaste from home, and here in the Alexanderplatz or in the Tiergarten they disposed of them at fantastic prices to the Russian comrades. "Mickey Mouse" watches—whatever they are—fetched ten thousand marks apiece, Howard said, which a GI could convert into one thousand American dollars and send home. Now, however, the army was stepping in to stop the racket, and the Russians were also beginning to co-operate. Both commands were checking up not only on their own troops but on Germans who were palming off a weird assortment of knick-knacks on the property-hungry Red Army men.

Indeed, hardly had we entered the square and paused to see the sinister Gestapo jail and headquarters, which had been nicely smashed, before a large squad of Russian military police began rounding up a hundred or so black-market operators, about a third of whom were Soviet soldiers and the rest German civilians.

One little incident followed that I did not much like. The Russians, as every American soldier here knows, do not let you take photographs in their sector without a special permit. But an American lieutenant colonel was blandly photographing the round-up of the black-marketeers by the Russian M.P.'s. Two Russian guards immediately grabbed him and proceeded to march him off to the hoosegow. He was a rather elderly fellow and evidently not a combat officer; but he grew combative enough with the Russians. What I did not like was that the German civilians on the platz gathered around with obvious glee to see the spectacle of a couple of Russian soldiers arresting an American colonel. A Russian officer intervened and appeared to explain in Russian that if the colonel would give up his film he would be freed. But either the American did not understand or he did not want to part with his film. So off to the jug he was marched while the Germans guffawed. Perhaps, I thought, they saw their first glimmer of hope in this little incident. In the end—*Ja?*—The Russians and Americans would never understand each other, never get along. If so, that was a German's chance.

We came home by way of Wedding, a German workers' district in northern Berlin and now part of the Russian sector. At every street corner you saw a big Russian poster in German which read: "The Experience of History Shows That the Hitlers Come and Go, but That the People of the German Nation Live on." It was signed: "Stalin."

Now our Russian friends, I reflected, stand for a tough peace with Germany because they are determined not to have to defend themselves against any more German attacks. But they know something about propaganda. We Americans, alas, do not.

Berlin, *Thursday, November* 1

At the invitation of General James Gavin, commander of the U.S. 82nd Airborne Division, I sat in today on the seventeenth meeting of the Allied Kommandatura, which rules Berlin. 'Twas something of an experience. Here on a practical plane you could see the four victorious Allies, so different in their backgrounds, psychology, and national structures, trying to work together in peace as they had in war. The gulf between the East and the West was certainly there as the four generals tried to agree on various details of ruling the conquered city. But on the whole they did not get along badly at all. General Smirnov, the Russian, who presided, conducted himself, I thought, with tact, humor, and dispatch, though an American diplomat had solemnly assured me that the Russians were simply too ignorant really to know how to participate in an international meeting, much less conduct one.

All together, watching the Kommandatura meeting was a rather encouraging experience when you consider that the future peace of the world depends on the four major Allies getting along together especially here in Germany.

In the evening, with some colleagues, to General Robertson, the British deputy commander. He seemed anxious to see that the Germans were treated well, and moreover made it look as though that was official British policy.

Running into a host of old friends here—newspaper and diplomatic.

Berlin, *Friday, November* 2

I must try to get the story of how we Americans are running our part of Germany. Last night an earnest young American Army captain spoke bitterly and discouragingly on the subject. He thought we were doing a pretty lousy job. He said in Darmstadt our CIC had gone so far as to employ Nazi Gestapo agents to track down German Communists, though the Communist Party is recognized as legal in our zone, as in all the others. Nazi elements, he said, run the German prisoner-of-war camps and ill-treat anti-Nazi prisoners just as they did in the POW camps at home. He stressed how badly German anti-Nazi refugees in the U.S. were needed here—yet we do not allow them to return. He told a weird story about one of our chief political advisers here, a sinister German, he thought, a former protégé of Schacht, a former S.S. man and a rabid German nationalist. Now this singular fellow advises us on what to do with the Germans!

Walter Kerr, Howard, and I had another look at the ruins today. Driving up Budapesterstrasse toward the Lützowplatz, someone noted that the house of ill fame on the right side of the street was the only building in the block left habitable, as if the fates—in their inscrutable ways—had been kind to the world's oldest profession.

The Lützowplatz, once one of the prettiest squares in Berlin, is smashed beyond recognition. Hardly a house is standing. The Nazis, in their wrath, blew up the broad bridge, the Herkulesbrücke, to the north of the platz, as indeed they blew up all of these bridges over the Landwehrkanal. I looked for the studio of Carlos, from which we had watched the air-raids in the first part of the war. The building on whose fifth floor it had been was razed to the ground. The Herkuleshaus, where Sinclair Lewis and other old-timers used to stay, has simply been erased.

We turned down the Nettelbeckstrasse toward Wittenbergplatz to see how the Taverne, to which we American and British correspondents had repaired on many a night of crisis to quiet our shaky nerves, had fared. It was a hopeless quest. The whole area had been leveled into an ugly mass of debris. The Courbièrestrasse, on which the tavern had fronted, was gone—just part of the rubble….

Going into Wittenbergplatz, I noticed a sign put up by the Russians. (We Americans, obviously, did not go in for such stuff.) It was in German and said: "No foreign enemy ever brought so much misery to the Germans as Hitler." Misery there was, such as no living German had ever dreamed was possible. These middle-class German women toiling over there in the rubble on half-empty stomachs, passing broken bricks all day long with their once dainty hands, were an example of just part of it. And yet how many Germans realized *why* this misery had come? Didn't they blame the foreign enemy for it? Wasn't the only blame they had for Hitler merely that he had lost, not won, the war? Walter and Howard, who have been here some time, said that it was. The German people they had talked to, they said, blamed the Nazis not for starting this incredibly destructive war, but merely for having lost it. As a German woman, with hungry eyes, I fell to talking to at the Press Club last night kept saying: "If only Hitler had let the generals run the war; if only we hadn't attacked Russia, or, if after we had, you Americans had not come in to help them, we might have won and been spared this."

The German people, I fear, have not—by a hell of a long way—learned the lessons of this terrible war. They have no sense of guilt and are sorry only that they were beaten and must now suffer the consequences. They are sorry only for themselves; not at all for those they murdered and tortured and tried to wipe off this earth.

Howard wanted to have a look at Wittenbergplatz, where he had lived. We found what he thought was the approximate spot. But the building was gone.

I was curious to see what had happened to the little pub on the south side of the platz that Hitler's half-brother, Alois Hitler, had started shortly before the war, much to the disgust of the Führer, who did not like the people to be reminded of the lower-middle-class origins of the Hitler family. It was still there, and open for such business as pubs, without suitable food or drink, conduct at the moment. But we could not find Alois Hitler within. Somehow that name did not seem to ring the bell in anyone's mind, though it had struck terror up and down Europe and indeed the world. I remembered Alois Hitler was a harmless enough fellow, a typical pub-keeper, whose chief fear was that his half-brother would fly into a rage and order him to get out of business. But no one inside seemed to remember him. Outside, on the sign over the Establishment, his famous name had, in fact, been hastily rubbed out. The new name was "FENT," if you please—though when I looked a second time I could make out the smeared letters that had been there when I was last here: "A. HITLER."

The great K.D.W. department store on the west side of the square, where I had done my meager Christmas shopping in the days when I lived across the street and was broke, was battered and burnt out. So was the house in the Tauentzienstrasse opposite it where in 1934 Tess and I had rented a studio from a cultivated German Jewish couple. He had been a sculptor and she an art historian, and they had had the good sense to beat it hurriedly for England and later for the United States at the time when many of their Jewish friends thought things could still be arranged with the Nazis.

In the little studio atop the building, which had now been bombed to ground level, we had given refuge and what help we could to certain victims of the Nazi barbarism. One of them, a half-Jewish lawyer who had lost an arm for the Fatherland in World War I, had wisely come to us first, I remembered, on his release from the dreaded Gestapo prison of tortures in the Columbiahaus. He was out of his head, though he was one of the bravest men I ever knew, and we kept him until he had become a little normal, a little human, a little like himself, before we took him back to his wife and children. That, of course, was in the beginning of Nazism and we were quite shocked at the time. Innocent we were—then.

All of Berlin's railway stations have been smashed, but most of them are functioning after a sort. We took a look at some of them—the Potsdamerbahnhof and the Anhalterbahnhof. Before the Anhalter station hundreds of German refugees were milling around with their great bundles full of what earthly goods they had managed to save. We stopped a moment to question them. They had come in from the east, they said, from Poland, from Czechoslovakia, from the Russian zone. Where they were going, or how, they did not know, nor, apparently, did anyone else. They looked very forlorn, these same sturdy German folk who had rushed so joyously, many of them, in 1939 and the ensuing good war years, to settle on land that the Germans had stolen from the Poles, Russians, and Czechs. Now the rightful owners had taken back their land, and these German conquerors, in their rags and their hunger, were looking for refuge in the shrunken, already crowded German land.

We drove and prowled for hours through the prostrate city. On the whole, one began to see, the residents of Berlin themselves—as distinguished from the refugees pouring into the capital—were better dressed than the people one saw in the liberated western countries, or even in London. In Paris still the women went stockingless. In Berlin almost all women wear stockings, many of them, no doubt, leftovers from the huge stocks sent back by German soldiers from Holland, Belgium, and especially France in 1940-1. I had seen them buying out the stores in these countries then. I remarked how many German women sported stylish fur coats, though, to listen to some Germans and their American friends here, the Russians were supposed to have torn all the fur coats off all the backs of all the German women in Germany.

In that respect I am beginning to question the tales one heard in Washington, New York, London, and Paris about how the Russians raped. In Budapest, one hears here, it was pretty bad. But it does not appear to have been very excessive here in Berlin. There is always some rape when an army overruns a land. Our own army has done a little on occasion. But when you consider what the Germans did to the Russian population when *they* overran half of European Russia—and that the Red Army soldier may have remembered this—and taking into account that the Soviet troops had been in the field constantly fighting for two or three years and that capturing Berlin was a costly operation and that some of the Russian divisions were made up of very inferior material not to mention a weird assortment of Asiatic troops, then the amount of raping by Russian troops here apparently was not above the average to be expected.

I have met only one German woman who admits she was raped (and she does not take it very tragically, I must say, perhaps because she is well on in years). I have talked to several who say that while the Russians took their watches and some of the junk out of their houses, there was no attempt to rape them. A lot of houses where Germans complain of Russian looting have a surprising amount of good furniture and other things still about.

The German women in the street, then, look pretty well, though I am not implying, God knows, that they were ever a beautiful race. The men look more dilapidated, probably because of their clothes. Many of them, demobilized, found their homes destroyed and their civilian clothes gone.

The people in the streets of Berlin amble along at even a slower gait than they used to when things were good. Our officers think it is partly because they are still dazed from the bombings and their personal catastrophes—loss of homes and of their much-loved property, loss of their menfolk, sudden defeat when victory looked so near for so long—and because the German's reflexes, never very speedy, are slowed down by his hunger and cold. He plods along the street, pays little attention to the snorting, speeding Allied military vehicles careening up and down, and sometimes gets run over, without making much effort to avoid it.

The most sorry-looking folk on the street (to say pitiful would be dishonest for me, since I have no pity for *them*) are the demobilized German soldiers. They hobble along in their rags, footsore from walking in worn out shoes stuffed with newspaper, their uniforms, which in my day they kept so smart, tattered and filthy. They make an impressive picture of defeat and desolation. On a street in Wedding we stopped to talk to a group of them scraping along. God! Were these the crack soldiers who goosestepped so arrogantly through Poland, France, Russia, and other temporarily conquered lands? These the *Herrenvolk*? God, they are certainly not arrogant now. They are bent, dirty, tired, and hungry.

"Where you come from?" I asked them.

"From Stalingrad," they said. "*Alles kaputt.*" They grinned and you could see that few of them, though they were young men, had any teeth left. They begged for cigarettes and we passed a pack around. Then they shuffled and hobbled away.

We lunched at W.'s, and later I went to X.'s office to peruse some documents. Rather interesting, I must say.

One was an interrogation of Dr. Schacht, now in the hoosegow in Nuremberg waiting trial with twenty-two other Nazi gangsters. (Ley, one of the worst Nazi thugs around Hitler, couldn't take it and hanged himself the other day; Hess, one of the pillars of the Nazi regime before he flew to England on his foolish errand, feigns amnesia—so conveniently. Old Krupp von Bohlen und Halbach, another defendant and one of Hitler's chief supporters in German big business, lies stricken with something at Salzburg and has no stomach for a trial.)

Schacht, according to this confidential American report, paces his cell, fuming against the Nazis. Admitted that he never loved them, the fact is he did more than almost anyone else to bring them to power in 1933, and for many years his peculiar financial talents served Hitler well. How often have I seen him on the platform of the Reichstag beaming with pleasure and approval as Hitler harangued and excused some new treaty broken, some new country murdered. Now he rages that he was always against the Nazis and whimpers at the Americans for having locked him up.

All these Nazi thugs, it is evident, are going to blame each other for Nazism's crimes in order to save their skins.

Ah, and some interesting dope on Ribbentrop, the former German Foreign Minister and one of the most truculent and stupid of the Hitler gang, and a mean little liar to boot! I remember how he used to prance into the Foreign Office press room to tell us in his most arrogant fashion of some new Hitlerite aggression. And now here's his preliminary interrogation at Nuremberg, which makes clear that he was not only a liar but a monstrous ignoramus. Only a Hitler would have made such a worm his Foreign Minister.

Some hasty notes scrawled from Ribbentrop's interrogation:

"Hitler told me for the first time on April 22 or 23 that the war was lost...."
But early in April, Ribbentrop says, he and Hitler were still talking about making a deal with Britain! He quotes Hitler as telling him: "We must make some sort of arrangement with England." Were there ever such fools as those Germans!

Ribbentrop claims that after the fall of France, Hitler still spoke of a "quick peace" with England that would leave the British their "prestige." He discourses at length on the theme that Hitler always sought an understanding with Britain. The idiot is still rattling off the old Nazi propaganda line, probably partly because he is too enmeshed in the big Nazi lie to extricate himself and partly because, being an incredibly stupid man, he thinks such silly talk may save his neck.

Now, in the interrogation, Ribbentrop squirms and comes through with a typical whopper. "It is false," he whines, "that I ever said England wouldn't fight. I said she would. Always I had violent disagreements with the Führer on this." Everyone knows he never *dared* to disagree with Hitler, even timidly, let alone violently. And everyone knows that it was his assurance to Hitler that Britain would not fight that helped turn the tables for war in August 1939. He claims Hitler's speeches on foreign affairs were always made without his advice. He even claims that on August 25, 1939—six days before Hitler began his war—he asked the Führer "to stop the advance against Poland"!

This is a good place to get in extracts from a letter Ribbentrop, after Germany's demise, handed to Field-Marshal Montgomery to be forwarded to "Mr. Vincent Churchill"—the lout didn't even know the Christian name of the British Prime Minister!—and Mr. Eden. "Its contents refer—as you will see—" he writes Montgomery, "to a message the Führer gave me before his death."

The letter, in part (written in Ribbentrop's inimitable English), is as follows:

PERSONAL AND CONFIDENTIAL

Sirs:

Radio reports, etc., which I do not quite understand... would come to it, that former collaborators of the Führer... are trying to depreciate the Führer, falsify his ideas about England.... [I wish] to inform you about my last political conversation with the Führer.

This conversation—during which—as so often lately—the Führer's deep disappointment and embitterment about the failure of a political conception was evident, culminated in a kind of last appeal and a message to the leaders of the British Empire. This appeal represents at the same time— one may well say—the last political will of a man, who as a great idealist has loved his people above all, who has lived and fought for his people to his last gasp and in whose conception of the world the English-German question has always been the central point of his political meditations.

I do not know, if the old and noble English custom of fair play is also applicable for a defeated foe. I also do not know if you wish to hear the political testament of a deceased man. But I could imagine that its contents might be adapted to heal wounds, which in the course of this bitter war, have been inflicted and I further believe that its ultimate fulfillment might in this perilous epoch of our world be able to help bring about a better future for all people.

As far as I am concerned I have the duty to do everything I can, to fulfill this last wish the Führer has expressed to me and therefore give myself into the hands of the British occupation army. Should you be willing to give me the opportunity of bringing last conversation with Adolf Hitler to your knowledge, I would be grateful, if I could do this personally and verbally....

[Needless to say, Ribbentrop was never able to see Churchill or Eden on this matter. Several ensuing pages of his letter are taken up to prove that unfortunately Hitler did not follow his Foreign Minister's advice on relations with Britain, Russia, and the U.S.A., which, he says, he wanted to be peaceful. Finally he gets back to what he claims was Hitler's final conversation with him and describes the leader as "having suddenly turned around to me and said: 'You will see, my spirit will arise from my grave and one will see that I have been right.'"]

About one point there has always been entire agreement between the Führer and myself and that was that a strong and united Germany... could only exist in the long run by a close collaboration with Great Britain. What the Führer and myself have done... for the realization of this English-German conception during the last quarter of a century is known to all people concerned. I believe, it was very much....[8]

In spite of all disappointment and embitterment about the repeated English rejection of the German offers the English-German collaboration has to this last hour always been the political creed of the Führer. He has spoken often in vehement terms about British politics, which he did not understand, but everyone who knew the Führer was well aware that it was one of the most outstanding features of his character that—impulse [R. wrote the word this way] though he was—he never changed his fundamental convictions. For this reason in all those years I worked for him and in all our discussions on foreign politics he always came back to this cardinal point. Every step, political, military, etc., during these years was always taken with an eye on this final issue, that is to say to bring Great Britain to terms. To the outside world this may at times not have been recognizable and yet it was so. That England declared war on Germany over the Polish question, a war which we both wanted to avoid by all means and which I tried and almost succeeded to prevent at the last moment, came lastly as a great shock to the Führer.

Now shortly before the bitter end and before his death Hitler has shown himself once more and in spite of his very poor state of health in his old ingenious way. He has with extraordinary clearness quite detached from the events of the day, the war situation and the political combinations given to me an extensive survey of the coming developments of world politics, as he saw it. He has in an almost prophetic way pointed out the decisive importance, which in this century of the formation of large combined political areas must be attached to English-German relations and herewith also to the relations with the present enemies the U.S.A., Soviet Union, France etc. He said, what after this lost war could be contributed by the German side, to establish a stable balance of power between the big political areas, in order that not again and irresistibly new war catastrophes would come over Europe, over the British Empire and over the whole world.

We spoke of Russia and the Führer mentioned the gigantic display of power of the Soviet Union and its doctrines and... he repeatedly referred to the creation of the Red Army by Stalin and called this a "grandiose" deed. And he further said, that "in spite of the divergencies in the Weltauffassung" Germany simply had to come to a good relationship with Soviet Russia, as both people had to live side by side on the long run....

We also spoke at length of the U.S.A. Hitler regretted the war with America, because we had no possible divergencies with this big nation. We had always regretted this war from the beginning and have done everything we could to prevent it even when our ships were being attacked. The Führer said, that good and lasting relations with the U.S.A. absolutely had to be found.... But always again during that conversation the Führer came back to the question of the English-German relations....

Sirs, you have won the war and you hold all power in your hands. May I, as the last foreign minister of a defeated nation and as a man, who in spite of all bitterness of war and of all untruths about his alleged antagonism or "hatred" of England, has always considered England as his second home and who always has wanted the English-German alliance just as much as the Führer himself, point out this:

An enormous to me not comprehensible wave of hatred is at present overwhelming the defeated German nation... concentration camps are taken as the cause of a very serious campaign against the German people... it is difficult for me to say anything at all on this question. But in this letter which is meant personal and confidential I would like to say this: Any inhuman treatment of a prisoner is an impossible way of acting and every decent German will like me deplore such acts and condemn them wholeheartedly.... Neither I nor, I am certain, most of my colleagues in the former government had any idea, what was happening in concentration camps.... This may perhaps surprise, but for a person acquainted with our government system this is quite comprehensible.... I ask myself, can one charge a whole nation with such excesses committed by individuals, as is being done now, excesses which I believe have occurred in the history of all nations? As far as my attitude... in the question of prisoners... I have stood up for the carrying out of the Geneva Convention....

A few days ago it was published that the Wehrmacht had not fought honourably and that the German people should have to learn decency again.

Sirs, can one say this of a defeated enemy, who has fought bravely and of a people who have made superhuman efforts for their country and have lost everything? Can one put down Germans who as patriots... have only done their duty towards their country as war criminals and punish them as such? I would like to appeal to the generosity of the victors.

I have been a patriot all my life.... I have always opposed the policy against Jews, churches, freemasons.... When very much against my will, war broke out after all, I have of course taken an attitude of hard determination and complete conviction in the German victory for internal and external reasons.... But this attitude has not prevented me, to continuously keep an eye on the question of an arrangement with the enemies, in order to seize the first occasion for a peace feeler. In my more intimate conversations with the Führer I continuously placed this point before him and stressed him to allow me to do something about it, but he, after the fruitless attempt for peace in the Reichstag 1940, was sceptical about my plans and endeavors in this direction. In spite of various confidential peace tentatives there has (owing to the uncompromising attitude of the enemy) never been a serious occasion to end this war. The war is lost for Germany. In spite of this fact I am of the holy conviction, that the bringing about of a real friendship between the English and the German people is a fundamental necessity, if both nations will live on the long run. The Führer was of the same opinion and has therefore entrusted me with the mission to inform you—if possible, about his reasons and ideas concerning this collaboration and the quite new form, which in his opinion should be found for it. In order to fulfill this last mission I lay my fate into your hands.

[signed] *Joachim von Ribbentrop*

I would be grateful, if this letter could not be published. I will ask field-marshal Montgomery to send it to you under "personal and confidential."

For unadulterated hypocrisy, this letter by this lying scoundrel takes the prize! And yet—ah! how revealing nevertheless not only of the German Foreign Minister but of German character!

Berlin, *Monday, November* **5**

Is Hitler dead?

The British called us in the other evening to say they thought he was. The Russians claim to be skeptical. They would like to see, they say, the dead man's molars, if he is dead.

No trace has been found of the body that reportedly was burned with that of Hitler's mistress, Eva Braun, in the garden of the Reichs Chancellery on or about May 1 last.

Today I am convinced the evil man *is* dead. I think two documents I have just seen pretty well prove it. They tell the story so much better than I could, since the authors lived through the last fantastic days of the dictator in the underground bunker beneath the Chancellery here in Berlin, that I shall put them in here.

They will make a chapter in this record, and we will call it simply "The Last Days of Hitler."

The first document is the story told by Hanna Reitsch, the German woman flier. It is her account of Hitler's end, but, as will be noted, it is written by an unidentified American officer who interrogated her and then wrote a summary of the interrogation. I wish I had his name. He is a gifted writer.

THE FIRST DOCUMENT

October 8, 1945

SUMMARY OF INTERROGATION
THE LAST DAYS IN HITLER'S AIR-RAID SHELTER

This report is the story of the last days of the war as they were experienced by Hanna Reitsch, the well-known German test-pilot and aeronautical research expert. Her account of the flight into Berlin to report to Hitler and of her stay in the Führer's bunker is probably as accurate a one as will be obtained of those last days, although the "Is he dead or is he not dead?" fate of Hitler is answered only to the extent of describing the mental state and the hopelessness of the last-minute situation, from which individual opinions must be drawn. Her own opinion is that the tactical situation and Hitler's own physical condition made any thought of his escape inconceivable....

The Trip to Berlin: Hitler had sent a telegram to Munich on the 24th of

April to Lieutenant General Ritter von Greim, instructing him to report to the Reichs Chancellery on a highly urgent matter. The problem of getting into Berlin was then already a very precarious one, as the Russians had practically encircled the city. Greim, however, decided that by availing himself of Hanna Reitsch as pilot, the entrance might be accomplished by means of an autogiro, which could land on the streets or in the gardens of the Reichs Chancellery.

During the night of the 25th to the 26th of April Reitsch and Greim arrived at Rechlin, prepared immediately to fly into Berlin. As, however, the only available autogiro had been damaged that day, it was decided that a Feldwebel pilot, who had taken Albert Speer to the Führer two days before, should fly Greim in because of the experience the previous flight had given him. Some sense of responsibility to Greim, as his personal pilot and friend, made Reitsch beg to be taken along. A Focke-Wulf 190 was to be used, which had a pig-a-back space for one passenger arranged behind the pilot's seat. Reitsch was stuffed into the tail through a small emergency opening.

Forty fighters were taken to fly cover. Almost immediately upon take-off they were engaged by Russian aircraft. A running hedgehopping flight got them to the Gatow airfield, the only Berlin field still in German hands. Their own craft got through with nothing more than a few wing shots, but the cost was heavy to the supporting fighters.

The landing at Gatow was made through further heavy attacks by Russian fighters who were strafing the field when they arrived. What was left of the German planes engaged the Russians while the Greim craft made a successful landing. Immediately attempts were made to phone the Chancellery but as all the lines were out, it was decided to fly an available Fiesler-Storch for the remaining distance and land within walking distance of Hitler's shelter. With Greim at the controls and Reitsch as passenger, the plane took off under a whirling cover of German-Russian dogfights. At a height of a few meters Greim managed to get away from the field and continue at treetop level toward the Brandenburger Tor.

Street fighting was going on below them and countless Russian aircraft were in the air. After a few minutes of flight, heavy fire tore out the bottom of the plane and severely injured Greim's right leg. By reaching over his shoulders, Reitsch took control of the craft and by dodging and squirming closely along the ground, brought the plane down on the East-West Axis. Heavy Russian artillery and small-arm fire was sheeting the area with shrapnel as they landed. A passing vehicle was commandeered to take them to Hitler's shelter, with Greim receiving first aid for his shattered foot on the way.

*Arrival at Hitler's Shelter:*Greim and Reitsch arrived in the bunker between 6 and 7 o'clock on the evening of the 26th of April. First to meet them was Frau Goebbels, who fell upon Reitsch with tears and kisses, expressing her astonishment that anyone still possessed the courage and loyalty to come to the Führer, in stark contrast to all those who had deserted him. Greim was immediately taken to the operation room, where Hitler's physician tended the injured foot.

Hitler came into the sickroom, according to Reitsch, with his face showing deep gratitude over Greim's coming. He remarked something to the effect that even a soldier has the right to disobey an order when everything indicates that to carry it out would be futile and hopeless. Greim then reported his presence in the official manner.

Hitler's Denunciation of Göring:
HITLER: "Do you know why I have called you?"
GREIM: "No, *mein Führer.*"
HITLER: "Because Hermann Göring has betrayed and deserted both me and his Fatherland. Behind my back he has established connections with the enemy. His action was a mark of cowardice. And against my orders he has gone to save himself at Berchtesgaden. From there he sent me a disrespectful telegram. He said that I had once named him as my successor and that now, as I was no longer able to rule from Berlin, he was prepared to rule from Berchtesgaden in my place. He closes the wire by stating that if he had no answer from me by nine thirty on the date of the wire he would assume my answer to be in the affirmative."

The scene Reitsch describes as "touchingly dramatic," that there were tears in the Führer's eyes as he told them of Göring's treachery, that his head sagged, that his face was deathly pallid, and that the uncontrolled shaking of his hands made the message flutter wildly as he handed it to Greim.

The Führer's face remained deathly earnest as Greim read. Then every muscle in it began to twitch and his breath came in explosive puffs; only with effort did he gain sufficient control to actually shout:

"An ultimatum!! A crass ultimatum!! Now nothing remains. Nothing is spared me. No allegiances are kept, no 'honor' lived up to, no disappointments that I have not had, no betrayals that I have not experienced, and now this above all else. Nothing remains. Every wrong has already been done me."

As Reitsch explains it, the scene was in the typical *"et tu, Brute"* manner, full of remorse and self-pity. It was long before he could gather sufficient control to continue.

With eyes hard and half-closed and in a voice unusually low he went on: "I immediately had Göring arrested as a traitor to the Reich, took from him all his offices, and removed him from all organizations. That is why I have called you to me. I hereby declare you Göring's successor as Oberbefehlshaber der Luftwaffe. In the name of the German people I give you my hand."

*"To Die for the 'Honor' of the Luftwaffe":*Greim and Reitsch were deeply stunned with the news of Göring's betrayal. As with one mind they both grasped Hitler's hands and begged to be allowed to remain in the bunker, and with their own lives atone for the great wrong that Göring had perpetrated against the Führer, against the German people, and against the Luftwaffe itself. To save the "honor" of the fliers who had died, to re-establish the "honor" of their land in the eyes of the world, they begged to remain. Hitler agreed to all of this and told them they might stay and told them too that their decision would long be remembered in the history of the Luftwaffe. It had been previously arranged with operations at Rechlin that an aircraft was to come in the next day to take Greim and Reitsch out of Berlin. Now that they decided to stay it was impossible to get the information out. Rechlin, in the meantime, was sending plane after plane, each shot down in turn by the Russians. Finally on the 27th a JU 52, loaded with SS guards and ammunition, managed to land on the East-West traffic axis, but because Reitsch and Greim had intended to stay, was sent back empty. (The order cashiering Göring was released from the underground headquarters some time on the 23rd of April.)

Hitler Sees the Cause as Lost: Later that first evening Hitler called Reitsch to him in his room. She remembers that his face was deeply lined and that there was a constant film of moisture in his eyes. In a very small voice he said: "Hanna, you belong to those who will die with me. Each of us has a vial of poison such as this," with which he handed her one for herself and one for Greim. "I do not wish that one of us falls to the Russians alive, nor do I wish our bodies to be found by them. Each person is responsible for destroying his body so that nothing recognizable remains. Eva and I will have our bodies burned. You will devise your own method. Will you please so inform von Greim?"

Reitsch sank to a chair in tears, not, she claims, over the certainty of her own end but because for the first time she knew that the Führer saw the cause as lost. Through the sobs she said: *"Mein Führer,* why do you stay? Why do you deprive Germany of your life? When the news was released that you would remain in Berlin to the last, the people were amazed with horror. 'The Führer must live so that Germany can live,' the people said. Save yourself, *mein Führer,* that is the will of every German."

"No, Hanna, if I die it is for the 'honor' of our country, it is because as a soldier I must obey my own command that I would defend Berlin to the last. My dear girl, I did not intend it so, I believed firmly that Berlin would be saved at the banks of the Oder. Everything we had was moved to hold that position. You may believe that when our best efforts failed, I was the most horror-struck of all. Then when the encirclement of the city began, the knowledge that there were three million of my countrymen still in Berlin made it necessary that I stay to defend them. By staying I believed that all the troops of the land would take example through my act and come to the rescue of the city. I hoped that they would rise to superhuman efforts to save me and thereby save my three million countrymen. But, my Hanna, I still have hope. The army of General Wenck is moving up from the south. He must and will drive the Russians back long enough to save our people. Then we will fall back to hold again."

It appeared almost as if he believed this himself and as the conversation closed he was walking about the room with quick, stumbling strides, his hand clasped behind him and his head bobbing up and down as he walked. Although his words spoke of hope, Hanna claims that his face showed that the war was over.

Hanna returned to Greim's bedside, handed him the poison, and then decided with him, should the end really come, that they would quickly drink the contents of the vial and then each pull the pin from a heavy grenade and hold it tightly to their bodies.

Late in the night of the 26th to 27th of April the first heavy barrage bracketed the Chancellery. The splattering of heavy shells and the crashing of falling buildings directly above the air-raid shelter tightened the nervous strain of everyone so that here and there deep sobbing came through the doors. Hanna spent the night tending Greim, who was in great pain, and in getting grenades ready in the event that the Russians should enter the Chancellery grounds before morning.

Hitler's Guests in the Shelter: The next morning she was introduced to the other occupants and learned for the first time the identity of all those who were facing the end with the Führer. Present in the elaborate shelter on the 27th of April were Goebbels and his wife and their six children; State Secretary Naumann; Hitler's right hand, Reichsleiter Martin Bormann; Hevel from Ribbentrop's office; Admiral Voss as representative from Doenitz; General Krebs of the infantry and his adjutant Burgdorf; Hitler's personal pilot, Hansel Bauer; another pilot, Baetz; Eva Braun; SS Obergruppenführer Fegelein as liaison between Himmler and Hitler and husband of Eva Braun's sister; Hitler's personal physician, Dr. Stumpfegger; Oberst von Below, Hitler's Luftwaffe adjutant; Dr. Lorenz representing Reichspresse chief Dr. Deitrich for the German press; two of Hitler's secretaries, a Frau Christian, wife of General der Flieger Christian and a Fräulein Kreuger; and various SS orderlies and messengers. Reitsch claims that these composed the entire assembly.

A regular visitor during the last days was Reichsjugendführer Axman, who was commanding a Hitlerjugend division committed to the defense of the city. From Axman came current information as to the ground situation against the Russians, which was well mirrored by the increasingly despondent manner of each visit.

Another Betrayal: Late in the afternoon of the 27th Obergruppenführer Fegelein disappeared. Shortly thereafter it was reported that he had been captured on the outskirts of Berlin disguised in civilian clothes, claiming to be a refugee. The news of his capture was immediately brought to Hitler, who instantly ordered him shot. The rest of the evening Fegelein's betrayal weighed heavily on the Führer and in conversation he indicated a half-way doubt as to Himmler's position, fearing that Fegelein's desertion might have been known and even condoned by the SS leader.

*Observations on Shelter Occupants:*Reitsch had little contact with most of the people in the shelter, being mostly occupied in nursing von Greim, but she did have the opportunity to speak to many of them and observe their reactions under the trying conditions of the last days in the bunker. It is believed that she attempts to relate her observations truthfully and that her reactions are honestly conceived. It must be remembered that prior to her arrival in the bunker Reitsch had but small contact with most of these individuals and that her previous opinions regarding them were at a rather low level. Of the people she was able to observe closely the Goebbels family probably stands out.

Doctor Goebbels: She describes Goebbels as being incensed over Göring's treachery. He strode about his small, luxurious quarters like an animal, muttering vile accusations concerning the Luftwaffe leader and what he had done. The precarious military situation of the moment was Göring's fault. Should the war be lost, as it certainly now seemed it would be, that too would be Göring's fault.

"That swine," Goebbels said, "who has always set himself up as the Führer's greatest support, now does not have the courage to stand beside him. As if that were not enough, he wants to replace the Führer as head of the State. He, an incessant incompetent, who has destroyed his Fatherland with his mishandling and stupidity, now wants to lead the entire nation. By this alone he proves that he was never truly one of us, that at heart he was always weak and a traitor."

All this, as Hanna saw it, was in the best theatrical manner, with much hand-waving and fine gestures, made even more grotesque by the jerky up-and-down hobbling as he strode about the room. When he wasn't railing about Göring he spoke to the world about the example those in the bunker were setting for history. As on a platform and gripping a chair-back he said:

"We are teaching the world how men die for their 'honor.' Our deaths shall be an eternal example to all Germans, to all friends and enemies alike. One day the whole world will acknowledge that we did right, that we sought to protect the world against Bolshevism with our lives. One day it will be set down in the history of all time."

It appears that Goebbels exercised his greatest ability to the very last. The rooms of Goebbels and Reitsch adjoined each other and doors were usually open. Through them the Goebbels oratory would sound out at any hour of the day or night. And always the talk was of "honor," of "how to die," of "standing true to the Führer to the last," of "setting an example that would long blaze as a holy thing from the pages of history."

One of the last things Reitsch remembers hearing from the lips of the propaganda master was: "We shall go down for the glory of the Reich so that the name of Germany will live forever." Even Reitsch was moved to conclude that the Goebbels display, in spite of the tenseness of the situation, was a bit overdrawn and out-and-out theatrical. She claims that in her opinion Goebbels, then as he always had, performed as if he were speaking to a legion of historians who were avidly awaiting and recording every word. She adds that her own dubious opinions regarding Goebbels's mannerisms, his superficiality and studied oratory, were well substantiated by these outbursts. She claims, too, that after listening to these tirades she and von Greim often asked each other, with a sad, head-shaking attitude: "Are these the people who ruled our country?"

Frau Goebbels: Frau Goebbels she described as a very brave woman, whose control, which was at most times strong, did break down now and then to pitiful spasms of weeping. Her main concern was her children, and in their presence her manner was always delightful and cheery. Much of her day was occupied in keeping the children's clothes clean and tidy, and as they had only the clothes they wore, this kept Frau Goebbels occupied. Often she would quickly retire to her room to hide the tears. It appears from Hanna's description that Frau Goebbels probably represented the epitome of Nazi indoctrination.

If the Third Reich could not live she preferred to die with it, nor would she allow her children to outlive it. In recognition of the example she embodied of true German womanhood, Hitler, in the presence of all the occupants of the bunker, presented her with his personal golden party insignia. "A staunch pillar of the 'honor' upon which National Socialism was built and the German Fatherland founded," was his approximate remark as he pinned it to her dress.

Frau Goebbels often thanked God that she was alive so that she could kill her children to save them from whatever "evil" would follow the collapse. To Reitsch she said: "My dear Hanna, when the end comes you must help me if I become weak about the children. You must help me to help them out of this life. They belong to the Third Reich and to the Führer and if those two things cease to exist there can be no further place for them. But you must help me. My greatest fear is that at the last moment I will be too weak."

It is Hanna's belief that in the last moment she was not weak.

Conclusions that can be safely drawn from Hanna's remarks are that Frau Goebbels was simply one of the most convinced subjects of her own husband's rantings; the most pronounced example of the Nazi influence over the women of Germany.

The Goebbels Children: The Goebbels children numbered six. Their names and approximate ages were: Hela, 12; Hilda, 11; Helmut, 9; Holde, 7; Hedda, 5; Heide, 3. They were the one bright spot of relief in the stark death-shadowed life of the bunker. Reitsch taught them songs which they sang for the Führer and for the injured von Greim. Their talk was full of being in "the cave" with their "Uncle Führer," and in spite of the fact that there were bombs outside, nothing could really harm them as long as they were with him. And anyway "Uncle Führer" had said that soon the soldiers would come and drive the Russians away and then tomorrow they could all go back to play in their garden. Everyone in the bunker entered into the game of making the time as pleasant as possible for them. Frau Goebbels repeatedly thanked Reitsch for making their last days enjoyable, as Reitsch often gathered them about her and told them long stories of her flying and of the places she had been and the countries she had seen.

Eva Braun: It seemed to Reitsch that Hitler's "girl friend" remained studiously true to her position as the "showpiece" in the Führer's circle. Most of her time was occupied in fingernail-polishing, changing of clothes for each hour of the day, and all the other little feminine tasks of grooming, combing, and polishing. She seemed to take the prospect of dying with the Führer as quite matter-of-fact, with an attitude that seemed to say: "… had not the relationship been of twelve long years' duration and had she not seriously threatened suicide when Hitler once wanted to be rid of her? This would be a much easier way to die and much more proper…." Her constant remark was "Poor, poor Adolf, deserted by everyone, betrayed by all. Better that ten thousand others die than that he be lost to Germany."

In Hitler's presence she was always charming, and thoughtful of his every comfort. But only while she was with him was she completely in character, for the moment he was out of earshot she would rave about all the ungrateful swine who had deserted their Führer and that each of them should be destroyed. All her remarks had an adolescent tinge and it appeared that the only "good" Germans at the moment were those who were caught in the bunker and that all the others were traitors because they were not there to die with him. The reasons for her willingness to die with the rest were similar to those of Frau Goebbels. She was simply convinced that whatever followed the Third Reich would not be fit to live in for a true German. Often she expressed sorrow for those people who were unable to destroy themselves, as they would forever be forced to live without "honor" and reduced instead to living as human beings without souls.

Reitsch emphasizes that Braun was very apparently of rather shallow mentality, but she also agrees that she was a beautiful woman. Beyond fulfilling her purpose, Reitsch considers it highly unlikely that Braun had any control or influence over Hitler. The rumor of the last minute marriage ceremony Reitsch considers as highly unlikely, not only because she believes that Hitler had no such intention, but also because the circumstances in the bunker on the last days would have made such a ceremony ludicrous. Certainly, up to the time Reitsch left the bunker, hardly a day before Hitler's death was announced, there had not been the slightest mention of such a ceremony. The rumor that there had been children out of the union, Reitsch quickly dismisses as fantastic.

Martin Bormann: Bormann moved about very little, kept instead very close to his writing desk. He was "recording the momentous events in the bunker for posterity." Every word, every action went down on his paper. Often he would visit this person or that to scowlingly demand what the exact remark had been that passed between the Führer and the person he had just had an audience with. Things that passed between other occupants of the bunker were also carefully recorded. This document was to be spirited out of the bunker at the very last moment so that, according to the modest Bormann, it could "take its place among the greatest chapters of German history."

Adolf Hitler: Throughout Hanna's stay in the bunker Hitler's manner and physical condition sunk to lower and lower depths. At first he seemed to be playing the proper part of leading the defense of Germany and Berlin. And at first this was in some manner possible as communications were still quite reliable. Messages were telephoned to a flak tower and from there were radioed out by means of a portable, balloon-suspended aerial. But each day this was more and more difficult until late on the afternoon of the 28th and all day on the 29th communications were almost impossible. On about the 20th of April, at what was probably the last Hitler war council in the Reichs Chancellery, the Führer is said to have been so overcome by the persistently hopeless news that he completely broke down in the presence of all the gathering. The talk in the bunker, where Hanna heard of the collapse, was that with this display even the most optimistic of Hitler's cohorts tended toward the conviction that the war was irretrievably lost. According to Reitsch, Hitler never physically nor mentally recovered from this conference-room collapse.

Occasionally he still seemed to hold to the hope of General Wenck's success in breaking through from the south. He talked of little else, and all day on the 28th and 29th he was mentally planning the tactics that Wenck might use in freeing Berlin. He would stride about the shelter, waving a road map that was fast disintegrating from the sweat of his hands and planning Wenck's campaign with anyone who happened to be listening. When he became overly excited he would snatch the map from where it lay, pace with a quick, nervous stride about the room, and loudly "direct" the city's defense with armies that no longer existed (as even Wenck, unknown to the Führer, had already been routed and destroyed).

Reitsch describes it as a pathetic thing, the picture of a man's complete disintegration. A comic tragedy of frustration, futility, and uselessness. The picture of a man running almost blindly from wall to wall in his last retreat, waving papers that fluttered like leaves in his nervous, twitching hands, or sitting stooped and crumbled before his table moving buttons to represent his nonexistent armies, back and forth on a sweat-stained map, like a young boy playing at war.

The Possibility that Hitler Still Lives: The possibility that Hitler might have got out of the bunker alive, Reitsch dismisses as completely absurd. She claims that she is convinced that the Hitler she left in the shelter was physically unable to have got away. "Had a path been cleared for him from the bunker to freedom he would not have had the strength to use it," she says. She believes, too, that at the very end he had no intention to live, that only the Wenck hope stayed his hand from putting the mass-suicide plan into operation. News that Wenck could not get through, she feels, would immediately have set off the well-rehearsed plans of destruction.

When confronted with the rumor that Hitler might still be alive in Tyrol and that her own flight to that area, after she had left the bunker, might be more than coincidental, she appears deeply upset that such opinions are even entertained. She says only: "Hitler is dead! The man I saw in the shelter could not have lived. He had no reason to live and the tragedy was that he knew it well, knew it perhaps better than anyone else did."

Hanna's Opinion of the Führer: It is apparent from Reitsch's conversation that she held the Führer in high esteem. It is probably also true when she says that her "good" opinion suffered considerably during the closing stages of the war. She is emphatic when she describes the apparent mismanagement she observed and learned in the bunker. For instance, Berlin had been depleted of arms to hold the Oder. When that line fell, it appeared that no coherent defense plan of Berlin had been prepared, certainly adequate arrangements had not been made to direct the defense from the bunker. There was no other communication equipment available than the telephone that led only to the flak tower. It appears that only in the last moment had he decided to direct the battle from the shelter and then did not have the first tools with which to operate. No maps. No battle plans. No radio. Only a hastily prepared messenger service and the one telephone were available. The fact that, unknown to Hitler, the Wenck army had been destroyed almost days before was only one example of the inadequacies. All of which resulted in the Führer of Germany sitting helplessly in the cellar impotently playing at his table-top war.

Reitsch claims that Hitler the idealist died, and his country with him, because of the incompetence of Hitler the soldier and Hitler the statesman. She concludes, still with a faint touch of allegiance, that no one who knew him would deny his idealistically motivated intentions nor could they deny that he was simply infinitely incompetent to rule his country, that one of his great faults was proper character analysis in the people about him, which led to the selection of persons equally incompetent to fill important positions. (Most important example: Göring.)

She repeatedly remarked that never again must such a person be allowed to gain control of Germany or of any country. But strangely enough she does not appear to hold him personally responsible for many of the wrongs and evils that she recognizes completely and is quick to point out. She says rather: "A great part of the fault lies with those who led him, lured him, criminally misdirected him, and informed him falsely. But that he himself selected the men who led him can never be forgiven."

A Criminal against the World: "Hitler ended his life as a criminal against the world," but she is quick to add: "he did not begin it that way. At first his thoughts were only of how to make Germany healthy again, how to give his people a life free from economic insufficiencies and social maladjustments. To do this he gambled much, with a stake that no man has the right to jeopardize—the lives of his people. This was the first great wrong, his first great failure. But once the first few risks had been successful, he fell into the faults of every gambler; he risked more and more, and each time that he won he was more easily led to the next gamble." According to Reitsch it all began with the occupation of the Ruhr. [*She undoubtedly means Rhineland here.*—W. L. S.] This was the first and most difficult gamble of all, and when the world did not answer his Ruhr [*Rhineland*] bluff with war, every succeeding risk became progressively easier.

Each success made the enthusiasm of the people greater and this gave him the necessary support to take the next step. The end-result, Reitsch claims, was that Hitler himself underwent a character change that transformed him from an idealistically motivated benefactor to a grasping, scheming despot, a victim of his own delusions of grandeur. "Never again," she concludes, "in the history of the world must such power be allowed to rest with one man."

Suicide Council: On the night of the 27th to 28th the Russian bombardment of the Chancellery reached the highest pitch it had yet attained. The accuracy, to those in the shelter below, was astounding. It seemed as if each shell landed in exactly the same place as the one before, all dead-center on the Chancellery buildings. As this indicated that the Russian ground troops could overrun the area at any moment, another suicide council was called by the Führer. All plans as to the destruction of the bodies of everyone in the shelter were gone over again. The decision was that as soon as the Russians reached the Chancellery grounds the mass suicide would begin. Last instructions were given as to the use of the poison vials.

The group was hypnotized with the suicide rehearsal and a general discussion was entered into to determine in which manner the most thorough destruction of the human body could be performed. Then everyone made little speeches swearing allegiance again and again to the Führer and to Germany. Yet, through it all, still ran the faint hope that Wenck might get in and hold long enough to effect an evacuation. But even on the 27th, Reitsch claims, the others paid lipservice to the Wenck hope only to follow the lead of the Führer. Almost everyone had given up all thoughts of being saved, and said so to each other whenever Hitler was not present. Closing the discussions on the destruction of the bodies there was talk that SS men would be assigned to see that no trace remained. Throughout the day of the 28th the intensity of the Russian fire continued while the suicide talk kept pace with the shelling in the shelter below.

The Himmler Betrayal: Then on the 29th fell the greatest blow of all. A telegram arrived which indicated that the staunch and trusted Himmler had joined Göring on the traitor list. It was like a death blow to the entire assembly. Reitsch claims that men and women alike cried and screamed with rage, fear and desperation, all mixed into one emotional spasm. Himmler, the protector of the Reich, now a traitor was impossible. The telegram message was that Himmler had contacted the British and American authorities through Sweden to propose a capitulation to the San Francisco Conference. Hitler raged as a madman. His color rose to a heated red and his face was virtually unrecognizable. Additional evidence of Himmler's "treachery" was that he had asked not to be identified with the capitulation proposals; American authorities were said to have abided by this request, while the British did not.

After the lengthy outburst Hitler sank into a stupor and for a time the entire bunker was silent.

Later came the anticlimactic news that the Russians would make a full-force bid to overrun the Chancellery on the morning of the 30th. Even then small-arm fire was beginning to sprinkle the area above the shelter. Ground reports indicated that the Russians were nearing the Potsdamerplatz and were losing thousands of men as they fanatically prepared the position from which the attack of the next morning was to be launched.

Reitsch claims that everyone again looked to his poison.

Orders to Leave the Shelter: At one thirty on the morning of the 30th of April, Hitler, with chalk-white face, came to Greim's room and slumped down on the edge of the bed. "Our only hope is Wenck," he said, "and to make his entry possible we must call up every available aircraft to cover his approach." Hitler then claimed that he had just been informed that Wenck's guns were already shelling the Russians in Potsdamerplatz.

"Every available plane," Hitler said, "must be called up by daylight, therefore it is my order to you to return to Rechlin and muster your planes from there. It is the task of your aircraft to destroy the positions from which the Russians will launch their attack on the Chancellery. With Luftwaffe help, Wenck may get through. That is the first reason why you must leave the shelter. The second is that Himmler must be stopped," and immediately he mentioned the SS Führer his voice became more unsteady and both his lips and hands trembled. The order to Greim was that if Himmler had actually made the reported contact, and could be found, he should immediately be arrested.

"A traitor must never succeed me as Führer! You must get out to insure that he will not."

Greim and Reitsch protested vehemently that the attempt would be futile, that it would be impossible to reach Rechlin, that they preferred to die in the shelter, that the mission could not succeed, that it was insane.

"As soldiers of the Reich," Hitler answered, "it is our holy duty to exhaust every possibility. This is the only chance of success that remains. It is your duty and mine to take it."

Hanna was not convinced. "No, no," she screamed, "what can be accomplished now, even if we should get through? Everything is lost, to try to change it now is insane." But Greim thought differently. "Hanna," he said, "we are the only hope for those who remain here. If the chance is just the smallest, we owe it to them to take it. Not to go would rob them of the only light that remains. Maybe Wenck is there. Maybe we can help, but whether we can or cannot, we will go."

Hanna, still convinced as to the absurdity of attempting an escape, went alone to the Führer while Greim was making his preparations. Through her sobbing she begged: "*Mein Führer*, why, why don't you let us stay?" He looked at her for a moment and said only: "God protect you."

The Leave-Taking: Preparations were quickly made and Reitsch is graphic in her description of the leave-taking. Colonel von Below, late Göring's liaison officer with the Führer and now a staunch Greim-man, said: "You must get out. It depends upon you to tell the truth to our people, to save the 'honor' of the Luftwaffe: to save the meaning of Germany for the whole world." Everyone gave the departing duo some token, something to take back into the world. Everyone wrote quick, last-minute letters for them to take along. Reitsch says that she and Greim destroyed all but two letters, which were from Goebbels and his wife to their eldest son, by Frau Goebbels's first marriage, who was then in an Allied prisoner-of-war camp. These Reitsch still had. Frau Goebbels also gave her a diamond ring from her finger to wear in her memory.

Thirty minutes after Hitler had given the order they left the shelter.

The Flight out of Berlin: Outside, the whole city was aflame and heavy small-arm fire was already plainly audible a short distance away. SS troops, committed to guarding Hitler to the end, were moving about. These men brought up a small armored vehicle which was to take Reitsch and Greim to where an Arado 96 was hidden near Brandenburger Tor. The sky was filled with the thunder of shells, some of which landed so close that their vehicle was knocked out several yards short of the revetment where the Arado was stationed. (Reitsch claims that she is certain that this was the last craft available. The possibility of another plane having got in and possibly out again with Hitler as passenger, she dismisses as highly unlikely as Greim would certainly have been informed. She knows, too, that Greim had ordered other planes in but that each craft was shot down in the attempt, and as Russian troops already solidly ringed the city, she is certain that Hitler never left Berlin.)

The broad street leading from Brandenburger Tor was to be used for take-off. About 400 meters of uncratered pavement was available as runway. The take-off was made under hailing Russian fire and as the plane rose to rooftop level it was picked up by countless searchlights and at once bracketed in a barrage of shelling. Explosions tossed the craft like a feather, but only a few splinters hit the plane. Reitsch circled to about 20,000 feet from where Berlin was a sea of flames beneath her. From that altitude the magnitude of the destruction of Berlin she describes as stark and fantastic. Heading north, 50 minutes saw them in Rechlin, where the landing was again made through a screen of Russian fighter craft....

The News of Wenck's Non-Existence: Keitel was found in the early morning of the 1st of May and gave them the news that Wenck's army had long been destroyed or captured. And that he (Keitel) had sent word to Hitler to that effect the day before (30th of April).

Greim and Reitsch now knew that Hitler must surely have given up all hope and both fully expected that the well-rehearsed suicide plans had already been put into operation.

The New Government: The advance of the English necessitated a retreat into Schleswig late on the first day of May. Here, the same evening, Reitsch and Greim learned that the announcement of Hitler's death had been made and that he had been succeeded by Doenitz. On the 2nd of May the new government was called to Plön. Greim and Reitsch, to receive orders from Doenitz as to immediate Luftwaffe activities, had the additional purpose of meeting Himmler and confronting him with the betrayal story.

Himmler's Capitulation Explanation: Himmler arrived late so that all the others were in the conference room, leaving Reitsch alone when he walked in.

"One moment, Herr Reichsführer, a matter of the highest importance, if you can spare the time?" Reitsch asked.

Himmler seemed almost jovial as he said: "Of course."

"Is it true, Herr Reichsführer, that you contacted the Allies with proposals of peace without orders to do so from Hitler?"

"But of course."

"You betrayed your Führer and your people in the very darkest hour? Such a thing is high treason, Herr Reichsführer. You did that when your place was actually in the bunker with Hitler?"

"High treason? No! You'll see, history will weigh it differently. Hitler wanted to continue the fight. He was mad with his pride and his 'honor.' He wanted to shed more German blood when there was none left to flow. Hitler was insane. It should have been stopped long ago."

"Insane? I came from him less than thirty-six hours ago. He died for the cause he believed in. He died bravely and filled with the 'honor' you speak of, while you and Göring and the rest must now live as branded traitors and cowards."

"I did as I did to save German blood, to rescue what was left of our country."

"You speak of German blood, Herr Reichsführer? You speak of it now? You should have thought of it years ago, before you became identified with the useless shedding of so much of it."

A sudden strafing attack terminated the conversation.

Why the "Redoubt" was Not Utilized: In response to the question as to why the Austria and Southern Germany last stand of resistance was never put into operation, Reitsch has little to add to what is already known. She states that as late as the 15th of April it still seemed that there was every intention of moving the government and military headquarters to Berchtesgaden. All of the bureaus and headquarters in Berlin at that time were on a constant two-hour alert. From what she heard from Oberst Below and others it appeared that the conference mentioned above was to decide on the full particulars covering the move. She claims that the reports Hitler received at that time were so shocking that he was convinced that preparations to make "Redoubt" resistance a success would never be completed in time. It was believed that the realization that "Redoubt," of which so much was expected, would have to be crossed off as useless was the major cause of Hitler's breakdown. It was also said that Göring and Hitler had had a strained conversation regarding this, with Göring insisting on an early evacuation to the "Redoubt" area and Hitler declining in the hope that the Oder would hold. Göring was to have claimed that "Redoubt" was ready for occupancy while Hitler preferred to wait until he could have its readiness confirmed at the above-mentioned conference. It was the talk later at the Doenitz war council and elsewhere that Göring's departure was governed solely by his realization that the Oder would be crossed and by his unfulfilled hope that the partially completed "Redoubt" area would hold.

Had Göring's coup succeeded, it is believed that "Redoubt" might have been more actively defended. The reasons that it was not: First—Göring's failure. Second—Hitler's belief that continued resistance in Berlin might be more eventful than the sure collapse he saw in an uncompleted "Redoubt."...

Evaluation of Source: It is the opinion of the interrogator that the above information is given with a sincere and conscientious effort to be truthful and exact. The suicide of her family, the death of her closest friend, von

Greim,[9] the physical pain of Germany, and the trying nature of her experiences during the closing days of the war combined to seriously tempt her to commit suicide as well. She claims that the only reason she remained alive is for the sake of the truth; to tell the truth about Göring, "the shallow showman," to tell the truth about Hitler, "the criminal incompetent," and to tell the German people the truth about the dangers of the form of government that the Third Reich gave them....

Hanna Reitsch, then, did not actually see Hitler die. But we have the sworn testimony of one who says he saw the dead body. I must say I find it convincing. Here it is:

THE SECOND DOCUMENT

Berchtesgaden, June 20th, 1945

TESTIMONY OF MR. ERICH KEMPKA ON THE LAST DAYS OF HITLER

...Being a member of the NSDAP (Nazi Party) since May 1930, I came as a chauffeur to Adolf Hitler.... Since 1936 I was the sole chauffeur of the Führer. The Führer himself never drove a car. When Hitler stayed in Berlin with his headquarters I was supervisor of the Reichs Chancellery garage, to which about 40 vehicles belonged. Already in the days before April 20, 1945, I also passed the nights in the garage situated in the basement of the Reichs Chancellery. On April 20th I went for about one quarter of an hour to the Führer's bunker in order to congratulate the Führer upon his birthday....

In the days after April 20th, I have still seen Hitler several times in his bunker in the Reichs Chancellery. He had not changed in his behavior and gave a quiet impression. Eva Braun stayed with the Führer. After April 28th, there were rumors in the Reichs Chancellery that the Führer had been married during the night from the 28th to the 29th to Eva Braun.... Only on May 1st, Secretary of State Dr. Naumann confirmed the fact of the marriage.

I spoke to the Führer for the last time on April 29, 1945. I reported to him that I was engaged in bringing food into the inner part of Berlin in order not to let the food fall into the hands of the Russians and in order to provide the hospitals situated in the government district.

On April 30th, at 1430 hours SS-Sturmbannführer Guensche telephoned me and asked me to come to the Führer-bunker. I was to take care that five cans of gasoline, that is to say 200 ltr., were brought along. I at once took along two or three men carrying the cans. More men were following because it took some time to collect 200 ltr. of gasoline. By order of Guensche the cans were brought by these men to the entrance of the Führer-bunker located in the garden of the Reichs Chancellery, which was next to the so-called tower-home and about 20 meters from the so-called Haus Kempka, my quarters. There was a sentry of the SD[10] at the entrance of the bunker. I then went into the antechamber of the briefing-room, where I met Guensche. *Guensche told me that the Führer was dead.*[11]He explained he had got the order from the Führer to burn him at once after his death, "so that he would not be exhibited at a Russian freak-show." A short time after that SS-Sturmbannführer Linge (valet of the Führer) and an orderly whom I do not remember came from the private room of the Führer... carrying a corpse wrapped in an ordinary field-gray blanket. Based on the previous information from Guensche, I at once supposed that it was the corpse of the Führer. One could only see the long black trousers and the black shoes which the Führer usually wore with his field-gray uniform jacket.

Under these circumstances *there was no doubt that it was the corpse of the Führer.* I could not observe any spots of blood on the body wrapped in the blanket. Thereupon came Martin Bormann from the living-room of the Führer and carried in his arms the corpse of Mrs. Eva Hitler, nee Braun. He turned the corpse over to me. Mrs. Hitler wore a dark dress. I did not have the feeling that the corpse was still warm. I could not recognize any injuries on the body. The dress was slightly damp only in the region of the heart. The orderly now went upstairs with the corpse of the Führer to the bunker exit towards the garden of the Reichs Chancellery.... I followed with the corpse of Mrs. Hitler. Behind me came Bormann, Dr. Goebbels, and Guensche. Linge and the orderly carried the corpse of the Führer from the westwardly directed bunker exit in the tower-house and put the wrapped corpse on the flat ground in a small depression which was about four to five meters distant from the bunker exit.... There was no lawn, rather bare sand. *I put the corpse of Mrs. Hitler next to the Führer's. Immediately Guensche poured the complete contents of the five cans over the two corpses and ignited the fuel.* Martin Bormann, Dr. Goebbels, Guensche, Linge, the orderly, and I stood in the bunker entrance, looked towards the fire, and all saluted with raised hands. The stay in the bunker exit lasted only a short time because the garden of the Reichs Chancellery was under heavy artillery-fire.

In order to return to the garage I had to pass through the Führer-bunker and wanted to look once more at the rooms in which the Führer had lived last. Opposite the entrance of the room, the dimensions of which are only 3×4 meters, stood a narrow sofa.... Before the right leg of the sofa lay a Walther-Pistol, 6.35 mm cal., which, as I knew, belonged to Miss Eva

Braun. Also on the floor approximately before the middle of the sofa lay a Walther-Pistol, 7.65 mm cal. I supposed that this pistol belonged to the Führer.... According to the situation it was clear to me that the Führer and Miss Eva Braun shot themselves. From the location of the two pistols I concluded that the Führer sat about on the middle of the sofa before firing the shot and that Eva Braun had sat on the right part of the sofa.

And finally there is the conclusion of British military intelligence, as of November 1, which reads as follows:

November 1, 1945

PR Branch
C.C.G. (BE),
BERLIN

THE LAST DAYS OF HITLER AND EVA BRAUN

Available evidence sifted by British Intelligence and based largely on eye witness accounts, shows (as conclusively as possible without bodies) that Hitler and Eva Braun died shortly after 2.30 on April 30th, 1945, in the bunker of the Reichs Chancellery, their bodies being burned just outside the bunker.

HITLER'S original intention had been to fly to BERCHTESGADEN on 20th April and from there continue the struggle. When that day came he postponed his departure. On 22nd April, at about 4.30 p.m., he held a staff conference at which he made it clear to his advisers that he considered the war was lost and that he intended to remain in BERLIN to the last in defence of the capital. If BERLIN fell he would die there. It is clear that HITLER at that time suffered from an attack of nervous prostration, during which he blamed everyone but himself for the failure of Germany to win the war. His advisers, both military and civil, endeavoured to persuade HITLER to change his mind and leave BERLIN. This was of no avail. GOEBBELS took the same decision and with Martin BORMANN, Dr. Ludwig STUMPFEGGER (HITLER'S surgeon), and others of the personal staff, remained behind to the end, while the generals retired to their new H.Q.

HITLER'S breakdown on 22nd April was the beginning of the end. From that time he never left the bunker, surrounded no longer by soldiers and politicians, but by his "family circle," and those officers responsible directly to him for the defence of BERLIN. His state of mind was reported by all who saw him to have been very much calmer after the crisis on 22nd April. He had made his decision. He even gained more confidence as to the outcome of the battle of BERLIN. Every now and again, however, his calm was interrupted by tantrums when he recalled old treacheries and found new ones. His physical health, on the contrary, was poor. The nervous strain, unhealthy living conditions and eccentric hours told on him. Apart from the reported trembling of the hands, from which he had suffered for some time, and his general decrepitude, he was as "normal" as ever in his mind.

On the night of April 23/24, HITLER was visited by SPEER, to whom he disclosed that he had made all plans for his suicide and for the complete destruction of his body by burning. About the same time, HIMMLER sent GEBHARDT, his personal doctor, to HITLERin order to persuade him to leave BERLIN before it was too late, but HITLERrejected this.

On the evening of April 26th Field Marshal RITTER VONGREIM reported to HITLER'S bunker to receive his commission as C.-in-C. German Air Force in succession to GÖRING, the latter having fallen into complete disfavour by his endeavour to take over control from HITLER a few days earlier. HITLER informed GREIM, as he had SPEER, that he had made all arrangements for the destruction of his body and that of Eva BRAUN so that they would not fall into enemy hands, and "that nothing recognizable remains." He gave GREIM and REITSCHpoison capsules, which the former has since used. Such capsules had already been issued to all in the bunker.

On 28th April the inmates of the bunker heard with a mixture of incredulity and disgust of HIMMLER'Sapproach to the Allies through Sweden.

During the previous three days, the battle of BERLIN had been drawing nearer the centre of the city. Shells were falling round the bunker and in the early hours of 29th April it was reported that Russian tanks had broken into the Potsdamerplatz. HITLER then ordered GREIM to return to RECHLIN to mount a Luftwaffe attack in support of Wenck's 12th (German) Army which was reported also to be within shelling distance of the Potsdamerplatz. (In fact, it was not, but this was probably not known at the time). GREIM, with REITSCH, took off from the Charlottenburger Chaussée in an Arado 96, which had been flown in to collect them.

Later on 29th April, any hope of the effective relief of BERLIN by Wenck's Army had to be abandoned. Captured telegrams sent to Doenitz at the time disclose the hysterical recrimination of despair. On the evening of 29th April HITLER married Eva BRAUN, the ceremony being performed by an official from the Propaganda Ministry in a small conference room in the bunker. Eva BRAUN may have suggested the marriage for she had apparently always wished for the peculiar glory of dying with HITLER, and had used her influence to persuade him to die in BERLIN.[12]

After the ceremony, the newly married couple shook hands with all present in the bunker and retired to their suite with HITLER'S secretary for a marriage feast. According to her the conversation which had been confined to suicide, was so oppressive, that she had to leave. It was about this time that HITLERhad his Alsatian dog destroyed.

At about 2.30 a.m. on 30th April HITLERsaid goodbye to about 20 people, about 10 of them women, whom he had summoned from the other bunkers in the Old and New Chancelleries. He shook hands with the women and spoke to most of them.

On the same day at about 2.30 p.m., though the exact time is uncertain, orders were sent to the transport office requiring the immediate despatch to the bunker of 200 litres of petrol. Between 160 and 180 litres of petrol were collected and deposited in the garden just outside the emergency exit of the bunker. At about the same time HITLER and Eva BRAUN made their last appearance alive. They went round the bunker and shook hands with their immediate entourage and retired to their own apartments, where they both committed suicide, HITLER by shooting himself, apparently through the mouth, Eva BRAUNapparently by taking poison, though she was supplied with a revolver.

After the suicide the bodies were taken into the garden just outside the bunker by GOEBBELS, BORMANN, perhaps STUMPFEGGER and one or two others, HITLERwrapped in a blanket presumably because he was bloody.

The bodies were placed side by side in the garden about three yards from the emergency exit of the bunker and drenched with petrol. Because of the shelling, the party withdrew under the shelter of the emergency exit and a petrol soaked and lighted rag was thrown on the bodies which at once caught fire. The party then stood to attention, gave the HITLERsalute and retired.

From then on the evidence is more circumstantial. How often the bodies were resoaked or how long they burnt is not known. One witness was informed that they burnt until nothing was left, more probably they were charred until they were unrecognizable, and the bones broken up and probably buried.

On the evening of 1st May, BORMANN sent a telegram to DOENITZ informing him that HITLER'Swill[13]was now in force (i.e. that HITLER was dead). This was amplified later by a telegram from GOEBBELS which stated that HITLER had died at 3.30 p.m. on the previous day, and that his will appointed DOENITZ as Reichspresident, GOEBBELS as Reichschancellor, BORMANN as Party Minister and SEYSS-INQUART as Foreign Minister. GOEBBELS added that BORMANN was trying to go to DOENITZto inform him of the situation.

CONCLUSION

The above evidence is not complete; but it is positive, circumstantial, consistent and independent. There is no evidence whatever to support any of the theories which have been circulated and which presuppose that HITLER is still alive. All such stories which have been reported have been investigated, and have been found to be quite baseless; most of them have dissolved at the first touch of fact and some of them have been admitted by their authors to have been pure fabrication. Nor is it possible to dispose of the existing evidence which is summarized above. It is considered quite impossible that the versions of the various eyewitnesses can represent a concerted cover-story; they were all too busy planning their own safety to have been able or disposed to learn an elaborate charade which they could still maintain after five months of isolation from each other and under detailed and persistent cross-examination. Nor is it considered possible that the witnesses were mistaken in respect of HITLER'S body (of the identity of Eva BRAUN'S body no doubt is considered possible; not being blanketed she was easily recognized). Such a theory would require that HITLER escaped after 2.30 p.m. on 30th April and that Eva BRAUN was fobbed off with the corpse of a double which had been secretly introduced. But escape after 2.30 p.m. was almost certainly impossible. Even if it was still possible to fly a training-plane from the Charlottenburger Chaussée, there was no pilot to fly it; for HITLER'S two pilots, who were in the bunker on 30th April, both took part in the attempted escape on the night of May 1st. In any case, there is no valid reason for constructing such theories, which are contrary to the only positive evidence and supported by no evidence at all.

Berlin, *Tuesday, November* **6**
With Nicky Nabokoff, who is helping to guide our Military Government in its cultural endeavors, to see the premiere of an American play, Robert Ardry's *Thunder Rock*, at the Hebbel Theater. It is the first American play the Berliners have seen in more than ten years, and the audience liked it. Ernst Busch, who played the lead, and who, I gathered, had not been seen on the stage in these parts for a long time, got a great reception. The theater, of course, was unheated and it was surprising how many fur coats these well-dressed Berlin women turned up in. I thought I recognized many old faces from prewar first nights.

The play, which was due to start at five p.m., was delayed a little because of a bit of a rumpus with four Russian officers. They arrived with carbines slung over their shoulders and a little in their cups, no doubt in anticipation of the anniversary of the Russian Revolution tomorrow. The play had been sold out, but the frightened German manager hastily found four seats for them. The trouble was they were in the balcony, and when the Russians saw that scores of American officers were sitting downstairs, they descended to the box office and proceeded to make a row. The German manager, not understanding Russian and not liking the way the Russians fingered their carbines, became definitely nervous until Nabokoff, who has not forgotten his native Russian, stepped in, kidded the irate officers, and finally induced them to depart, which they did after stiff salutes and not without dignity. I was touched that Soviet officers should be so interested in seeing an American play; how many of our own would walk across town to see a Russian play?

Talks these last days with some of the German Socialists and Communists. Though AMG, whose top men are either American businessmen or professional soldiers, may not know it yet, the best hope for a decent, peaceful and—eventually— democratic Germany lies in its working class. The trouble is that in a land where even before Hitler all workers were either Socialists or Communists, the latter are under the heel of the Russians and the former do not seem to have learned anything from the war and from the long Nazi tyranny. The Communists strike me as seeing things more clearly. They admit, for example, that one of their first jobs is to convince the German people—including the working class—of their share of responsibility for the war and—yes—of their complicity in Hitler's crimes.

But Otto Grotewohl, chairman of the Social Democratic Party, says not only that the German workers are not responsible for what Hitler did, but that the German people have no responsibility. He puts the blame for the war exclusively on "German big business" and the Nazi Party, conveniently overlooking (though I don't) that Hitler never could have built up his great war machine nor even marched off to war had not the German workers given him their full support.

Berlin, *Thursday, November* 8

Somewhat of a head this morning. Blame the Russian Revolution. Last evening, with Ray [Daniell] and Anne [McCormick] of the *New York Times*, I went out to Cäecilienhof at Potsdam. The Hohenzollerns, to whom it once belonged, are, of course, no longer around. The palace at the moment is occupied by the Russians and it was they, beginning with Marshal Zhukov, who were hosts for the celebration of the anniversary of the Russian Revolution. They almost drowned their guests with vodka and stuffed them with some very choice food.

Despite all the talk you hear in anti-Russian Allied circles here about Red Army men being forbidden to fraternize with their allies, there was certainly a lot of it last night. I have never drunk so many toasts in my life nor seldom seen so much conviviality. I must confess that one Russian major, a correspondent, I think, from *Isvestia*, gave me a particular kick when, after someone had told him I was the author of *Berlin Diary*, he embraced me like a bear and shouted in broken German: "It is you! You! You! Why, I used to read your diary day after day in the trenches at Stalingrad. It came out daily for weeks in one of our army papers there." And he dragged me over to the buffet table with some of his fellow officers, where we up-ended many too many tumblers of vodka.... A chat with the Russian garrison commander, General Smirnov, who ever since General Gavin took me to a meeting of the Kommandatura at which Smirnov presided, mistakes me for an officer in Gavin's airborne division whom he met when his army corps made contact with the 82nd Airborne in central Germany. I try to explain I am just a civilian scribe in uniform, but he will have none of it.

An interesting chat at noon today with Johannes Becher, the German poet. He almost floored Howard [Smith] and me with his frankness. We had got the impression from our talks with Germans that they had no sense of guilt or even remorse for Germany's crime in making war and regretted merely having lost it. But since one reporter can talk to but relatively few Germans, one could be wrong. Becher made it clear at once that we couldn't be more right. In fact, he put it much stronger than even I had felt it.

"With a few exceptions, there is no feeling of guilt in the entire people," he said. We had not put the question to him. He started right off talking about it on his own.

"It is not these ruins," he said, pointing to a block of debris along the adjoining Kurfürstendamm, where once homes of the complacent bourgeoisie undoubtedly had stood, "that are the worst thing about Germany's present condition. Far worse is the deadness of the German soul. It has been poisoned beyond belief by twelve years of Nazism. Today it has no spiritual connection either with our German past—the world of Goethe and Schiller, for example—or with the outside world of the present. And while it is true that everyone is preoccupied with finding shelter, warmth, and food (his office, in which we talked, was bitter cold), this cannot excuse the German people for having dead souls and nitwit minds and not the slightest desire to make good their awful crimes or even recognize them for crimes or even think about how Germany eventually can get in step with the rest of the world and its civilization."

And then he made the most cynical remark I have yet heard in Berlin.

"Why, these people," he said, pointing out to the passers-by on the street, "regret the loss of their little flats and their ugly furniture from the bombings more than they do their men, or even their women, who were killed in the war. It pains me, believe me, as a German to have to say these things," he said, apparently noticing our slight shock, "but it's better to be brutally frank, I think."

Becher said the working class, though it was the only hope of a decent Germany, had been as poisoned by Goebbels and Hitler as the middle classes. The workers too, he said, could not understand that they had helped in the perpetration of Nazi crimes. They had not minded much—or done anything about—the loss of freedom in Germany. As for the whole German people, they had not given a hoot when they were told by the Nazis what to think and read and write.

Becher is a Communist and like all party members he talks a lot about eventual democracy for Germans. But having spent long years of exile in Moscow, he must have known, I could not help thinking, that there too a writer, a poet, was scarcely free to write what he pleased.

We got to talking about writers in Germany. Like most other men of letters who have returned to the ruins of the Reich, he was somewhat resentful of Thomas Mann's decision not to come home. I asked about the man who had been to German drama what Mann was to the novel—Gerhart Hauptmann. For some reason the Russians have been making quite a hero of him and this has been inexplicable to me. For Hauptmann, who even before 1914 had been persecuted by the Kaiser for being a Socialist, had weakened in his declining days and had seemed to make his peace with the Nazi butchers. Had they not put on his last play, *The Daughter of the Cathedral*, and had not Goebbels made Nazi capital of this? Had the Nazis not boasted that Germany's greatest living playwright, a former Socialist, could remain in Hitlerite Germany and write and have his plays produced? Hauptmann had bitterly disappointed his followers throughout the world. Yet when the Russians arrived, they lost no time in letting it be known that Hauptmann should be honored. And only last month, on October 6, the aged playwright had sent a message to the new "*Kulturbund* for the Democratic Revival of Germany" wishing it well and expressing the hope that it would succeed in bringing about a "spiritual rebirth" of the German people—a message that seems to have been accepted with deep gratitude.

A turncoat he seemed to me, lacking the guts that Thomas Mann and Heinrich Mann and so many other German writers had shown at a moment when the integrity of the German artist was at stake.

However, Becher said he thought there were extenuating circumstances in Hauptmann's favor. He had learned, he said, that for every concession the great playwright had made to the Nazis, he had courageously rejected eleven other demands to exploit him. Maybe so. One hears the same talk about Wilhelm Furtwängler, conductor of the Berlin Philharmonic Orchestra, who carried on under the Nazis and thereby served them. The Russians have already approved his return, but the Americans, for the moment, refuse to clear him.

It is easy, of course, for an American writer, who was never put to the test the Germans were, to take a high-handed position. But Mann's course does seem more honorable than Hauptmann's or Furtwängler's.

It occurred to me that among eighty million Germans there must have been a few rebel souls among the youth who had poured out their hearts in writing a new literature that would see the light of day when the Hitler evil had perished. Had it not always been so in all countries in all such periods of suppression of the human spirit? I asked Becher about this. "You must have uncovered some interesting writing," I said.

His eyes glared at me. "That's what I thought too when I returned," he said. "I was absolutely certain that many a young, unknown writer—as well as some of the older ones—would flood us with manuscripts kept in hiding during the repression. But I was wrong. Nothing, apparently, was written—by anyone."

We did not nearly finish our talk and agreed to meet soon for a further one.

Berlin, *Friday, November* 9

Today the anniversary of Hitler's Munich beer-house *Putsch*—a day of great celebration in the Nazi time. How many endless speeches full of wind and lies have I heard Hitler give from the Bürgerbräukeller on this day. And I was here, I remember, on November 9, 1939, nine weeks after Hitler had started his war, when word came through that a bomb had gone off just after he and all the other bigwigs of the party had left the beer-house after the usual celebration and speech.

We correspondents always thought that Himmler set the bomb off—it killed seven of the lesser Nazi fry and wounded sixty-three others—to rally the Germans around the Führer and his war. Today one of the German editors in a local paper remarks that nothing more was ever heard of the poor chap, Georg Elser by name, whom Himmler designated as the man who planted the bomb on behalf of the British Intelligence Service. Well, the Germans will be hearing of what happened to him shortly, as soon as the German secret documents are made public at Nuremberg.

Just as we suspected, the Nazis did the job. And they made Elser, a carpenter by profession, the goat just as they had done with van der Lubbe in the Reichstag fire. The records show that Elser, who had absolutely nothing to do with the bombing, was confined to a concentration camp and treated exceptionally well, though kept separate from other prisoners. The Nazis had promised him 40,000 marks and release on the termination of the war. But of course it never would have done for the man to survive a *lost* war. So a month before the end Himmler ordered Elser "liquidated" immediately and decreed that an announcement be given the press that the hapless fellow had been killed in an Allied "terror attack" on Dachau. It does not surprise me.

Today too was the anniversary of the German "revolution" of 1918 when the Kaiser fled and the Germans sued for peace and the Socialists (there were no communists then) took over power in Germany. A couple of editors try to draw the lesson from the failure of that "revolution"—the failure of the Socialists, who had the power, to appreciate it and use it. Instead, they had called in the reactionaries and the men of the discredited army—a false and stupid move that eventually paved the way to these ruins of the Third Reich among which the Germans, in their dazed helplessness, now live.

Last night at dinner with an old friend I had a long confab with one of the top Russian political advisers, who shall be nameless here. I got the impression from him that the Soviet policy for Germany was quite clear: to treat Germany in such a manner that she would never again be strong enough to attack Russia.

Afterward I sat up most of the night reading the diary of Count Lutz von

Schwerin-Krosigk, the German Minister of Finance throughout the twelve years of the Nazi regime. Though he was, as I recalled, a dull fellow, his notes of the last feverish days of the thousand-year Reich are strangely exciting. And how revealing! The fool believed to the last minute that the Pope, with the backing of American Catholics, might still save Germany, and that the Wehrmacht could team up with the British and American armies to fight the Russians!

He reveals that he, Hitler, Goebbels, and the rest of the Nazi gangsters received the news of Roosevelt's death as though it were a gift from God, the very break they had been waiting for to enable them to snatch victory from defeat!

Now, I recalled that Schwerin-Krosigk was not originally a Nazi. A Rhodes scholar at Oxford before the first war, a permanent official in the Finance Ministry after it, he had been Minister of Finance in the shortlived Papen government and had continued on under Hitler apparently because he had a reputation as a financial expert and as an honest man. I remember that Ambassador Dodd was impressed by him and seemed to consider him an anti-Nazi force in the cabinet. I recall too that Schwerin-Krosigk had the reputation of being a deeply religious man and that he was the father of an unusually large number of children—twelve, I believe.

The morals of such Germans (the so-called "good Germans," so beloved at home), who did not start as Nazi gutter-bums, come to light in this diary. Because of that and because this account by an important cabinet member is the best first-hand report we have of what happened inside the German government in the last fifteen feverish days of the Third Reich, I think it may be of historical importance and of some general interest to insert it, in part at least, in these notes.

THE DIARY OF COUNT LUTZ VON SCHWERIN-KROSIGK

April 15, 1945

I had a very long talk with Goebbels on Monday. He told me with regard to the military situation that a concentrated attack on the Oder front is expected within the next few days. General von Busse, commander of the army defending the Berlin sector, is convinced that he will be able to repel the Russians. In the west, in about one week, an army of excellently equipped divisions will thrust deep into the flank of the advancing Americans: this will bring about a welcome diversion if not a reversal of the situation.

With regard to the political situation he declared that the divergencies between the Bolsheviks and the Anglo-Americans were deepening daily, that the only important thing for us to do was to remain on the alert for the actual break that was bound to occur. According to his conviction this was a matter of three to four months.[14]

I replied that I also believed in a forthcoming break. However, I was afraid it would come only when we were prostrate and not one minute sooner. In any case it would be a mistake to assume that such a development would be automatic. It was necessary, I said, to engage in active politics. There was no time to be lost since, as a consequence of the loss of our most important armament bases and because of the decreasing resistance and fighting spirit of the troops, the military situation was to be considered desperate. I elaborated on thoughts that I had already exposed to Goebbels in my last letters. I said it was impossible to engage in active politics with a Foreign Office sending second-rate representatives abroad. Instead, unofficial personalities, preferably from economic circles, should make contacts with similar personalities on the neutral or enemy side. Or they should approach men who could possibly act as intermediaries. The only ones I could see in such a role were the Pope, the Swiss Dr. Burckhardt, and Salazar, the Portuguese Prime Minister. However, only adequate men on our side such as Neurath, Papen, Lindemann-Bremen could deal with those men.

Goebbels agreed wholeheartedly. Confidentially he told me that certain steps leading to a contact had already been taken. From the first scanty information the following impression had been gained: one did not have to fear complete rejection from the Americans and, strangely enough, not from the Soviets either; however, England, though more strongly endangered as a result of the threatening preponderance of the Soviets and Americans, was showing a completely negative attitude. Negotiations on our side, however, were handicapped by the person of von Ribbentrop, the Foreign Minister.

Goebbels criticized the policies of the Foreign Office and the personality of its chief in a manner that could not possibly be more outspoken.... He was handicapped, however, in his criticism of the Foreign Minister, since there were repeated attempts to persuade the Führer that he, Goebbels, wanted the Foreign Office in addition to his Propaganda Ministry. This accounted for the fact that it was impossible for him, when discussing foreign policy, to be as frank and blunt in his talks with the Führer as he was on all other questions. Could I not speak to the Führer?

...Goebbels said one had to comprehend that the Führer could not and would not let himself be advised by inappropriate persons. Besides, the 20th of July had very badly affected him, physically—one hand still unusable and trembling—as well as, and more so, psychologically. The break of confidence had been a terrible shock and had made him even more suspicious and lonely. But Goebbels said he knew how greatly the Führer valued my honesty and sincerity and how much he appreciated my advice, knowing that I never wanted anything for myself. Would I agree to his suggesting an audience for me with the Führer? In this case I should start the conversation with a short report on my particular field. The Führer would soon start discussing the general situation and would thus give me an easy starting-point for entering into my subject. True, the Führer could not stand defeatism. As soon as he got the impression of being talked into capitulation, he would end the conversation immediately. Therefore one had to choose one's words carefully and tactfully.

While realizing that this point rendered any intervention difficult, I immediately agreed to Goebbels's speaking to the Führer on my behalf.

Goebbels told me how he recently had read to the Führer Carlyle's grandiose description of the desperate days of the Seven Years' War. The great King himself [Frederick the Great] no longer could see any way out. His statesmen and generals became convinced of his defeat. His enemies, considering Prussia defeated, already busied themselves with more important matters. He saw a dark future ahead of him and wrote a last letter to the Minister, Count Finkenstein, setting himself a final ultimatum: if by February 15 no change should take place, he would then give up and take poison. And Carlyle writes: "Brave King, wait a little while and the days of your suffering will be over; the sun of your luck is already hiding behind the clouds and will soon show itself to you." On February 12, the Czarina died, the miracle of the Brandenburg House happened. The Führer's eyes were filled with tears.

As the result of an inquiry, Goebbels went on, the Führer's horoscope of January 30, 1933, and the "Republik Horoskop" of September 9, 1918, had been thoroughly examined. An amazing fact had become evident, both horoscopes predicting the outbreak of the war in 1939, the victories until 1941, and the subsequent series of reversals, with the hardest blows during the first months of 1945, particularly during the first half of April. In the second half of April we were to experience a temporary success. Then there would be stagnation until August and peace that same month. For the following three years Germany would have a hard time, but starting in 1948 she would rise again.

The following day he sent me the horoscopes. I myself could not detect all these things. I only read them in the attached "analysis," which, however, has been done only recently. I am very curious now to see what is going to happen in the second half of April.

Before separating I gave Goebbels the thesis on our relations with England and on England's guilt that I have written in the past weeks.... I had also given this treatise to Ottfried Dewitz. He had passed it on to his chief, SS commander Schellenberg, who had succeeded Canaris as head of Counter-Intelligence. Dewitz wrote me I should shorten the thesis and write a second part to it on Germany's guilt, concluding that it was time to settle the accounts of guilt on both sides by letting bygones be bygones.

Germany's guilt? Ah! We now learn from the German Finance Minister that with the war lost—but not a second before, remember—the Nazis begin to scurry about to see what can be saved. Perhaps the Russians and their western allies will fall out. Perhaps peace can be negotiated with the west. Of course things will have to be changed a little in Germany too, the extermination of the Jews halted, the rigors of the dictatorship softened.

The count at this juncture has what he calls "a very interesting conversation with Schellenberg." He describes him as "a quite young, very intelligent and likable man." Actually Walter Schellenberg, chief of Himmler's dreaded Security Service for the Occupied Territories, is one of the worst and bloodiest of the Nazi gangsters, a killer of the first order. But even a sturdy German Christian like Schwerin-Krosigkno longer has any standards by which to judge human beings.

> Of course, we discussed the possibility of negotiations with the enemy. Schellenberg said right now he could see no starting-point, not because of a lack of possibilities but because of our silly Foreign Minister, who was promptly sabotaging any suggestions that were not his own—while the ones he put forward were just impossible. Another reason was that our top authorities apparently were not yet facing the fact that they, too, would have to make sacrifices. Schellenberg was very frank in criticizing our attitude toward foreign states, which, quite unnecessarily, had provoked hatred; our Jewish policy, for instance. One can treat a people the way we treated the Jews, he said, only when one has complete power over this people. Since we had power over but one third—the remainder living outside our jurisdiction—our treatment of the Jews had been a stupidity worse than crime. The same held true for the policies applied to our own people, the quarrel with the church, the reign of the big shots (Bonzentum), etc. As a matter of fact, abroad one objected passionately to the leading personalities of the German "system." *Confirming this, I added that while it was quite possible to find substitutes for all our leading men, one might understand abroad that the Führer and the Reichsführer (Himmler) had to stay.* For if they were to go, a vacuum would arise, and with such a vacuum, the situation of the German people being what it now was, there would always be a danger of chaotic and bolshevistic development. The difficulty was that these two personalities were just the ones to which foreign countries objected the most violently....
>
> Franz Seldte, the former Stahlhelm (steel helmet) leader, came last week to discuss the situation with me. In the opinion of Seldte it would soon become necessary to do away with certain regulations that branded our system as a dictatorship; for instance, the one that laws could be made, not only by the Reichstag, but also by the Führer alone. Then the one-party

system should be abolished and other parties be admitted, together with the National Socialist Party.

On Wednesday night, after an especially long alert, I met Dowandt, who told me that American tanks had already appeared that day on the Dessau-Berlin *Autostrade*. Consequently the High Command had ordered the closing of the powder factories of Croswig and Wittenberg-Bitterfeld. These had been the last powder factories in Germany, he said. The available stocks would last but a short time; then everything would be over, since even the bravest soldier could not fight without ammunition. I was deeply depressed. Was that really to be the end? My intellect had told me long ago that the coming of this end was inevitable, but instinctively I had strongly rejected such a possibility.

At that moment the telephone rang with a shrill tone: the Secretary of State wanted me. Why, at this late hour? Only a short sentence: *Roosevelt is dead! ...This was the angel of history. We felt its wings flutter through the room. Was not that the turn of events we awaited so anxiously?*—The next morning I called Goebbels. After presenting my congratulations I asked him to take the press in tow at once. While it must not be allowed to revile the new President, it should also refrain from exaggerated praise and especially from mentioning the controversy between Goebbels and Roosevelt. There might arise new possibilities now, and the press must not spoil them by clumsiness.

Goebbels was of the same opinion; he had already given new instructions. He said that on Wednesday he had paid a visit to the Busse army. Busse had asserted that a Russian break-through was impossible. His chosen watchword was: we hold out until the British kick us in the ass— which sums up the situation in a short, soldier-like formula. In the evening they had sat together at Busse's headquarters and Goebbels had developed his thesis—namely, according to historical logic and justice, things were bound to change, just as in the Seven Years' War there had been the miracle of the Brandenburg House. One of the General Staff officers, a skeptic, had asked ironically: "Well, which Czarina is going to die this time?" Goebbels had answered he didn't know, but that fate holds all kinds of possibilities.

He had driven back home, where he received the news of Roosevelt's death. He had called up Busse right away: the Czarina is dead! Busse said this would be a terrific stimulant for his men, who now could have new hope. *According to Goebbels, this news would provoke a complete change in the entire German people's morale, for one could and must consider this event a manifestation of historical fate and justice.* I interrupted him: "Why don't you say of God!" Since he was rushing around, I immediately wrote him a letter. *I myself, I said, see in Roosevelt's death a divine judgment, but it is also a gift from God that we shall have to acquire in order to possess it.*[Allusion to Goethe's: *Was du ererbt von deinen Vätern hast*, erwirbes *um es zu*besitzen.—W. L. S.] This death, I continued, eliminates the block that has obstructed all roads leading to contacting America. Now they'll have to exploit this God-sent opportunity and do everything to get negotiations started. *The only promising way, it seemed to me, was through the intermediary of the Pope.* As the American Catholics formed a strong, united block—in contrast to the Protestants, who were split into numerous sects—the Pope's voice would carry great weight in the U.S.A. Considering the seriousness of the military situation, we must not hesitate.

And yet they do hesitate. Hitler will not listen to peace-feelers being sent through the Pope or anyone else. As we already know, the mad Führer wants to pull Germany and the German people down with him in a fiery, pagan end. Count Schwerin-Krosigk sees Secretary of State Dr. Wilhelm Stuckart, a veteran Nazi Party member, and finds him "deeply shocked and embittered" at the turn of events. Stuckart rants that "victory was already ours, but senselessly and foolishly we squandered it." The State Secretary reveals that Pétain had offered Hitler "an alliance and a declaration of war against England." Had it been accepted, "no American would ever have come to Africa, let alone Europe. We could have won over the peoples of the occupied territories in the east and recruited armies to fight on our side, whereas now these armies are storming against us...."

And at home in the Fatherland? The veteran Nazi thug is full of remorse: "A small circle possessed with ambition and lust of power has tyrannized over and trampled on the German people, which has fought this war so bravely and nobly." At this point Stuckart makes a terrible confession to the Finance Minister.

Small wonder then, he said, that the people in Hesse and Franconia, formerly faithful followers of the party, had now greeted the Americans as their liberators, not only from the bombing terror but from the party's yoke. It was enough to make one cry. I could only join him in this outbreak. Did he still see any hope? I wondered. *To be saved there was only one way left open to us: to choose either the west or the east, he replied. Against both they could not fight. Whereas such a choice might enable us, under the greatest sacrifices though, to save the substance of the German people.* It would not matter if they established international control over the Rhineland, and even over the Ruhr region. The people there would remain German and there would come a day when they would win again. But if we were to lose the east, depopulated by ourselves, this region would fill up with Slavs and remain lost to us forever. To this, too, I could only agree.

Segeberg, April 22, 1945

A new phase of life begins: I have left Berlin. When and how shall I see it again?

On Thursday I had a long talk with Himmler.... He mentioned the deep impression my notes on "England's guilt" had made on him.... Then I developed my viewpoint. The military collapse could not be delayed much longer. Following the loss of our production bases and of our armament works, there existed a shortage of arms that would make itself felt more and more. The army in the west was still fighting, but in a disorderly manner and no longer possessed of the firm will to resist to the last. This was not surprising, I pointed out. Large parts of the population had acclaimed the arrival of the Americans as a liberation, not alone from bombing terror but from suppression. It was the party's fault that things should have gone so far. Up to now I myself had been convinced that resistance should be carried on to the utmost, provided, however, that the delay thus gained would be utilized for negotiations. *The sacrifice in blood that had been imposed on the German people could only be justified by the determination to pursue a policy that would bring about and hasten the break between the Bolsheviks and the Anglo-Americans.*

When Himmler inquired what I thought such a policy should be like, I outlined various ways to him: the Pope should use his influence on the Catholic bloc in America. We should approach the personalities who in my opinion were the only suitable ones for the role of possible mediators: Dr. Burckhardt, and Salazar of Portugal—and, interjected Himmler, the King of Sweden. And there should be unofficial contacts by economists—for certain countries their place might be taken by professors, artists, etc.—with corresponding personalities on the enemy side. *The Americans, for instance, could be made to understand that the increase in power the Bolsheviks would derive from the German economic potential and from the German population, was a threat to them, that the military inventions that we had no time to use in battle would make the Soviets invincible, and that the Americans were wrong in the assumption that they could sufficiently pacify the Soviets by giving them a morsel of Europe, to have their own hands free in the Far East. The contrary holds true: once strengthened, Soviet Russia will throw herself upon the Far East.*

I said that notwithstanding the heavy territorial sacrifices that would be imposed on us, we would also be forced to pipe down considerably in our internal policies. In my opinion it was not even the Jewish problem that would give us the biggest headache. The British won't insist that we allow the Jews to return. True, we would have to pay a heavy fine for what we did to the Jews. A bigger problem was the one relative to the position and the person of the Führer, and the party problem. In this connection it suffices to recall the problem of the restoration of the people's right to elect the president and of doing away with the one-party system.

Himmler completely agreed with my judgment of the situation. He criticized our foreign policy and the Foreign Minister very sharply, but at the same time he admitted grave mistakes in the domain of internal policy. He, too, was doubtful about the automatism of a break between Russia and the Western powers. He mentioned that for two years nothing more had happened to the Jews still remaining in Germany; they were to serve as a barter in all future negotiations. But it was his belief that in questions of internal policy the Führer was not going to make any concessions.

I told him that to me this was a psychological puzzle. Was the Führer not a realist, in spite of his often high-strung plans? Wasn't he capable of considering the situation soberly, without illusions? I wondered what he might well be waiting for. These remarks apparently embarrassed Himmler and he talked himself out by saying that it was just that the Führer had a different conception. But he would not reveal what this conception was like. He added that he himself, letting his instinct gain the upper hand over all arguments of reason, believed in a happy ending of the war.

When leaving, Himmler remarked that, while his reputation was that of a gay and godless person, in the depths of his heart he really was a believer in Providence and in God. In the course of the past year he had learned again to believe in miracles. The preservation of the Führer on July 20 had been a true miracle. He had personally experienced a second one last spring when, under unimaginable difficulties, he had taken over the Vistula army group. There one night he had told his staff that now he himself could see no further possibilities or hope. At that moment it started to drip outside, the thaw set in, and we gained time to build up the defense of the Oder. The miracle of our deliverance had happened, Himmler related. Since that time a happy end seemed absolutely certain to him.

I told him that I believed in miracles myself, but that such miracles are always a Godly challenge at the same time: I give you a chance, you make the most of it. It was so with Roosevelt's death. That was another chance, maybe the last one, given us by God.

Seldte, who was with me when Himmler arrived, later on continued to put pressure on Himmler, once alone with him. *He* had to act, it was he who had to use any possible means for influencing the Führer. This was no longer something concerning individuals. It was the substance of the entire German people that was at stake.

Segeberg, Monday, April 23, 1945

Continued writing my memoirs, which I started years ago and then abandoned.... Should anything untoward happen to me in this time, my descendants at least shall know what the man was like who belonged to the Reich cabinet in its years of greatest ascendancy as well as through its most sinister collapse. For our people seems to be faced with the darkest fate. The entire week was a chain of Job's tribulations.

What had happened in Berlin during this fateful week that had sent the German cabinet ministers scurrying for safety to the north while Hitler and Goebbels remained in the capital? We know from the British Intelligence report on Hitler's end that on April 22 the Führer suffered an attack of nervous prostration after he had called in his advisers to tell them he considered the war lost. His followers had tried to persuade him to leave Berlin, but to no avail. What should they do, then? Desert the leader? Opinions differed. Schwerin-Krosigk tells—though not very well—what happened.

April 24, 1945

On Tuesday I met with the other ministers who now form the government of the Reich in the north and who have settled in the environs of Eutin and Plön, with the exception of Rosenberg and Rust, who immediately "fled" to the northernmost part of the province, Flensburg. Poor Kritzinger related several times the developments of that night, when he had received the most contradictory orders from the ministers. He had had a violent clash with Goebbels on April 21. Goebbels had claimed he had been left ignorant of the move to the north. Now he was protesting violently against the flight from Berlin by all responsible authorities. This was rendering his defense extremely difficult. Maybe it had been this outcry of Goebbels that had determined the Führer to stay.

Kritzinger had explained to Goebbels that the transfer to the south had long been a foregone conclusion. But after it had become impracticable to move in that direction, the Führer, on Bormann's suggestion, had left it up to the ministers to go north, to be evacuated to the south by plane later on. In the written order Kritzinger had then chosen an expression that was absolutely in line with the whole situation: that it was *desirable* for the ministers to make for the north as soon as possible.

I myself had not paid any particular attention to these various nuances. I regarded the communication as a measure to maintain, outside of doomed (?)[15] Berlin, a government fit to negotiate and act. Only the technical infeasibility of moving the entire government, including the Führer and his close entourage, to the south had at the last moment led to the detour via the north. When, therefore, on the critical night Rust called to tell me of his intention to stay in Berlin no matter what, I had emphasized that such an action would isolate him from the government and might one day be pinned on him as desertion. The Führer's surprise decision to remain in Berlin had put all of us in an awkward situation. It now looked as if we had abandoned him and fled to the north. But this was not our fault. In any case we can confirm that Kritzinger's action was absolutely correct and that the formulation of his order had been in exact conformance with the situation at *that time*...[16]

April 25, 1945

In the afternoon Gauleiter Wegener came to see the ministers of the Reich. He painted the situation as gloomy. In the northwest the front could not be held longer than a few days. If the Americans on the Elbe should mean business and push forward to Hamburg, it would be over, there too, in a short time, with the insufficient forces we had in that sector. Just as it was impossible, even for a limited time, to hold the line of the Lübeck-Trave Canal. We now had to negotiate with the British, he said. It was still his conviction that they could at least be made to stand by, with their guns at ease, in case we should throw all our forces against the Russians.

Last night in a telephone conversation with the Führer he had discussed the situation in a completely undisguised manner. But the Führer was still opposing any negotiation with the western powers. He wanted to wait for the issue of the decisive battle being waged in Berlin. According to Wegener it was terrifying to observe how the walls put up around the Führer's inner thoughts were impenetrable to any advice, argument, or reason and even to hints of the atrocious suffering of our poor people. Nobody was allowed to glance behind those walls. What if there was nothing behind them, nothing maybe but the impotent titanic stubbornness of a genius who, cheated of his illusions, was sacrificing everybody to the deification of his own ego?

In the afternoon I had a conversation with Doenitz. He declared himself to be a soldier, carrying out definite orders given him by the highest state authority. As long as the political leaders approved of it, he would defend the western front against the British and send his submarines against England. It would necessitate an order to the contrary to make him act differently. I told him my belief that with the intensification of the battle in Berlin he would be forced very soon to take the initiative in political action himself. Our talk was short and revealing.

April 26, 1945

I reported my conversation with Doenitz to the ministers in Eutin.... In a confidential conference with Stuckart I stated that it was of the utmost importance for the Reichsführer (Himmler) to come to this sector as soon as possible. Constant contact with Doenitz was indispensable. Furthermore, I considered his presence necessary in view of the strong separatist tendencies that, according to what I had heard in the past few days, were becoming evident. Everybody was thinking of his own safety, without consideration for the situation as a whole. Hamburg and Bremen were said to be thinking already of a northwest German Reich, possibly one to be ruled by a British prince. Stuckart, sharing my views, promised to use his influence with the Führer accordingly, either by telephone or by telegram.

On Friday, April 27, our diarist receives the "sensational news" that Göring has "resigned" and even been "arrested." He reveals that the pompous Reichsmarshal at the last moment tried to coax the members of Hitler's cabinet to fly south to join him. But Admiral Doenitz, faithful to the Führer to the last, crossed him up by turning over Göring's message to Hitler.

And what did the pious Finance Minister, who had bowed and scraped to Göring for so long, really think of the Number Two man of Nazi Germany? At last he dares, on April 27, to speak out in his diary:

April 27, 1945

It is a pity that a man with the talents, the authority, and the popularity of Göring should not have profited by all those qualities during the war, that instead he should have allowed things to drag and let himself be dominated by his passion for hunting and collecting. He has "collected"—I am afraid, in a manner not always beyond reproach—big quantities of paintings and jewelry in the occupied territories of the west. Meanwhile he was resting on the laurels his Luftwaffe had earned during the first years of the war. He alone was responsible for the failure to provide fighter planes in time to protect the Reich against the aerial terror. Warnings and remonstrances went unheeded. *Since we lost the war militarily as a result of the Luftwaffe's failure, Göring must be regarded as responsible for the disaster the German people have met with. The main responsibility in the political field lies with Ribbentrop. It was he who, by his conceitedness and immoderation, alienated the neutral powers; it was he who failed to reply to Pétain's offer of peace, an alliance, and a declaration of war on England—which would have made the enemy invasions of Africa, Italy, and France impossible. It was he who declined a Russian peace offer in 1942.*

Others responsible are men like Erich Koch. His criminally false policies in the east made us appear, not as liberators, but as suppressors. As a result, men from the Ukraine and other parts of Russia, inclined to collaborate and even fight with us, instead became partisans and fought fanatically against us. Finally, men of the type of Bormann, whom I consider the Führer's evil spirit, the shadowy "brown eminence." On the enemy side, Stalin was very clever and successful in mobilizing the entire people's forces and in rallying them to the flag of the country. Instead of acting like him, Bormann overemphasized the party angle—the party was even allowed to organize the Volkssturm, with the results known to everybody. Party rivalries sharpened the lust for power of the small fry of the party, and the political divergencies existing between party members, often of doubtful character, grew boundless.... So, finally, large parts of the loyal and brave German population hailed the invading armies of the western powers as liberators, not only from the bombing terror but from the terror of the big shots....

April 28, 1945

I had a long talk with Stuckart and Kritzinger. I pointed out to them that now—all communications with Berlin, telephone as well as wire, being out—we had to face the possibility that the Führer might disappear any moment, either through death or some other circumstance, and that no vacuum must be allowed to arise. Every lost minute would cost the German people streams of blood and might become a question of to be or not to be. With regard to the possibilities of negotiating with the outside world and to the conservation of internal unity, a legal and constitutional succession would be indispensable. It was possible, I said, that at the last hour the Führer might change his original will, which had designated Göring as successor, and, as a second choice, Hess, and it might be possible to make this change public in an unquestionable manner. Since Hess, as well as Göring, was out of the question—change or no change of will—I thought that Himmler was the only possible legal successor....

April 29, 1945

In a conversation with Stuckart and a high SS leader we elaborated further on the subject discussed yesterday. I was very frank. While I myself could not think of anyone but Himmler who would be fit to exercise supreme power in Germany under the present circumstances, I felt it my duty to point to the grave objections that would be raised, abroad as well as at home, against Himmler's person, because of his past. Rightly or wrongly, his name was being related to some of the darkest chapters that, unfortunately, stained German history in the past years. The country regarded him as responsible for many actions of the Gestapo, the latter a special object of the people's wrath, and rightly so. One might assume that foreign countries, if willing to negotiate at all, would not let themselves be disturbed by the name of Himmler. On the other hand, if they did not want to negotiate, even the finest democratic name would not help. Yet I was afraid that mentioning the Reichsführer's name might complicate and delay any negotiation. Both reasons, in my opinion, would make it necessary for Himmler at the time of his taking office to announce a whole series of measures that would signify a change of policy and a repudiation of many things that had shocked people abroad and at home.

In the afternoon I took a walk to see Seldte, whose judgment is good and clear. We discussed all problems, including the changes to be suggested to Himmler. It was clear that he would immediately dismiss Ribbentrop. But who was to succeed him as Foreign Minister? I thought he might possibly ask me, but did not think I would be quite the right man.... I did not feel up to the task of playing all the more or less dirty tricks one would need at present....

April 30, 1945

Stuckart informed me yesterday that Field Marshal von Greim, the Luftwaffe's new commander-in-chief, left Berlin during the night of Saturday to Sunday in a *Storch* piloted by Hanna Reitsch. His descriptions of the completely destroyed town are terrible. I spent the evening at Dorpmueller's with Backe and Speer. We discussed all the possibilities of the government that was to liquidate the desperate situation. We all agreed not to announce any new testament of the Führer. The old one, nominating Göring as successor, had to be considered as impracticable, because of Göring's "ill health," which had provoked his resignation from all offices, and also because of his responsibility for the war's unfortunate ending. Himmler, then, was the only one who, under the present circumstances, could exercise the power of government. Both men asked me to take over the Foreign Office and possibly also the direction of the cabinet, under no matter what circumstances. We did not expect to receive any more news from Berlin.

May 1, 1945

On Tuesday we received the news of the Führer's death. It was not unexpected and, after so many trepidations, worn down as we are, it hardly came as a shock. Yet the accompanying announcement of his nomination of

Admiral Doenitz as his successor was a surprise. So it wasn't Himmler, but Doenitz, after all. Speer... told me that Doenitz was looking for a foreign minister. Speer had recommended me as the most suitable gentleman.... I outlined my objections against my own nomination to him. I was a minister *étranger aux affaires*[*sic*], especially since the whole apparatus of the Foreign Office was missing. Furthermore, my nomination would be considered abroad as a *solution de convenience*, dictated by the obvious intention of selecting a colorless personality, not compromised in the field of foreign policy and unobjectionable to foreign countries, a person who did not stand for any definite policy.

If one was looking for a man known abroad, why not send for old Neurath?

The diary ends abruptly here. Schwerin-Krosigk did become Foreign Minister, but a quick end was made of his silly illusions shortly afterward when all the members of the absurd "Doenitz government" were arrested and jailed by Allied military authorities.

It may be, of course, that Schwerin-Krosigk is not such a fool as his diary seems to reveal. His hope—the hopes of all the Nazi criminals—that Germany may somehow be saved by a falling out between Russia and her western Allies already does not seem as absurd as it did a few months ago. Well, if we and the Russians are as stupid as the Germans are counting on us to be, we *deserve*another German war, or, at least, to lose the peace.

Berlin, *Saturday, November* **10**
Cold and raw today, and the Germans in their unheated homes, many still roofless, windowless, must be feeling it. Our military kicked the owner of our house out of the place today and hired a German worker to heat it with our meager coal ration. The house was much warmer.

Spent part of the day going over a batch of German newspapers. They, at least, have changed. The Russians, British, French, and Americans see to that. It seems incredible that the German people could have read their Nazi press with its bilge, its lies, its utter emptiness, for twelve years. But some of the old Nazis are changing their colors pretty fast. Bumped into Hasendorff the other day. He was a very able assistant to Goebbels in the Propaganda Ministry, specializing on American affairs, when I was last here.

"I've fallen on my feet," he laughed, when I told him I was surprised to see him even at large, considering his past.

"How come?" I said.

"I'm managing editor of the British-licensed daily newspaper here," he chuckled. His attitude seemed to be: if the British are stupid, why should I be?

His talk reminded me of a recent evening at John Scott's. Victor de Kowa, the theater producer, was there. I remembered him as having done very well in the theater business under the Nazis. Now, he said, the British had just given him two theaters to direct in the British section of Berlin.

"How come?" I had asked, hardly surprised any more.

"I was in the underground. Didn't you know it?" he said.

"No," I said. "What did you do in the underground?"

"Raised money," he said.

The girl with him was very beautiful. She spoke German, but I soon gathered from her accent that she was French. In fact, it came out, she was a French movie actress. She spoke of the pictures she had made in Berlin during the war. Now, she said, she was going back to Paris. The war was over, after all. It was—apparently even for the collaborators.

The French, who have been fairly tough on their collaborators, puzzle me. The girl was small fry—though pretty. But Hasendorff says that the managing editor of a new French-licensed newspaper here, the *Kurier*, which will begin publishing next week, is one Vaudoin, the same individual who was, he adds, Vichy correspondent of the Berlin newspaper *Deutsche Allgemeine Zeitung* and an ardent Pétainist. Surely the French are not that stupid—assuming that Hasendorff is correct.

Martha Gellhorn, apparently just divorced from Hemingway, is back. She says Marlene Dietrich flew in with her to see her dying mother, but arrived too late.

Howard [Smith] and I again went to see Becher, who complained that his German cultural committee and its new publishing house find it difficult to make cultural contacts with the American Military Government. He says the British and the Russians have been most helpful. The Germans, he declares, are starving for foreign books and are especially anxious to fill the void of the last twelve years. They want to read again Hemingway and Steinbeck and Dos Passos and Upton Sinclair and Sinclair Lewis and others. But AMG, he says, apparently hasn't heard of America's best writers.

It became clear that Becher and his crowd are really quite bitter at Thomas Mann for not rushing back to Germany. They are pretty sore at him for a letter he wrote to a local author the other day explaining why he wasn't coming back.

But what a commentary on German culture and character in our time when the country's greatest living author has to become an American citizen, and has to tell his former fellow countrymen that what they did to him in the past and what they failed to do as decent men and honest artists under the Nazis does not make him feel much like returning! Somehow I am moved by the tragedy of this great estrangement between a German artist and the German people. Must translate Mann's letter and put it in here.

[A clipping of Mann's letter got lost among my effects in Germany, but on my return to America the author kindly lent me his copy. It is so important for the understanding of what has happened to Germany and to the Germans, and so profoundly moving in itself, that I give it here. It is addressed to Walter von Molo, a minor German poet and a former president of the German Academy of Poetry.]

My dear Herr von Molo:

I thank you for your very friendly birthday greetings, as well as for the Open Letter addressed to me, which was published in the German press, and was also reprinted, in part, by the U.S. papers. In the latter you express even more strongly and urgently the wish—I could even say the formal demand—that I return to Germany and live there again, to "advise and act." You are not the only one to address this appeal to me; the Russian-controlled Berlin radio, I am told, and the official newspaper of the United Democratic Parties of Germany have done so too, basing their argument on the greatly exaggerated motivation that I had "a historical task to perform in Germany."

Now, I should surely be glad that Germany wants to have me again— not only my books, but myself, as a human being and as a person. However, I feel that in these appeals there are disturbing, disquieting elements, and I sense something that is illogical, even unjust and rather ill-considered. You know only too well, my dear Herr von Molo, that "advice and action" are at a premium in Germany today, in the almost hopeless situation that our unfortunate people have brought upon themselves. It seems rather doubtful to me whether an old man on whose heart muscles these troubled times have, after all, made their demands could contribute much, directly, personally, through his presence, to raise up the prostrate men whom you describe so movingly. But this is beside the point. However, in these appeals the technical, civic, and moral handicaps that impede my return do not appear to me to have been given mature consideration.

Can these twelve years and their consequences thus be wiped from the slate, and can we act as if they had never occurred? Hard enough and breath-taking enough was the shock in 1933 of the loss of my accustomed way of life, my home and my country, my books, souvenirs, and property, accompanied as it was by all the wretched happenings, expulsions, desertions. I will never forget the illiterate and murderously vindictive radio and press campaign against my Wagner essay which was contrived in Munich and which made me realize for the first time that the road back was cut off; my struggle for expression, my attempts to write, to reply, to explain myself, the "letters into the night," as René Schickele, one of the many lost friends, called these smothered monologues. Hard enough was what followed, the life of wandering from country to country, the passport worries, the nomadic existence in hotels, while my ears were ringing with the tales of shame that daily came from the lost, estranged homeland now reverted to barbarism. All of you who swore fidelity to the "charismatic Führer" (ghastly, ghastly this besotten erudition) under Goebbels's directives, have not gone through all of this. I do not forget that you went through something far worse, later, which I escaped; but you have not known this asthma of exile, the uprooting, the nervous fears of homelessness.

Sometimes I revolted when I thought of the advantages that you enjoyed. I saw in them a denial of solidarity. If at that time the German intellectuals, everyone who had a name and a world repute, doctors, musicians, teachers, writers, artists, had risen against the disgrace as one man, had proclaimed a general strike, the course of events might have been different. However, the individual, if he did not happen to be a Jew, was always tempted to ask: "Why? After all, the others collaborate. It can't be as bad as it seems."

I said that I felt outraged sometimes. But I never envied you, you who lived in Germany, not even during the days of your triumphs. For I knew only too well that these great days were but bubbles of blood and that they would very soon explode. I did envy Hermann Hesse, with whom I associated during the first weeks and months, and with whom I found solace and courage. I envied him, for he had been free for a long time. He had liberated himself long ago on a basis that was only too well motivated: "Who denies that the Germans are a great and important people? The salt of the earth? Perhaps. But they are quite impossible as a political nation. Once and for all, I don't want to have anything to do with them as such." And he lived in serene security in his Montagnola home, and in his garden he played boccia with his distracted guest.

Slowly, very slowly, my life became settled and organized again. I found first a home in France, then another in Switzerland. To a certain extent, quietude, the sense of "belonging," of settling down grew from the emotion of being utterly lost. I took up again the work that I had forsaken, which I believed no longer existed. Switzerland was traditionally hospitable, but suffered from the menacing pressure of powerful neighbors, and was bound to neutrality even to the point of morality. She always remained understandably embarrassed and anxious because of the presence of the guest without papers who was on such bad terms with his own government, and tact was therefore necessary. Then, however, came the invitation from the American university, and suddenly, in the immense free country, there was no question of "tact" any longer, there was nothing but open, uninhibited, declared friendliness, cheerful and unreserved. The standing motto was: "Thank you, Mr. Hitler!" I have some reason, my dear Herr von Molo, to be grateful to this country, and reason to prove myself grateful.

Today I am an American citizen, and long before Germany's terrible downfall I declared publicly and privately that I had no intention ever to turn my back on America. My children—two of my sons are now in the

United States Army—are deeply rooted in this country. English-speaking grandchildren grow up around me. I, too, am in many ways anchored in this country and have, here and there, honorary responsibilities—toward Washington and toward the leading universities of the country, which awarded me honorary doctor's degrees. I have built my home on this beautiful coast that looks toward the future, and it is under this shelter that I hope to bring my life's work to an end—as part of an atmosphere of power, reason, abundance, and peace. Frankly, I do not see why I should not profit from the advantages of my strange destiny, after having tasted its bitterness to the very dregs. I do not understand why I should not, for I do not see what service I could render the German people that I cannot do from the shores of California.

That everything has happened as it did is certainly not of my doing. It is the result of the character and the destiny of the German people—a people strange enough and so tragically fascinating that they are worthy of a good deal of forbearance. Admitting this, one should recognize the consequences, and not dismiss everything with a commonplace "Come back, all is forgiven!" Far from me to be self-righteous! It was easy for us, abroad, to follow the path of virtue, and to say what we meant about Hitler. I shall not cast a stone against anybody. I am only rather shy and "afraid of strangers," as we say of little children. Yes, Germany has become very foreign to me during all these years. It is, you must grant, a rather alarming country. I admit that I am afraid of German ruins—the ruins of stone and the human ruins. And I fear that there is little in common between a person who has looked at the witches' Sabbath from the outside and you who have danced with and waited upon Master Urian. I do not remain unmoved— how could I?—when I receive long letters, full of long-suppressed affection, which are now sent to me from Germany. These are genuine and moving adventures of the heart. But my joy is somewhat diminished when I think that none of them would ever have been written if Hitler had triumphed. Moreover, the writers of these letters are particularly naïve and callous in the way they resume contact immediately, as if the twelve years (of the Nazi regime) had never existed. Books, too, are sent to me. May I admit that I do not like to look at them and very soon put them aside? It may be superstition, but, in my view, books that were printed in Germany from 1933 to 1945 are less than worthless and not good to touch. A smell of blood and shame clings to them. They should all be destroyed.

It was forbidden and impossible to "produce" culture in Germany while all around the things occurred that we know. It meant adorning depravity and crime. Among the tortures we suffered belonged the realization that the German spirit and art were constantly offering themselves as the shield and protector for the most absolute corruption. It seems utterly inconceivable that no more honorable occupation could be found than the creation of Wagner settings for Hitler's Bayreuth. It proves a complete lack of feeling. To go to Hungary, with Goebbels's permission, or to some other European country and promote *Kulturpropaganda* for the German Reich by giving clever lectures—I do not say that this was reprehensible; I only say that I do not understand it and shy away from meeting certain people again.

A conductor dispatched by Hitler to conduct Beethoven in Zürich, Paris, or Budapest is thereby guilty of an obscene lie when he uses the pretext that he was a musician and that his concern was music alone. But, above all, at home his music was already a lie. How could it happen that Beethoven's *Fidelio*—this opera destined for the day of German self-liberation—was *not*forbidden in the Germany of the last twelve years? It was a scandal that it was not forbidden and that highly cultured performances were given, that singers could be found to perform, musicians to play, a public to listen. For what utter stupidity was required to be able to listen to *Fidelio*in Himmler's Germany—without covering one's face and rushing out of the hall!

Indeed, many a letter is brought to me from the foreign and strange-seeming homeland by American sergeants and lieutenants—not only from important people, but also from young and simple people, and, strangely enough, none of these suggests that I should come back to Germany so soon. "Remain where you are," they simply say. "Spend the rest of your life in your new, happier homeland! Here life is full of sorrows...." Full of sorrows? If that were all! But there is also unavoidably continuing evil and hostility. As a kind of trophy, a back number of a magazine published by a highly placed Nazi professor and *Doctor Honoris Causa*was recently sent to me by an American (*Volk im Werden*, March 1937, Hanseatische Verlagsanstalt, Hamburg). The name of this professor was not KRIEG, but Krieck, with "ck." It was frightening to read. Life cannot be easy among people who have been fed with this type of drugs for twelve years. "You would have there, no doubt, many good and faithful friends, both old and young ones," I said to myself. "But you would also have enemies in ambush—beaten enemies, it is true, but these are the worst and the most venomous."

And yet, my dear Herr von Molo, all this is only one side. The other side demands a hearing. The deep curiosity and anxiety with which I receive news, whether direct or indirect, from Germany and the greater importance it has for me than news out of any other part of the world, indifferent as it is to Germany's unimportant fate, bring me daily a fresh realization of the unspeakable bonds which, in spite of all, unite me with the country that deprived me of citizenship. An American world citizen? Well and good. But I cannot deny that my roots are there, that, in spite of all my fruitful admiration for foreign ways, I live and create within German tradition,

WILLIAM L. SHIRER

even though the times may not have permitted my works to be anything but a somewhat morbid parody and an echo of all that is German.

I shall never cease to consider myself a German writer, and even during the years when my books survived only in English translations, I remained faithful to the German language—not only because I was too old to change languages, but also because I was conscious that my work has its modest place in the history of German literature. My novel on Goethe, written in Germany's darkest days, a few copies of which were smuggled into Germany, is not exactly a document of oblivion or of repudiation. And I don't need to say to you, either: "I am ashamed of my days of peace—to suffer with you was far more worth while." Germany never left me in peace. I have "suffered with you," and I did not exaggerate when I spoke in my letter to Bonn of an anxiety and torment, a soul- and thought-filling distress "from which, for four years, not an hour of my life has been free, and against which I have had to struggle daily to be able to continue my creative work." Often enough I did not even try to struggle. The fifty or more broadcasts to Germany, now being published in Sweden—these pleas repeated time and again—may testify that often enough something besides "art" seemed more urgent to me.

Some weeks ago I made a speech in the Library of Congress about "Germany and the Germans." I wrote it in German, and it will be published in the next issue of the *Neue Rundschau*, reborn in June 1945. It was an attempt to show to an educated American public, from the psychological point of view, how it all could happen in Germany. I had to admire the quiet readiness with which the public accepted my explanations, so soon after the end of a terrible war. It was not easy, of course, to find my way between an unseemly apology and a disavowal that would have looked just as bad. But I managed, more or less. I spoke of the blessed fact that often, on earth, good comes out of evil, and of the devilish fact that the bad often springs from the good. I outlined briefly the story of Germany's soul. I repudiated the theory of the "two Germanys"—a "good" Germany and a "bad" Germany. The bad Germany, I stated, is the good Germany which failed, the good Germany in misery, in a state of guilt and downfall. I did not speak, I said, to commend myself, to praise myself, according to the despicable custom, as the representative of the Good, the Just, the Noble Germany in white robes. Nothing of what I was trying to say to my audience came from the outside or was cold, impartial wisdom. Every single element was part of myself. I had experienced it all within myself.

This was, perhaps, what is called a declaration of solidarity—in the most difficult moment. I did not identify myself with National Socialism, but with a Germany that finally succumbed to its temptation and made a pact with the devil. The pact with the devil is a deeply traditional German

160

temptation, and a German novel based on the sufferings of the last few years would have to take as theme this terrible contract. But in our greatest poetical work the devil is finally cheated even of the individual soul of Faust, and let us reject the idea, emphatically, that Germany has finally gone to the devil. The grace of God is a higher law than any contract written in blood. I believe in the grace of God, I believe in Germany's future, however desperate the present seems to be, however hopeless the ruins. Let us not speak any longer about the end of German history! Germany is not to be identified with the short, dark episode that bears the name of Adolf Hitler. She is not to be identified with the Bismarckian era of the Prusso-German Reich, itself a short episode. Neither is she to be identified with the period of a mere two centuries which one could call the era of Frederick the Great. She is in a process of taking a new shape, of finding a new way of life, which may, after the first distress of transformation and transition is over, promise more happiness and true prestige, may be more in tune with the innermost tendencies and needs of the nation, than the old one.

Is world history at an end? We are now in a most active era of world history, and the future of Germany is involved with it. Power politics continue, indeed, to give us drastic warnings of exaggerated expectations. But does there not remain a hope that by way of compulsion and suffering the first tentative steps will be made toward a world situation in which the national individualism of the nineteenth century will dissolve itself and finally disappear? A world economy, a diminishing importance of national boundaries, a degree of "depolitization" of the state as such, the awakening of mankind to a consciousness of its genuine unity on the practical plan—the first consideration by humanity of the idea of a world state—how should all this *social humanism*, which is so far in advance of the concepts of bourgeois democracy and is the great issue of our time, be foreign and repugnant to the German soul? In Germany's fear of the world there has always been so much world affinity. Behind this isolation, which made her evil, is the wish to love and be loved, and who would deny it? Let Germany renounce her vainglory, hatred, and egoism, let her find again her love, and she will be loved. In spite of all, she remains a country of mighty values, a country that can count on the ability of her population as well as on the help of the world, and to whom, once the present trial is over, a new life, full of achievements and prestige, is promised.

I have digressed a good deal in this letter, my dear Herr von Molo. However, many things must be said in a letter to Germany. I will add one more remark. The dream of feeling the soil of the old continent under my feet is not foreign to me by day or by night, in spite of my spoiled life in America. And when the hour comes—if I live and transportation conditions as well as the authorities permit it, I hope to come over. Once I am back, I

WILLIAM L. SHIRER

suspect that the fears and feelings of estrangement—the result of a mere twelve years—will not resist an attraction that has longer than a thousand years of memories on its side. Therefore, if God wills, *Auf weider sehen.*

[Mann, as my diary notes indicate, was immediately attacked for writing this letter by a number of second- and third-rate German writers. He answered them in a broadcast to Germany over the BBC as follows:]

MANN'S BROADCAST

...I am ready to defend my stand before God, and posterity will call it reasonable.

It seems that one could give proof of egoism as much by remaining in Germany as by fleeing. I was far removed from the monumental callousness such as Richard Strauss manifested in an interview with American journalists for the amusement of the world. The devil's spawn that is National Socialism has taught me to hate—to hate for the first time in my life with a genuine, deep, inextinguishable, deadly hatred, a hatred that, I fancy in a mystical way, was not without influence on the course of events. From the very first day I have worked for the downfall of this evil, not only through my broadcasts to Germany, which were a single sincere appeal to the German people to rid themselves of it. And what do you believe was my purpose, among other things, in doing this? That I should return as I am now being asked to do, now that it is too late?

To return home! How for years, as a guest of Switzerland, I hoped for it, dreamed of it, how eagerly I accepted every sign that Germany had had the fill of its degradation! How different it would have been if it had been given to Germany to liberate herself! If between 1933 and 1939 the revolution of deliverance had broken out among you, do you think I would not have taken the very first train home?

This could not and did not happen. It was impossible—every German says so—and so I must believe it. I must believe that a highly cultured people of seventy million, under certain circumstances, can do nothing but accept for six years a regime of bloody savagery which is revolting to the depths of its soul and then follow it into a war that it recognizes as utter insanity. And this same people, for six more years, does its uttermost, strains all its inventive powers, courage, intelligence, love for discipline, military ability—in short, throws its entire strength into helping this regime to victory and thus to immortality. That is what had to be, and entreaties such as mine were utterly worthless. "The blind," says the writer Frank Thiess, a member of the Inner Emigration, "would not listen and the wise were always one step ahead of the spoken word"—at least, at the very end. That is how it was in Germany.

In oppressed Europe and in the rest of the world more than one tortured heart found solace in my superfluous talks, and so I have no regrets. But, however meaningless the love's labor lost of these appeals may have been for Germany, they cannot now be my compelling reason for returning. "You have posed as a spiritual leader of the German people," so they say. "Well now, live among this people. Do not merely share their sufferings, but relieve them, and oppose the foreigners who are responsible for them."

But where is Germany? Where is it to be found, even only geographically? How can one return to a fatherland that does not even exist as a unit, to a country torn asunder into occupation zones, which hardly know each other? Should I go to the Russians, or to the French, or to the English, or to my fellow citizens, the Americans, and ask for the protection of their bayonets against National Socialism which is far from being buried and even today is hard at work at corrupting our soldiers? Should I, in the face of the impudence that is exhibited and that is unfortunately encouraged in certain quarters, protest against the sufferings of Germany, and point out to the occupation powers the mistakes they commit in the treatment and administration of Germany? This is exactly what I cannot do. I was able to speak as a German to the Germans, and to warn them of the approaching nemesis. But just because I am a German who feels deeply that everything German is involved in the terrible national guilt, I cannot feel free to criticize the policy of the victors, for my criticism would always be interpreted as being the expression of egocentric patriotism and of apathy toward the years of suffering imposed by Germany on other nations. One who has long ago been frightened by the mountains of hate that established themselves all around Germany, and who, long ago, during sleepless nights, anticipated and tried to imagine the terrible way the inhuman acts of the Nazis and their armies would one day backfire throughout Germany, cannot now wring his hands in patriotic horror at the actions of the Russians, Czechs, and Poles toward Germany. It is a mechanical and unavoidable reaction to the misdeeds committed, for which a whole people is being punished, and where individual justice, or the guilt or innocence of the individual, unfortunately is of no account.

It is far better to act from here to help Europe, to save German children from starving to death, than to agitate in Germany to soften the lot of the Germans—an agitation that might unwittingly promote German nationalism. For I am not a nationalist. You may forgive this or not, but I have suffered as much over the misery of the countries oppressed by Germany as I now do over German misfortune. As far as my living abroad is concerned, the time granted to me by my country for this purpose has led me not only to accustom myself to it with resignation, but also to accept, with sincerity, the dictates of fate as being for the best. I have in the past impatiently awaited the opportunity to return home. I have just seen again a letter I wrote early in 1941 to a Hungarian friend, in which I said: "Exile has become something quite different from what it was in the past; it is no more a state of expectation, a concentration on return, but hints already at the dissolution of nations and the unification of the world." This is true. Everything national has long ago become provincial, and the atmosphere that is but the air of the fatherland has become prison air!

"Germany, Germany, and without Germany one must decay!" This is the call of those who never opened their mouths to warn of the coming catastrophe and therefore were allowed to remain in Germany in 1933. But this is a grave error. Living away from home has been good for me. I have taken with me my German heritage, I have not missed anything that the Germans experienced these past years, even though I was not in Munich when my house was destroyed. Grant to me my World Germanism, which came naturally to me when I was still at home, and grant to me my outpost of German culture, which I hope to maintain honorably for the remaining years of my life.

[Thus a great German soul crying out in the terrible German wilderness! And the soul seared and sorrowed, but courageously facing the hideous fact of what has happened to his fellow countrymen and of the awful plight their collective crime against humanity has put them in. The American and British people, in the depths of their stupid sentimentality and of their ignorance, will try to forget the fact, and soon, I am afraid, the integrity of Thomas Mann will be but a small voice in the complacent Anglo-American wilderness.

[In his letter Mann refers to a conductor who was sent abroad by the Nazis to direct the music of Beethoven as being "guilty of an obscene lie." He mentions no names, but he could mean Wilhelm Furtwängler, Germany's greatest symphony-orchestra conductor, whose concern for art did not prevent him from serving the Nazis well. On December 17, 1946, nevertheless, Furtwängler was acquitted by a German denazification court in Berlin, and most Germans, it was evident, were greatly pleased with the verdict. Why not? Furtwängler's real crime was one that the frightened little denazification tribunal in Berlin did not even attempt to assess: lack of moral sense and integrity. Was that not the chief crime of the whole German people?

[Was that not what was wrong with the greatest composer of our time, Richard Strauss, whom Mann, in his broadcast, castigates for his "monumental" cynicism and callousness? Here were Germany's two greatest artists in the art in which modern Germans were pre-eminent—music—(Walter Gieseking, the pianist, was a third), lending their world-wide reputations, their magnificent talents, their great names, to a barbarous German regime that was murdering and prostituting art and crucifying mankind, from which art springs.

[Gerhart Hauptmann, it seemed to me, was guilty of the same crime. The writers who stayed in Germany were no better than the musicians, though in literature, at least, the greatest figures (except for Hauptmann)—the brothers Mann, Hermann Hess, Bert Brecht, Leonhard Frank, Fritz von Unruh, and others—had the guts to emigrate rather than to knuckle down to the inanities of Dr. Goebbels. In most cases, uprooted as they were, they were not able to write very much. But those who remained in Germany, the authors Mann refers to as the "Inner Emigration"—a term incidentally that they like very much—produced nothing of worth—a frightening phenomena. A few, like Ernst Wiechert, once a rabid German nationalist, showed courage. Wiechert himself went to a concentration camp and now appears to be emerging as the most significant writer in Germany.

[On the stage and screen it was the same story. Gustav Gruendgens, perhaps Germany's most popular actor and director, who during the Republic had had left-wing sympathies and who had been a disciple of the great Max Reinhardt, became a darling of Göring and one of the titans of the Nazi theater. Werner Krauss, a sort of German Barrymore, became another. Gruendgens recently made a triumphal return to the Berlin stage, his prodigious services to the Nazis having been forgiven, if not forgotten. Only the other day the Berlin Actors Association petitioned the Allied Kommandatura to permit Krauss to return to the stage.

[I suspect Emil Jannings, most popular of German film actors, will be back in business soon too. After the German collapse innocent young American war correspondents sought him out at his picturesque villa on Wolfgangsee near Salzburg and fell easily for his pose that he, of course, had been anti-Nazi all along. Even Klaus Mann, son of Thomas Mann, who should have known better, was taken in by Jannings when, as a soldier-correspondent for *Stars and Stripes*, he went to see the famous actor. Jannings told Mann of how he had been persecuted by the Nazis and of what a good liberal democrat he had always been at heart. Later, after further evidence of Jannings's kowtowing to Goebbels had come in, Mann changed his mind. I myself, especially during the first year and a half of the war, had seen Jannings gloating in the company of the Nazi bigwigs, had been disgusted by his taking the leading role in the Nazi propaganda war film *Ohm Kruger* and by his boasting of how he liked this ridiculous movie of the Boer War; and, finally, I had noted in the Nazi press a little item announcing that Jannings had been made head of a big Nazi film company—a most lucrative post.

[Alas, Germany's artists had been as lacking in personal guts and integrity as other Germans and it was merely further proof that the German people, at heart, had not changed, had not reformed, when they demanded the return to the limelight of their artists who had served Hitler's barbarism so well. There will always be a Germany, I guess, and, in our lifetime at least, it will always be the same.]

Berlin, *Sunday, November* **11**

Armistice Day—and cold, gray, and drizzly. This morning the Russians unveiled their mammoth monument in the Tiergarten commemorating the men of the Red Army killed in the Battle of Berlin. You could almost hear Hitler's Bolshevik-hating bones rattling in the grave.

This morning Field Marshal Montgomery called the correspondents to his villa. His mind seemed to be preoccupied with another battle. He kept talking about the "Battle of Winter." 'Twill be a tough winter for the Germans, he said. Something must be done to get them more food and heat. Everyone here agrees that the Allies must not let Germans starve or freeze. We Americans are now furnishing the Germans one third of their food supplies. This morning I noticed in the corner grocery store sacks of flour piled up to the roof. They were all stamped: "Buffalo, U.S.A."

What stumps me, though, is that the Allies don't seem to give a damn about the liberated people, who also are cold and hungry, after having been deliberately starved (and frozen) by the German government for years. Shouldn't we help *them*first? According to UNRRA, the liberated peoples will get this winter, on an average, three hundred less calories a day than we provide for the Germans.

Yet only the other day there were shocking outbursts in the House of Commons, especially from my Labour friends, protesting about the Allied failure to give the Germans more food. No wonder that wise old man Jan Christiaan Smuts was moved to say recently: "You see today a ruined Europe. If tomorrow you hear of suffering, disease, starvation, and death on a large scale unknown before in time of peace, remember that that was, in the first place, the curse of Hitler, and in the second place the dreadful responsibility of the German people who allowed such a monster to become their master. The dreadful responsibility rests on us to do all we can to save what can still be saved. But do not forget where the chief responsibility lies."

But we are forgetting.

I said to a German woman the other day: "It must be nice to have white bread again after that sawdust you got from the Nazis during the war."

"Nice? I find it tasteless," she said, smugly. "Why don't the Americans give us nice brown bread?"

After Montgomery's remarks my mind kept going back to a little item in yesterday's Berlin newspapers. It came from Czechoslovakia. It was about that former little Czech town, Lidice. Almost forgotten now, isn't it? How the Nazi gangsters erased it from the face of the earth and murdered the entire male population above the age of fifteen. What ever happened to the women and children? The women, the newspapers now divulge, were shipped to a concentration camp at Ravensbrück. And their children? Well, they, the papers say, were torn from their mothers by the Gestapo and scattered around, nameless, in Germany. There were ninety-three of them. *Not a one of them has been found to this day.* That's what the little piece in the local papers was about. It was a pitiful appeal from the mothers of Lidice to the German people to help them locate their children and send them home.

I've been wondering since I came here how many of the 540,000 Jews who lived in Germany when the Nazis came to power in 1933 are still alive. I can't get the figures for today, but I have found the Nazi government's own figure for a year ago. On July 1, 1944, there were 20,000 Jews left in Germany—20,000 out of 540,000. Hitler thus failed by only four per cent to make good his boast of wiping them all out.

Which reminds me of another item in the local press. It tells of the testimony of a fifteen-year-old German lad, the son of the former SS commander of the Mauthausen concentration camp. Questioned about his father, the boy said: "For my birthday, my father put forty inmates at my disposal to teach me how to shoot. I took shots at them until they were all lying around dead. Otherwise, I have nothing else to report about my father."

After my recording today Howard and I went out to see Friedrich Wolf, the anti-Nazi playwright and author of the play *Professor Mamlock*. We found him at the home of Fritz Wisten, a Jewish regisseur. Wisten is a bit puzzled that none of the Allies will give him a theater, though the British have given de Kowa two, despite his having done well under the Nazis. We found the two hungry for news—especially literary and theater news—from the outside world.

Berlin, *Monday, November* 12

I have had several talks with American economic and financial experts, and had better put some of their amazing revelations down.

In the first place, the bomb damage to Germany's industrial plant is not nearly so great as it looks, or as we were all led to believe by the British and American air forces. In fact, our people state flatly that German industry is virtually intact and that, if left to her own devices, Germany could—in five years—make herself stronger industrially than she was when she marched off to war in 1939. The Allied bombers, it develops, did not *destroy* the German industrial plant. They merely curtailed production temporarily in a number of key industries—above all, aircraft and synthetic oil. Actually at the very moment that Allied bombing approached its peak, in the latter part of 1944, German production was higher than it had ever been in history! Today, according to our experts, most of the big German plants could get back to normal production with very little repairing.

For example: one single I.G. Farben plant, with a capacity for producing nearly as much dye annually as all the chemical works in the United States put together, is completely intact. It didn't even suffer a broken window. It could start full operations tomorrow.

Almost all the iron and steel furnaces of Germany are either in a position to start producing immediately or could be put into operation in a short time after minor repairs. It is this industry that is the basis of a war-making machine. Its capacity of some 25,000,000 tons of steel a year is easily five times what Germany herself could consume for peaceful uses.

Here are some facts about the state of other German industries that most of us in America thought had been destroyed by Anglo-American bombing:

COAL-TAR BY-PRODUCTS, which include hundreds of materials used in warfare (explosives, for example). Germany's production in this field, the world's greatest, has scarcely been affected by the bombing.

NITROGEN. Germany produced about half the world's output. It could do so again, after a little repair-work.

OIL. At the height of the war Germany was manufacturing 5,500,000 tons a year of synthetic oil. Our bombers put out of action a good part of the plant producing it, but most of it can be repaired and normal production restored in a short time.

ALUMINUM. If allowed to, Germany can produce 250,000 tons a year, compared to 40,000 tons in 1933, the year Hitler came into power.

MACHINE TOOLS. Production of these, as everybody knows, is the key to all great modern war machines. In 1939 Germany surpassed every other great power, including the United States, in its supply of machine tools and its capacity to manufacture them. Today, despite some bomb damage to the industry, Germany has more than 4,000,000 tons of machine tools on hand and a vast undamaged plant to produce more.

It is plain, therefore, that unless the Allies do something about it, Germany in five years can become again a great military power, able to produce more deadly machines of war than she turned out for a war that almost destroyed the rest of the world. It will not solve the problem to propose, as many more or less innocent souls in Britain and America do, that this great German industrial plant be put back to work to produce for the prosperity of Europe. That is, it will not do if you leave the control of this vast plant in German hands. For if you do, you automatically guarantee Germany's military power.

My own feeling is that some of the plant should be removed to the liberated lands as compensation for the destruction visited upon them by the Nazis. As for the heart of German industry, which lies in the Ruhr and Rhineland, this should be placed under permanent international control and its superb production facilities made to work not only for the Germans but for all of Europe.[17] We should never again allow it to become the basis of Germany's ability to wage gigantic wars.

I wish I had the time to get down here some of the fantastic tales our economic and financial experts tell: of American businessmen suddenly turning up in army uniform to reclaim their factories or acquire new ones; of AMG officers sabotaging the job of getting the Nazis out of the big-business posts. (They tell of a certain American lieutenant colonel in Württemberg who stoutly declares that our official denazification policy will drive the Germans to Communism and who therefore opposes our denazification whenever he can.)

The story of I.G. Farben, the world's greatest chemical trust, which not only furnished Hitler with the materials to make war but carried on a gigantic economic and political warfare against the rest of the world, is gradually being ferreted out by our American investigators. It would make a fascinating book, but is too vast a story even to attempt to summarize here.

Perhaps, also, it is too strong stuff to be published at home, for I.G. Farben had many connections with big American corporations, and according to the evidence so far uncovered (including the testimony of various I.G. directors) made monkeys out of some of our leading businessmen. It obtained from the latter some of the most vital secret processes for such essentials to modern war as lead tetraethyl while at the same time refusing, on the advice of the Wehrmacht, to give us in return some of *its* secrets, such as the buna process for making synthetic rubber—a product that was to become a life-and-death matter for our country in 1941.

Berlin, *Tuesday, November* 13

Lunch with Bob Murphy in a very charming villa he has taken over. Somehow, we never got around to talking much about what is going on here. Afterward a long talk with General Lucius Clay, deputy military governor, a most competent administrator. His latest headache, he said, was the refusal of the French to set up central German administrations in Berlin. He has many other headaches, of course. The magnificent American Army which landed on the Normandy beaches and swept to the Elbe in less than a year is deteriorating at a frightening pace. Officers and men have but one thought: to get back home. Those who stay are pretty inferior. They know nothing of Germany or Germans and they are not fit to govern our zone. Too many of them have already been taken in by German propaganda. Few of them have the faintest idea of what Nazism was. Most of them therefore either are opposed to denazification, even though it is a military order that they are supposed to carry out, or are uninterested in doing anything about it. Their passion for "creature comforts" is tremendous. They think of little else....

Afterward, at X's, perused a somewhat startling document. The British had proposed a list of suitable Germans for responsible positions in the information setup of the planned central German authority. This group will be largely responsible for the future of the German press, the theater, movies, music, and art in the new Reich. The British had proposed some fifty German names and my American friends had been assigned to check up on them. The first forty-nine were all Nazi Party members!

I've found Hilda, who saved my neck on many an occasion when I was here during the war. Though as Aryan as they come, she had fallen in love with a Jew, who had escaped to a neighboring country. When it was overrun by the Germans, she gave him up for dead. I have promised to try to find out for her if the man is alive, as soon as I get out of this country. It was good to see her again and to be reminded that there are Germans of noble character, capable of every sacrifice for fellow human beings, able to distinguish evil when they see it, and brimming with courage. She had sustained me at many moments when hope seemed lost. She had fantastic tales to recount here....

Berlin, *Wednesday, November* 14

Here in the ruins of the capital of the conquered Reich one can see the end of the Road to War that Hitler took. But how did it begin? How did he proceed? Was there ever a thought of turning back? Did he, from the start, know his goal and realize that war—war against the world—was the only means of attaining it? Did the others in high position in Germany? If so, did they ever try to halt their mad genius? And, once embarked on war, did the Germans themselves ever realize where the turning-point came, and when, and why?

This day, I believe, I have found the complete answers to such questions. History can no longer have any doubts. For the Germans, with true Teutonic thoroughness, wrote everything down and now we have captured their secret archives—fourteen hundred tons of them, at least. I have spent much time the last few days wading through them, the ones that tell the story of Germany's Road to War. They would fill several fascinating volumes. But one can get down here, perhaps, a few of the more important documents, thus leaving it to the Germans themselves to tell their own story in their own way of how the German war came, what it aimed to achieve, and why it was lost. The principal recorder here—as will be seen—is the man who was largely responsible for the war, Adolf Hitler. Is it not fitting that he himself should unfold most of the story?

I should start, I suppose, with *Mein Kampf*. Hitler did not hide his aims in his book. But what he said in it is already known, though few on our side paid any attention until too late. We have to do today with the secret documents.

We might start with September 30, 1934, a year and a half after Hitler came to power. On that date Dr. Schacht, who in Nuremberg is now cursing the Allies for daring to try him as a war criminal, submits to Hitler a secret "Report on the State of Preparation for War-Economic Mobilization." Schacht, as Minister of Economy, is enthusiastic and realistic about his job. Eight months later, on May 3, 1935, he writes another memo to the Führer. "The execution of the armament program," he says, "is, by its speed and extent, *the*[18] mission of German policy, and everything else must be subordinated to this purpose."

One skips a wealth of material, which the historians can deal with in due time, to a document dated November 5, 1937. On that day Hitler called to the Reich Chancellery in Berlin his top military men, Field Marshal von Blomberg, the Minister of War, Colonel General von Fritsch, commander-in-chief of the army, Admiral Dr. Raeder, commander-in-chief of the navy, Colonel General Göring, commander-in-chief of the air force and von Neurath, the Foreign Minister.

Colonel Hossbach, Hitler's aide, was also present and drew up the minutes of the meeting. Those minutes I have just now read. They show that after Hitler had harangued his leading military and political advisers for four hours and fifteen minutes—from 4.15 p.m. to 8.30 p.m.—they could have had no more doubts that he had chosen irrevocably the road to war. Hitler himself considered his statement so important, Hossbach noted, that he requested it to "be looked upon in the case of his death as his last will and testament."

Here is the essential part of the remarkable document:

Berlin, November 10, 1937

Notes on the Conference in the Reich Chancellery on November 5, '37 from 1615 to 2030 hours

PRESENT: The Führer [etc.]

The Führer stated:

…The German future is dependent exclusively on the solution of the need for living-space. Such a solution can be sought naturally only for a limited period, about 1-3 generations.

Before touching upon the question of solving the need for living-space, it must be decided whether a solution of the German position with a good future can be attained either by way of an autarchy or by way of an increased share in universal commerce and industry.

Autarchy:

A. In the sphere of raw materials, only limited, but NOT total autarchy can be attained.…

B. In the case of foods, the question of an autarchy must be answered with a definite "NO." …

…Consequently autarchy becomes impossible, specifically in the sphere of food supplies as well as generally.

Participation in World Economy: There are limits to this that we are unable to transgress. The market fluctuations would be an obstacle to a secure foundation of the German position; international commercial agreements do NOT offer any guarantee for practical execution.…

…The only way out, and one that may appear imaginary, is the securing of greater living-space, an endeavor that at all times has been the cause of the formation of stakes and of movements of nations. Should the security of our food position be our foremost thought, then the space required for this can only be sought in Europe, for we will not copy liberal capitalist policies, which rely on exploiting colonies. It is NOT a case of conquering people, but of conquering agriculturally useful space. It would also be more to the purpose to seek raw-material-producing territory in Europe directly adjoining the Reich and not overseas, and this solution would have to be brought into effect in one or two generations. The history of all times—Roman Empire, British Empire—has proved that every space expansion can only be effected by breaking resistance and taking risks. Even setbacks are unavoidable; neither formerly nor today has space been found without an owner; the attacker always comes, up against the proprietor.

The question for Germany is where the greatest possible conquest can be made at lowest cost.[19]

German politics must reckon with its two hateful enemies, England and France, to whom a strong German colossus in the center of Europe would be intolerable. Both these states would oppose a further reinforcement of Germany, both in Europe and overseas, and in this opposition they would have the support of all parties....

England is NOT in a position to cede any of her colonial possessions to us owing to the resistance that she experiences in the Dominions.... A serious discussion regarding the return of colonies to us could be considered only at a time when England is in a state of emergency and the German Reich is strong and well armed. The Führer does not share the opinion that the Empire is unshakable....

France's position is more favorable than that of England. The French Empire is better placed geographically, the population of its colonial possessions represents a potential military increase. But France is faced with difficulties of internal politics. At the present time only 10 per cent approximately of the nations have parliamentary governments whereas 90 per cent of them have totalitarian governments. Nevertheless we have to take the following into our political considerations as power factors:

Britain, France, Russia, and the adjoining smaller states.

The German question can be solved only by way of force, and this is never without risk. The battles of Frederick the Great for Silesia, and Bismarck's wars against Austria and France were a tremendous risk, and the speed of Prussian action in 1810 prevented Austria from participating in the war. If we place the decision to apply force with risk at the head of the following expositions, then we are left to reply to the questions "when" and "how." In this regard we have to decide upon three different cases.

Case 1. Period 1943-5. After this we can only expect a change for the worse. The rearming of the army, the navy, and the air force, as well as the formation of the officers' corps, are practically concluded. Our material equipment and armaments are modern; with further delay the danger of their becoming out of date will increase. In particular the secrecy of "special weapons" cannot always be safeguarded....

In comparison with the rearmament, which will have been carried out at that time by the other nations, we shall decrease in relative power. Should we not act until 1943-5; then, dependent on the absence of reserves, any year could bring about the food crisis, for the countering of which we do NOT possess the necessary foreign currency. This must be considered as a "point of weakness in the regime." Over and above that, the world will anticipate our action and will increase countermeasures yearly.

What the actual position would be in the years 1943—5 no one knows today. It is certain, however, that we can wait no longer.

On the one side the large armed forces, with the necessity for securing their upkeep, the aging of the Nazi movement and of its leaders, and on the other side the prospect of a lowering of the standard of living and a drop in the birth rate, leaves us no other choice than to act. If the Führer is still living, then it will be his irrevocable decisions to solve the German space problem no later than 1943-5. The necessity for action before 1943-5 will come under consideration in Cases 2 and 3.

*Case 2.*Should the social tensions in France lead to an internal political crisis of such dimensions that it absorbs the French Army and thus renders it incapable for employment in war against Germany, then the time for action against Czechoslovakia has come.

Case 3. It would be equally possible to act against Czechoslovakia if France should be so tied up by a war against another state that it cannot "proceed" against Germany.

For the improvement of our military political position it must be our first aim, in every case of entanglement by war, to conquer Czechoslovakia and Austria simultaneously, in order to remove any threat from the flanks in case of a possible advance westwards…. Once Czechoslovakia is conquered—and a mutual frontier, Germany-Hungary is obtained— then a neutral attitude by Poland in a German-French conflict could more easily be relied upon….

Assuming a development of the situation that would lead to a planned attack on our part in the years 1943-5, then the behavior of France, Poland, and Russia would probably have to be judged in the following manner:

The Führer believes personally that in all probability England and perhaps also France have already silently written off Czechoslovakia, and that they have got used to the idea that this question would one day be cleaned up by Germany. The difficulties in the British Empire and the prospect of being entangled in another long-drawn-out European war were decisive factors in the non-participation of England in a war against Germany. The British attitude would certainly NOT remain without influence on France's attitude. An attack by France without British support is hardly probable assuming that its offensive would stagnate along our western fortifications. Without England's support, it would also NOT be necessary to take into consideration a march by France through Belgium and Holland….

Naturally, we should in every case have to bar our frontier during the operation of our attacks against Czechoslovakia and Austria…. Although the population of Czechoslovakia in the first place is not a thin one, the embodiment of Czechoslovakia and Austria would nevertheless constitute the conquest of food for 5-6 million people, on the basis that a compulsory emigration of 2 million from Czechoslovakia and of 1 million from Austria could be carried out. The annexation of the two states to Germany militarily and politically would constitute a considerable relief, owing to shorter and better frontiers, the freeing of fighting personnel for other purposes, and the possibility of reconstituting new armies up to a strength of about 12 divisions, representing a new division per 1 million population.

No opposition to the removal of Czechoslovakia is expected on the part of Italy; however, it cannot be judged today what would be her attitude in the Austrian question since it would depend largely on whether the Duce were alive at the time or not.

The measure and speed of our action would decide Poland's attitude. Poland will have little inclination to enter the war against a victorious Germany, with Russia in its rear.

Military participation by Russia must be countered by the speed of our operations; it is a question whether this need be taken into consideration at all in view of Japan's attitude.

Should Case 2 occur—paralyzation of France by a civil war—then the situation should be utilized *at any time*[20]for operations against Czechoslovakia.

The Führer sees Case 3 looming nearer; it could develop from the existing tensions in the Mediterranean, and should it occur he has firmly decided to make use of it any time, perhaps even as early as 1938.

What Hitler means, he explains to his chieftains at this point, is that the civil war in Spain may well bring on a conflict between Great Britain and Italy in the Mediterranean. That is why, he emphasizes, a "100 per cent victory by Franco is not desirable, from the German point of view. We are more interested in a continuation of the war and preservation of the tensions in the Mediterranean." Why? So that these tensions will provoke an Italo-British war, and perhaps draw France into it too.

If Germany profits from this war by disposing of the Czechoslovakian and the Austrian questions, the probability must be assumed that England—being at war with Italy—would not decide to commence operations against Germany. Without British support a warlike action by France against Germany is not to be anticipated.

The date of our attack on Czechoslovakia and Austria must be made dependent on the course of the Italian-English-French war; …by exploiting this unique favorable opportunity he wishes to begin to carry out operations against Czechoslovakia. The attack on Czechoslovakia would have to take place with the "speed of lightning" (*blitzartig schnell*).

This is only 1937, remember, and a top German general this early in the game still dares to question the Führer's genius. Both Field Marshal von Blomberg and General von Fritsch, the notes disclose, proceed at this point to cast some doubts on Hitler's estimate of the military factors involved.

> They stated that the war with Italy would NOT bind the French Army to such an extent that it would NOT be in a position to commence operations on our western frontier with superior forces. General von Fritsch estimated the French forces that would presumably be employed on the Alpine frontier against Italy to be in the region of twenty divisions, so that a strong French superiority would still remain on our western frontier. The French, according to German reasoning, would attempt to advance into the Rhineland. We should consider the lead that France has got in mobilization, and quite apart from the very small value of our existing fortifications—which was pointed out particularly by von Blomberg—the four motorized divisions that had been laid down for the west would be more or less incapable of movement. With regard to our offensive in a southeasterly direction, von Blomberg draws special attention to the strength of the Czechoslovakian fortifications, the building of which had assumed the character of a Maginot Line and which would present extreme difficulties to our attack.

Not only the generals disagree with Hitler, but even Foreign Minister von Neurath summons up enough courage to tell the Führer that an "Italian-English-French conflict is not as near as the Führer appears to assume." But Hitler will not listen to him. He sees this war as a distinct possibility by "summer, 1938." As to the curious views of his generals—

> The Führer repeated his previous statements and said that he was convinced of Britain's non-participation and that consequently he did not believe in military action by France against Germany. Should the Mediterranean conflict already mentioned lead to a general mobilization in Europe, then we should have to commence operations against Czechoslovakia immediately....
>
> The second part of the discussion concerned material armament questions.
>
> [*Signed*] HOSSBACH

Thus for Hitler's Germany (and for the world, though it didn't know it), the die was cast on November 5, 1937. Germany would go to war for additional "living-space." To wait much longer would be to her disadvantage. Perhaps war would come in the following summer of 1938. It could not come "later than 1943-5."

We pass over (though I hope to return to them) Hitler's plans for war against Austria and Czechoslovakia. Both countries fell without a war, though in each case Hitler was determined to take them even if it meant a European armed conflict. (We must revise our judgment that Munich was a bluff. It was not. Hitler *preferred*to begin his war then.)

We come, then, to the fateful year of 1939. On March 15 the Germans had seized the rest of Czechoslovakia. At Easter, Poland feared it might momentarily be the next victim. On May 23 Hitler again convoked his generals and admirals to the Reich Chancellery. Poland would be attacked "at the first suitable opportunity," he announced. And this time, he warned his followers, there would be war. We have the minutes of this meeting, kept by Hitler's adjutant, Lieutenant Colonel G. S. Schmundt. They read as follows:

TOP SECRET
TO BE TRANSMITTED BY OFFICER ONLY
Minutes of a Conference on May 23, 1939

*Place:*The Führer's study, New Reich Chancellery.

Adjutant on duty: Lt.-Col. (G.S.) Schmundt.

Present: The Führer, Field Marshal Göring, Grand Admiral Raeder, Col.-Gen. von Brauchitsch, Col.-Gen. Keitel, Col.-Gen. Milch, Gen. (of Artillery) Halder, Gen. Bodenschatz, Rear-Adml. Schniewindt, Col. (G.S.) Jeschonnek, Col. (G.S.) Warlimont, Lt.-Col. (G.S.) Schmundt, Capt. Engel (Army), Lieut.-Comd. Albrecht, Capt. v. Below (Army).

*Subject:*Indoctrination on the political situation and future aims.

The Führer's observations are given in systematized form below.

Our present situation must be considered from two points of view:

1. The actual development of events between 1933 and 1939;
2. The permanent and unchanging situation in which Germany lies.
   In the period 1933-9 progress was made in all fields. Our military situation improved enormously.
   Our situation with regard to the rest of the world has remained the same....

A mass of 80 million people has solved the ideological problems. So, too, must the economic problems be solved. No German can evade the creation of the necessary economic conditions for this. The solution of the problems demands courage. The principle by which one evades solving the problems by adapting oneself to circumstances is inadmissible. Circumstances must rather be adapted to aims. *This is impossible without invasion of foreign states or attacks upon foreign property.*[21]

Living space, in proportion to the magnitude of the state, is the basis of all power. One may refuse for a time to face the problem, but finally it is solved one way or another. The choice is between advancement and decline. In 15 or 20 years' time we shall be compelled to find a solution. No German statesman can evade the question longer than that.

We are at present in a state of patriotic fervor, which is shared by two other nations: Italy and Japan.

After 6 years the situation is today as follows:

The national-political unity of the Germans has been achieved, apart from minor exceptions· *Further success cannot be attained without the shedding of blood.*

The Pole is no "supplementary enemy." Poland will always be on the side of our adversaries. In spite of treaties of friendship, Poland has always had the secret intention of exploiting every opportunity to do us harm.

Danzig is not the subject of the dispute at all. It is a question of expanding our living-space in the east and of securing our food supplies, of the settlement of the Baltic problems. Food supplies can be expected only from thinly populated areas. Over and above the natural fertility, thoroughgoing German exploitation will enormously increase the surplus.

There is no other possibility for Europe.

Colonies: Beware of gifts of colonial territory. This does not solve the food problem. Remember—blockade.

If fate brings us into conflict with the west, possession of extensive areas in the east will be advantageous. Upon record harvests we shall be able to rely even less in time of war than in peace.

The population of non-German areas will perform no military service, and will be available as a source of labor.

The Polish problem is inseparable from conflict with the west.

Poland's internal power of resistance to Bolshevism is doubtful. Thus Poland is of doubtful value as a barrier against Russia.

It is questionable whether military success in the west can be achieved by a quick decision, questionable too is the attitude of Poland.

The Polish government will not resist pressure from Russia. Poland sees danger in a German victory in the west, and will attempt to rob us of the victory.

There is therefore no question of sparing Poland, and we are left with the decision:

To attack Poland at the first suitable opportunity.[22]

We cannot expect a repetition of the Czech affair. *There will be war.* Our task is to isolate Poland. The success of the isolation will be decisive.

Therefore, the Führer must reserve the right to give the final order to attack. There must be no simultaneous conflict with the western powers (France and England).

If it is not certain that a German-Polish conflict will not lead to war in the west, then the fight must be primarily against England and France.

Fundamentally, therefore: Conflict with Poland—beginning with an attack on Poland—will only be successful if the western powers keep out of it. If this is impossible, then it will be better to attack in the west and to settle Poland at the same time.

Japan is a weighty problem. Even if at first for various reasons her collaboration with us appears to be somewhat cool and restricted, it is nevertheless in Japan's own interest to take the initiative in attacking Russia in good time.

Economic relations with Russia are possible only if political relations have improved. A cautious trend is evident in press comment. It is not impossible that Russia will show herself to be disinterested in the destruction of Poland. Should Russia take steps to oppose us, our relations with Japan may become closer.

If there were an alliance of France, England, and Russia against Germany, Italy, and Japan, I would be constrained to attack England and France with a few annihilating blows. The Führer doubts the possibility of a peaceful settlement with England. We must prepare ourselves for the conflict. England sees in our development the foundation of a hegemony that would weaken England. England is therefore our enemy, and the conflict with England will be a life-and-death struggle. What will this struggle be like?

England cannot deal with Germany and subjugate us with a few powerful blows. It is imperative for England that the war should be brought as near to the Ruhr Basin as possible. French blood will be spared (West Wall). The possession of the Ruhr Basin will determine the duration of our resistance.

The Dutch and Belgian air bases must be occupied by armed force. Declarations of neutrality must be ignored. If England and France intend the war between Germany and Poland to lead to a conflict, they will support Holland and Belgium in their neutrality and make them build fortifications, in order finally to force them into co-operation.

Albeit under protest, Belgium and Holland will yield to pressure.

Therefore, if England intends to intervene in the Polish war, we must occupy Holland with lightning speed. We must aim at securing a new defense line on Dutch soil up to the Zuider Zee.

The war with England and France will be a life-and-death struggle.

The idea that we can get off cheaply is dangerous; there is no such possibility. We must burn our boats, and it is no longer a question of justice or injustice, but of life or death for 80 million human beings.

Question: Short or long war?

Every country's armed forces or government must aim at a short war. The government, however, must also be prepared for a war of 10-15 years' duration.

History has always shown that the people have believed that wars would be short. In 1914 the opinion still prevailed that it was impossible to finance a long war. Even today this idea still persists in many minds. But, on the contrary, every state will hold out as long as possible, unless it immediately suffers some grave weakening (e.g., Ruhr Basin). England has similar weaknesses.

England knows that to lose a war will mean the end of her world power.

England is the driving force against Germany. Her strength lies in the following:

1. The British themselves are proud, courageous, tenacious, firm in resistance, and gifted as organizers. They know how to exploit every new development. They have the love of adventure and bravery of the Nordic race. Quality is lowered by dispersal. The German average is higher.

2. World power in itself. It has been constant for 300 years. Extended by the acquisition of allies. This power is not merely something concrete, but must also be considered as a psychological force, embracing the entire world. Add to this immeasurable wealth, with consequential financial credit.

3. Geopolitical safety and protection by strong sea power and a courageous air force.

England's weaknesses:

If in World War I we had had two battleships and two cruisers more, and if the Battle of Jutland had begun in the morning, the British fleet would have been defeated and England brought to her knees. It would have meant the end of world war. It was formerly not sufficient to defeat the fleet; landings had to be made in order to defeat England. England could provide her own food supplies. Today that is no longer possible.

The moment England's food-supply routes are cut, she is forced to capitulate. The import of food and fuel depends on the fleet's protection.

If the German Air Force attacks English territory, England will not be forced to capitulate in one day. But if the fleet is destroyed, immediate capitulation will be the result.

There is no doubt that a surprise attack can lead to a quick decision. It would be criminal, however, for the government to rely entirely on the element of surprise....

The final date for striking must be fixed well in advance. Beyond that time the tension cannot be endured for long....

An effort must be made to deal the enemy a significant or the final decisive blow right at the start. Considerations of right and wrong, or treaties, do not enter into the matter.

In addition to the surprise attack, preparations for a long war must be made, while opportunities on the Continent for England are eliminated.

The army will have to hold positions essential to the navy and air force. If Holland and Belgium are successfully occupied and held, and if France is also defeated, the fundamental conditions for a successful war against England will have been secured.

England can then be blockaded from western France at close quarters by the air force while the navy with its submarines can extend the range of the blockade. Consequences:

England will not be able to fight on the Continent;

Daily attacks by the air force and navy will cut all her lifelines;

Time will not be on England's side;

Germany will not bleed to death on land.

Such strategy has been shown to be necessary by World War I and subsequent military operations. World War I is responsible for the following strategic considerations, which are imperative:

1. With a more powerful navy at the outbreak of the war, or a wheeling movement by the army toward the Channel ports, the end would have been different.

2. A country cannot be brought to defeat by an air force. It is impossible to attack all objectives simultaneously, and the lapse of time of a few minutes would evoke defensive countermeasures.

3. The unrestricted use of all resources is essential.

4. Once the army, in co-operation with the air force and the navy, has taken the most important positions, industrial production will cease to flow into the bottomless pit of the army's battles and can be diverted to benefit the air force and navy....

The aim will always be to force England to her knees....

We shall not be forced into a war, but we shall not be able to avoid one.

Secrecy is the decisive requirement for success. Our object must be kept secret even from Italy or Japan....

Certified correct record
(*Sgd*) SCHMUNDT, Lt.-Col.

So on May 23, 1939, Hitler burns his bridges. Peace is doomed. Further success cannot be obtained, he says, "without the shedding of blood." Good, it will be shed against Poland "at the first suitable opportunity." Danzig has nothing to do with the war at all. Germany needs living-space in the east. While getting it, the Reich will settle with the west as well. England is the real enemy of Germany there. She must be forced to her knees!

Note that the whole plan for the war in the *west* as it was actually carried out a year later is outlined by the mad Führer (No matter that in London the complacent Chamberlain does not know it, does not suspect it, and that in Washington the venerable Senator Borah says he knows, from his own special sources of information in Europe, that there will be no war.)

All through the late spring and the summer the finishing touches are put to the Nazi war machine. In Moscow the British and French representatives dawdle with the Russians. Do not Chamberlain and Daladier still hope that German aggression may yet be turned on Russia so that the civilized west will be saved? Before June is up, General Keitel, chief of the Supreme Command of the Armed Forces, submits the timetable for "Operation White"—against Poland. We have these interesting documents, but there is no space for them here.

August, the fateful month, arrives. It is time to let the ally, Italy, in on the secret, for she has a role to play in Hitler's calculations. Count Ciano is summoned to Berchtesgaden. Stunned at what he hears from the Führer's lips, he remains there two days, August 12 and 13. We have the German records of the two-day meeting. They are remarkable on several accounts. They show that Hitler has now picked his date for the attack on Poland, that he is ready for war with the west, that he has Russia in the bag (though the world will not learn of it for ten days), and that Ciano and Mussolini are taken completely by surprise. They obviously had no idea that war was so near. Ciano comes out in this meeting better than I expected. He talks up to Hitler. He tells him bluntly that Italy is not ready for war. And he stands up to the Führer and argues for peace—indeed, proposing instead of war a peace conference!

The secret German minutes of the two meetings of Hitler and Ciano on August 12 and 13, 1939, read (with a few deletions of unimportant details) as follows:

Minutes of the conference between the Führer and the Italian Minister for Foreign Affairs, Count Ciano, in the presence of the Reich Foreign Minister at Obersalzberg on August 12, 1939.

At the beginning of the conference the Führer with the aid of maps explained to Count Ciano the present situation of Germany from the military standpoint. He emphasized particularly the strength of the German fortifications in the west. There are three break-through points in the west at which the French had in former times always attempted to break through for geographical and strategic reasons, which have now been protected with particular care, so that a break-through seems impossible....

The third possibility of attacking Germany is a blockade by the British Navy. But it must be kept in mind that ships used for the blockade would be attacked from the air from Germany, since all of England is within the radius of attack of the German Air Force, because of the long range of the latest German bombers. There are no further possibilities of attack on Germany. The Nordic countries would no doubt remain neutral and are safe from air attack from any side, since there is hardly any question of occupying such large areas as Norway and Sweden. In the same way Switzerland would certainly defend her neutrality to the last against any invader.

Germany has likewise built strong fortifications in the east.... Of course the capital (Berlin) is exposed to air attacks, since it lies only 150 km. from the Polish border....

Proceeding to the military situation of the western powers and Poland, the Führer again pointed out England's vulnerability from the air. Although some progress has been made in aircraft production, the anti-aircraft defense is still quite backward.... Moreover, London and other great cities and industrial centers have the same disadvantage that character-izes Berlin's position in regard to Polish air attacks: from high altitude, out of range of the present English AA guns which are left from the [first World] war, bombing can be carried out in absolute safety, which would be successful in any case in the general target area.

At the present time England has no increase in sea power to record. The first units of the ships under construction cannot be put in service for some time. As for the land army, 60,000 men have been called up since the introduction of compulsory military service. If England keeps the necessary troops at home, she will be in a position to put at the disposal of France only two infantry divisions and one armored division. Furthermore, she can transfer a few groups of bombers to France but hardly any groups of fighters, since the German air fleet would attack England immediately upon the outbreak of war, and the English fighter planes would be urgently needed for the protection of their own country.

In regard to France's situation—the Führer said that in a general conflict after the expected conquest, within a short time, of Poland, Germany would be in a position to assemble 100 divisions at the West Wall, which would force France to assemble all available forces from the colonies, from the Italian border and elsewhere at the Maginot Line for the life-and-death struggle that would then begin. Moreover, it is his opinion that the French cannot overrun the Italian fortifications any more than the West Wall.

At this point Count Ciano showed signs of extreme doubt.[23]

The Polish Army varies greatly in its value. Besides several crack divisions there are a number of inferior units. Poland is very weak in AA and anti-tank defense. At present France and England cannot supply her. If, however, Poland is supported economically for a considerable period of time by the west, she could acquire these weapons, and Germany's superiority would be reduced. The fanatics of Warsaw and Cracow are opposed by the indifferent peasant population of other districts.... Under these circumstances, Poland would be conquered by Germany in a very short time.

As Poland makes it clear by her whole attitude that in case of conflict she will in any event be on the side of the enemies of Germany and Italy, quick liquidation at this moment would only be of advantage *for the unavoidable conflict with the western democracies. Generally speaking, it would be best to liquidate the pseudo-neutrals one after another.* This is fairly easily done, if one Axis partner protects the rear of the other, who is just finishing off one of the uncertain neutrals, and vice versa. Italy may consider Yugoslavia such an uncertain neutral.... Among the Balkan countries the Axis can completely rely on Bulgaria, which is in a sense a natural ally of Italy and Germany. That is why Germany has supported Bulgaria as much as possible with supplies of weapons and will continue to do so. Yugoslavia would stay neutral only as long as it would be dangerous to take the side of the western democracies openly. At the moment when there would be a turn for the worse for Germany and Italy, however, Yugoslavia would join the other side openly, hoping thereby to give matters a final turn to the disadvantage of the Axis. Rumania is afraid of Hungary and is militarily very weak and internally corrupt. King Carol would doubtless not give up his neutrality unless absolutely necessary.

Hungary is friendly and Slovakia is under German influence and even has German garrisons in some parts.

Returning to the question of Danzig, the Führer explained to Count Ciano that it is impossible to yield on this point.... Danzig, the Nordic Nuremberg, is an old German city, which awakens sentimental feelings in every German, and just this psychological element forces the Führer to respect public opinion. To make the situation easier to understand for an Italian, Count Ciano should imagine that Trieste is in the hands of Yugoslavia and a strong Italian minority on Yugoslavian territory is being treated with brutal force. It can hardly be supposed that Italy would look on calmly for very long. [*Recall that on May 25 Hitler told his generals flatly that "Danzig is not the subject of the dispute at all."*—W. L. S.]

Count Ciano replied to the Führer's explanations by first pointing out the great surprise among the Italians at the absolutely unexpected seriousness of the situation. Neither in the Milan conversations nor in the talks on the occasion of his visit to Berlin was any indication given by the Germans that the situation with regard to Poland was so serious. On the contrary, the Reich Foreign Minister had declared that in his opinion the question of Danzig would be settled in the course of time. On the basis of this state of affairs, the Duce, true to his conviction that a conflict with the western democracies was unavoidable, decided to make his preparations for that eventuality, and made his plans for a certain period of time of 2 to 3 years. If a conflict is unavoidable now, Italy would of course be on Germany's side, as the Duce reemphasized just before Count Ciano's departure, but for various reasons, enumerated in detail, *Italy would welcome a postponement of the general conflict.*

Count Ciano then explained, with the aid of a map, the Italian position at the outbreak of a general conflict. *Italy believes, he said, that a conflict with Poland would not be restricted to that country, but would grow into a general European war.*

The Führer remarked that opinions differ on that point. He personally is firmly convinced that the western democracies will in the end shy away from precipitating a general war.

Count Ciano replied that he hoped the Führer was right, but he did not believe it. In any case, one should adapt one's reflections to the worst possibility—i.e., to general conflict. Since the Abyssinian conflict Italy has actually been constantly living in a state of war and therefore urgently needs a breathing-spell. Count Ciano proved with the aid of figures how great Italy's material effort had been, especially in the Spanish conflict. Italy's stock of raw materials is now exhausted. She needs time to restock her warehouses.

She must also transfer her war industries, all of which are in an exposed location, to the south, in order to be better able to defend them. In the same way the Italian artillery, particularly the AA defense, is greatly in need of modernization. The long coast line and other exposed points are not sufficiently defended.

The strength of the fleet is also extremely unfavorable. At the moment Italy can put against the combined English and French 11 to 12 battleships only 2 of its own, while in a few years a total of 8 battleships will be available.

At this point the Führer remarked that of course England and France will have additional battleships of 35,000 and 40,000 tons.

Count Ciano pointed out the long Italian coast line, which is hard to defend, and the numerous bases at the disposal of the English and French fleets, giving particular attention to the Greek ports.

The Italian colonies are especially vulnerable at present…. Though Abyssinia is almost pacified, with the exception of certain regions along the border of the English territory, where the English create difficulties among the population with their money and propaganda, this pacification is only on the surface. It would be sufficient, in a general conflict for a few English airplanes to drop leaflets over Abyssinia, saying that the world had risen against Italy and that the Negus would return, to make the revolt of the Abyssinians flare up again. Besides, Abyssinia would be cut off completely from the motherland in case of a conflict, and the fate of the 200,000 Italians in Abyssinia would be very uncertain....

Italy has plans of economic autarchy that cannot be realized for several years and that would then put Italy in a position to withstand even a prolonged war without difficulties. Another reason for the Duce's desire to postpone the conflict is the Italians abroad, who are to be brought back to Italy according to plan.

Besides, the Duce personally attaches great importance to the World's Fair in 1942, for which Italy has made big preparations and from which she hopes for good results in the economic field, especially as regards the inflow of foreign currency.

Besides these considerations, which are based on Italy's position, there are others of a general political nature that recommend postponement of a general conflict. The Duce is convinced that the encirclement system of the western democracies would doubtless work at the present time. But after a certain length of time the points of friction and the seeds of disunity would come to the fore among the partners of the encirclement front, and the front would gradually disintegrate.

Moreover, the Duce is convinced that the present enthusiasm in England and France will not last very long. Soon, particularly in France, the *union sacrée* will once more be replaced by party discord, on condition that the Axis keeps quiet for a time. At the present time it is only due to the Axis that internal differences have been buried in the respective countries.

Japan's position would also be much stronger after the termination of the China conflict, which is to be expected in two years, while Roosevelt's position in America would be seriously weakened after a period of calm in the field of foreign policies, so that he could not be elected President for a third time, which would certainly be the case if a conflict should break out soon.

Spain, which has just acquired a government friendly to the Axis, needs peace after the civil war, but would stand at the side of the Axis in 2 to 3 years as a power not to be neglected. Thus, for example, within 2 years Spain would build 4 battleships of 35,000 tons each, the plans for which have just been taken to Spain by an Italian general. The construction is to take place in El Ferrol.

For these reasons the Duce insists that the Axis powers should make a gesture that would emphasize anew the will for peace of Italy and Germany. This could be done by the publication of a communiqué that Count Ciano had given to the Reich Foreign Minister on the previous day and that he now presented again….

Count Ciano said in connection with this tentative communiqué that the Duce had at first contemplated a proposal for a conference, but conscious of the Führer's misgivings, he now makes another suggestion in a milder form and is very much interested in its acceptance.

The Führer declared concerning the conference plan that in future meetings of the powers it will not be possible to exclude Russia. In the German-Russian conversations the Russians had made it plain, with reference to Munich and other occasions from which they had been excluded, that they would not tolerate this any more….

Count Ciano replied that the Duce is of the opinion that the one who wins at a conference is the one who is ready to let the conference fail if necessary and to accept war as a possible result. Moreover, the Duce took the Führer's misgivings into consideration and modified his proposal…. The suggested gesture of Germany and Italy represents a face-saving way out for the western powers, which they will certainly use, for there are wide circles that warn against war and that would be backed up by a peace gesture. This means, however, that Poland, which would doubtless be abandoned by the western powers, would be isolated after a time and would have to agree to reasonable solutions of the existing difficulties.

The Führer replied that there was no time to be lost in the solution of the Polish problem. The farther we get into fall, the harder military operations in the east of Europe will be. *Count Ciano asked by what time the question of Danzig would have to be settled, in the Führer's opinion. The Führer replied that this question would have to be settled one way or the other by the end of August.…* In the long run it is unbearable for a big power to tolerate such a hostile neighbor at a distance of only 150 km. from its capital. *The Führer is therefore determined to use the opportunity of the next political provocation, in the form of an ultimatum, brutal mistreatments of Germans, an attempt to starve out Danzig, or something similar, to attack Poland within 48 hours and to solve the problem in this way.…*

Count Ciano asked when such an undertaking against Poland was to be expected, since Italy must of course prepare for all eventualities. *The Führer replied that under the prevailing circumstances an attack on Poland was to be expected at any moment.*

A telegram from Moscow and one from Tokyo were handed to the Führer during this exchange of opinions. The conference was interrupted for a short time, and then Count Ciano was informed of the contents of the Moscow telegram. The Russians agreed to the sending of a German political mediator to Moscow. The Reich Foreign Minister added that the Russians were completely informed about Germany's intentions against Poland. He himself had informed the Russian chargé d'affaires, by order of the Führer.

The Führer remarked that in his opinion Russia would not be willing to pull chestnuts out of the fire for the western powers. Stalin's position is endangered as much by a victorious Russian Army as by a defeated Russian Army. Russia is, at the most, interested in enlarging her access to the Baltic a little. Germany has no objection to that. Besides, Russia would hardly take the part of Poland, whom she hates from the bottom of her heart. The sending of the English-French military mission to Moscow has only the purpose of averting the catastrophic state of political negotiations.

After further discussion of the communiqué proposed by Count Ciano, the Führer said that he wanted to think over for a day, this proposal as well as Count Ciano's explanation of the general situation, and he therefore suggested that the discussion be resumed the next day.

Salzburg, August 12, 1939
[*Signed*] SCHMIDT

It was.

Hitler tries to appear conciliatory with the frightened Italian messenger boy, but it is evident from the German minutes of this second meeting that his mind is made up. He will not only attack Poland in a fortnight but he will make this first conquest by German arms the beginning of his larger strategical action the goal of which is nothing less than the occupation of the East and the smashing of the West—that is, the conquest of Europe. As for Italy, he holds out a most attractive bait. The Italians can replace the British in the Mediterranean.

The essential part of the secret German minutes of this second Hitler-Ciano meeting at Obersalzberg on August 13, 1939, reads as follows:

The Führer said that since the last conversation he had been considering the whole position and… had come to two definite conclusions: (1) In the event of any further provocation he would immediately attack Poland. (2) If Poland did not clearly and plainly state her political intention, she must be forced to do so…. If the western democracies had already decided to move against the Axis, they would not in any case wait for three or four years before carrying out their plan and attack only at a time when the Axis powers had completed their necessary preparations. If, however, they had not yet come to a decision in the matter (and the Führer thought that with the state of their armaments they had not come to this decision), the best way of preventing them would be to deal with the Polish matter quickly….

The strengthening of the Axis by these individual operations was of the greatest importance *for the unavoidable clash with the western powers.* As matters now stand, Germany and Italy would simply not exist further in the world through lack of space: not only was there no more space, but existing space was completely blockaded by its present possessors. They sat like misers with their heaps of gold and deluded themselves about their riches. The western democracies were dominated by the desire to rule the world and would not regard Germany and Italy in their class. The psychological element of contempt was perhaps the worst thing about the whole business.... It could only be settled by a life-and-death struggle, which the two Axis partners could meet more easily because their interests did not clash at any point. The Mediterranean was obviously the most ancient domain for which Italy had a claim to predominance. The Duce himself had summed up the position to him in the words that Italy already was the dominant power in the Mediterranean.

On the other hand, the Führer said that Germany must take the old German road eastwards and that this road was also desirable for economic reasons, and that Italy had geographical and historical claims to permanency in the Mediterranean. Bismarck had recognized it and had said as much in his well-known letter to Mazzini. The interests of Germany and Italy went in quite different directions, and there never could be a conflict between them. Ribbentrop added that if the two problems mentioned in yesterday's conversations were settled, Italy and Germany would have their backs free for work against the west. The Führer said that Poland must be struck down so that for (50?) years long she would be incapable of fighting. In such a case, matters in the west could be settled.

Ciano thanked the Führer for his extremely clear explanation of the situation. He had, on his side, nothing to add and would give the Duce full details. He asked for more definite information on one point in order that the Duce might have all the facts before him. The Duce might indeed have to make no decision because the Führer believed that the conflict with Poland could be localized on the basis of long experience. He (Ciano) quite saw that so far the Führer had always been right in his judgment of the position. If, however, Mussolini had no decision to make, he had to take certain measures of precaution and therefore Ciano would put the following question:

The Führer had mentioned two conditions under which he would take Poland: (1) if Poland were guilty of serious provocation, and (2) if Poland did not make her political position clear. The first of these conditions depended on the decision of the Führer and German reaction could follow it in a moment. The second condition required certain decisions as to times. Ciano therefore asked what was the date by which Poland must satisfy Germany about her political condition. He realized that this date depended upon climatic conditions.

The Führer answered that the decision of Poland must be made clear at the latest by the end of August. Since, however, the decisive part of military operations against Poland could be carried out within a period of 14 days and the final liquidation would need another 4 weeks, it could be finished at the end of September or the beginning of October. These could be regarded as the dates. It followed therefore that the last date on which he could begin to take action was the end of August....

Ciano, the frightened playboy now, hurries back to Rome to tell the Duce that Hitler is going to war in a fortnight. The fateful August days tick off. The magnificent German war machine is poised for the blow, supremely confident it can smash Poland in a fortnight.

There is one little sour note, the documents show. On August 17 Admiral Canaris, chief of German Counter-Intelligence (strangled to death for treason in the last months of the war), sees General Keitel. The admiral is worried about the western powers coming into the war. We have his notes on the conversation. He finds Keitel altogether too certain that Britain will stay out of the conflict. Canaris tries to argue to the contrary, pointing out especially the dangers of a British blockade. But Keitel is cocky this day. Canaris gets nowhere.

On August 22 Hitler convokes his commanders-in-chief to Berchtesgaden for a final war conference. It is a date to remember. The newspapers around the globe are telling in screaming headlines the ominous news from Moscow that Germany and Russia have decided to conclude a non-aggression pact. Hitler knows that in a day or two a virtual alliance with Russia to destroy Poland and frighten the west from coming into the war will be signed at Moscow. He is in even a more swaggering mood than usual. He is carried away by his own success, his own personality. The secret German minutes of his speech to his generals on this occasion—the eve of the war—read as follows:

The Führer's speech to the Commanders-in-Chief on August 22, 1939

I have called you together to give you a picture of the political situation, in order that you may have insight into the various elements on which I have based my decision to act, and in order to strengthen your confidence.

After this we will discuss military details.

It was clear to me that a conflict with Poland had to come sooner or later. I had already made this decision in (the) spring, but I thought that I would first turn against the West in a few years, and only afterward against the east. But the sequence cannot be fixed. One cannot close one's eyes even before a threatening situation.... I enumerate as reasons for this reflection:

First of all, two personal constitutions:

My own personality and that of Mussolini.

Essentially it depends on me, my existence, because of my political activities. Furthermore the fact that probably no one will ever again have the confidence of the whole German people as I do. There will probably never again be a man in the future with more authority than I have. My existence is therefore a factor of great value. But I can be eliminated at any time by a criminal or an idiot.[24]

The second personal factor is the Duce. His existence is also decisive. If something happens to him, Italy's loyalty to the alliance will no longer be certain. The basic attitude of the Italian court is against the Duce. Above all, the court sees in the expansion of the empire a burden. The Duce is the man with the strongest nerves in Italy.

The third factor favorable for us is Franco. We can ask only benevolent neutrality from Spain. But this depends on Franco's personality. He guarantees a certain uniformity and steadiness of the present system in Spain....

On the other side a negative picture as far as decisive personalities are concerned. There is no outstanding personality in England or France.

For us it is easy to make a decision. We have nothing to lose: we can only gain. Our economic situation is such, because of our restrictions, that we cannot hold out more than a few years. Göring can confirm this. We have no other choice. We must act. Our opponents risk much and can gain only a little. England's stake in a war is unimaginably great. Our enemies have men who are below average. No personalities. No masters, no men of action.

Besides the personal factor, the political situation is favorable for us; in the Mediterranean rivalry between Italy, France, and England; in the Orient tension, which leads to the alarming of the Mohammedan world.

The English Empire did not emerge from the last war strengthened. From a maritime point of view, nothing was achieved. Conflict between England and Ireland. The South African Union became more independent. Concessions had to be made to India. England is in great danger. Unhealthy industries. A British statesman can look into the future only with concern.

France's position has also deteriorated, particularly in the Mediterranean.

Further favorable factors for us are these:

Since Albania there is an equilibrium of power in the Balkans. Yugoslavia carries the germ of collapse because of her internal situation.

Rumania did not grow stronger. She is liable to attack and vulnerable. She is threatened by Hungary and Bulgaria. Since Kemal's death Turkey has been, ruled by small minds, unsteady, weak men.

All these fortunate circumstances will no longer prevail in 2 to 3 years. No one knows how long I shall live. Therefore conflict better now.

The creation of Greater Germany was a great achievement politically, but militarily it was questionable, since it was achieved through a bluff of the political leaders. It is necessary to test the military. If at all possible, not by general settlement, but by solving individual tasks.

The relation to Poland has become unbearable. My Polish policy hitherto was in contrast to the ideas of the people. My propositions to Poland (Danzig corridor) were disturbed by England's intervention. Poland changed her tone toward us. The initiative cannot be allowed to pass to the others. This moment is more favorable than in 2 to 3 years. An attempt on my life or Mussolini's could change the situation to our disadvantage. One cannot eternally stand opposite one another with cocked rifle. A suggested compromise would have demanded that we change our convictions and make agreeable gestures. They talked to us again in the language of Versailles. There was danger of losing prestige. *Now the probability is still great that the west will not interfere. We must accept the risk with reckless resolution.* A politician must accept a risk as much as a military leader. We are facing the alternative to strike or to be destroyed with certainty sooner or later....

Now it is also a great risk. Iron nerves, iron resolution.

The following special reasons strengthen my idea. England and France are obligated to go to war; neither is in a position for it. There is no actual rearmament in England, just propaganda. Much damage has been done by what many reluctant Germans said and wrote to Englishmen after the solution of the Czech question. The Führer carried his point because you lost your nerve, because you capitulated too soon. This explains the present propaganda war. The English speak of a war of nerves. It is one element of this war of nerves to emphasize the increase of armament. But how is British rearmament in actual fact? The construction program of the navy for 1938 has not yet been filled. Only mobilization of the reserve fleet. Purchase of fishing steamers. Considerable strengthening of the navy, not before 1941 or 1942.

Little has been done on land. England will be able to send a maximum of 3 divisions to the Continent. A little has been done for the air force, but it is only a beginning. AA defense is in its beginning stages. At the moment England has only 150 AA guns.... England is still vulnerable from the air. This can change in two to three years. At the moment the English air force has only 130,000 men, the French 72,000 men, the Polish 15,000 men. England does not want the conflict to break out for two or three years.

The following is characteristic for England. Poland wanted a loan from England for rearmament. England, however, only gave credit in order to make sure that Poland buys in England, although England cannot deliver. This means that England does not really want to support Poland.

She does not risk 8,000,000 pounds in Poland, although she put half a billion into China. *England's position in the world is very precarious. She will not accept any risks.*

France lacks men (decline of the birth rate). Little has been done for rearmament. The artillery is antiquated. France did not want to enter on this adventure. The west has only two possibilities to fight against us:

1. Blockade: It will not be effective because of our autarchy and because we have sources of aid in the east.

2. Attack from the west from the Maginot Line: I consider this impossible.

Another possibility is the violation of Dutch, Belgian, and Swiss neutrality. I have no doubts that all these states as well as Scandinavia will defend their neutrality by all available means. England and France will not violate the neutrality of those countries. Actually England cannot help Poland. There remains an attack on Italy. A military attack is out of the question. No one is counting on a long war. If Herr von Brauchitsch (the commander-in-chief of the German Army) had told me that I would need 4 years to conquer Poland I would have replied: then it cannot be done. It is nonsense to say that England wants to wage a long war. We will hold our position in the west until we have conquered Poland. We must be conscious of our great production. It is much bigger than in 1914-18.

The enemy had another hope, that Russia would become our enemy after the conquest of Poland. The enemy did not count on my great power of resolution. *Our enemies are little worms. I saw them in Munich.*

I was convinced that Stalin would never accept the English offer. Russia has no interest in maintaining Poland, and Stalin knows that it is the end of his regime no matter whether his soldiers come out of a war victoriously or beaten. Litvinov's replacement was decisive. I brought about the change toward Russia gradually. In connection with the commercial treaty we got into a political conversation. Proposal of a non-aggression pact. Then came a general proposal from Russia. *Four days ago I took a special step, which brought it about that Russia answered yesterday that she is ready to sign. The personal contract with Stalin is established. The day after tomorrow von Ribbentrop will conclude the treaty. Now Poland is in the position in which I wanted her.*

We need not be afraid of a blockade. The east will supply us with grain, cattle, coal, lead, and zinc. It is a big arm, which demands great efforts. *I am only afraid that at the last minute some Schweinehund(literally, swineherd's dog; figuratively, filthy person)[25]will make a proposal for mediation.*

The political arm is set farther. A beginning has been made for the destruction of England's hegemony. The way is open for the soldier, after I have made the political preparations.

Today's publication of the non-aggression pact with Russia hit like a shell. The consequences cannot be overlooked. Stalin also said that his course will be of benefit to both countries. The effect on Poland will be tremendous.

Göring answers with thanks to the Führer and the assurance that the armed forces will do their duty.

Another German participant in this meeting describes Göring's "thanks" with possibly more accuracy. "The speech [of Hitler] was listened to enthusiastically," he writes. "Göring jumped on the table. Bloodthirsty thanks and bloody promises. He danced around like a savage. The few doubtful ones remained silent."

This eyewitness, in fact, gives a slightly different version of the August 22 outburst of Hitler. His account, I believe, was first obtained by Louis Lochner, Berlin A.P. correspondent, during the war. It reads, in part, as follows:

Contents of Hitler's Talk to the Supreme Commander and Commanding Generals, Obersalzberg, August 22, 1939

…Since autumn 1938… I have found out that Japan does not go with us without conditions, and that Mussolini is menaced by the weak-headed King and the treacherous scoundrel of a Crown Prince, I have decided to go with Stalin. On the whole, there are only three great statesmen in the world: Stalin, myself, and Mussolini. Mussolini, the weakest, has not been able to break either the power of the crown or of the church. *Stalin and I are the only ones that see only the future. So I shall shake hands with Stalin within a few weeks on the common German-Russian border and undertake with him a new distribution of the world.*[26]

Our strength is in our quickness and our brutality. Genghis Khan had millions of women and children killed by his own will and with a gay heart. History sees in him only a great state-builder. What weak western European civilization thinks about me does not matter. I have given the order and will have everyone shot who utters even one word of criticism that the aim of the war is not to attain certain lines, but consists in the physical destruction of the opponent. Thus for the time being I have sent to the east only my "Death's-Head units" with the order to kill without pity or mercy all men, women, and children of Polish race or language. Only in such a way shall we win the vital space that we need. Who still talks nowadays of the extermination of the Armenians?

Colonel General von Brauchitsch has promised me to bring the war against Poland to a conclusion within a few weeks. If he had told me that it would take me two years or even one year only, I would not have issued the order to march and would have temporarily entered into an alliance with England instead of Russia. For we cannot conduct a long war. In any case, a new situation has now been created. I have witnessed the miserable worms Daladier and Chamberlain in Munich. They will be too cowardly to attack. They will not go any farther than blockade. Against it we have our autarchy and the Russian raw materials. Poland will be depopulated and colonized with Germans. My pact with Poland was only meant to stall for time. *And besides, gentlemen, in Russia will happen just what I have practiced with Poland. After Stalin's death(he is seriously ill) we shall crush the Soviet Union.*

The small countries do not frighten me. Since Kemal's death Turkey has been ruled by morons and half-idiots. Carol of Rumania is a thoroughly corrupted slave of his sexual desires. The King of Belgium and the northern kings are weak puppets, depending on the good digestion of their overfed and tired peoples.

We must take into account the defection of Japan. I have left to Japan a whole year's time to decide. The Emperor is the companion piece of the late czars. Weak, cowardly, irresolute, he may fall before a revolution. My association with Japan was never popular. We will furthermore cause unrest in the Far East and Arabia. Let us think of ourselves as masters and consider these people at best as lacquered half-monkeys, who need to feel the knout.

The occasion is favorable now as it has never been. I have only one fear and that is that Chamberlain or some other dirty swine comes to me with propositions or a change of mind. He will be thrown downstairs. And even if I must personally kick him in the belly before the eyes of all the photographers.

No, for this it is too late. The invasion and the extermination of Poland begins on Saturday morning. I will have a few companies in Polish uniform attack in Upper Silesia or in the Protectorate. Whether the world believes it doesn't mean a damn to me. The world believes only in success.

Glory and honor are beckoning to you, gentlemen, as they never did for centuries. Be hard. Be without mercy. Act quicker and more brutally than the others. The citizens of western Europe must quiver in horror. That is the most human warfare, for it scares them off.

The new warfare corresponds to the new border status. A wall from Reval, Lublin, Kaschau to the Danube estuary. The Russians get the rest. Ribbentrop has received instructions to make any offer and to accept any demand. In the west I reserve the right to ascertain the line strategically best. Here, there will be something to do with Holland, Belgium, French Lorraine as protectorate areas.

And now, on to the enemy! In Warsaw we will celebrate our meeting again....

There is a third German document on this August 22 meeting. It consists of rough notes of a second speech Hitler made, but to whom is not indicated. From its tenor I gather it was probably delivered to the top field-commanders of the army who were to lead the assault on Poland. It reads as follows:

Second Speech by the Führer on August 22, 1939

It may also turn out differently regarding England and France. One cannot predict it with certainty. I figure on a trade-barrier, not on a blockade, and with severance of relations. Most iron determination on our side. Retreat before nothing. Everybody shall have to make a point of it that we were determined from the beginning to fight the western powers. Struggle for life or death. Germany has won every war as long as she was united. Iron, unflinching attitude of all superiors, greatest confidence, faith in victory, overcoming of the past by getting used to heaviest strain. A long period of peace would not do us any good. Therefore it is necessary to expect everything. Manly bearing. It is not machines that fight each other. We have the better quality of men. Mental factors are decisive. The opposite camp has weaker people. In 1918 the nation fell down because the mental prerequisites were not sufficient. Frederick the Great secured final success only through his mental power.

Destruction of Poland in the foreground. The aim is elimination of living forces, not the arrival at a certain line. Even if war should break out in the west, the destruction of Poland shall be the primary objective. Quick decision because of the season.

I shall give a propagandistic cause for starting the war—never mind whether it be plausible or not. The victor shall not be asked, later on, whether we told the truth or not. In starting and making a war, not the right is what matters, but victory.

Have no pity. Brutal attitude. Eighty million people shall get what is their right. Their existence has to be secured. The strongest has the right. Greatest severity.

Quick decision necessary. Unshakable faith in the German soldier. A crisis may happen only if the nerves of the leaders give way.

First aim: advance to the Vistula and Narev. Our technical superiority will break the nerves of the Poles. Every newly created Polish force shall again be broken at once. Constant war of attrition.

New German frontier according to healthy principles. Possibly a protectorate as a buffer. Military operations shall not be influenced by these reflections. Complete destruction of Poland is the military aim. To be fast is the main thing. Pursuit until complete elimination. Conviction that the German Wehrmacht is up to the requirements. The start shall be ordered, probably, by Saturday morning.

From the documents it is plain that Hitler meant Saturday, August 26, for "the start," and that he postponed it until the following Friday in order, as he told Göring, "to see whether we can eliminate British intervention." On August 23 Nevile Henderson, the British Ambassador, flies down to Berchtesgaden to inform Hitler that the British government will honor its pledge to Poland if Germany attacks her, regardless of the German deal with Russia. The Führer gives him a contemptuous answer, but Henderson, who has staked his all on appeasement, keeps on trying, calling on the mad dictator in Berlin twice during August 25 and flying off to London on August 26 to confer with Chamberlain.

It is of no use. At dawn on Friday, September 1, the German armies pour into Poland. On Sunday, September 3, Great Britain and France come into the war against Germany.

Hitler has his World War! Poland is annihilated in eighteen days.

And now the German documents reveal a surprising thing. Contrary to what we had always believed, Hitler finds no consolation in the phony war in the west. He orders a German onslaught on the west before the coming of winter. To waste time is to Germany's disadvantage. The first date fixed for the western offensive is November 7. This is postponed to November 9 on account of weather. It is postponed again and again—all through the winter of 1939-40.

At noon on November 23, 1939, Hitler convokes all his supreme commanders to listen to his latest thoughts. His head is full—of the past, present, and future—and his talk is long. As you read through the amazing secret text of his speech, which we have in full, you get a magnificent résumé of all that has gone through his diseased mind and made him and Germany what they are, as of November 1939. The future course of the war, including the attack in the west, the violation of Dutch and Belgian neutrality, the eventual blow against Russia "when we are free in the west," is outlined with utter clarity and ruthlessness. The conqueror of the world is now certain that his day has come. He speaks as follows:

TOP SECRET

The purpose of this conference is to give you an idea of the world of my thoughts, which governs me in the face of future events, and to tell you my decisions.... When I started my political task in 1919, my strong belief in final success was based on a thorough observation of the events of the day and the study of the reasons for their occurrence. Therefore I never lost my belief in the midst of setbacks that were not spared me during my period of struggle. Providence has had the last word and brought me success. On top of that I had a clear recognition of the probable course of historical events, and the firm will to make brutal decisions.

The first decision was in 1919 when after long internal conflict I became a politician and took up the struggle against my enemies. That was the hardest of all decisions. I had, however, the firm belief that I would arrive at my goal. First of all, I desired a new system of selection. I wanted to educate a minority, which would take over the leadership. After 15 years I arrived at my goal, after strenuous struggles and many setbacks. When I came to power in 1933, a period of the most difficult struggle lay behind me. Everything existing before that had collapsed. I had to reorganize everything beginning with the mass of the people and extending it to the armed forces. First, reorganization of the interior, abolishment of appearances of decay and defeatist ideas, education to heroism.

While reorganizing the interior, I undertook the second task: to release Germany from its international ties. Two particular moves are to be pointed out: secession from the League of Nations and denunciation of the disarmament conference. It was a hard decision. The number of prophets who predicted that it would lead to the occupation of the Rhineland was large, the number of believers was very small. After that, the order for rearmament. Here again there were numerous prophets who predicted misfortunes, and only a few believers. In 1935 the introduction of compulsory armed service. After that, militarization of the Rhineland, again an action believed to be impossible at that time. The number of people who put trust in me was very small. Then the beginning of the fortification of the whole country, especially in the west.

One year later, Austria came. This step also was considered doubtful. It brought about a considerable reinforcement of the Reich. The next step was Bohemia, Moravia, and Poland. This step also was not possible to accomplish in one campaign. First of all, the western fortifications had to be finished. It was not possible to reach the goal in one effort. *It was clear to me from the first moment that I could not be satisfied with the Sudeten-German territory. That was only a partial solution.*[27] The decision to march into Bohemia was made. Then followed the erection of the protectorate and with that the basis for the action against Poland was laid, but I wasn't quite clear at that time whether I should start first against the east and then the west or vice versa. Moltke often made the same calculations in his time. Under pressure the decision came to fight with Poland first.

One might accuse me of wanting to fight and fight again. In struggle I see the fate of all beings. Nobody can avoid a struggle if he does not want to lose out. The increasing number of people requires a larger living-space (Lebensraum). My goal was to create a logical relation between the number of people and the space for them to live in. The struggle must start here.

No people can get away from the solution of this task or else it must yield and gradually die out. That is taught by history.... No calculated cleverness is of any help. *Solution only with the sword. A people unable to produce the strength to fight must withdraw.*

Struggles are different from those of 100 years ago. Today we can speak of a racial fight. Today we fight for oil fields, rubber, treasures of the earth, etc. After the Peace of Westphalia Germany disintegrated. Disintegration, impotence of the German Reich, was determined by decree. This German impotence was removed by the creation of the Reich when Prussia realized her task. Then the opposition between France and England began. Since 1870 England has been against us. Bismarck and Moltke were certain that there would have to be one more action. The danger at that time was of a two-front war.... The basic thought of Moltke was the offensive. He never thought of the defense. Many opportunities were missed after Moltke's death. *The solution was only possible by attacking a country at a favorable moment.* Political and military leadership always declared that it was not yet ready. In 1914 there came the war on several fronts. It did not bring the solution of these problems.

Today the second act of this drama is being written. For the first time in 67 years it must be made clear that we do not have a two-front war to wage. That which has been desired since 1870 and considered as impossible of achievement has come to pass. For the first time in history we have to fight on only one front. *But no one can know how long that will remain so.*I have doubted for a long time whether I should strike in the east and then in the west. *Basically I did not organize the armed forces in order not to strike. The decision to strike was always in me. Earlier or later I wanted to solve the problem.*

Under pressure it was decided that the east was to be attacked first. If the Polish war was won so quickly, it was due to the superiority of our armed forces. The most glorious appearance in history. Unexpectedly small expenditures of men and material. Now the eastern front is held by only a few divisions. It is a situation which we viewed previously as unachievable. Now the situation is as follows: The opponent in the west lies behind his fortifications. There is no possibility of coming to grips with him. The decisive question is: how long can we endure this situation?

*Russia is at present not dangerous. It is weakened by many factors today. Moreover, we have a pact with Russia. Pacts, however, are only held as long as they serve the purpose. Russia will hold herself to it only so long as Russia considers it to be to her benefit. Even Bismarck thought so. Let one think of the pact to assure our back. Now Russia has far-reaching goals; above all, the strengthening of her position in the Baltic. We can oppose Russia only when we are free in the west.*Further, Russia is striving to increase her influence on the Balkans and is striving toward the Persian Gulf. That is also the goal of our foreign policy. Russia will do that which she considers of benefit to her. At the present moment she has retired from internationalism. In case she renounces this, she will proceed to Pan-Slavism. It is difficult to see into the future. It is a fact that at the present time the Russian Army is of little worth. For the next one or two years the present situation will remain.

Much depends on Italy; above all, on Mussolini, whose death could alter everything. Italy has a great goal for the consolidation of her empire. Those who carry this idea are Fascism and the Duce, personally. The court is opposed to that. As long as the Duce lives, it can be calculated that Italy will seize every opportunity to reach her imperialistic goal. However, it is too much to ask of Italy that she should join in the battle before Germany has seized the offensive in the west. Just so Russia did not attack until we had marched into Poland. Otherwise Italy will think that France has only to deal with Italy, since Germany is sitting behind its West Wall.

Italy will not attack until Germany has taken the offensive against France. Just as the death of Stalin, so the death of the Duce can bring danger to us. Just how easily the death of a statesman can come I myself have experienced recently.[28] The time must be used to the full, otherwise one will suddenly find oneself faced with a new situation. As long as Italy maintains this position, then no danger from Yugoslavia is to be feared. Just so is the neutrality of Rumania achieved by the position of Russia. Scandinavia is hostile to us because of Marxistic influence, but is neutral now. *America is still not dangerous to us because of its neutrality laws. The strengthening of our opponents by America is still not important.* The position of Japan is still uncertain. It is not yet certain whether she will join against England.

Everything is determined by the fact that the moment is favorable now; in 6 months it might not be so any more.

As the last factor I must name my own person, in all modesty: irreplaceable. Neither a military nor a civil person could replace me. Assassination attempts may be repeated. I am convinced of the powers of my intellect and of decision. Wars are always ended only by the destruction of the opponent. Everyone who believes differently is irresponsible. Time is working for our adversary. Now there is a relationship of forces which can never be more propitious, but can only deteriorate for us. The enemy will not make peace when the relationship of forces is unfavorable for us. No compromise. Sternness with ourselves. I shall strike and not capitulate. *The fate of the Reich depends only on me. I shall deal accordingly.* Today we have a superiority such as we never had before.

At this point the mad dictator digresses to impress the point on his generals. For a quarter of an hour he rattles off figures and historical data to prove Germany's military superiority. The minute details need not concern us here. But his general line of thought is interesting. He is contemptuous of the Allies for having "disarmed themselves after 1918 of their own accord." The British, he explains to his military chieftains, "neglected the construction of their fleet." The French reduced the length of military service so that "after 1918 the French Army deteriorated." As for the British Army, it has, he says, "only a symbolic meaning."

In the Polish campaign that has just come to an end, the German infantry, we learn from the Führer, "did not accomplish what one would have expected from it. Discipline was lax.... I am told that our troops will only advance if the officers lead the way. In 1914 that was also the case." Still, he concludes, the Wehrmacht has no match in all the world today.

Five million Germans have been called to the colors. Of what importance if a few of them collapse. Daring in the army, navy, and Luftwaffe. I cannot bear it when one says the army is not in good shape. Everything lies in the hands of the military leader. I can do anything with the German soldier if he is well led. We have succeeded with our small navy in clearing the North Sea of the British....

The land army achieved outstanding things in Poland. Even in the west it was not shown that the German soldier is inferior to the French.

Revolution from within is impossible. We are superior to the enemy numerically in the west. Behind the army stands the strongest armament industry of the world.

I am disturbed by the stronger and stronger appearance of the English. The English are a tough enemy. Above all on defense. There is no doubt that England will be very much represented in France, at the latest in six to eight months.

We have an Achilles' heel: The Ruhr. The progress of the war depends on the possession of the Ruhr. If England and France push through Belgium and Holland into the Ruhr, we shall be in the greatest danger. That could lead to the paralyzing of the German power of resistance.

Every hope of compromise is childish: Victory or defeat! The question is not the fate of a National Socialist Germany, but who is to dominate Europe in the future. The question is worthy of the greatest efforts. Certainly England and France will assume the offensive against Germany when they are armed. England and France have means of pressure to bring Belgium and Holland to request English and French help. In Belgium and Holland the sympathies are all for France and England....

One more thing. U-boats, mines, and the Luftwaffe (also for mines) can strike England effectively if we have a better starting-point. Now a flight to England demands so much fuel that sufficient bomb loads cannot be carried. The invention of a new-type mine is of greatest importance for the navy. Aircraft will be the chief minelayers now. We shall sow the English coast with mines that cannot be cleared. This mine warfare with the Luftwaffe demands a different starting-point. England cannot live without its imports. We can feed ourselves. The permanent sowing of mines on the English coasts will bring England to her knees. *However, this can only occur if we have occupied Belgium and Holland. It is a difficult decision for me. No one has ever achieved what I have achieved. My life is of no importance in all this. I have led the German people to a great height, even if the world does hate us now.*

I am setting this work on a gamble. I have to choose between victory or destruction. I choose victory. Greatest historical choice, to be compared with the decision of Frederick the Great before the first Silesian War. Prussia owes its rise to the heroism of one man. Even there the closest advisers were disposed to capitulation. Everything depended on Frederick the Great....

My decision is unchangeable. I shall attack France and England at the most favorable and quickest moment. Breach of the neutrality of Belgium and Holland is meaningless. No one will question that when we have won. We shall not bring about the breach of neutrality as idiotically as it was in 1914. If we do not break the neutrality, then England and France will. I consider it as possible to end the war only by means of an attack. Everything depends upon the favorable instant. The military conditions are favorable....

The whole thing means the end of the World War, not just of a single action. It concerns not just a single question, but the existence or non-existence of the nation....

The spirit of the great men of our history must hearten us all. Fate demands from us no more than from the great men of German history. As long as I live I shall think only of the victory of my people. *I shall shrink from nothing and shall destroy everyone who is opposed to me. I have decided to live my life so that I can stand unashamed if I have to die. I want to destroy the enemy. Behind me stands the German people, whose morale can only grow worse. Only he who struggles with destiny can have a good intuition. Even in the present development I see the prophecy.*

If we come through this struggle victoriously—and we shall come through victoriously—our time will enter into the history of our people. I shall stand or fall in this struggle. I shall never survive the defeat of my people. No capitulation to the outside forces, no revolution from the interior forces.

On one thing the mad German dictator is right in his prophecies. He himself will not survive the defeat of his people.

For exactly two years, though, there is not the faintest shadow of defeat. Hitler goes from one fantastic victory to another. In the spring Denmark and Norway are overrun. In early summer, Holland, Belgium, and France. The invasion of Britain has to be postponed in the fall. But all during the winter of 1940-1 the cities and towns of England, which is now standing alone against the Axis might, are battered unmercifully from the air by German bombers.

During this winter Hitler is feverishly pushing his secret plans to fall upon Russia. The confidential German documents show that before the six weeks' war in the west was scarcely finished—indeed, "during the western campaign," according to General Jodl—the Führer made his fateful decision to attack the Soviet Union in 1941. By October 1, 1940, the German General Staff is back in Zossen and "working intensively on the problem," General Franz Halder, chief of the General Staff, will later reveal.

The "problem" is called "Operation Barbarossa," which becomes the code word for the plan of attack against Russia. Hitler and his generals can think of nothing else. "Operation Sea Lion"—for the invasion of Britain—is all but forgotten. By December 5, the German documents show, General Halder has given Hitler the General Staff's plan for the Russian campaign. On December 18 Hitler issues his "Directive 21—Operation Barbarossa," which begins: "The German armed forces must be prepared to crush Soviet Russia in a quick campaign before the end of the war against England." Hitler orders all preparations completed by May 15, 1941. The unexpected resistance of Yugoslavia to being swallowed up by the Germans postpones the date by five weeks—the documents make plain—and probably thereby saves Russia.

General Halder, whom Hitler hates, but whose brilliance he cannot dispense with, warns that "Russia's strength in military personnel is completely unknown." But the Führer has no patience with such warnings. He calls in his top generals on February 3, 1941, and, according to the captured minutes of the meeting, exclaims: "*When Barbarossa commences, the world will hold its breath and make no comment.*"

In the early morning of June 22, 1941, it commences. The German armies hurtle through Russia. It seems that nothing can stop them. In Washington, General Marshall calls in the editors and correspondents to warn them, confidentially, that Russian collapse is only a matter of a few weeks. Hitler is sure it will come before winter. By the end of September the Nazi hordes are deep in Russia. Kiev, capital of the Ukraine, has fallen. Von Rundstedt's southern group of armies is pressing toward Rostov and Kharkov. On October 2 Hitler launches his great offensive on Moscow. On October 4 he is in Berlin for a speech. "The enemy is already broken and will never rise again," he proclaims.

A few days later, on October 9, he sends his press chief, Dr. Otto Dietrich, pell-mell back to Berlin to tell the correspondents, hastily convened in the Propaganda Ministry, that the last fully effective remnants of the Red Army are trapped in two German pockets before Moscow and "undergoing swift, merciless annihilation," and that, further, "for all military purposes Soviet Russia is done with."

Hitler believed it himself, as General Halder later will confirm. In fact, Halder, in a report written after the end of the war, makes the sensational revelation that Hitler secretly ordered the "dissolution of about forty army divisions, the manpower to return to industry." So sure was he that Russia was finished, says Halder, that he also ordered a halt in munitions production.

The Russians, as the Germans soon learned, were far from finished. In the south Timoshenko had taken over from Budenny at the end of October and within a month had driven von Kleist's victorious armies out of Rostov. But the crucial battle of the war was being fought before Moscow. Though Hitler and Dr. Dietrich had "destroyed" the last remnants of the Red armies on this front early in October, ferocious fighting, with heavy losses on both sides, continued all through October and November.

On December 5 and 6 the tide turned. On December 5 a German armored column from Istra fought its way into the outskirts of the Russian capital. It was the nearest the Germans ever got to Moscow. The next day the Russian counter-offensive was in full swing, the Germans in retreat. The greatest army the world had ever seen had at last been stopped. It would never recover from the blow. December 6 was the turning-point in the war.

Where did the German plans to finish Russia before the winter snows go wrong? On our side, during the war, we knew that the severity of the winter and the unexpected strength of the Red Army had upset Hitler's plans. But what we did not know was: what his plans were, and how—in the opinion of the German General Staff—they went awry.

I think I have found the answers in a report drawn up after the end of hostilities by General Halder, chief of the German General Staff at the time, and, in my opinion, the greatest German strategist of the war. (He was dismissed by Hitler in the midst of the Russian campaign and in 1944, arrested, and placed in solitary confinement.) His comments on the turning-point of the war, taken from his lengthy report, follow. They destroy, incidentally, once and for all, the Nazi myth that Hitler was a military genius.

At the start of operations Hitler's belief in his own infallibility and the omnipotence of his will had grown. So had his nervous irritability. His interference in the directing of the army, even in small matters, increased, and tense debates about strategical and even tactical questions… became more and more frequent in the course of the Russian campaign.

There was no doubt that Hitler was under considerable pressure because of the advanced season…. The Yugoslav campaign [had] delayed the beginning of the Russian campaign by about two months…. I am firmly convinced that he entered the Russian campaign with the preconceived idea, which was not shared, still less encouraged, by the Army General Staff, that Russia could be forced to make peace even in 1941, and that thus the further prosecution of the war would be hopeless for the Allies.

Spoiled by the quick successes of the previous campaigns, he expected operations to be carried through in a space of time that ignored completely the conditions of terrain and roads in the east. He obstinately refused to take notice of the results obtained from studying the map and working with a compass. The advance on Russian territory could never be fast enough for his impatience.... In a conference with all *Gauleiter*, held immediately before the beginning of operations, Hitler promised to be in Leningrad within eight weeks....

The number of divisions employed for the initial attack on Russia was sufficient for the frontier battles, but was not enough to cover later needs that were going to arise when the front advanced farther to the east....

Hitler was continually dominated by the illusion that there was a continuous front....

The interference of Hitler that had the most decisive influence on the Russian campaign was the official order of the Supreme Command for the "Battle of Kiev."...[29] The Army Group North was at that time advancing south of Leningrad.... In front of Army Group Center there was still a considerable portion of the original Russian forces in the area between Smolensk and Moscow. [*These were the troops Hitler and Dr. Dietrich had "destroyed."*—W. L. S.] These forces had expended much of their strength, it is true, in useless frontal counterattacks, but had also proved the will of the commands and the unbroken combat spirit of the troops. Feverish activity was shown in building rear positions between Smolensk and Moscow, which proved the sensitiveness of the Russians against thrusts in this direction. It was known that farther to the rear considerable new formations were being organized. A considerable portion of these were near Moscow, to the west of the Volga. The center of gravity of Russian strength was therefore in front of Army Group Center....

The General Staff had been brought up with the idea that it must be the aim of an operation to defeat the military power of the enemy, and it therefore considered the next and most pressing task to be to defeat the forces of Timoshenko by concentrating all available forces at Army Group Center, to advance on Moscow, to take this nerve center of enemy resistance, and to destroy the new enemy formations. The assembly for this attack had to be carried out as soon as possible because the season was advanced. Army Group North was in the meantime to fulfill its original mission and to try to contact the Finns. Army Group South was to advance farther east to tie down the strongest possible enemy forces.

The commander-in-chief of the army [Field Marshal von Brauchitsch] was of the same opinion and, after oral discussions between the General Staff and the Leadership Staff of the Supreme Command [the latter headed by General Jodl—W. L. S.] had failed, submitted a memorandum of the General Staff to Hitler. *The effect was explosive.*

Hitler himself prepared a counter-memorandum, full of insults, in which he stated that only minds fossilized in out-of-date theories could overlook that the slowness of Army Group South compared with Army Group Center had created a break in the front that simply asked for a decisive action against the forces of Budenny. It would be possible to defeat the enemy decisively there and to open the way for the German Army into the industrial area of the eastern Ukraine, so vital for the Russians. The strongest possible forces from Army Groups Center and South were to be concentrated for a great pincer movement against the forces east of the Dnieper....

The clear line that aimed at destroying the Russian center of strength was therefore abandoned in favor of a second-rate undertaking, which under the most favorable conditions would lead only to a quick collapse of an already weakened enemy front, paying for this success with irreparable losses in time and strength. The aim of defeating the Russian forces decisively was subordinated to the desire to obtain a valuable industrial area and to advance in the direction of the Russian oil.

After the "Battle of Kiev" had been fought (making unsparing use of the already severely worked military transport engines) the Supreme Command ordered the attack in the direction of Moscow. For this, strong forces had again to be brought up from the Ukraine. By now, however, the military transport engines had reached their limits of endurance. The autumn mud period delayed the movement after the successful attack on Vyazma. The winter, unusually early and severe, acted as a powerful ally of the Russians before the objective was reached.

The result of "his battle" at Kiev revived Hitler's confidence. He never did recognize the importance of Moscow as a military nerve center of the Russians.

Hitler made little use of the news of the reinforcement of the enemy front by forces from the east and of the imminent employment of the new Russian formations. Any hints concerning the now noticeable fatigue of the German troops and the dangerous condition of the military transport were branded as defeatism. Hitler was convinced that the Russians were militarily finished after the Battle of Kiev.... Hitler at that time gave the order for the dissolution of about forty army divisions, the manpower to return to industry, and the order to stop munitions production for the army....

Further tension arose over the question of prisoners. The General Staff of the Army had made all preparations for the transport of the prisoners back in the approved manner. Ample accommodation to house the prisoners in the home area had been provided. The sudden order from Hitler, when operations were already under way, not to take any Russian prisoners back into the home area came as a complete surprise. The reason given was the danger of Bolshevik contamination.... The Supreme Command [Keitel] therefore took over the forwarding of Russian prisoners outside the narrow limited area of operations and the responsibility for their welfare. The result was the death of masses of Russian prisoners.... The repercussions of this unpleasant development could be felt right down to the troops.

A series of military reverses set in soon after the early and unusually severe beginning of winter. The main causes were: the results of the strategically wrong decision taken before the Battle of Kiev, the tired condition of troops who, with full confidence in their leaders, had exerted their full strength without hesitation in unsuccessful attempts to accomplish the tasks set them; and the enemy countermeasures, which could be foreseen by the expert eye, but which Hitler in blind arrogance refused to see. Mistakes made by the local German commanders did the rest.

The reverse suffered at Rostov was sufficient to induce sensible German leaders to withdraw the front to the Mius. When this decision was reported by Army Group South, Hitler vetoed its execution and, from his command post in East Prussia and working only from a map, fixed a line in the eastern Ukraine which had to be held "to the last man." Rundstedt asked for and was granted his retirement. The commander-in-chief of the army was never consulted....

Army Group North had reached the southern point of Lake Ladoga and had therefore cut off Leningrad, but had not been in a position to contact the Finns. The High Command of the army refused to make new demands on the overtired troops. Hitler personally gave the commander-in-chief of the army the order for motorized formations to advance across the Volkhov in the direction of Tikhvin, hoping to force the Russians to withdraw from the small area between the German and Finnish fronts.... The result was a complete failure, which cost the numerically already weakened Army Group North further heavy losses in men and material.

The first heavy Russian counterattacks around Moscow were launched toward Army Group Center. These were soon followed by further German reverses farther south (Orel, Kursk).... The commander-in-chief [Brauchitsch] was extremely worried.... The myth of the invincibility of the German Army was broken. The enemy appeared with strong and fresh, if frequently only improvised, forces. He was filled with the impetus of new confidence. The German troops, on the other hand, had reached the limit of endurance. The equipment was worn out, and communications with the homeland were threatened by a transport crisis that caused much worry. The morale of the army had deteriorated....

The myth of the invincibility of German arms was broken, then, in the Russian snows before Moscow and it was never restored—even in the German Army, as General Halder makes clear. There would be more German victories, to be sure—battles won here and there—but they did not recreate the myth, and each triumph on this front or that weakened the German armies more than it did those of the Allies, which, now that America, the world's greatest arsenal, was in the war, were rapidly growing in strength.

By the end of October 1942 the British had smashed Rommel's bid for Suez and the shattered African corps was in disorderly retreat toward Libya. On November 8 an Anglo-American army under Eisenhower had landed in North Africa. In the Mediterranean, as in Russia, the tide had turned against the hitherto invincible Axis arms.

The summer of 1942, indeed, had seen smashing German victories deep in Russia. By the end of August, Hitler's armies had smashed into the Caucasus and appeared to have the Soviets' richest oil fields within their grasp. Worse, they had driven to the outskirts of Stalingrad, on the Volga. But again the final, decisive victory eluded the Germans. In November the Russians hit back, and as the year ended the Nazi armies in the south of Russia were in retreat and the massive Sixth Army was surrounded and doomed at Stalingrad.

The situation did not improve for the Germans in 1943. How did the war look at the end of four years to the German command? During the war we could only guess amidst the fog of propaganda emanating from Berlin. But today we know. One of the most remarkable documents I have seen this day gives us a good picture. It consists of a lengthy lecture given by General Alfred Jodl to the provincial political leaders at Munich on November 7, 1943—on the eve of the anniversary of Hitler's beer-house *Putsch*.

It is entitled "The Strategic Position in the Beginning of the Fifth Year of the War." It is no mere pep speech such as was usually given at Munich on this anniversary. General Jodl admits that defeatism in Germany is rife, that the "devil of subversion" strides the Reich. It is obvious that on Hitler's orders he intends, for once, to tell the Nazi political authorities the stark truth—or at least more of it than they have ever heard. The seriousness of the situation can no longer be hidden.

We have here no ordinary "lecture." We have, indeed, a document prepared with typical Teutonic thoroughness which is, in effect, a short history of the war as experienced and analyzed by the German Supreme Command. Here we can see in broad but specific outline the Nazi military and political objectives and why they were not always reached. The detail is almost overwhelming. The lecture is full of figures on the disposition of German troops all over Europe and of the Allied forces all over the world. The disposition of American divisions is given not only for Europe but in the Pacific and at home. The length of coast lines to be defended, the position and state of fortifications, the nature of German and enemy armament, the probable strategy of the Allies—all these and many other matters are gone into with an array of figures, charts, and maps.

It was General Jodl's lecture, but it is obvious from the captured documents we have that it was Hitler himself who supervised its preparation. We have dozens of memoranda marked "TOP SECRET" or "VERY SECRET" and stamped "Führer's GHQ." On each is a notation: "Material for the Lecture by the Chief of the Armed Forces Operations Staff on 7.11.1943."

It is thus evident that in General Jodl's lecture we really are getting the picture of the war as Hitler saw it at the beginning of the fifth year.

The picture, obviously then, is not always truthful. There are evasions and excuses. But it is probably the most honest document ever prepared by Hitler. He already sees the Anglo-American invasion in the west coming and to his selected few admits that it "will decide the war" and at the same time "that the forces at our disposal will not be adequate."

This, then, is the first authentic history of the war—for the first four years—that we have had from the Germans. It is too long to give here in full. I shall copy, though, the most essential parts:

THE STRATEGIC POSITION IN THE BEGINNING OF THE 5TH YEAR OF WAR

Reichsleiter Bormann has requested me to give you a review today of the strategic position in the beginning of the 5th year of war....

No one—the Führer has ordered—may know more or be told more than he needs for his own immediate task, but I have no doubt at all in my mind, gentlemen, but that you need a great deal in order to be able to cope with your tasks. It is in your Gaus, after all, and among their inhabitants that all the enemy propaganda, the defeatism, and the malicious rumors concentrate among our people. Up and down the country the devil of subversion strides. All the cowards are seeking a way out, or—as they call it—a political solution. They say we must negotiate while there is still something in hand, and all these slogans are made use of to attack the natural sense of the people that in this war there can only be a fight to the end. Capitulation is the end of the nation, the end of Germany....

The necessity and objectives of this war were clear to everyone at the moment when we entered upon the War of Liberation of Greater Germany and, by attacking, parried the danger that menaced us both from Poland and from the western powers. Our further incursions into Scandinavia, in the direction of the Mediterranean, and in that of Russia—these also aroused no doubts concerning the general conduct of the war so long as we were successful. It was not until more serious setbacks were encountered and our general situation began to become increasingly acute that the German people began to ask itself whether perhaps we had not undertaken more than we could do and set our aims too high. To provide an answer to this questioning is one of the main points of my lecture.... In view of my position as military adviser to the Führer, I shall confine myself in my remarks to the problems of my own personal sphere of action, fully appreciating at the same time that, in view of the protean nature of this war, I shall in this way be giving expression to only one side of events....

The bloodless solution of the Czech conflict in the autumn of 1938 and spring of 1939 and the annexation of Slovakia rounded off the territory of Greater Germany in such a way that it now became possible to consider the Polish problem on the basis of more or less favorable strategic premises.

This brings me to the actual outbreak of the present war, and the question that next arises is whether the moment for the struggle with Poland—in itself unavoidable—was favorably selected or not. The answer to this question is all the less in doubt since the opponent—after all, not inconsiderable himself—collapsed unexpectedly quickly, and the western powers who were his friends, while they did declare war on us and form a second front, made no use of the possibilities open to them of snatching the initiative from our hands....

The main effect of this success was that we now had no opponent in the east and that in view of the agreement with Russia the two-front problem might be regarded as for the time being solved.

As a result of all this the point of gravity in the conduct of the war naturally shifted to the west, where the most urgent task was clearly defined as the protection of the Ruhr area from the invasion of Holland by the British and French. Even before the Polish campaign had been concluded, the Führer had already decided upon an attack against the enemy, the aim of which could only be complete subjection of the opponent. The circumstance that this decision was not carried out as originally planned—that is, in the late autumn of 1939—was mainly due to weather conditions, but in part also was influenced by our situation with regard to armaments.

In the meantime, however, we were confronted by yet another problem which had to be settled promptly: the occupation of Norway and Denmark.... In the first place, there was danger that England would seize Scandinavia and thereby besides effecting a strategic encirclement from the north would stop the import of iron and nickel, which was of such importance to us for war purposes. Secondly, it was imperative for us to secure for ourselves free access to the Atlantic with a number of air and naval support points on the Norwegian coast. Here, too, therefore, defensive and offensive requirements combined to form an indissoluble whole.

The course and conclusion of this campaign are known. In the main it was completed in such good time that it was possible to start upon the campaign in the west with the setting in of the most favorable season of the year, in May 1940.

The decisive success of this campaign improved our position in the best possible way. We gained possession not only of the French potential of armaments—destined to do us important service in the further course of the war—but, above all, the entire Atlantic coast fell into our hands, with its naval ports and air support points. Direct threat to the British motherland had by this means become possible.

The question now arose whether or not we should carry the war into England by a landing on the grand scale. Furthermore—in view of the possible eventuality of the U.S.A. entering the war—it was necessary to take into consideration the occupation of a number of advanced support points in the Atlantic (for instance, Iceland and the Azores, on which in the meantime the enemy had laid his hand).... However, very wisely the Führer refrained from adopting these objectives. Not alone their initial execution but the subsequent maintenance of communications by sea would have involved a measure of strength that our naval and air equipment could not have provided permanently.

Instead of these considerations the winter of 1940-1 provided another opportunity of combating England. Although outwardly our action only took the form of aid to our Italian ally, yet ultimately the point at issue was British command of the seas in the Mediterranean, which in turn represented a heavy menace to the southern flank of the European continent. As the weakness and failure of Italy became more and more manifest, North Africa became more and more a German theater of war....

What was less acceptable, however, was the necessity of affording our assistance as an ally in the Balkans in consequence of the unnecessary expedition of the Italians against Greece. The attack that they launched in the autumn of 1940 from Albania with totally inadequate means was contrary to all agreement but in the end led to a decision on our part which—taking a long view of the matter—would have become necessary in any case sooner or later. The planned attack on Greece from the north was not executed merely as an operation in aid of an ally. Its real purpose was to prevent the British from gaining a foothold in Greece and from menacing our Rumanian oil area from that country.

Parallel with all these developments realization was steadily growing of the danger drawing constantly nearer from the Bolshevik east—that danger which has been only too little perceived in Germany and latterly, for diplomatic reasons, had deliberately to be ignored. However, the Führer himself always kept this danger steadily in view and *even as far back as during the western campaign*[30] had informed me of his fundamental decision to take steps against this danger the moment our military position made it at all possible.

Following on the interlude of the overthrow in Yugoslavia, the Balkan campaign that followed this, and our occupation of Crete, this decision was translated into action. If put into effect at all, it had of necessity to take us deep into Russian territory—a circumstance entailing dangers to an extent not yet encountered in our previous campaigns.

In spite of the fact that we were not able either in 1941 or in 1942 completely to annihilate the enemy's fighting forces and thereby to force Russia to her knees, yet we can definitely claim it as a positive result that the Bolshevist danger has been driven back far from our frontiers.

If today, in view of the repeated and prolonged setbacks of the year 1943, the question comes up again and again whether we had not thoroughly underestimated the strength of the Bolshevik opponent, the answer to this question in regard to the execution of individual operations may certainly be said to be yes. But as regards the decision to attack as a whole and that of holding on to this decision for as long as possible, there can be no doubts…. One can only think with a shudder of what would have happened if we had adopted a waiting attitude in the face of this danger and, sooner or later, been overrun by it.[31]

Within the framework of this short sketch of the sweep of our strategy all that remains to mention is the occupation of Tunis effected as a counter-measure to the landing of Anglo-American forces on the north and west coasts of French North Africa, the rapid loss of which position is probably especially likely to evoke doubt in the correctness of our wider strategy.

Taking it all in all, however, fighting along the periphery has built up for us a capital sum of space which we are now living upon.

In recapitulation, a brief summary of the course of the great tactical events up to the autumn of 1943:

The first two years of war saw Germany and its later allies running a victorious course almost unparalleled in history. The campaigns in Poland, Norway, France, in North Africa, in the Balkans, and the attack on Russia as far as to the Donetz, up to the gates of Moscow and up to the Volkhov, created a wide forefield for the defense of Europe and, as a result of the occupation and making safe of rich areas of raw materials and food, provided the premises for a long war. Superior leadership, better employment of the modern means of war, a superior air arm, and the exceptionally high fighting value and morale of our troops faced by opponents inferior on each of these counts have produced these successes.

Nevertheless, during this period of the war, in which our superiority on land was undisputed, and our superiority in the air was able, at all events in the coastal district, to make up for our hopeless inferiority at sea, *in our last grasp at the palm of victory success has eluded us.* The landing in England, prepared for down to the smallest detail, but with improvised transport resources only, could not be dared while the British air arm had not been completely beaten. And this we were not able to do, just as we have not been able completely to shatter the Soviet armed forces. Later generations will not be able to reproach us with not having dared the utmost and spared no effort to achieve these aims which would have decided the war.

But no one could take it upon himself to allow the German air arm to bleed to death in the Battle of Britain in view of the struggle that still lay before us against Soviet Russia.[32]

In the east, however, the natural catastrophe of the winter of 1941 imposed an imperative halt on even the sternest resolution.

Our third objective, that of drawing Spain into the war on our side and thereby creating the possibility of seizing Gibraltar, was wrecked by the resistance of the Spanish or, better say, Jesuit Foreign Minister Serrano Suñer.

It therefore became clear that we could no longer count upon an early end to the war, but that it would be hard and difficult and confront the whole nation with great hardships.[33]

After the first setbacks on the eastern front and in the North African theater of war, the Reich and its allies once again gathered together all their strength in order to defeat this eastern enemy finally by a new assault and to deprive the British of their Egyptian base of operations. The great operation against the Caucasus and the Delta of the Nile failed, however, owing to insufficient strength and inadequate supplies. For the first time our western opponents showed themselves to be superior both on the technical side and numerically in the air over the Mediterranean. The Soviet Russian command also continued to stabilize the front at Stalingrad and before the Caucasus, and after that in wintertime, using newly formed strong reserves, continued to break through the petrified, overextended fronts on the Volga and along the Don—largely occupied, moreover, by the troops of our allies. The 6th Army, consisting of the best German formations, inadequately supplied and exposed to the storms of winter, succumbed to enemy superiority (at Stalingrad).

Similarly, the western powers were able to bring together in Egypt a concentration of land, sea, and air forces which held us up at the very gates of Egypt and after the Battle of El Alamein forced us to retreat, and finally, following the landing of strong Anglo-American armies in French North Africa, to surrender the entire African position. Again, some of the best German divisions fell a victim to the stranglehold of a superior enemy air force on our supplies by sea, although not before they had won for us a certain gain in time, which was worth every sacrifice.

At the end of the winter fighting of 1942-3 and after the loss of the African army the armed forces of Germany and her allies were strained to the utmost. It proved possible to re-form the 5th Armored Army and the 6th Army—but four armies of our allies were lost for good.

Gone was the great mobility of the army and, excepting in the Russian theater of war, gone also our superiority in the air. The superior economic strength of our opponents and their greater reservoir of manpower, concentrated to form a point of gravity against Europe, was beginning to tell. The complete failure of Italy in all domains and the absence of any munitions production worthy of the name among our other allies could not be adequately compensated by the tremendous efforts made by Germany.

Of necessity, therefore, the initiative was bound to pass over to the opposing side, and the Reich and the European nations fighting at Germany's side to go over to the defensive.

So when the position pushed out beyond the European front to the south had been taken by the enemy, in July 1943, the enemy attack started: in the east to regain the territories lost there, and in the south against the Fortress Europe proper at its weakest point. In the meantime the air arms of the Anglo-Americans had already begun the grand assault on the production hearths and morale of our people at home....

It was at this stage of the war that the Italian betrayal took place. Actually it was even more dramatic than the newspapers showed. For the Supreme Command it was perhaps one of the hardest problems that it had as yet to master. That the removal and arrest of the Duce could not end otherwise than by the defection of Italy was completely clear to the Führer from the first, although many politically less well-trained eyes thought to see in it rather an improvement in our position in the Mediterranean and our co-operation with the Italians. There were many personages at this time who failed to understand the Führer's GHQ in its political and military actions. For these were directed toward overthrowing the new government and liberating the Duce. Only the smallest possible circle might know of this. On the military side in the meantime everything was to be done to stop enemy penetration of the southern front as far south as possible—that is, on Sicily....

If the enemy were successful in a landing in northern Italy, then all the German formations in central and southern Italy would be lost. Moreover no grounds must be given which might serve the Italians as a moral pretext for their betrayal, or by premature hostile action to commit the betrayal ourselves. In the meantime the traitors simply oozed with amiability and assurances of faith, and even got as far as to make some of our officers who daily came in contact with them doubtful of the truth of the betrayal hypothesis. This was nothing to be wondered at, for to the German officers such depths of infamy were simply incomprehensible.

The situation became more and more difficult. It was perhaps the only time in this war when at times I myself hardly knew what I should suggest to the Führer. The measures to be taken in the event of an *open* betrayal had been decided in every detail. The watchword "Axis" would set them in motion…. How much meanwhile we had been able to find out through our troops and through the bordering gaus—keen as sleuthhounds on the track of Italian machinations—in the matter of manifestly hostile actions and preparations is known to you all. However, somehow or other the Italians explained it all ways, either as a misunderstanding or with excuses.

In this insupportable position the Führer agreed to slash through the Gordian knot by a political and military ultimatum. Then on the morning of September 7 the enemy landing fleet appeared at Salerno, and on the afternoon of September 8 news of the Italian capitulation flew through the ether. Even now, however, at the last moment, the freedom of action of the command was still held up: the Italians refused to admit the authenticity of the wireless message. The password itself therefore could not be given, but only the "stand-by" for the troops, until at last at 19.15 this most monstrous of all betrayals in history was confirmed by the Italian political authorities themselves. What followed was both a drama and a tragedy. Only at a later date will it be possible to gather together and set forth all the grotesque details. The more disillusioned the troops and the *German command*,[34] the harder the reaction.

At this point General Jodl's set speech breaks off and we have page after page of "top secret" memoranda from the Führer's headquarters outlining in great detail the situation on every front. A penciled note in the margin of the manuscript by Jodl explains: "Delivered extempore with the help of maps."

Nothing seemingly is forgotten by the Teuton general. One memorandum is marked: "List of Italian Booty." It is an exhaustive list of everything grabbed from the Italians after their collapse, from artillery to destroyers, trousers, and tallow.

Students of the war will want to pore over these papers and examine them in detail. In this book of general notes there is room for mention of only a very few salient points brought out in them.

One document shows how clearly the German command realized the danger of an Anglo-American invasion in the west seven months before it actually took place. The paper is marked:

VERY SECRET
Armed Forces Operations Staff/Op Army/West

Führer's GHQ,
November 2, 1943
2 draft copies
draft copy

Western Theater of War including the Netherlands and Belgium.

Subject: *Lecture by Chief of Armed Forces Operations Staff.*

It reads in part as follows:

…In all areas the enemy has at his disposal locally superior forces. The enemy formations are fresh and have gained experience in the campaigns in North Africa, Sicily, and Italy. He has developed his landing technique and tactics to a high level, so that we must now reckon at all times with a landing on the grand scale.

Enemy Air Arm: Numerically greatly superior. Will enable the enemy both to defend his own forces and their supply and to effect the employment of air landing forces on a big scale.

Possibilities for the enemy: Successful penetration of the western defenses would very soon break through to the Belgian, north French, and west German industrial areas and so prove fatal [italics, Jodl's]…. Even a minor enemy success involving the creation of a bridgehead would spell danger, since in view of the enemy's superiority in equipment and personnel he would have no difficulty in extending this bridgehead into a breach of our defenses….

However, in the event of an attack in force in the west, even if the said tactical reserves are there, the forces at our disposal will not be adequate. It will be necessary in this event, which will decide the war, to employ every German able to bear arms, laying the home country largely bare.

Jodl reveals German strength in the west at 1,374,000 men. British and American forces are given in detail. But in the east, Jodl states, the Germans have 200 divisions, amounting to 4,183,000 men. The Russians, it is plain, are still bearing the main brunt of the war on the Allied side.

A "top secret" memorandum prepared at the Führer's GHQ on October 31, 1943, for Jodl's lecture provides fascinating material on how the Russian front looked to the German command. It notes a "large-scale building up of Russian artillery." It finds "especially unpleasant for our troops… the new

Russian battle airplane now appearing in large numbers." It refers, no doubt, to the Stormovik.

How serious was Russian partisan warfare behind the German lines? The Jodl memorandum mentions it and notes in particular how it affects communications and transport. He has one GHQ memorandum that reads—in italics—"*Railway sabotage: July 1,560, August 2,121, September 2,000 line demolitions with far-reaching effect on operations and evacuation transport.*"

And here at last we get the German estimate of the strength of the various partisan groups in Yugoslavia and Greece, which the Allies are still arguing about. A November 1 memorandum from the Führer's GHQ marked "Very Secret" comments: "The bands are all anti-German but not in agreement among themselves. A distinction should be made between:

"a. Croatia and Serbia:
aa. Communist band under the command of Tito to a strength of about 90,000.
bb. Chetniks under the command of Drazha Mihailovich to a strength of 30,000.
"b. Greece.
"Nationalist bands under the command of Zervas to a strength of 10,000 men, and approximately 15,000 Communists."

Having spoken extempore from his memoranda at some length, General Jodl then resumed the prepared part of his lecture:

According to my experience, there is yet another anxiety stalking the land. It concerns the morale of our own allies and the fear that yet other, as yet neutral states might join the ranks of our enemies.

Of the neutral countries, we are not loved by *Sweden*and *Switzerland*. The latter is surrounded, of no danger to us from the military point of view, and will not harm us. She lives on our bounty and we benefit from her.

The same does not apply to *Sweden*. In the last few years she has been arming hard, and has, in all, 400,000 men under arms. Sweden sways between fear of Bolshevism and hope of British-American aid. This latter is far away for as long as we are in the Skagerrak and cut off Sweden's contact with England.

Should an enemy landing in Norway or Denmark prove successful, Sweden may become dangerous—but not before.

*Spain and Portugal*have decided to remain neutral. They have not the necessary strength to defend themselves against England and America. Everything depends on the goodwill of our western opponents as to the measure in which they recognize this neutrality....

Turkey so far has maintained a clear policy of neutrality.... Attack by surprise on the part of Turkey against the Axis powers is not to be expected....

Our own allies, on the other hand, are united and kept at our side by the fear of Bolshevism. That is understandable, for no people fights for another, but only for his own existence....

In *Hungary*, as a feudal state on the old pattern, social contrasts are still present in their acute form. The country is therefore particularly liable to infection with the Communist idea. In no city in Europe, however, does this fact appear to be less recognized than in Budapest. In that city a dissolute, strongly Judafied society stratum is living and dancing on a volcano. However, in contradistinction to Italy, here the main mass of the officer caste at least has recognized the danger. For the present, at all events, for Hungary there is no political way out.

Japan: There a heroic people is fighting decisively for its existence just as we are. From the political-strategic point of view a great gap yawns in the Far East in the clear line of the fronts. Roosevelt and Churchill want Russia to join in the fight against Japan. We ourselves, from the purely military point of view, would be glad to see the Manchurian armies cross the Amur or advance against Vladivostok. But on this point both the Asiatic powers stop their ears to the siren songs of the West. The reasons for this do not lie solely in the supplementary military burdens that both states would have to take upon themselves by such a decision, but more probably in their own long-term political considerations. For why should Japan start a war against Russia for as long as it can be certain that there will be no American-British air base at Vladivostok and while on the distant horizon there still looms large a conflict of the western powers against Soviet Russia?[35]

Leaving the slippery grounds of politics, I now turn to the problem that confronts the High Command today and will confront it in the near future. We are fighting along the *inner* line; that is, we are in a position to transfer strong forces from one theater of war to another in a much shorter time. Our great successes in the east in 1917–18 and in Italy in 1917 we owe to able exploitation of the inner line. Today this tactical advantage of the inner line is not so marked; at the moment the enemy is so strong on all fronts that in spite of our shorter lines of communication we are scarcely in a position to produce more than local superiority.... The hardest task of all of the command is to distribute its forces throughout the theater of war as a whole in such a way that we may be sufficiently strong at those points at which the enemy delivers the blow.... We have won advanced positions in Finland, Norway, Denmark, in the west, in Italy and the southeast in order to keep the core of the Reich itself alive.

The same reasons that compelled us to take these positions also compel us now, when the superior range of the enemy air arm is inflicting grave injury to the center of the Reich, to maintain them. To do so a certain measure of strength is necessary. That things are getting warm on the east front must be admitted; however, no success gained by the enemy is directly fatal there, with the exception of the loss of the Rumanian oil region. *None the less the command cannot close its eyes to the fact that the brand is now held in readiness at some time or other to start a conflagration in the west which if not extinguished then and there will pass beyond control....*

No theater of war can be weakened below a certain level. Our uttermost efforts can therefore only take the form of creating, in spite of all our manpower problems, new tactical central reserves over and above the necessary minimum of occupying forces. That is now being done....

This, however, brings us to the next difficult problem, which always arises in every long war: the interplay and conflict between the need for soldiers at the front and the need for workers at home. Never before has this problem presented itself in so acute a form as in this highly mechanized war....

How, therefore, is the command to decide? The front needs soldiers and the front needs weapons....

The dilemma of manpower shortage has led to the idea of making more thorough use of the manpower reserves in the territories occupied by us.... *In my opinion, the time has now come to take steps with remorseless vigor and resolution in Denmark, Holland, France, and Belgium also, to compel thousands of idle ones (Nichtstuer) to carry out the fortification work, which is more important than any other work. The necessary orders for this have already been given.*

The question of recruiting alien peoples as fighting men should, however, be examined with the greatest caution and skepticism. There was a time when something in the nature of a neurosis emanated from the east front with the slogan "Russia can be conquered only by Russians." [In the typescript the word was typed as "liberated." This has been scratched out in favor of "conquered."] Many heads were haunted by the notion of an immense Vlasov army.[36] At that time we recruited over 160 battalions. Our experiences were good while we were ourselves attacking successfully. They became bad when the position changed for the worse and we were compelled to retreat. Today only about 100 eastern battalions are available, and hardly one of these is in the east....

However, what weighs most heavily today on the home front, and consequently by reaction on the front line also, is the enemy terror raids from the air on our homes and so on our wives and children. In this respect the war—and this cannot be repeated often enough—has assumed forms solely through the fault of England[37] such as were believed to be no longer possible since the days of the racial and religious wars.

The effect of these terror raids, psychological, moral, and material, is such that they must be relieved if they cannot be made to cease completely. It is true that they—like any other great trouble—have had some good effects. In face of the ruins of one's own possessions all social problems, all enviousness, and all the petty impulses of the human soul die down. But this is no consolation for us. Asking too much of our air arm and inability on the technical side to keep pace with the aircraft development and radio location of our enemies have brought us to this pass. The efforts of the Führer and the Reichs Marshal [Göring] will overcome this crisis also. We shall counter the heavy and powerful armament of the 4-engined bombers by speed and the annihilating effect of fire at long range. Our enemies have realized this danger and are endeavoring to meet it by destroying the hearths of production.

It is enough if the enemy bombers can be made with absolute certainty in all day and night raids to lose 10-12 per cent of the aircraft put in. They might perhaps replace this loss on the equipment side, but not in personnel: *and, above all, the morale of the crews, most of whom have no idea of what they are fighting for and who among the Americans are mainly materialists, will not hold out against it.* I am fully convinced that, thanks to our new weapons and technical progress, *the raids in close-squadron formation, which alone by means of their bomb-carpets have been able to produce so annihilating an effect,* will not escape their fate.

Nevertheless the greatest hopes of all have been stamped by the military command and the German people in U-boat warfare, and that with every right, since within the first week of the general large-scale strategic defensive into which we have been forced by the development of the war and the gradual coming into effect of the superior war potential of our enemies, *submarine warfare may be regarded as the only offensive sector of the German command.* Here too, heavy setbacks have had to be recorded in the course of the last few months, setbacks that have resulted in the successes of the tonnage war no longer being able to keep up with the rate at which the enemy is able to build his merchantmen.

The reason for the decline in U-boat successes lies in the anti-U-boat defense measures that the enemy has been driving forward with the uttermost energy, making use for this purpose of wide-scale support by the air arm and new highly efficient detector equipment, together with high-efficiency bombs and submarine weapons. *The present crisis in the German U-boat war is therefore directly traceable to the enemy's air superiority over the Atlantic.* The crisis must and will be overcome. The extraordinary importance of the tonnage war remains unassailable, as before…. On our side, measures have been instituted, or are already being developed and driven forward with the utmost resolution, with a view to breaking the enemy defense and bringing about a radical improvement in the fighting value of the U-boat.

There is every reason to believe that they will lead to success in the near future and in this way put an end to the present slackening in the U-boat war….

THE GROUNDS FOR OUR CONFIDENCE IN FINAL VICTORY

When at the end of my considerations I come to sum up the general situation in a few words, I am bound to describe it quite candidly as difficult; moreover, I cannot gloss over the fact that I expect further severe crises….

In particular, however, our confidence is built up on a series of points of views to be set forth objectively. At the head comes the *ethical and moral foundation of our struggle*, which leaves its mark upon the general attitude of the German people and makes our armed forces a definitely reliable instrument in the hands of its command. The force of the revolutionary idea has not only made possible a series of unprecedented successes; it also enables our brave troops to achieve feats in defense and in retreat according to plan such perhaps as the Russians but certainly no other people could achieve and which drive off into the realm of Utopia and hope on the part of our opponents for a military breakdown.

As against this, the moral, political, and military tendencies of our opponents by no means form a closed, uniformly directed whole. This shows most clearly in the fighting morale of the English and Americans, whose successes in Africa, Sicily, and Italy are solely ascribable to the weakness and treachery of our Italian ally. Where they have met German forces in battle, they have shown themselves inferior throughout and gained the advantage only as a result of multiple numerical advantage. This shows particularly clearly from the point of view of their conduct of the war, *for according to our ideas it is totally incomprehensible that the Anglo-Americans should have avoided forming the second front in the west that their Russian allies have been demanding for over 2 years*, and they have by no means extracted from their opportunities in the Mediterranean that which according to the true state of affairs, and by German standards of activity, they might have extracted….

My most profound confidence, however, is based upon the fact that at the head of Germany there stands a man who by his entire development, his desires and striving, can only have been destined by fate to lead our people into a brighter future. In defiance of all views to the contrary, I must here testify that he is the soul not only of the political but also of the military conduct of the war and that the force of his will-power and the creative riches of his thought animate and hold together the whole of the German armed forces, with respect to strategy, organization, and munitions of war. Similarly the unity of political and military command, which is so important, is personified by him in a way such as has never been known since the days of Frederick the Great.

That no command is free of errors has often been said by the Führer himself; moreover, the history of war—to use an aphorism of Schlieffen's—consists in general only of a series of errors, and every war situation, naturally, can only be the product of errors.

What matters ultimately is constant readiness to act, the determination never to let oneself be beaten and always to stick to the enemy. That is so now, I am able to assure you from the bottom of my heart....

It behooves us all, therefore, to crush down within ourselves all faintheartedness and by so doing to create within ourselves the foundations of that confidence out of which alone victory can grow. After all, the other fellow is just a bit more frightened still, and a war is only lost when it is given up.

How this war will end, that no man can foretell. What imponderables it may yet bring with it, how many hopes may be disappointed, and how many troubles may turn to the contrary lie hidden in the darkness of the future. All that is sure is that we shall never cease to fight, for through the history of the world there run, like a bronze law, progress and advance upward. In these Europe has led, and at the head of Europe—Germany. A Europe under the whip of American Jews or Bolshevik commissars is unthinkable.

Berlin, *Thursday, November* 15

Though my time has been much too short, I guess I have found out some of the things I came here to find out: what happened after I left—indeed, first of all what went on in secret during the tumultuous years I was here—and then what the physical damage has been and the moral damage and finally the state of the German spirit after defeat and collapse.

There is so much more I could learn if I could linger on. The picture is so black. Are there no shadings? Could I not find some? Are there no "good Germans," for instance, on which to build one's hopes? Ah, surely! Was there not the poet Adam Kuckhoff, who did not give in? Who was convicted of "high treason"? Who was hanged on the gallows at Plötzensee on the morning of August 5, 1943? Who, before he was led away, wrote his wife, Greta, one of the most moving poems and one of the most courageous letters ever penned by man? Yes, there was Kuckhoff and the poet Bonhoeffer and others in this sad land who gave their lives in the name of human decency.

But amidst these ruins I do not hear their names. Was the sacrifice of these few of no account? Is it not rather the spirit of Hitler and Himmler that is rising again from the debris? Is it not *their*deaths and their deeds that count among these tragic people? And are the Germans not already waiting to follow another diabolical Führer to still another destruction? Alas, so it seems to me.

Tomorrow I shall leave Berlin—perhaps for the last time. I am weary of the Berlin story I started to chronicle so long ago, which has been the core of my life for more than a decade. I was lucky, though, that it turned out to be the most important story of my generation, starting, almost unnoticed, here in this city and in the end engulfing the world, uprooting the lives of the mechanic in Stalingrad, the farmer near Cedar Rapids, Iowa, and the sheep-grower in Australia on the other side of the planet.

I am weary and have had enough of it. Surely there must be something less ugly, not so brutal and evil, that I can concentrate on in the remaining years. The sprawling, crazy, wonderful land of America, certainly. My family, which I hardly know, the children whom I have scarcely seen. And perhaps poetry and music and the theater and, above all, Peace.

At home, maybe, they will say the German story is not finished, the German problem still not solved, a third German war not too far off, and one must not abandon thinking of it and writing of it. They will be right. The German story will never be finished. But there are others who can write of it better than I. It has been easy to exaggerate my meager contribution because of the lucky sales of a book of hasty notes and because of the peculiar range of radio. Now to come down to earth. To clear out of this German land for good. To seek another life.

A postscript there must be. Tomorrow I shall set out for Nuremberg, there to see justice try to catch up with some of the vile little men who have wrought this awful destruction to the human race. Will it—can it—overtake them?

Frankfurt am Main, *Saturday, November* 17

The stench of the dead under the ghastly ruins of Kassel last night beneath the winter's full moon! ...the first sight, in the early-morning moonlit fog, of the rubble of this once great German city of Frankfurt, the birthplace of Goethe, the seat of election of the German kings, the capital of the German Confederation, a stronghold of the nineteenth-century German liberals, a great business center and, just before its end, a bulwark of Nazism.... Dead it is, in the cold ruins....

Nuremberg, *Sunday, November* 18

It is gone! The lovely medieval town behind the moat is utterly destroyed. It is a vast heap of rubble, beyond description and beyond hope of rebuilding. As the prosaic U.S. Army puts it, Nuremberg is "91 per cent dead." The old town, I should say, the old Nuremberg of Dürer and Hans Sachs and the Meistersingers and the venerable churches of St. Lorenz and St. Sebald and Our Lady and the old Rathaus and my favorite inn, the Bratwurstglöcklein (dating from A.D. 1400 or thereabouts), is 99 per cent "dead."

I crawled for hours today in the debris looking for familiar landmarks. Few were left, and none intact. The façade of the Gothic Frauenkirche on the market place (known as Adolf Hitler Platz when I was last here, in 1937) stands precariously, supported by two side walls. The rest of the church has been smashed into dust. St. Lorenz, one of the oldest and most beautiful Protestant churches in Germany, probably still can be saved, though it has been badly smashed. Half the wonderful old frame dwellings along the river Pegnitz have caved into the stream. Most of old Nuremberg's winding little streets are completely blotted out. The Deutscher Hof, where Hitler always stayed during the annual Nazi Party rallies in September, I could not find at all. The whole block was gone.

What had happened? It was a sunny, pleasant afternoon, the burghers were out for a breath of air and a little solar warmth, and I asked some of them. The first big bombings had come in October 1943, they said. The last one, the biggest of all, the one that really completed the destruction of Nuremberg, had come, they recalled, the day after New Year's Day in 1945. That was the day the medieval city finally died and was buried in its own ruins.

The gripping beauty, the great charm, the very soul of the ancient city, though, had departed—I always felt—when the Nazis came. Spiritually Nuremberg had died then. The Nazis had made of it the city of their annual party rallies—those obscene orgies of the Teutonic herd in which the German man and woman had joyously shed their individuality, their decency, their dignity as human beings, and become merged in the putrid, inhuman mass that Hitler was shaping.

Oh, I had seen it with my own eyes! In 1934 and again in 1937 I had been sent here as an American newspaperman to describe the foul performance. Night after night under the arc of searchlights (which really had been built for the approaching war), by the glare of the barbarian torchlights and between the blood-curdling shouting ("We are strong and will get stronger!" they kept yelling in the night), I had heard Hitler rave and Göring rant and watched the miserable Jew-baiter Streicher brandishing his horsewhip. Was it not proof of its utter degradation and final death that in this once great center of European culture, where the incomparable Albrecht Dürer had lived and created, the repulsive, debauched Julius Streicher, who boasted of his pornographic publications and his pornographic "library" and his own lecherous fornications, had become supreme political boss and indeed the first citizen of Nuremberg?

In this town, once esteemed throughout the civilized world, I had heard the frenzied shouting of the madmen when on September 5, 1934, Hitler had made his ridiculous "announcement" that "the German form of life is definitely determined for the next thousand years. There will be no revolution in Germany," he told them, "for the next one thousand years!"

The once sturdy burghers of Nuremberg, like all the rest of the Germans, had become intoxicated by the evil Nazi gospel and they were proud their beautiful city had become the scene of the monstrous annual party rally.

Now in their grotesque ruins did they recall it all? What was in their minds this Sunday afternoon? It was difficult to tell. They seemed a bit more dignified, a little more cool toward us in enemy uniform, than the Berliners or the people of Frankfurt. Resentful they were, naturally, and sullen. Oh, they had applauded wildly the dire threats against the foreign lands that Hitler had uttered from this place. They had hurrahed and tossed flowers at the SA brown-shirts and the SS black-coats and the gray-clad soldiers parading through their ancient, winding streets. But like everyone else throughout the German wasteland they had never wanted to face the consequences of all that had been hatched and nurtured here.

The consequences had come late and sudden and with terrible fury. All that loving, knowing hands had wrought here in stone and wood, in shape and color, for nine hundred years, had been pulverized into dust and ashes in a brief, fiery moment by a flick of the hand of youths from the distant Anglo-Saxon lands whose short lives, probably, had never been touched by this particular flowering of civilization and whose bomb-sights, at any rate, had been aimed not at it but at a deadly arsenal near by, which was helping to keep Hitler's Germany in the war and which therefore had to be destroyed.

It was a fearful consequence. Saturation bombing, which the Germans had originated over London and Coventry, had never been an ideal solution for the Allies, and an American could feel sick in the stomach and the heart and the mind at the contemplation of its inaccuracy here. But was it not a fate of war, the fate that Warsaw and Rotterdam and so many other innocent non-German cities had first experienced, a fate determined by those who bred the war in the German places such as Nuremberg?

A bit dazed still, I went over late in the afternoon to the Courthouse to do my Sunday broadcast. The tiny radio "studio" looked directly on the courtroom. It was cold and bare. Raucous GI's were testing the lights and shoving furniture about, making ready for the trial of Göring, Hess, Ribbentrop, Rosenberg, and the seventeen other Nazi leaders whom I had seen strut so arrogantly about this town and who, day after tomorrow, will face the consequences of all the blood of this world they helped to spill.

Nuremberg, *Monday, November* 19

Are we, in this shattered old German town, on the eve of a great event in history? Will the trial of the Nazi war criminals, which starts tomorrow in the local Courthouse, establish—as some believe—principles as important to mankind as Magna Carta, the Bill of Rights, and habeas corpus? Is it just barely possible that this trial may make a greater contribution to the outlawing of war than all the past pious resolutions of nations and men, than the Hague Conventions, than a thousand solemn treaties, than the Charter and the machinery of the new United Nations organization?

Exciting questions! All day long today they kept bobbing up in my mind. Certainly, nothing of this kind has ever been attempted before. Never was there an International *Criminal*Court. The World Court at The Hague did not deal with the *crimes*of men and nations. In fact, no generally recognized code of world criminal law has ever existed, strictly speaking.

How did we arrive at the stage we are in at Nuremberg, then? A lawyer versed in history could, I suppose, trace a gradual development over two or three thousand years, or for as long as men have been insane enough to carry on wars. But even at the end of the first World War we had not progressed very far. There was a feeble attempt then to punish the German war criminals. It turned out to be a farce, though not a very funny one. In 1919, as I recall, the Allies drew up a list of 3,000 Germans accused of war crimes. The number was quickly reduced to 892. Of these, only *twelve* were finally brought to justice before a German court at Leipzig. Three of the twelve failed to show up for their trial. Charges against three others were dropped by order of the German court. The six remaining men, all minor offenders, got off with light sentences. To most Germans the whole affair was a joke, just another example of how dumb the victors could be.

This time it looks as though we were going to do better. And for this the whole world is indebted to Justice Robert H. Jackson, who, with a perseverance rare in our fickle times, succeeded in convincing first his own government and then the governments of our British, French, and Russian allies of the wisdom and of the necessity of haling the Nazi culprits before the International Military Tribunal. Few at home realize the magnitude of his accomplishment, and fewer over here. But I suspect history some day will give him credit.

The most important thing about this trial, as Jackson has never tired of pointing out, is not the conviction and sentence of the miserable Nazi thugs, desirable though it is that retribution overtake them, but that the four great powers on this earth (Russia included) have committed themselves to the principle that a war of aggression is a crime and that those who plot it and wage it are liable to be prosecuted, and convicted and punished after due and fair trial. The four powers agreed to that in London on August 8 last.

There are some, of course, especially among the timid hairsplitters of the legal profession in Great Britain and the United States, who complain that this cannot be a fair trial because, after all, there has never been an internationally recognized law forbidding aggressive war or even certain savage practices of war, and that therefore we are trying the Nazi leaders by *ex post facto*law—that is, making them liable for crimes that were not punishable when they committed them. We are, these timid souls assert, making the rules after the crimes were perpetrated.

It does seem to a layman like myself that there are two mighty arguments against these legal hairsplitters. First, there have been for a long time rules against murder, torture, and enslavement generally recognized by all civilized peoples and indeed embodied in their domestic laws. As Jackson said in his report to the President on June 7: "We propose to punish acts which have been regarded as criminal since the time of Cain and have been so written in every civilized code."

In the second place—and most people seem already to have forgotten this—the Allies did give the Nazi barbarians fair warning that they would be held accountable for their criminal acts. This warning was issued by Roosevelt, Churchill, and Stalin in a statement given out in Moscow on November 1, 1943. Their governments, they said, had been shocked by the evidence of atrocities, massacres, and cold-blooded mass executions being perpetrated by the Hitlerite forces.

"Accordingly," the Moscow statement continued, "the three Allied powers, speaking in the interests of the thirty-three United Nations, hereby solemnly declare and give full warning of their declaration as follows: At the time of granting of any armistice to any government which may be set up in Germany, those German officers and men and members of the Nazi party who have been responsible for or have taken a consenting part in… atrocities, massacres and executions will be sent back to the countries in which their abominable deeds were done in order that they may be judged and punished according to the laws of these liberated countries…."

The major criminals whose offenses had no particular geographical localization, it was laid down at Moscow, would be punished by joint decision of the Allies. It is these who will go on trial here tomorrow.

"Let those who have hitherto not stained their hands with innocent blood," the warning, which surely was written by Churchill, concluded, "beware lest they join the ranks of the guilty, for most assuredly the three Allied Powers will pursue them to the uttermost ends of the earth and will deliver them to their accusers in order that justice may be done."

And so tonight, here in Nuremberg, we stand, as Jackson so eloquently put it in his report to the President, "at one of those rare moments when the thought and institutions and habits of the world have been shaken by the impact of world war on the lives of countless millions. Such occasions rarely come and quickly pass."

Nuremberg, *Tuesday, November* 20

This, then, is the climax! This is the moment you have been waiting for all these black, despairing years! To see Justice catch up with Evil. To see it overtake these barbaric little men who almost destroyed our world. This, really, is the end of the long night, of the hideous nightmare.

And how the mighty have fallen! Shorn of the power and the glory and the glittering trappings of Nazidom, how little and mean and mediocre they look—the twenty defendants in the dock this day! How was it possible, you ask yourself in amazement, that these nondescript-looking individuals, fidgeting nervously in their rather shabby clothes, wielded, when last you saw them, only five years ago, such monstrous power? How could *they*, so measly of countenance as they slump in their seats, have conquered a great nation and almost the world? Their metamorphosis staggers you. Were *these* the conquerors, the strutting leaders of the Master Race? Why, the sudden loss of power seems to have stripped them clean of the arrogance, the insolence, the truculence that was their very being in all the years I knew them. How quickly they have become broken, miserable little men!

They are already seated in the prisoner's dock when I enter the courtroom at nine forty a.m. The first sight of them is indescribable.

There is Göring. He sits in the first seat in the first of the two rows that compose the dock. It is the number-one place and it strikes you that at last he has achieved his long ambition of being Number One in the Nazi hierarchy, though not precisely as he had once dreamed. At first glance I scarcely recognize him. He has lost much weight—eighty pounds, a U.S. Army doctor whispers to me. The fat, pouchy face I knew is much thinner now. He looks younger and healthier, with his excess weight gone and his drug habit cured—an achievement of our army medical corps. His faded air-force uniform, shorn of the insignia and of the medals he loved so childishly, hangs loosely on him. He could hardly strut in it now. And gone is his burliness, the old arrogance, the flamboyant air. Indeed, he sits through the five-and-a-half-hour opening session of court quite subdued, though attentive and alert to the proceedings. Often he reaches for his earphones and with a gesture that is almost meek, almost humble, clasps them over his head so that he can listen to the simultaneous German translation of something that is being said in English or French or Russian. At such moments, I cannot help thinking, he looks more like a genial radio operator on a ship at sea than the former tyrant I had heard so often thundering his threats against the world. It is wonderful how a twist of fate can reduce a man to normal size.

Next to Göring sits Rudolf Hess, the number-three man of the Third Reich until his ridiculous flight to England. How on earth, you ask again, could *that* man have been one of the top leaders of a great nation? Here is really a broken man, his face so emaciated it looks like a skeleton, his mouth twitching nervously, his once bright eyes staring vacantly and stupidly around the courtroom. It is the first time I have ever seen Hess out of uniform. In the black coat of the SS he always seemed a strapping fellow. Today in a threadbare civilian suit he looks small and wizened. Unlike the others, he pays little attention to what is going on and sits for most of the time reading a novel balanced on his knees. We know that he claims to have lost his memory, but he seems to me to behave normally enough. He was never very bright and he certainly does not appear bright today. It is his deterioration that startles you. Here is the wreck of a man whom Hitler not so long ago wanted to succeed him as dictator of Germany.

Next in line is the insufferable mountebank Joachim von Ribbentrop, Hitler's former Foreign Minister. How often in the grim years have I sat in the Foreign Office in the Wilhelmstrasse and watched this arrogant nincompoop strut in to a press conference to announce in a snarling voice that another innocent, decent land had "provoked" Germany into attacking it! He was an evil, pompous little ignoramus, this former champagne-salesman who had married the boss's (the German champagne king, Henkell's) daughter, and only in the underworld of the Nazi gangsters could such a creature attain prominence. Even among most of them his vanity and arrogance were too much, but Hitler, for some reason, liked him and kept him on as his errand-boy at the Foreign Office until the very end. One glance today shows that the turn of events has shattered this scheming little worm too. Ah, now he is bent and beaten and aged beyond belief. During a recess he shuffles past me as two guards escort him to the toilet. His body is stooped, his face pale, his eyes vacant—a defeated, broken man if I have ever seen one.

In the dock on Ribbentrop's left sits Wilhelm Keitel in an army officer's faded uniform stripped of all markings. He had been something of a jaunty Prussian, this former field marshal and chief of the Supreme Command. I had last seen him at close quarters at Compiègne when he, on Hitler's behalf, dictated armistice terms to France in the sad June days of 1940. I remember how cocky he was then, like all Germans when they are on top, always prancing when he walked and wearing his cap at a rakish angle. There is nothing prancing or jaunty about the old field marshal today. He too is subdued, though he is not a broken man as are most of the others. The massacre of so many souls does not seem to weigh on him unduly. His appetite obviously is still good. He keeps munching crackers—from an American Army K-ration kit.

On his left squats Alfred Rosenberg, the phony "philosopher" and once the mentor of Hitler and the Nazi movement. He too has lost weight, the puffiness on the sallow, square face is gone, and he looks younger and healthier than when I saw him last. Dressed in a dark-brown suit, this dull, confused, but dangerous Balt who contributed so much to the Nazis' race hatreds, who superintended the loot of art objects from the conquered lands, and who finally helped direct the dreadful extermination of the Slav people in the conquered Russian territories, is nervous in the dock, lurching forward to catch every word, his hands shaking.

Next is a real barbarian in captivity for you! Hans Frank, the lawyer, who as Governor General of occupied Poland decimated the Polish people and wiped out millions of Jews. He strikes you immediately as the type of refined murderer who, like Himmler, could kill and kill without getting excited about it or even appearing, personally, as particularly brutal. Today he is easily the most self-assured man in the dock. He keeps his back half-turned on the prosecutors as they read the lengthy indictment of his crimes.

At his side farther down is Wilhelm Frick, a cold and ruthless man behind his rather modest exterior. He was one of Hitler's chief henchmen, but toward the end of the regime became somewhat forgotten. Today he seems a forlorn figure in his checkered sport coat. But one could not forget his brutality as Hitler's first Minister of Interior and, in the end, as the "Protector" of Bohemia and Moravia.

It is difficult to recognize the next man in the dock, Julius Streicher. The former undisputed master of this town, who strode through its ancient streets brandishing a whip and waxed fat on pornography and Jew-baiting, has rather wilted away. He sits there, an obscene, bald, decrepit old man, perspiring profusely. Occasionally the old scowl comes back as he glares at the judges. The guards tell me Streicher is convinced they are all Jews. It fortifies your belief in ultimate justice to see this repulsive German at last brought to judgment.

Walther Funk, who shouldered Schacht out of the presidency of the Reichsbank and of the ministership of Economics, comes next. He merely looks like a more aged toad than before, still coarse, greasy, and shifty-eyed. Next to him, and the last one in the first row, is a man who would not speak to him for ten years until today—the inimitable Dr. Hjalmar Horace Greeley Schacht. It is evident from the very start that the wily banker, who did more than any other individual in Germany to bring Hitler to power, is furious at having to stand trial with men he now—conveniently—considers as thugs. Sitting erect, his head separated from the rest of his body by his high choker collar, he folds his arms defiantly across his chest. Knowing English, he follows the reading of the indictment without earphones and with rapt attention. Occasionally he deigns to turn to Funk, whom he despises, to exchange a word. I am told Schacht is sure he will be acquitted.

We can dispose of the second row of accused more quickly. The first two gentlemen are the two Grand Admirals, Karl Doenitz and Erich Raeder. Doenitz, an able naval officer who worked out the wolf-pack technique for German submarines before he succeeded Raeder as commander-in-chief of the navy, sits erect in a civilian suit and looks for all the world like a grocery clerk. Hard to imagine him as the successor of Hitler, which he was—for a brief moment. Raeder, still in uniform, still clinging to his high upturned collar, has aged beyond his already considerable years. The spark that enabled him to build up the German Navy after World War I has gone out of him completely. He is a bewildered old man today.

Beside him is the most personable-looking and the youngest of the defendants, Baldur von Schirach, leader of the Hitler Youth and, during the war, the hated *Gauleiter* of Vienna. He looks more American than German, his parents having been American, I believe, and one of his grandfathers a soldier in the Union Army during the American Civil War. Young Schirach actually believed in the Nazi nonsense, serving Hitler with fanatical loyalty and great ruthlessness, particularly in corrupting the youth of Germany with the poison of Nazism. Today he seems a bit dazed at finding himself in this place.

Fritz Sauckel, next to him, the boss of slave labor, looks like a pig, with his narrow little slit-eyes. If Germany had been a normal land, he would have found his place in life behind the counter in a butcher shop, for he looks like a small-town butcher. He is nervous today and sways to and fro. The stiff back of the man next to him, Alfred Jodl, does not sway. He sits gravely in his faded army uniform, this tight-lipped Bavarian who became the most powerful general in the German

Army and the closest to Hitler. Like Keitel, he could never say no to Hitler, which was probably the principal reason for his advancement, as it was of Keitel's.

And next comes old Franz von Papen, incredibly aged, the eyes sunk in, the skin taut over the wizened face, the shoulders stooped, but still looking the part of the old fox. He has had many narrow escapes in his life, but here at last justice seems to have nailed him. He does not like it at all, you can see. Arthur Seyss-Inquart, the Austrian traitor and, during the war, the brutal oppressor of the Dutch, and Albert Speer, Hitler's Minister of Armament and Munitions, are next in line and show little emotion of any kind.

Next to the last is Baron Konstantin von Neurath, the typical career diplomat, without convictions and without integrity. Hitler had used him for a time as Foreign Minister and then as a front man for his butchery in Prague, where Neurath was the first "Protector." He sits in the dock today, a broken old man, apparently dazed by the discovery that one can come to the end of the road to compromise. He hardly knows how to stand up and be counted, for this forlorn remnant of a conservative old German family has never stood for anything in his life except serving whoever was his master. Last in the dock is the most unimportant, one Hans Fritzsche, whose voice on the radio was so like his master's, Goebbels's, that it was often difficult to tell them apart. He is here, I take it, as a sort of substitute for Goebbels and appears to be taken aback by the importance attached to him.

Promptly at ten a.m. the bailiff, whose manner and voice make plain he could only have been imported from an English law court, bawls to the occupants of the courtroom to come to attention and rise. The prisoners, quick to respond to any orders, leap to their feet. The judges file in.

They are an interesting lot. Lord Justice Lawrence, who will preside, is a fine old chunk of Britain with an ample Gladstonian forehead and the restrained self-assurance of all eminent British judges. He looks like a cross between Gladstone and Stanley Baldwin. Within a moment's passing he has stamped his dominance of the courtroom on all present, including the prisoners, you feel. He will be firm, unemotional, and fair. His alternate is Sir Norman Birkett, probably the keenest legal mind in the room, a thin, gangling fellow whom I had often seen at court in my younger days in London, where he was among the two or three greatest trial lawyers of the time.

Francis Biddle, our former Attorney General, is a bit self-conscious, almost tripping on his robe as he mounts the bench. At his side is Judge John J. Parker, a homespun North Carolinian, whom an irate Senate once kept out of the Supreme Court. Europe and especially the insane Nazi world are a bit strange to him, you feel, but he takes them in his even stride. The French judge, Donnedieu de Vabres, resembles Clemenceau one minute and Pétain the next. His alternate, Robert Falco, looks like any French lawyer one used to see crowding the halls of the Palais de Justice in Paris. He seems to have a tendency to drool.

All these judges wear black, judicial robes, but the Russian judge, Major General Iona Timofeevich Nikitchenko, vice-president of the Supreme Court of the U.S.S.R., and his alternate, Lieutenant Colonel Alexander Fedorovich Volchkov, are in military uniform, resplendent with decorations.

Without ado, Justice Lawrence raps for order and proceeds to read an opening statement. "The trial," he says, "which is now about to begin is unique in the history of jurisprudence of the world, and it is of supreme importance to millions of people all over the globe. For these reasons, there is laid upon everybody who takes part in this trial a solemn responsibility to discharge their duties without fear or favor in accordance with the sacred principles of law and justice.... It is the duty of all concerned to see that the trial in no way departs from those principles and traditions which alone give justice its authority and the place it ought to occupy in the affairs of all civilized states."

He warns that the Tribunal "will insist upon the complete maintenance of order and decorum, and will take the strictest measures to enforce it."

Whereupon, getting down to business with dispatch, he directs the reading of the indictment. Everyone in the courtroom knows it almost by heart, but this is a trial by due process and it must be read. Justice Jackson picks his first assistant, Sidney S. Alderman, to begin the tedious task of reading, and later the British, French, and Russian attorneys pitch in to carry on with it. "The United States of America," Alderman intones, "the French Republic, the United Kingdom of Great Britain and Northern Ireland, and the Union of Soviet Socialist Republics *against* Hermann Wilhelm Göring, Rudolf Hess, etc., defendants...."

One by one the four counts are read: count one, the charge of conspiracy to commit crimes against peace, war crimes, and crimes against humanity; count two, the detailed charge of crimes against peace; count three, war crimes; count four, crimes against humanity. All the obscene atrocities, to which we seem to have become hardened, are described and enumerated. The prisoners are bored. So is everyone else.

One's eyes wander over this strange, unprecedented scene. On the right, as I look from the press box, the raised bench of the tribunal. Directly across the room, facing the judges, is the prisoners' dock. Back of the defendants, who sit on hard, bare, wooden benches, are eight American M.P.'s, in neat GI uniforms, white belts, and helmets, carrying nightsticks and side arms. They are on the alert to see that no materials for suicide pass between the prisoners and their lawyers, who are crowded at small tables immediately in front of them. Directly before us sit the prosecutors of the four nations. And at the opposite end are the interpreters, behind glass partitions, jabbering away into microphones in English, French, German, and Russian. You can adjust your earphone to whichever language you please. This setup, installed by the U.S. Navy, should save years of time, since it does away with the tedious business of waiting for every word spoken here to be translated into three other languages. Now the translation is simultaneous. Judge Lawrence, for example, poses a question in English to a German lawyer who understands only his own tongue. The question comes over his earphones in German. He answers in German and simultaneously the judge gets the answer in English. Thus international trials in our day, with the awful barriers of language practically wiped out.

Over the main entrance to the courtroom, one notices there is some rather bad German art work representing, I take it, eternal justice with the sword. The miserable little men in the dock and the system they built up had denied justice to all who stood in their way. Perhaps, in a rough sense, it was eternal, a durable thing you could not forever do away with despite your strength and your tyranny. Had it not, quietly and decently, returned to this little room today, as sure as death itself?

Nuremberg, *Wednesday, November* **21**

I think we have heard today one of the great trial addresses of history. The opening statement for the United States, delivered by Justice Jackson, was not, to be sure, a masterly oration, for in his public speaking he is no Cicero. The necessity to proceed slowly so that the interpreters could keep up made it impossible to deliver an impassioned oration even had Mr. Jackson felt so inclined and been able to do so. He did speak out in a clear, even voice. It was what he had to say that was so eloquent, the words and the phrases and the sentences ringing out by themselves, on their own, so that they matched the sentiments and the hopes and the aspirations and the great challenge of this moment and of this fleeting opportunity.

Listening to him, I felt the thrill I had as a youth when I had taken to reading in my father's law books the texts of some of the great trial speeches of the past: Cicero's orations against Catiline, the magnificent onslaughts of Richard Brinsley Sheridan (who was also a fine playwright) in the trial of Warren Hastings, and so on. Later I had come across the moving address of Sir Roger Casement at the end of the trial in which he was condemned to death for treason, with its sublime and unforgettable phrases ("Ireland has outlived the failure of all her hopes"... "the painful stairs of Irish history—that treadmill of a nation whose labors are as vain for her own uplifting as the convict's execution are for his redemption"). And there was the throb in the spine at the mere reading, years later in India, of Gandhi's historic speech to the court at Allahabad before receiving his prison sentence.

My spine throbbed today as Jackson, neatly dressed in a morning coat and striped trousers, stood at the prosecutor's stand midway between the judges and the defendants and used the power of language to build up, hour after hour, his masterly case against the Nazi barbarism and these twenty lost men who had helped to perpetrate it. They had not in recent years heard this kind of reasoned talk nor been forced to hear a recital of the gruesome details of their crimes. All except Hess listened attentively.

The speech, I understand, will be published at home tomorrow, so I will not put it in here. Perhaps a word or two, though, for this little record:

"May it please Your Honors," he began.

"The privilege of opening the first trial in history for crimes against the peace of the world imposes a grave responsibility. The wrongs which we seek to condemn and punish have been so calculated, so malignant and so devastating, that civilization cannot tolerate their being ignored because it cannot survive their being repeated. That four great nations, flushed with victory and stung with injury, stay the hand of vengeance and voluntarily submit their captive enemies to the judgment of the law is one of the most significant tributes that Power ever has paid to Reason.

"…The common sense of mankind demands that law shall not stop with the punishment of petty crimes by little people. It must also reach men who possess themselves of great power and make deliberate and concerted use of it to set in motion evils which leave no home in the world untouched….

"In the prisoners' dock sit twenty-odd broken men. Reproached by the humiliation of those they have led almost as bitterly as by the desolation of those they have attacked, their personal capacity for evil is forever past. It is hard now to perceive in these miserable men as captives the power by which as Nazi leaders they once dominated much of the world and terrified most of it. Merely as individuals, their fate is of little consequence to the world.

"What makes this inquest significant is that these prisoners represent sinister influences that will lurk in the world long after their bodies have returned to dust. They are living symbols of racial hatreds, of terrorism and violence, and of the arrogance and cruelty of power…. They have so identified themselves with the philosophies they conceived and with the forces they directed that any tenderness to them is a victory and an encouragement to all the evils which are attached to their names."

He launches into the heart of the case, the Nazi conspiracy to make aggressive war and commit crimes against humanity. Facts and figures and recitals from the most incriminating of secret Nazi documents pour forth. "Our proof will be disgusting," he warns the court, "and you will say I have robbed you of your sleep…. To cruel experiments the Nazis added obscene ones…. At Dachau… victims were immersed in cold water until their body temperature was reduced to 28 degrees centigrade (82.4 degrees Fahrenheit), when they all died immediately. This was in August 1942. But the 'doctor's' technique improved. By February, 1943, he was able to report that thirty persons were chilled to 27 to 29 degrees [centigrade], their hands and feet frozen white, and their bodies 'rewarmed' by a hot bath. But the Nazi scientific triumph was 'rewarming with animal heat.' The victim, all but frozen to death, was surrounded with bodies of living women until he revived and responded to his environment by having sexual intercourse. Here Nazi degeneracy reached its nadir."

Justice Jackson reveals, in passing, that captured German documents will show that in October 1940, "Hitler was occupied with the question of the occupation of the Atlantic islands with a view to the prosecution of war against America at a later date."

He has started speaking at 11.05 a.m., and after the luncheon interval he continues until late in the afternoon. Now he reaches his peroration.

"This trial represents mankind's desperate effort to apply the discipline of the law to statesmen who have used their powers of state to attack the foundations of the world's peace.... This [is]... another step... to ensure that those who start a war will pay for it personally.... The real complaining party at your bar is Civilization...."[38]

A noble conception, and it could be contrasted to the shabby concept of law and morals presented by the rather motley crew of German defense attorneys in their motion to dismiss the indictment at the beginning of this morning's session. Their argument was just one more reminder of how little the Germans have learned from the disaster of the Nazi experiment. Their joint motion argued that trying individuals for the actions of states in launching wars "goes further than even the strictest legal minds since the early Middle Ages"! It contended further "that international law has never even thought of incriminating statesmen, generals, economic leaders of a state using force, and still less bringing these men before an international court.... As far as crimes against the peace are concerned, the present trial, therefore, has no legal basis in international law but is a procedure based on penal law; a penal law created only after the act. This is in contradiction to a legal principle that is cherished in the world... Every defendant must feel treated unjustly if he is punished under a murder law created ex post facto."

And these learned German lawyers, some of whom are convinced Nazis still (and incidentally frightened to death, most of them, of their tough clients), end up with the ridiculous proposal that the whole trial, as such, be dropped, and that it "limit itself to investigation of what happened." They propose a further joker, that after the investigation "the community of law-abiding nations should *then*create law to establish punishment for such individuals who intentionally start *in the future*an unjust war."

Thus the Nazi culprits would automatically go scot free! Justice Lawrence is not impressed with the plea and patiently explains to the defense attorneys that it conflicts with Article III of the Charter, which stipulates that the Tribunal cannot be challenged by the prosecution or defense. The plea, therefore, he rules, will not be entertained.

After a brief recess to give the German lawyers an opportunity to confer with their clients about their pleas, the British judge announces: "I will now call on the defendants to plead guilty or not guilty."

Göring heaves himself up at the mention of his name and strides to a microphone in front of the prisoners' dock. You can see a dramatic speech mounting in his very loins.

"Before I make—" he starts to say, but Justice Lawrence lets him get no further. There is a heavy pounding of his gavel. "I have already explained," he remarks tartly, "that the defendants are not to make a speech." The mighty Reichsmarshal is taken aback. This is new treatment for him. He puffs. Then angrily: "I am not guilty."

Hess is next. He speaks but a single word, shouted defiantly: "*Nein!*"

"That," says Justice Lawrence with eloquent calmness, "will be entered as a plea of not guilty."

And so, in varying phrases, they all plead not guilty. Then Göring bobs up a second time, indicating he wishes to be heard. But Lawrence will not be cowed, even by Göring. "You are not entitled," he says softly, "to address the Tribunal except through your counsel at the present time." Glowering, the once mighty man clumps down in his seat. It is time for Jackson to open the argument for the prosecution.

Home to the "castle" tonight with flu and fever, but happy inside that in a world so full of bastards, the voice of decency can still rise and still be heard.

Nuremberg, *Thursday, November 22*

Thanksgiving. A raw, cold day, and I spent most of it in bed trying to lick my flu. Got up about dusk, which comes a little after four p.m. here now, and wandered up to the "castle's" bar. Ed Morgan of the *Chicago Daily News*, one of the most thoughtful of the new generation of correspondents, was there. We had a long talk. We tried, as newspapermen in a bar will do, to find an answer to a question: why the disintegration (as General Marshall called it the other day in his speech to the *Herald Tribune*Forum) of the U.S. Army so soon after its mighty conquests?

Fundamentally, we wondered, was it not a reflection of a disintegration at home in America, of our headlong rush to forget the war, get the boys back home, and return hell-bent to "normalcy"? It was, of course, a very human and natural thing for an American man to want to get back home, now that the war was over. But who would stay on in Germany, then—at least until he could be replaced—to do an unpleasant but necessary job if we did not want to have a *third*German war? (The Germans might win the third.)

Ed thought there were several reasons why we are doing such a lousy job of occupation.

1. American officers especially (but also GI's) think first of "creature comforts." (Ah, but was that not characteristic of all of us Americans with our mania for the material things?) Now, Ed said, our officers were busy holing up for the winter, expending most of their energies on getting a comfortable billet, plenty of heat for it, good food and drink for it, and a girl, of course, for it.

2. A typical American has a natural and healthy yen to get his immediate job done. Thus if the Germans in his town are not getting enough food or fuel, his first inclination is to try to see that they get it. If there is a factory silent in his town, he wants to get it humming. It would scarcely occur to

him to adjust his inclinations to the larger political picture of how Germany is to be treated; for instance, whether the additional food he may get for his Germans or the coal for his factory should not first go to the Dutch or Belgians or other victims of the Germans. He has no idea of what the victims in Europe went through under the hideous German occupation. Nor is he curious to learn.

This leads to point 3: our weird lack of political sense. Ed described a German motor-truck factory he visited the other day. It makes Daimler-Benz trucks. An American captain is in charge, but a young sergeant is the real American driving force in the plant. He has a knack "for getting things done." His factory is consequently turning out more than its quota of trucks. There is only one drawback. But he does not want to hear of it. The German manager of the plant is an out-and-out Nazi, a party member. General Eisenhower has issued strict military orders that no party members can remain in managerial positions. But our captain and sergeant pay no attention to Eisenhower, supreme chief though he may be. They will be judged by their immediate superiors, they say, on the number of trucks they turn out. It fills them with pride to turn them out ahead of schedule. The German workers protest. They threaten to strike unless the Nazi manager is turned out. The captain and sergeant crack down on the workers. No nonsense, no strikes, from them. And so the workers, Ed believes, come to the conclusion that the Americans either are political idiots or conquered Germany to save it for the Nazis.

In miniature, I'm afraid, this is the true picture of our occupation of Germany.

A lot of drinks, considering the wretched flu, and afterward quite a good turkey dinner, the first decent meal we have had in this mess. After dinner ran into Silliman, who used to be my debating coach in college. He's a major now and has been concerned with apprehending the Nazi criminals. Surprising, he thinks, how easily they gave themselves up. Probably they were fool enough to think the good-natured Americans would not be too tough on them compared, say, with the Russians.

Nuremberg, *Friday, November* **23**

Certainly no other trial in history can have been like this. The Nazi defendants are going to be convicted by their own words, their own records, their own foul deeds. The idiots wrote everything down, and in the chaos of the collapse were unable to destroy the damaging evidence.

This afternoon the American prosecution unloaded on the court (and on us) 91,000 words of secret Nazi documents tracing the road to aggressive war which the Nazis deliberately took. The defendants in the dock appeared flabbergasted. All the skeletons in all the dark closets were showing up. Here was not what Hitler or Göring or Ribbentrop or Hess said for public consumption—the propaganda lies about wanting peace. Here was what they said at their secret meetings at which war was plotted and planned. Here at last was the *truth* for the world to see.

Most of the material I saw in Berlin and it is already in these hasty notes. There was some new stuff today about a preliminary understanding reached in Berlin on April 4, 1941, between Hitler and the then Japanese Foreign Minister, Yosuke Matsuoka, for war against the United States. Hitler, we learn, on that day promised that Germany would go to war against the United States *without delay* in case Japan became involved in a conflict with America.

This, then—April 4, 1941—was the date on which America's involvement in the war became certain, and it is a terrible irony, I think, and a terrible indictment of the United States and its lack of political sense that our destiny in this instance was decided not by ourselves but by a German and a Jap sitting in an ornate room in Berlin. The two men had a very interesting conversation that day and, as usual, the German government preserved in its secret archives complete notes on the talk. The pertinent part reads as follows:

"The Führer pointed out [to Matsuoka] that Germany would immediately take the consequences if Japan got involved with the United States.... Therefore Germany would strike without delay in case of a conflict between Japan and America."

Matsuoka, for his part, left no doubt in Hitler's mind that Japan intended soon to attack the United States. The secret German minutes of the meeting make this very clear.

"As regards Japanese-American relations," they state, "Matsuoka explained that... sooner or later a war with the United States would be unavoidable.... In his opinion this conflict would happen rather sooner than later. His argument was: why should Japan not decisively strike at the right moment and take the risk upon herself of a fight against America?"

At this point the wily little Japanese Foreign Minister admitted to the Führer that there were some in Japan who "hesitate to follow these trends of thought" and who considered him "a dangerous man." Hitler apparently felt the need of bucking him up a little on the subject of the Americans. The German minutes continue:

"Germany [Hitler said] had made her preparations so that no American could land in Europe. Germany would conduct a most energetic fight against America with her U-boats and her Luftwaffe, and owing to her superior experience... she would be vastly superior, and that quite apart from the fact that the German soldier naturally ranks high above the American."

We know from previous notes that Hitler had already decided to attack Russia and that in fact the date for the beginning of the war with the Soviet Union was but a couple of months off at the time of his talk with the Japanese Foreign Minister. Naturally, he did not disclose his plans to his Japanese ally. But he did throw out a hint. "He would not hesitate a moment," the secret minutes quote him as telling Matsuoka, "to reply instantly to any widening of the war, be it by Russia, be it by America."

This may be the place to bring up the question: how much did Russia know of Hitler's real intentions? There is an interesting document here in that connection which undoubtedly will not be admitted into evidence at this trial since we have both a Russian judge and a Russian prosecutor. It is a secret German memorandum on the conversation between Hitler, Ribbentrop, and Molotov in Berlin on November 12, 1940. Nazi Germany and Communist Russia were allies then, and though even the German minutes of the meeting show that a definite coolness had developed in their relations, they also show the Soviet Union begging to be allowed to become a partner in the tripartite alliance of Germany, Italy, and Japan, which, in reality, was directed mainly against the United States! The German memorandum on that point reads as follows:

"Then he [Molotov] spoke of the significance of the Three-Power Pact. What was the meaning of the New Order in Europe and Asia, and in what respect could the U.S.S.R. be a participant? Questions with regard to Russia's interests in the Balkans and the Black Sea would have to be cleared up. In relation to Rumania, Bulgaria, and Turkey it would be easier for the Russian government to take a definite position if they were given explanations. They were interested in the New Order in Europe, particularly in the tempo and form of this New Order. They would also like to have some idea of the New Order in Asia.

"Hitler answered that the Three-Power Pact would arrange matters in Europe in relation to the natural interests of the European states and that Germany would consult the Soviet Union before a settlement was reached. This was also true for Asia, where Russia would take part. Hitler thought it possible in conjunction with Russia to raise the question of the Black Sea, the Balkans, and Turkey. The crux of the matter was to prevent all attempts of America to dominate Europe.

"*Molotov said that he was fully in agreement with Hitler's remarks about the roles of the U.S.A. and England. He thought that Russia could take part in a Three-Power Pact on the condition that she came in as a partner.*"[39]

It is something to contemplate that but for Hitler's foolish decision to attack Russia, the Soviet Union, the citadel of socialism, the paradise of the workers, would in all probability have become an active partner of the Nazi-Fascist regimes of Germany, Italy, and Japan! The United States would have been in the soup then. But no doubt the party comrades at home would have found some means of justifying and even defending such a foul alliance.[40]

Nuremberg, *Sunday, November* 25

All day working on the broadcast. Sandwiched in some recordings of the actual proceedings of the trial during the past week—the first time I've done this on the Sunday show. This is a field radio could do wonders in, but until recently the network banned recordings. As a result we muffed a magnificent opportunity during the war to bring the sound and feel of battle and of combatant armies right into American homes. Here we could take the listeners right into the courtroom if there was any interest back home. Guess there isn't.

Waiting to go on the air this evening, had time to wade through some more secret German documents. Two items:

1. General Halder, in the memorandum he has drawn up at the request of the Allied High Command, claims that had Neville Chamberlain delayed his famous flight to Munich during the Czech crisis in 1938, a group of German generals would have carried out a well-planned attempt to depose Hitler and thus saved, as he puts it, the world from war. He contends that all arrangements had been made for General von Witzleben (who was later hanged for his part in the attempted assassination of the Führer on July 20, 1944) to march on Berlin with a Panzer division and arrest Hitler. The fact that the dictator remained longer than expected in Berchtesgaden held up the plan, but when he finally arrived in Berlin, the conspirators met in von Witzleben's office and decided to act immediately. Just as they were about to give the signal to set the plan in operation, the radio flashed the news that Chamberlain had agreed to fly to Munich the next day. The plot was postponed and after Chamberlain's capitulation at Munich—forgotten.

The former chief of the General Staff also speaks of a similar attempt by his predecessor, General Beck, and by Goerdeler (both of whom lost their lives in the abortive 1944 plot against Hitler's life) in 1939-40. General Halder then raises and answers a question most of us have pondered often:

"The question has frequently been asked—and particularly by the enemy—why the German officers' corps, and especially the generals, watched the development of affairs in Germany without interfering.

"The first answer is that any attempt at interference could only have been made by the army. No support could have been expected from the air force or the navy; rather the contrary.... The fight against the Supreme Commander [Hitler] had therefore to be carried out by single [army] personalities.... The number of these personalities was very small.... A single far-sighted personality [had] to take the consequences as far as his own person was concerned."

Alas, there were none willing to take the consequences and Halder gives various not very convincing excuses for this. Finally, he says, when the generals realized the army "was going to its doom, it was too late for collective measures by the military leaders, even if they had overcome their aversion to such a step, which, according to German conceptions, would be mutiny. Such an atmosphere explains July 20, 1944, when personalities who were willing to sacrifice themselves in their despair used means that cannot be approved.... But [otherwise] the clear will and determined leaders were lacking, [so the generals] did their military duty silently to the bitter end.

"The prediction," General Halder concludes, "made by General von Fritsch" (former commander-in-chief of the German Army, who committed suicide before Warsaw in September 1939) "has been fulfilled. In 1937 Fritsch said resignedly, in reply to my impassioned demand for a fight against Hitler:

'It is useless. This man is Germany's destiny, and this destiny must run its course to the end.'"

In other words, the German military went along. Not a single general, until it was too late, had the guts really to stand up to Hitler.

The truth about who sank the Cunard liner *Athenia* on the very first day of the war with the loss of more than 100 lives, including 28 American, has finally come out! The Germans, of course, did it. We have it now on the word of Admiral Doenitz.

But for years the German government officially maintained that the British sank it themselves with a time bomb in order to awaken American sentiment for themselves and against the Germans—a piece of foul propaganda still believed by many Americans when I returned home from Germany in 1941. I still remember one Sunday night in Berlin—October 22, 1939, it was—when Goebbels went on the air suddenly and without warning to angrily denounce Churchill for having sunk the *Athenia*.

Now Admiral Doenitz, in a sworn statement, tells what really happened: "U-30 returned to harbor about mid-September. I met the captain, Oberleutnant Lemp, on the lockside at Wilhelmshafen… and he asked permission to speak to me in private.... He told me at once that he thought he was responsible for the sinking of the *Athenia* in the north Channel area.... He had torpedoed a ship he afterward identified as the *Athenia* from wireless broadcasts.... I dispatched Lemp at once by air to report to headquarters at Berlin. In the meantime I ordered complete secrecy as a provisional measure. Later the same day, or early on the following day, U-boat captain had acted in good faith.

"1. The affair was to be kept a total secret.

"2. The Navy High Command considered that a court martial was not necessary as they were satisfied that the U-boat captain had acted in good faith.

"3. Political explanations would be handled by the Navy High Command.

"I had no part whatsoever in the political events in which the Führer claimed that no U-boat had sunk the *Athenia*."

However, the prosecution has found that the German admiral took good care to alter his diary on the day he reports the return of the U-30. He mentions only that she reported sinking two small freighters.

Another affidavit from a member of the U-30 crew, Adolf Schmidt, reveals that the crew was forced by its commander to sign the following oath: "I swear that I will shroud in secrecy all happenings of September 3, 1939, on board the U-30 from friend or foe and that I will erase from my memory all happenings of this day."

Such is German "honor," about which the German never ceases to prattle.

Last night I stumbled into a German newspaperman, an old acquaintance from the prewar days, a good anti-Nazi.

"How are the German people taking this trial of the Nazi war criminals?" I asked.

"They think it's propaganda," he said.

Nuremberg, *Monday, November* 26

Snow outside—the first of the year—and very lovely it looks too. Down with the flu.

Nuremberg, *Tuesday, November* 27

Woke up weak from fever, and before I had scarcely rubbed my eyes open, Howard Smith leaned over from his cot and said: "I have some bad news for you. Your mother is dead. New York told me over the feedback last night. I'm sorry." Poor Mother—I wonder how the end came. I hope it came decently and quickly and without pain.

Nuremberg, *Wednesday, November* 28

It did. Tess wires the end was "swift and painless." Later, another cable: "Mother felt well until last minute, fainted suddenly in middle of chat with neighbor, no pain, did not waken again, died twenty minutes later."

What a wonderful way to go! Tossing on this cot today, the grief recalling a thousand family pictures of the past, I thought of that time in our little Iowa town during the first German war when mother went into the downstairs bedroom and found *her*mother cold and dead. She too had passed peacefully in her sleep…. I last saw my mother the night that Roosevelt died—that spring evening… the shock… the grief….

Nuremberg, *Thursday, November* 29

A cable from Cedar Rapids, Iowa. The funeral there tomorrow, the pastor of the First Presbyterian Church officiating. I got off a cable to my brother telling of my despair at not being able to be there and setting down a few thoughts about my mother.

Up this evening, feeling a little better, and shall go back to work tomorrow. About time. I'm told I missed a dramatic scene at the trial this afternoon. An American Army film of the Nazi atrocities at the German concentration camps was shown the court. Before it started, Judge Lawrence announced no one could leave the courtroom during the showing of the picture "unless they became sick."

How did the Nazi thugs in the dock react to a pictorial presentation of some of their more obscene crimes? We have a rather accurate and even scientific report on that. When the lights in the courtroom were turned off, special hidden fluorescent lamps built in the ledges of the prisoners' dock were flashed on, casting a weird glow of soft light on the unhappy faces of the twenty men. Thus observation of their reaction was possible. It was done by two American psychiatrists, Major

Douglas M. Kelley of San Francisco and Lieutenant G.M. Gilbert of New York, who reported, in brief, as follows:

"All the defendants were obviously affected, and the majority felt profound shame at what they realized was Germany's disgrace before the world. For the most part they reacted with amazement and depression and showed the effects of severe emotional strain after viewing the film."

Specifically:

"Göring: Shielded his face with his right arm, and seemed especially upset as tortures were mentioned.

"Hess: Showed sustained interest, glaring at the screen.

"Keitel [the former field marshal, remember]: Was nervous and tense. Played with his earphone cord and mopped his face several times.

"Doenitz [the hard-boiled, thin-lipped former commander-in-chief of the German Navy, let us recall]: Was quite upset, clenching his fists, and covering his eyes with his hands.

"Schacht: Refused to look at the picture at all, turning his back on the screen. Showed no evidence of emotion.

"Funk: Broke down and cried.

"Frank [the butcher of Poland, in case we forget]: Quite overcome. He bit his nails, clenched his hands, and showed evidence of great emotion.

"Ribbentrop: Visibly depressed and quite tense. [The cold, calculating fellow couldn't take it most of the time, turning his head away from the screen. Neither could von Papen, who did the same.]

"Streicher [the whip-carrying Jew-baiter]: Kept watching without apparent emotion."

When the film had finished and the lights in the courtroom were turned on, one could see, I'm told, a stunned group of white-faced men in the prisoners' dock. The whole courtroom was as silent as a sepulcher. Justice Lawrence, hitherto equal to every occasion in his dry, matter-of-fact, judicial way, even forgot to adjourn court. The judges silently rose from their chairs and slowly strode out without saying a word. As the Nazi bigwigs were being led away, in twos, by the M.P.'s, Keitel was too overcome to move at first.

Kurt R., a former German journalist who is now a naturalized American citizen, I believe, came to my bedside this afternoon. He said he thought today marked a turning-point for the Nazi defendants. Until the film was shown, they had, after nearly two weeks of predominantly Anglo-Saxon justice, concluded, he thought, that they had a good chance of saving their necks. The British and Americans seemed to them such courteous and kind-hearted fools. But after these gruesome films proving their horrible crimes, the defendants, Kurt thought, realized that the Anglo-Saxons had the goods on them after all, and that for these hideous crimes they could never escape the noose.

Nuremberg, *Friday, November* 30

This was Rudolf Hess's day in court, and it was quite a day. Was the former number-three man of the Reich out of his mind or merely pretending to be? Judge Lawrence had promised the court would consider the matter at four p.m. today. Perhaps we would see.

The psychiatrists of America, Great Britain, France, and Russia had, we knew, been examining Hess on behalf of the court for some time. They had ascertained some curious facts and come to some interesting conclusions. These were perhaps best summed up in a report made to the Tribunal on November 17 by the Russian specialists, Dr. Eugene Krasnuchkin, Dr. Eugene Sepp, and Dr. Nicolas Kuraskov, professors of psychiatry, neurology, and medicine, respectively, at the Medical Institute of Moscow.

Reviewing first the report of Dr. T. Reece, chief consultant to the British War Office, who had had Hess under observation during his sojourn in England, the Russians disclose that "upon arrest and incarceration in England, Hess began to give expression to ideas of persecution. He feared he would be poisoned or killed and his death represented as a suicide, and that all this would be done by the English under the hypnotic influence of the Jews. Furthermore," the Russian report continues, "these delusions of persecution were maintained up to the news of the catastrophe suffered by the German Army at Stalingrad, when the manifestations were replaced by amnesia.... Furthermore there were two attempts at suicide. A knife wound, inflicted during the second attempt in the skin near the heart, gave evidence of a clearly hysterico-demonstrative character. After this there was again observed a change from amnesia to delusions of persecution, and during this period he wrote that he was *simulating*[41] his amnesia. Finally he again entered into a state of amnesia, which has been prolonged up to the present....

"Psychologically," the Russian report continues, "Hess is in a state of clear consciousness.... The loss of memory by Hess is not the result of some kind of mental disease, but represents hysterical amnesia, the basis of which is a subconscious inclination toward self-defense.... Such behavior often terminates when the hysterical person is faced with an unavoidable necessity of conducting himself correctly. Therefore, the amnesia of Hess may end upon his being brought to trial."

The Russian doctors did not want Hess exonerated "from his responsibility under the indictment." The British experts took a somewhat different view. Two days later, on November 19, a report signed by Lord Moran, president of the Royal College of Physicians, Dr. Reece and Dr. George Ruddock, chief consultant neurologist to the British War Office, advised the Tribunal that Hess "is not insane in the strict sense. His loss of memory will not entirely interfere with his comprehension of the proceedings, but it will interfere with his ability to make his defence, and to understand details of the past, which arise in evidence."

The British doctors, therefore, recommended "that further evidence should be obtained by narco-analysis."

That, as it happened, was just the kind of analysis Hess would not submit to, and that Justice Jackson—to his credit, I suppose—would not force him to submit to. It had been suggested to the American Army unit responsible for the security of the defendants on October 16 by Major Douglas M. Kelley of the Medical Corps, who was psychiatrist to the Nuremberg jail, that Hess's true condition could best be determined by a "narcohypnosis." Such a treatment was commonly used by all good psychiatrists, and though Major Kelley informed his superiors that "occasional accidents" happened, he had never seen one in one thousand cases he himself had treated.

But Hess would have none of it. After the trial maybe, but not before. Justice Jackson respected his wish, and on October 20 advised that "any treatment of this case involving the use of drugs which might cause injury to the subject is disapproved."

"This was not because I disapproved of the treatment," the American prosecutor told the court. "I approve of the treatment and would insist on it being employed if the victim were a member of my own family. But I was of the opinion that the private administration of any kind of drug to Hess would be dangerous because if he should thereafter die, even of natural causes, it would become the subject of public controversy."

That was how the case stood at four p.m. today when Justice Lawrence ordered the other prisoners sent back to their cells so that the insanity plea of Hess's lawyer could be heard. When we came back to the courtroom after a brief recess, the dock was empty of all but Hess, who sat there very composed and looking as sane as any Nazi I've ever seen. For the two weeks of the trial, it is true, he had paid little attention to the proceedings, sitting in his place on the hard wooden bench devouring novels. Now he appeared to follow what began to take place with the greatest of attention.

His German lawyer, a dull-witted fellow, embarked immediately upon a long speech. But he soon strained even his client's patience. Hess tore a sheet of paper from his notebook, scribbled something hastily, and angrily beckoned an M.P. to deliver it to his attorney. The latter looked at it, but proceeded to drone on. His plea was that Hess was suffering from a loss of memory and therefore could not follow court proceedings nor question witnesses nor indeed, generally speaking, properly defend himself.

As he said these things the defendant kept shaking his head until it got so embarrassing the bewildered lawyer stuttered something to the effect that Hess himself had not asked him to make this plea. Finally he sat down and the prosecution made brief statements. They thought, as Jackson put it, that Hess, at most, was a victim of voluntary amnesia and should stand trial.

The little German lawyer sprang up for a final word of rebuttal. Hess was now visibly peeved. He motioned his attorney to desist, which he finally did. Justice Lawrence then made as if to adjourn court for the day, but in what seemed a sort of afterthought asked the German lawyer, rather hesitantly, if he had any objection to Hess speaking for himself.

The whole courtroom was electrified. Justice Lawrence had hardly got the words out of his mouth before Hess bounded up and started to make for the lawyer's stand half-way between the dock and the bench. An M.P., with a wonderfully deadpan face, halted him and it looked for an instant as though Hess would try to push him aside. He pulled himself together and looked appealingly to the bench. Lawrence was not looking, but Justice Birkett, a nimble-witted fellow who misses nothing, was. Through the earphone we could hear him whisper to Lawrence: "He needs a mike. Get him a mike."

One was fetched by an M.P. and brought to the prisoners' dock. Hitler's former henchman, once again the center of attention and now fully conscious of it, was wonderfully composed and confident. His feeble-minded bearing of the past fortnight had vanished completely. Now he was the old Hess I had seen so often during the days of the Nazi power.

"Mr. President," he said in a clear, firm voice—and there was utter silence in the courtroom—"at the beginning of this afternoon's proceedings I handed my defense counsel a note stating that I am of the opinion that these proceedings could be shortened if I could speak briefly. What I have to say is as follows: In order to prevent any possibility of my being declared incapable of pleading, since I am willing to take part in the proceedings with the rest of them, I should like to make the following declaration to the Tribunal."

He paused for a second to scan some notes scrawled on the back of an old envelope.

"Originally I did not intend to make this declaration until a later time. *My memory is again in order.*"

Another well-timed pause to let this sink in.

"The reason why I simulated loss of memory was tactical. The truth is that only my capacity for concentration is slightly reduced. But as against that, I consider that my capacity to follow the trial, to defend myself, to put questions to witnesses or even to answer questions—in all these matters my capacities are not affected. I emphasize the fact that I bear full responsibility for everything I have done or signed or been cosignatory to. My fundamental attitude that the Tribunal is not legally competent to try me is not affected by the statement I have just made.

"Hitherto in my conversations with my official defense counsel I have affected a loss of memory. He was therefore acting in good faith when he asserted I had lost my memory."

Hess, not unconscious by a mile of the sensation he had created, stepped gingerly to his seat, a smile on his face, a light in the eyes that had stared so vacantly since the trial began. The courtroom was stunned and Judge Lawrence, looking for the first time a little taken aback himself, summoned his judicial manner sufficiently to announce that the court stood adjourned for the day.

Outside in the corridor I ran into Hess's lawyer, still perspiring freely and puffing a little.

"Who's crazy now?" he muttered.

Nuremberg, *Saturday, December* **1**

God! December here, as if it had raced in. But the day not so cold, the sun even trying to shine, and I suppose the Germans in their holes beneath the ruins are not suffering too much.

In court this morning Hess used his earphones for the first time since the trial began. He seemed positively interested in the proceedings following his star appearance yesterday. He heard the Tribunal rule that there were "no grounds whatsoever" for his not standing trial.

This afternoon, John Scott, Howard [K. Smith], Peggy Poore, and I drove out in John's luxurious Cadillac to see what had happened to the great Nazi superstructures that Hitler had ordered built out of imported Swedish granite (so they would last, as he said, a thousand years!) for the scene of the annual Nazi Party rally in this once cultured town. Irony! Unlike medieval Nuremberg, whose architectural beauties can never be replaced, the vast party structures, conceived in Hitler's ugliest style, were scarcely touched by the Allied bombing. The most spectacular building was the great auditorium, in which Hitler planned to celebrate some of his triumphs. It is so vast that you can easily pack half a dozen Madison Square Gardens into it. It appears to have been about half finished when the war broke out and work on it ceased. Mountains of blocks of Swedish granite, each block numbered, were piled all about. John said he had seen more of them in Sweden, the ones that had been cut but never sent because the war came. Like everything else Hitler attempted, this project too had failed. To be sure, he had wanted to go down in German history as a great builder and his plans for the rebuilding of Berlin, Hamburg, and a score of other German cities were staggeringly grandiose, if nothing else. But he had wanted to raise his titanic structures on the corpses of the non-German peoples of Europe. This does not appear to have caused many Germans to lose any sleep, nor does it seem to have occurred to them that it was a faulty foundation on which to erect great buildings—one that was almost certain to crumble.

German prisoners of war scampered about the gigantic half-finished auditorium today, boarding up the archways around the outer tiers, so that the American Army can use the building to store food for the German people this winter. They seemed to be especially resentful of their American guards. Probably they remembered that it was here at the scene of the party rallies that the famous Nuremberg racial laws to stamp out the Jews were proclaimed and where so much racial intolerance was hatched. The American guards, I noted, were Negro troops.

Nuremberg, *Sunday, December* **2**

At last a German—and a general at that (well, he's an Austrian, but let's overlook the difference)—has had the guts to stand up publicly before the world and brand Nazi Germany and the Nazis for what they were!

He is Major General Erwin Lahousen, of the German Counter-Intelligence, and confidant of one of the most fantastic characters of our time, Admiral Canaris, who was chief of German Counter-Intelligence and known to his intimates as the "Yellowbird" or "Canary." Canaris, it now seems certain, was the master mind behind several unsuccessful plots to kill Hitler. For his part in the last one, that of July 1944, which just missed succeeding, he was, as I may have mentioned before in these notes, tortured for nearly a year before the Gestapo, under the fine direction of Himmler, slowly strangled him to death. So far as he knows, Lahousen is the only important figure close to Canaris who is still alive. All the rest were done to death by the Nazis.

I must go back to Friday, when Lahousen was suddenly produced as the first prosecution witness of the trial. He was a curious figure under the glaring Klieg lights, which made the top of his shiny head look as though it were a part of his shiny perspiring face. And yet there was something sensitive in it, a quality of honesty, of integrity, of just plain human decency that attracted your attention, I suppose, because you suddenly realized that these very things, so common in more normal lands that you scarcely noticed them, were totally absent from the faces of those who had ruled the Third Reich and who now sat uneasily in the dock.

Göring, Ribbentrop, and Keitel glared angrily at the witness as he took the stand, and there were moments when you felt that if they could be granted one wish before they died it would be to wring the neck of this courageous Austrian until he was dead. However, their bearing did not intimidate him. He quickly showed that his contempt for them knew no bounds.

His weird account of the sheer savagery of the men who ruled Germany is too long and detailed, alas, to set down here. I can merely skip over the main points he made: that Hitler, Himmler, and the defendants Göring, Ribbentrop, Keitel, and Jodl at a conference held on September 12, 1939, in Hitler's train outside Warsaw agreed to deliberately bombard and destroy the Polish capital although all of them realized there was not the slightest military justification; that at this meeting they agreed on the extermination of the Polish intelligentsia, nobility, clergy, and, of course, the Jews; that later they gave orders for the mass branding and murdering of Russian prisoners of war; that the SS men who on the first morning of the war were sent in Polish Army uniforms to "attack" a frontier German radio station so as to give Hitler an excuse for marching into Poland were later all executed—so that they could tell no tales.

We have already seen here mountains of documents containing German plans for Operation So-and-so—against Austria, against Czechoslovakia, Russia, and so on. Lahousen sprang a new plan that I had never heard of before—"Operation Gustav." Operation Gustav turned out to be a plan whose execution was ordered by Field Marshal Keitel personally. It was to murder two famous French generals: Weygand and Giraud! The latter was to be "eliminated" in the prison where he was held captive; the former in North Africa.

The French prosecutor, a little skeptical, sprang up. "Who gave the orders to kill Generals Weygand and Giraud?"

"Keitel."

Judge Biddle intervened. "Were the orders to kill the Russian prisoners in writing?"

"As far as I know, yes...."

"Were they official orders?"

"Yes...."

Finally, just for good measure, Lahousen revealed that during the summer *before* the war started a special Luftwaffe squadron of high-altitude reconnaissance planes, operating from a secret airfield outside of Budapest, made reconnaissance flights over London and Leningrad! Apparently this is news to both the Russians and the British.

Nuremberg, *Monday, December* 3

In bed all day with fever and a chest cold, but got up this evening. Ran into David Low, the genius of the British cartoon world. He looks exactly as he often portrays himself in a stray corner of one of his masterly drawings. Until today he had never actually seen the Nazi culprits whom he had so often caricatured in his matchless cartoons.

"Did they look different from what you expected?" I asked him.

"Very much," he said. "They seemed much more ordinary little men than I had suspected."

Much good talk with him and with some of the Russian correspondents about the sad state of the world so soon after the glorious Allied victory.

It's rather interesting how well the Russian and American correspondents get along in this "castle" press headquarters where journalists from a score of nations are housed under one roof. Despite the gulf between our two worlds, a lot of us Americans find much in common with our Soviet confreres. For one thing, they are hard drinkers. For another, they like to sit up all night talking. And most of them are extremely intelligent and well-informed fellows. They keep asking me, for instance, to tell them what our major American writers have been up to since the war began. They have a surprising knowledge of the prewar works of most of our important authors. What has Steinbeck written, and Hemingway and Faulkner and Upton Sinclair and Sinclair Lewis and Dos Passos, they ask. What have our composers been doing in music?

The other night one of the Soviet correspondents, who, I'm told, is also a poet, proposed that we have a "Russian-American banquet."

"You fellows can tell us what your writers and musicians have been producing during the war and we'll try to tell you what our writers and musicians have done," he suggested. "Maybe I can show you on the piano some new things of Prokofiev and Shostakovich."

He had one other suggestion. "Let's make it a real banquet," he said. "You fellows bring a dozen bottles of whisky and we'll bring two dozen bottles of vodka—and we can talk all night."

I found it an excellent idea and I hope we can do it.

Nuremberg, *Tuesday, December* 4

It turned bitterly cold today, and in the afternoon it started to snow. Strange, the beauty of the ruined old city under the cold, white mantle of snow!

The Nazi thugs on trial for their life here, or rather those who were military men, received comfort and encouragement from a strange source today—from the *U.S. Army and Navy Journal.* Its curious remarks, quoted here in the *Stars and Stripes,* that Jackson was trying to discredit the "profession of arms" by bringing men like Keitel and Jodl to justice because of their service on the German High Command did not escape the notice of the culprits, who through their lawyers have access to what is published in *Stars and Stripes.*

Naturally the view of the *U.S. Army and Navy Journal* was pleasing to the Nazis, but it shocked the Allied prosecutors and drew a quick retort from Justice Jackson. He pointed out that the Nazi generals are not being prosecuted because they are soldiers but because they helped start a war that almost destroyed the world—something that you would have thought would be self-evident even to our brass hats.

Sir Hartley Shawcross, the rather suave Attorney-General of the new Labour government and chief British prosecutor here, opened the case for the prosecution under Count Two of the indictment today. I thought his speech, which took most of the day to deliver, lacked the polished eloquence of Justice Jackson's opening address, but it was packed with facts and logic. He accused the Germans of violating twenty-six specific international agreements, beginning with the Hague Convention of 1899 and ending with the German assurances given to Yugoslavia on October 6, 1939. Quite a record!

A cable from Carl Brandt saying *Reader's Digest* wants five thousand words from the notes I made on my return to Berlin. 'Twill be difficult selecting. The trouble with a writer, I guess, is that he thinks each sentence he puts down is so good and important that it ought to see print.

Nuremberg, *Wednesday, December* 5

The historians will now have to revise their judgment of the infamous pact at Munich that destroyed the first Czechoslovak Republic and staved off the World War for one year. This is clear from a mass of secret German documents introduced in the trial last week. They show beyond a shadow of doubt that the mad Führer was not bluffing during the "Munich crisis." He was quite ready to go to war. I myself had believed after personally covering the crucial meetings at Godesberg and Munich in the tense September days of 1938 that Hitler had pulled a gigantic bluff. But the confidential papers reveal that until the Sudetenland was handed to him on a platter at Munich with the connivance of Chamberlain and Daladier, Hitler and the German High Command were ready, and indeed intended, to attack Czechoslovakia with an overwhelming land and air force on or about October 1, 1938. What is more, the documents make clear that Hitler and his generals fully realized that an attack on the Czechs would engender a world war, and that they (with the exception of a few generals) were determined to risk *that* too in 1938!

For this information and much more we owe a debt of gratitude to the Führer's faithful adjutant, Major (and later Colonel) Schmundt, who assembled in one file most, if not all, of the secret orders, reports, and plans that comprised "Operation Green"—the planned attack on Czechoslovakia. The file was captured intact and has now been presented to the court. It would make a fascinating book in itself. Here I can only put down a few high lights.

The first is a discussion of "Operation Green" between Hitler and General Keitel on April 21, 1938, five weeks after the *Anschluss*. To begin with, they consider the political aspects of a German attack on Czechoslovakia:

"1. Strategic surprise attack out of a clear sky without any cause or possibility of justification has been turned down, as result would be: hostile world opinion, which can lead to a critical situation. Such a measure is justified only for the elimination of the *last* opponent on the mainland.

"2. Action after a time of diplomatic clashes, which gradually come to a crisis and lead to war.

"3. Lightning-swift action as the result of an incident (e.g., *assassination of German ambassador in connection with an anti-German demonstration*)."[42]

Coming to "military conclusions," the Führer and his general decide that "preparations are to be made for the political possibilities (2) and (3), but that the latter is best—that is, to provoke an "incident" for "lightning-swift action" by having their own Ambassador in Prague assassinated!

The first ominous note in Hitler's plans for aggression against the Czechs appears in a directive dated May 20. "It is very probable," he writes, "that attempts by Russia to give military support to Czechoslovakia are to be expected. If concrete successes are not achieved as a result of the ground operations during the first few days, a European crisis will certainly arise." Some of the generals, we learn, are more worried on this score than their leader. Jodl notes this in his personal diary—another interesting paper captured intact by the Allies.

On May 30 Jodl writes: "The Führer signs Directive Green, where he states his final decision to destroy Czechoslovakia soon.... The whole contrast becomes acute once more between the Führer's intuition that we *must*[Jodl's italics] do it this year and the opinion of the army that we cannot do it yet, as most certainly the western powers will interfere and we are not as yet equal to them."

This, incidentally, is the first we hear from an important military figure of Hitler's "intuition," which became so famous later and which, indeed, three years hence was to wreck the German armies in the snows of Russia.

We also have a covering letter dated May 30 written by Keitel which stresses that the "strategic concentration" against Czechoslovakia must be executed "as from October 1, 1938, at the latest." Thus we have the date for the planned German onslaught on the little Czech state. Hitler's May 30 directive is entitled "Two-Front War with Main Effort in the Southeast. (Strategic Concentration 'Green')" and begins:

"It is my unalterable decision to smash Czechoslovakia by military action in the near future…. An inevitable development of conditions inside Czechoslovakia or other political events in Europe creating a surprisingly favorable opportunity and one that may never come again may cause me to take early action…. Accordingly the preparations are to be made at once."

All through this May 30 directive appears just the slightest suspicion in Hitler's mind that Britain, France, and Russia may not sit idly by during the German war with Czechoslovakia. It is clear from the German military data that Germany in 1938 did not have the military strength to take on the three big powers. Hitler realizes this. But he draws back from reaching the necessary conclusions. Thus he emphasizes that the German forces in the west "must be limited in numbers," but fondly counts on them to handle the situation should the French and British move. He tells the Luftwaffe: "The *most important task* [his own italics] of the air force is the destruction of the Czech Air Force and their supply bases within the shortest possible time, in order to eliminate the possibility of its employment as well as that of Russian and French air forces." So he suspects military reaction from the Russians and French. He is not quite sure of the British, for he instructs the German Navy to take those measures "which appear necessary for the careful protection of the North Sea and the Baltic against a sudden intervention in the conflict by other states."

As the tense summer unfolds, the specter of a two-front war, the nightmare of German general staffs for a century, looms more and more in the mind of Hitler. Before the end of June the name of another "operation" begins to appear in the directives of Hitler and the High Command. It is called "Operation Red" and it concerns war in the west.

On June 18 a "Most Secret" directive from Hitler headed "Strategic Concentration" is issued. Article Two is called: "Two-Front War with the Main Effort in the West (Operation Red)." It says:

"Since even a war against us started by the western nations *must*[Hitler's italics], in view of the situation today, begin with the destruction of Czechoslovakia, the preparation of strategic concentration for a war with the main effort by the army and air force against the west is no longer of primary importance.

"The preparations made to date for the event ('Red'), however, remain in effect. They contribute... in the case of the Luftwaffe as a preparation of the shifting of the main effort from the east to the west, which may, under certain circumstances, suddenly become necessary. They also serve as preliminary work for future possibilities of war in the west."

Mention of the "tasks that arrive for the navy in Operation Red" is made. From other documents we know that the German Navy has been ordered to have a submarine screen in place in the North Sea and even in the English Channel by D-Day for the attack on Czechoslovakia.

So Hitler will face a war on two fronts. By July 7, as his audacity grows (or is it his stubbornness?), he is ready to face not only that but the very distinct possibility of having to fight Russia, as well as Czechoslovakia, in the east. His "Most Secret" memorandum of that date to the High Command admits for the first time that "how the political situation will develop during the execution, or after the conclusion, of 'Green' cannot be predicted....

"However," he continues, "it seems expedient to make at least theoretical considerations and calculations for several possible eventualities, to avoid being mentally unprepared."

What eventualities?

"If during the execution of 'Green,' France intervenes, the measures provided in 'Operation Red' come into force. The primary essential in this connection is to hold the western fortifications until the execution of the action 'Green' permits forces to be freed. Should France be supported by England, it will have small effect at first on the land war....

"Among the eastern powers, Russia is the most likely to intervene. This, in the beginning at any rate, will probably consist in reinforcement in the Czech Air Force and armament. However, the decision must not be neglected concerning what measures are to be taken if Russia were to come to the point of starting a naval and air war against us or even wish to penetrate into East Prussia, through the border states."

The German dictator is not even quite sure about Poland. "In the case of a penetration by Poland," he says, "we must hold the eastern fortifications and East Prussia."

If Hitler is slightly uncertain, some of his best generals are alarmed. Smash little "Czecho"—yes. But to take on France, Britain, and Russia—that is utter madness. That means a world war. General Ludwig Beck, chief of the General Staff, resigns "disgruntled," as his successor, General Halder, puts it, in August. Before he leaves, Beck sends a memorandum to Hitler warning him that his policies "will lead finally to a new World War and have a tragic end for Germany."

In fact, Halder later will claim that the whole General Staff was against the attack on the Czechs, which it regarded as a "military adventure."

At any event, matters came to a head on August 10. Hitler summoned his army chiefs to his Berghof retreat. The captured diary from General Jodl gives us an intimate picture of the meeting:

"After dinner the Führer makes a speech lasting for almost three hours, in which he develops his political thoughts. The subsequent attempts to draw the Führer's attention to the defects of our preparation, which are undertaken by a few generals of the army, are rather unfortunate. This applies especially to the remark of General Wietersheim... that the western fortifications can only be held for three weeks.

"The Führer becomes very indignant and flames up, bursting into the remark that in such a case the whole army would not be good for anything. 'I assure you, general, the position will not only be held for three weeks, but for three years.' The cause of this despondent opinion, which unfortunately is held very widely within the Army General Staff, is based on various reasons. First of all, it [the General Staff] is restrained by old memories; political considerations play a part as well, instead of obeying and executing its military mission. That is certainly done with traditional devotion, but the vigor of the soul is lacking because in the end they do not believe in the genius of the Führer.... This defeatism may not only possibly cause immense political damage, for the opposition between the generals' opinion and that of the Führer is common talk, but also constitute a danger for the morale of the troops."

This is a pretty state of affairs for military leaders about to embark on an uncertain war. But preparations and plans nevertheless proceed apace. On August 25 the General Staff of the Air Force circulates "through officer courier only... for commanders only" a top-secret directive entitled "Estimate of the Situation— Operation Green."

"The basic assumption," it begins, "is that France will declare war during Operation Green. It is presumed that France will only decide upon war if *active military assistance by Great Britain* [Luftwaffe's italics] is definitely assured. The Soviet Union will probably side immediately with the western powers.... The United States of America will immediately support the fight of the western powers with strong ideological and economic means. Italy, nationalist Spain, Hungary, and Japan are regarded as benevolent neutrals....

"*The war aim of the Entente Powers* [Luftwaffe's italics] is to be considered as the overcoming of Germany through attacking its war economy. In other words, through a *long* war."

The German aim, the directive states, "will be to bring about a decision by the defeat of the western powers."

We learn also from this directive that already in 1938 "basic target maps of British airfields are approximately 90 per cent ready.... The basic target maps for Belgium and the Netherlands are ready for printing." So the two little neutral states were to get it too—in 1938!

D-Day against Czechoslovakia—set for on or about October 1—approaches. On September 3 there is a conference at the Berghof between Hitler and Generals von Brauchitsch (commander-in-chief of the army) and Keitel (chief of the High Command). Major Schmundt again obliges with his notes. Brauchitsch reports the field army will be in position near the Czech border on September 28. Hitler promises he will choose D-Day by twelve noon on September 27. He also gives orders for the improvement of advance positions around Aachen and Saarbrücken in the west.

The west, it is clear, increasingly haunts the sleep of some of the German generals. On September 8 Jodl notes in his diary that General Stulpnagel "for the first time" begins to have some doubts about Hitler's plan because it "presupposed that the western powers would not interfere decisively." Jodl confesses: "I must admit that I am worrying too."

On the night of September 9, from ten p.m. to three thirty a.m., at Nuremberg, where the Nazi Party rally is coming to a close in a blaze of hysterical shouting against the Czechs, there is another meeting of Hitler with his top generals. The ubiquitous Major Schmundt is there to take his confidential notes. General Halder, the new chief of the General Staff, outlines in detail the latest version of Operation Green. Hitler, who does not like Halder, insists on changing the plans. He has to have, he says, a decisive success within eight days—for political reasons.

D-Day is now but little more than a fortnight off. Then Neville Chamberlain intervenes. On September 22 he is at Godesberg meeting with Hitler. The same evening, we learn in Jodl's diary, despite the frightened Prime Minister's plea for peace, General Stulpnagel, on behalf of Keitel, telephones to Berlin from Godesberg "to continue preparations according to plan." On the 26th, Hitler, shouting and shrieking in the worst state of excitement I have ever seen him in, tells his audience at the Sport Palace in Berlin that there will be war unless the Sudetenland is turned over to him by October 1.

The next document in the "Green" file reveals that the Führer himself believes it will be war. It reads: "Most Secret. At 1300, September 27, the Führer and Supreme Commander of the Armed Forces ordered the movement of the assault units from their exercise areas to their jumping-off points. The assault units must be ready to begin the action against 'Green' on September 30, the decision having been made one day previously by 1200 noon."

The die is cast. Jodl in his diary the next day, September 28, notes that Göring "states that a Great War can hardly be avoided any longer. It may last seven years, and we will win it."

There were a number of German generals who had their doubts. Some of them, as we know from a previous entry in my diary (November 25, 1945), were in Berlin on this fateful day of September 28 for the purpose of seizing Hitler, overthrowing the Nazi regime, and saving Germany—and the world—from war. Their own special D-Day had now arrived.

At five p.m. General Jodl halts whatever he is doing to scribble a second notation in his diary: "1700 hours. Tension relaxes. The Führer has decided on a conference with Chamberlain, the Duce, and Daladier in Munich."

I happened to be in Berlin too that day, and about the same hour confided to my own diary: "There is to be no war! Hitler has invited Mussolini, Chamberlain, and Daladier to meet him in Munich tomorrow. The latter three will rescue Hitler from his limb and he will get his Sudetenland without war."

The conspirators under General Witzleben, we would learn later from Halder, were consternated. "The execution of the plan," he would reveal, "was about to begin when news came, as a complete surprise, of the imminent meeting with Chamberlain in Munich. The foundations for the planned action had therefore collapsed."

Let Diarist Jodl finish the story: "September 29. The pact of Munich is signed. Czechoslovakia as a power is out…. The genius of the Führer and *his determination not to shun even a World War*[43] have again won the victory without the use of force. The hope remains that the incredulous, the weak, and the doubtful people have been converted and will remain that way."

Munich, then, was not a bluff, as most of us had believed. Hitler was ready to go to war and would have, had not Chamberlain and Daladier surrendered. Some may think this vindicates the bungling British Prime Minister. But I take the opposite view. Aside from the dishonorableness of his action in sacrificing Czechoslovakia so sordidly, he only postponed the World War by eleven months. Had Germany started it in 1938, I think we are justified in concluding from these German documents themselves that it would not have lasted long, that Germany would have been easily and quickly beaten, and that the world would have been spared the terrible devastation and suffering of the long war that began a year later. We see from these German archives that in the opinion of most of the German military experts themselves the Third Reich was not powerful enough in 1938 to take on Britain, France, Russia, Czechoslovakia, and probably Poland at one time. In 1938, it is fair to assume, this powerful coalition would have reacted to the German threat at once. When the World War actually came in 1939, Czechoslovakia, which a year earlier had had an excellent army defending formidable fortifications, was no more, and Hitler was able to attack the others one at a time, since Russia had fallen out of the potential coalition.

One is tempted to add a brief postscript to Operation Green. Two more "top-secret" directives of the Führer show the peculiar perfidy of the man whom General Jodl considered a "genius." He had repeatedly given his word that after he got the Sudetenland he had no more interest in the Czechs. Yet on October 21, just three weeks after he had signed the Munich Pact, Hitler issued a secret directive ordering the German armed forces to "be prepared at all times for the liquidation of the remainder of Czechoslovakia." On December 17 General Keitel issued a corollary to this directive, which begins as follows:

"Reference 'Liquidation of the Rest of Czechoslovakia'; the Führer has given the following additional order: The preparations for this eventuality are to continue on the assumption that no resistance worth mentioning is to be expected. To the outside world too it must clearly appear that it is merely an act of pacification and not a warlike undertaking."

On a blizzardy day of the following March the "Liquidation," as we know, was criminally carried out.

Nuremberg, *Thursday, December* 6

Dinner last night with George Biddle, the painter—and brother of the American judge here. Like Low, he finds the faces of the Nazi bigwigs much more common than he expected.

Another blizzard of documents at the trial today. Result: we now have the incredible inside story of the treacherous German conquest of Denmark and Norway in the spring of 1940. And we learn for the first time the real role of the sinister fellow whose name has become a synonym in all languages for a traitor: Quisling. This peculiar Norwegian, the German documents make clear, was more enthusiastic about a German occupation of Norway than were the Germans themselves. In fact, he seems to have spent a year trying to argue the Nazis into invading and occupying Norway. Even Hitler, at first, gave him a cold shoulder.

Vidkun Quisling, whom Alfred Rosenberg reveals as having been in touch with him for years, first saw Hitler on December 16, 1939. Another interview took place on the 18th. Rosenberg and Grand Admiral Erich Raeder, commander-in-chief of the German Navy, had, after some difficulty, finally induced the Führer to receive the little man who was to become the war's most notorious Fifth-Columnist.

"During the interview," Rosenberg writes in a captured memorandum, "the Führer emphasized repeatedly that the most preferable attitude for Norway, as well as for all of Scandinavia, would be one of complete neutrality. He had no intention of enlarging the theater of war to draw other nations into the conflict. If, however, the enemy were preparing an enlargement of the zones of war with the aim to throttle and threaten the Reich further, then, of course, he would be obliged to arm against such steps. The Führer promised Quisling financial support for his movement...."

The little Norwegian traitor, one assumes, must have been disappointed by the Führer's coolness at this first meeting. For he had been continually warning Rosenberg and Raeder that, in his opinion, the British intended to occupy Norway with the secret assent of the Norwegian government and that Germany must get in ahead of Britain. To accomplish this, he was in a position, he emphasized, to render extremely valuable support. In fact he already had a plan.

Admiral Raeder touches on it in a secret memorandum dated December 12, 1939, four days before Hitler received Quisling:

"Quisling has good connections with officers of the Norwegian Army," he notes, "and has supporters in important positions (e.g., railways). In such an event Quisling is ready to take over the government and to call upon Germany for help. He is also ready to promise preparations of a military character with the German armed forces."

Rosenberg reveals the plot itself, as evolved by Quisling: "A plan has been put forward which deals with the possibility of a coup, and which provides for a number of selected Norwegians to be trained in Germany with all possible speed for such a purpose, and provided with experienced and diehard National Socialists, who are practiced in such operations. These trained men should then proceed with all speed to Norway. Some important centers in Oslo would have to be taken over immediately, and at the same time the German fleet, together with suitable contingents of the German Army, would go into operation when summoned specially by the new Norwegian government in a specified bay at the approaches to Oslo. Quisling has no doubts that such a coup, having been carried out with instantaneous success, would immediately bring him the approval of those sections of the army with which he at present has connections…. As far as the King is concerned, he believes that he would respect it as an accomplished fact. Quisling gives figures of the number of German troops required, which accord with German calculations."

With the coming of the New Year, German interest in Quisling's project increases. On January 27, 1940, Keitel issues a "Most Secret" order: "The Führer… wishes that Study 'N' [Norway] should be further worked on under my direct and personal guidance…. All further plans will be made under the cover name 'Weser Exercise.'"

On February 5 Diarist General Jodl notes that "special staff 'Weser Exercise' meets…. Still no air-force representative." As we shall learn later, Göring has less than enthusiasm for the whole project.

There is another problem. Which should come first: Operation Yellow against the west or Weser Exercise against Denmark and Norway? On February 26 Jodl notes: "Führer raises the question whether it is better to undertake the Weser Exercise before or after Operation Yellow." On February 28 Jodl writes: "I propose that Operation Yellow and Weser Exercise must be prepared in such a way that they will be independent of each other…. Führer completely agrees, if this is in any way possible."

In the meantime General von Falkenhorst has been given the command of the whole expedition, and on March 1 Hitler signs the "Top Secret" directive for Weser Exercise. It reads in part as follows:

"The development of the situation in Scandinavia requires the making of all preparations for the occupation of Denmark and Norway by a part of the German armed forces ('Operation Weser Exercise'). This operation should prevent British encroachment on Scandinavia and the Baltic. Further, it should guarantee our ore base in Sweden and give our navy and air force a wider starting-line against Britain....

"In view of our military and political power in comparison with that of the Scandinavian states, the force to be employed... will be kept as small as possible. The numerical weakness will be balanced by daring actions and surprise execution. On principle we will do our utmost to make the operation appear as a *peaceful* [italics Hitler's] occupation, the object of which is the military protection of the neutrality of the Scandinavian states. Corresponding demands will be transmitted to the governments at the beginning of the occupation. If necessary, demonstrations by the navy and the air force will provide the necessary emphasis. If, in spite of this, resistance should be met with, all military means will be used to crush it....

"The crossing of the Danish border and the landings in Norway must take place *simultaneously*[Hitler's italics]. I emphasize that the operations must be prepared as quickly as possible.... It is most important that the Scandinavian states, as well as the western enemies, should be *taken by surprise*[Hitler's emphasis] by our measures. All preparations, particularly those of transport... must be made with this factor in mind. In case the preparations can no longer be kept secret, the leaders and the troops will be deceived with fictitious objectives. The troops may be acquainted with the actual objectives only after putting to sea...."

In one paragraph of this directive Hitler gives the following order: "The air force, after the occupation has been completed, will... make use of Norwegian bases for air warfare against Britain." On April 9, the day of the invasion of Norway, the German diplomatic note to the Norwegian government, one of the most cynical and impudent of all the Nazi state papers, will say: "The German High Command does not intend to make use of the points occupied by German troops as bases for operations against England...."

Now that he has decided to take the plunge into Scandinavia, Hitler is impatient to begin it as soon as possible. On March 3 General Jodl scribbles in his notebook: "Führer expressed himself very sharply on the necessity of a swift entry into N. [Norway] with strong forces. No delay by any branch of the armed forces. Very rapid acceleration of the attack necessary.... Führer decides to carry out 'Weser Exercise' before Operation 'Yellow,' with a few days' interval."

Scandinavia, that is, will get it before the Lowlands and France. Jodl notes something else on this day: "C.-in-C. of the air force [Göring] opposes subordination of units of the air force to 21st Army Corps." The fat field marshal is still not keen on the "Weser" adventure. This becomes more evident two days later. On March 5 Jodl confides to his diary: "Big conference with the three commanders-in-chief about 'Weser Exercise.' Field marshal [Göring] in a rage because not consulted till now. Won't listen to anyone and wants to show that all preparations so far made are worthless."

Worthless though they may be in the eyes of the bemedaled air-force chief, they go on anyway. But another problem arises. Our faithful diarist, Jodl, tells us what it is: "March 31. Führer does not give order yet for 'W.' *He is still looking for an excuse.*"[44]

This singular search continues. The next day Jodl jots down: "*Führer has not yet decided what reason to give for 'Weser Exercise.'*[44]Wrong news report in American press."

The poor Führer! Genius that he is in such matters, he cannot think up a good "excuse" for attacking peaceful Denmark and Norway. And there are other troubles. The navy itself, which first had had to urge Hitler to embark on the venture, now—with D-Day only a few days off—begins to get cold feet. Jodl notes down the navy's "doubts" and "misgivings." "March 14. C.-in-C. of the navy is doubtful.... Open to question whether it would not be better to undertake Operation 'Yellow' before 'Weser Exercise.' Danger that in that case the English would immediately land at Narvik, as we would have been the first to violate neutrality."

Even the army has its "misgivings." Thus Jodl on March 21 in his diary: "Misgivings of Task Force 21 (reinforced 21st Army Corps) about the long interval between taking up readiness positions at 0530 hours and close of diplomatic negotiations. Führer rejects any earlier negotiations, as otherwise calls for help go out to England and America...."

On March 28 it is the navy again. Jodl writes: "Individual naval officers seem to be lukewarm concerning the Weser Exercise and need a stimulus." So apparently do the army and the air force, for Jodl continues: "Also General von Falkenhorst and the other two commanders are worrying about matters that are none of their business. Kranke [navy] sees more disadvantages than advantages. In the evening the Führer visits the map room and roundly declares that he won't stand for the navy clearing out of the Norwegian ports right away. Narvik, Trondheim, and Oslo will have to remain occupied by naval forces. Bad impression on land troops." On the next day, Jodl tells us, Admiral Raeder "rejects Narvik."

But apparently these matters are straightened out. On April 2, Jodl notes, the "Führer orders carrying out of the Weser Exercise for April 9. Commander-in-chiefs of the air force, of the navy, and General von Falkenhorst all confirm preparations completed."

And what in the meantime has happened to the impatient Quisling? Rosenberg and Jodl supply us with some information. Toward the end of March, Rosenberg writes in a memorandum, Quisling sent him a message through his agent in Germany, an individual named Hagelin, "that any further delay would mean a grave risk." Schmundt, now a colonel and still the Führer's faithful adjutant, then suggested, Rosenberg writes, "a conference between Quisling and a colonel of the

General Staff at some neutral location." This conference was held in Copenhagen in the beginning of April.

Jodl confirms this in a diary entry on April 4: "Piepenbrock, chief of Military Intelligence I, returns with good results from the talks with Quisling in Copenhagen."

There is one final little deceit in this story of the deceitful attack on Norway. A secret German naval order dated March 24 orders all German craft in the Norwegian operation to pose at first as British ships.

"The disguise as British craft," it says, "must be kept up as long as possible. All challenges in Morse by Norwegian ships will be answered in English. In answer to questions a text with something like the following will be chosen: 'Calling at Bergen for a short visit. No hostile intent.'

"In case of a warning shot," the German naval commanders are told, they must answer in English: "Stop firing. British ship. Good friend."

"In case of an inquiry as to destination and purpose," the German naval officers are instructed to reply—in English—"Going Bergen. Chasing German steamers."

At dawn on April 9 Denmark and Norway were attacked. I still remember the flaming headline in Hitler's own paper in Berlin, the *Völkische Beobachter*, the next morning. It read: "GERMANY SAVES SCANDINAVIA!"

Nuremberg, *Friday, December 7*

Anniversary of Pearl Harbor. To think that in four years Japan destroyed herself! A Manila dispatch says General Yamashita has been condemned to death. That news will not be welcomed in the prisoners' dock here.

Apparently the secret documents of the German High Command for "Operation Sea-Lion"—the invasion of Britain—are not to be made available here. A pity—because we still don't know exactly why the Nazis never attempted the invasion. Or did they? Wasn't there a story about bodies of dead German soldiers being washed up on the British beaches in the fall of 1940?

(So far as I know, the papers regarding "Operation Sea-Lion" were never given out at Nuremberg. But on November 18, 1946, Prime Minister Attlee made a written statement on German plans for invading Britain, based on a study of captured German documents and the interrogation of German prisoners of war. It is a remarkable summary:

In July, 1940, Hitler had outrun his immediate plans and was faced with the first major unexpected check to his strategy. If he was to avoid a prolonged war—with the danger that, if forced to a final reckoning with Russia, he would be involved in a war on two fronts—he had to find means of compelling Britain to abandon the struggle. The military situation resulting from the fall of France seems to have encouraged Hitler to believe that

Britain would be ready to accept a compromise peace. But concurrently with his efforts to obtain such a peace, he directed that planning for the invasion of the United Kingdom should be begun and pushed rapidly forward, both as a threat to supplement the peace offer and as a practical alternative to be adopted if that offer should fail.

Until then the Germans had undertaken no long-term planning for the invasion of this country, apart from certain purely naval plans which had been elaborated by the Naval Operations Division since November, 1939. On May 21, 1940, Raeder discussed the subject with Hitler, and on July 2 Hitler ordered intelligence appreciations to be prepared and planning to begin for operation Sea-Lion (the invasion of England). The following is an extract from a directive issued by Hitler on July 16, 1940:—

"Since England, in spite of her militarily hopeless situation, shows no signs of coming to terms, I have decided to prepare a landing operation against England and, if necessary, to carry it out…. The preparations for the entire operation must be completed by mid-August."

The German staffs were, therefore, given little over a month in which to make all preparations.

It is clear that the General Staff of the German Army were apprehensive of the proposed operation. The German advance to the Channel coast had been unexpectedly rapid, and no plans had been prepared for such an ambitious undertaking. Part of the Luftwaffe had already been redeployed elsewhere. Assault shipping was limited to such barges and river boats as could be brought from Germany or the Netherlands. These craft were incapable of standing up to anything but a calm sea, or of disembarking tanks or vehicles without elaborate conversion. The troops had no training in amphibious assaults, nor had the staffs any experience in this unaccustomed technique. In the last resort, everything depended on the ability of the navy and air force to transport and cover the invading forces.

According to Doenitz, subsequently Commander-in-Chief of the German Navy, it was generally accepted by the German leaders that their navy would be no match for the Royal Navy, which they expected to be sacrificed to the last vessel and the last man to counter a landing. They thought it essential, therefore, that the German Air Force should accept the double role of both destroying the Royal Air Force and preventing the Royal Navy from attacking a landing force. Göring was confident that the German Air Force would be equal to both these tasks. Jodl and Keitel accepted his view, and were prepared to make the attempt on the basis that the German Navy would be asked to do no more than meet the army's essential requirements for transportation. According to Doenitz, the German Navy, though unequal to the larger task of protection, could have met these requirements.

The German Naval High Command appear, however, to have taken the view, in spite of the confidence of Göring, that even if the Luftwaffe had succeeded in defeating the Royal Air Force in the Battle of Britain, it would still have been incapable of carrying out its second task: namely, preventing the Royal Navy from attacking a seaborne landing force. They considered that the Luftwaffe had not the necessary weapons, and that the bombs in use at that time were of far too small a calibre to prevent heavy ships from coming to grips with the landing force. In spite of the view of the German Naval Command, it is probable that, if the Royal Air Force had been defeated, the operation would have been launched.

The preparatory phase of the whole operation was to be an air offensive, whose objectives were the destruction of the Royal Air Force in the air and on the ground, and the destruction of ports, communications, aircraft production plants, and food storage depots in London. The air offensive was to begin on August 13, though owing to naval factors it would be impossible for the invasion itself to take place until September 15. A decision would be taken later, in the light of the success gained in the preparatory phase, whether the operation could take place at all that year. This would depend on two factors: whether the German Air Force could neutralize the Royal Air Force and so obtain air mastery over the whole invasion area, and whether, given the inadequacy of the German Navy, the German Air Force could provide protection for the invasion forces and prevent attacks by the British Navy.

So far as it went, the general plan of operation Sea-Lion was for landings by two armies, with 25 divisions in all, between Folkstone and Worthing. Ten divisions were to be landed on the first four days to form the initial bridgehead. After about eight days an advance was to be made to the first objective, a line running from the Thames estuary along the hills south of London to Portsmouth. The course of the battle would then depend on circumstances, but efforts were to be made to cut London off from the west as quickly as possible. Parachute troops were to be used only for the capture of Dover. A third army might possibly be employed for a landing in Lyme Regis Bay if necessary.

The orders issued subsequently showed that Hitler was most reluctant to take a decision on operation Sea-Lion. On August 16 an order was issued to the effect that a decision was still delayed, but that preparations should continue up to September 15. On August 27 orders were issued to prepare for embarcation at Rotterdam, Antwerp and Le Havre. On September 3, D-Day was fixed for September 21, but it was provided that all operations were liable to cancellation 24 hours before zero hour. On September 17 Hitler decided on the further postponement of the operation, and on September 19 orders were given to discontinue the strategic concentration of shipping and to disperse existing concentrations of craft in view of allied air attacks. On October 12 the operation was called off until the spring, though deception measures were to continue.

The result of the Battle of Britain had been that the Luftwaffe had failed to carry out the first of the tasks assigned to it—namely, the destruction of the Royal Air Force. As this essential preliminary to invasion had not been achieved, the whole operation was postponed.

The deception measures mentioned above were maintained through the spring and early summer of 1941. In July of that year Hitler again postponed the operation until the spring of 1942, on the assumption that by that time "the Russian campaign would be completed." The project does not seem to have been seriously considered again.

It has been widely believed in this country that a German invasion attempt was actually launched in 1940. This belief is based partly on the fact that a number of German bodies were washed up on the south coast of England in August and September, 1940, and partly on the knowledge that the "invasion imminent" signal was issued by General Headquarters, Home Forces, on September 7, 1940. The facts are as stated in the following paragraphs:—

In August, 1940, the Germans were embarking their army in the barges in harbours along the French coast, but there is no evidence that they ever left harbour as a fleet to invade this country. Bombing raids on those harbours were carried out by Bomber Command, and some barges which put to sea, probably to escape the raids, were sunk either by bombing or on encountering bad weather. During the next six weeks bodies of German soldiers were washed up at scattered points along the coast between Cornwall and Yarmouth (amounting to about 36 over a period of a month).

On September 7, 1940, the British Chiefs of Staff considered a report on possible German action against the United Kingdom. The main features of this report were:—

a) The westerly and southerly movement of barges and small ships to ports between Ostend and Le Havre suggested a very early date for invasion, since such craft would not be moved unnecessarily early to ports so much exposed to bombing attacks.

b) The striking strength of the German Air Force disposed between Amsterdam and Brest had been increased by the transfer of 160 long-range bomber aircraft from Norway; and short-range dive-bomber units had been redeployed to forward aerodromes in the Pas de Calais area, presumably in preparation for employment against this country.

c) Four Germans captured on landing from a rowing boat on the south-east coast had confessed to being spies, and had said that they were to be ready at any time during the next fortnight to report the movement of British reserve formations in the area Oxford-Ipswich-London-Reading.

d) Moon and tide conditions during the period September 8-10 were most favourable for a seaborne invasion on the south-east coast.

This report indicated that German preparations for invasion were so advanced that it could be attempted at any time. Taking into account the German air attacks, which were at that time concentrated against aerodromes and aircraft factories, the Chiefs of Staff agreed that the possibility of invasion had become imminent, and that the defence forces should stand by at immediate notice.

At General Headquarters, Home Forces, there was then no machinery by which the then existing eight hours' notice for readiness could be adjusted to a state of readiness for "immediate action" by intermediate stages.

The code word "Cromwell" signifying "invasion imminent" was therefore issued by General Headquarters, Home Forces, that evening (8 p.m., September 7) to the Eastern and Southern Commands implying "action stations" for the forward (coastal) divisions. It was also issued to all formations in the London area and to the 4th and 7th Corps in General Headquarters Reserve, implying a state of readiness at short notice. The code word was repeated for information to all other Commands in the United Kingdom.

In some parts of the country certain Home Guard commanders, acting on their own initiative, called out the Home Guard by the ringing of church bells. This in turn gave rise to rumors that enemy parachutists were landing. There were also various reports, subsequently proved to be incorrect, that German E-boats were approaching the coast.

On the following morning (September 8), General Headquarters, Home Forces, gave instructions that the Home Guard were not to be permanently called out on receipt of the code word "Cromwell," except for special tasks: also, that church bells were to be rung only by order of a Home Guard who had himself seen at least 25 parachutists landing, and not because other bells had been heard, or for any other reason.

Nuremberg, *Saturday, December* 8

Bitterly cold today, and snow covering the earth. The youngsters, I noticed, were skating on the canal. But for the people living in the unheated cellars under the ruins the cold was cruel. I talked to some of them today, and to some whose houses, in the outskirts, are still intact.

The trial? *Ja*—propaganda! You'll hang them anyway. So you make a trial for propaganda. Why should we pay any attention? We're cold. We're hungry.

One man was a distinguished German engineer. He said: "Why was it wrong for Göring to build up his air force? If he'd done a better job, Nuremberg wouldn't be in ruins."

The enterprising A.P. staff obtained today an interesting statement from Rudolf Hess on why he flew to England on May 10, 1941. He shows himself unbelievably naive—about England—and generally confused and contradictory. Still, part of what he says is worth noting down in this informal record.

"*Q.* What was the purpose of your flight to England?

"*A.* During the campaign in France I expressed my view to the Führer, in June 1940, that on conclusion of the peace with England (which we then considered imminent) a demand should be made for the return of what had been taken from Germany by the Versailles Treaty....

"I said to myself that most likely reasons of prestige prevented England from entertaining the various proposals for understanding made by the Führer.

"Considering the military position then prevailing, England could negotiate without loss of prestige only if a reason visible to the whole world for entering into parleys with Germany could be provided. I therefore decided to supply this reason by going personally to England.

"I left a letter for the Führer at the moment of my departure giving my reason for the flight. In it I argued: After contact with me, the British government would be in a position to declare:

"'We have become convinced in talks with Herr Hess that proposals of the Führer looking toward an understanding have been made in earnest. Under these circumstances, England does not feel justified in assuming responsibility for prolonging the slaughter without having endeavored to bring the war to a conclusion acceptable to all parties. She therefore declares her willingness to enter upon negotiations looking to this goal.'

"What I wrote to the Führer, I repeated to such personages in England as I met there....

"*Q.* Did Hitler or any other top-flight Nazi know of the flight beforehand?

"*A.* Neither Hitler nor anybody else, except my adjutant, whom I took into my confidence.

"*Q.* In which way were Willy Messerschmitt and Prof. Haushofer implicated?

"*A.* Messerschmitt was not informed about my intention. I obtained a plane from him under the pretext that I needed the machine for long-range training flights within Germany. As to Haushofer, I merely asked him for a few lines of recommendation to the Duke of Hamilton under the pretext that I, with Hitler's knowledge, was to meet the Duke on neutral soil.

"*Q.* When did you decide to make the flight?

"*A.* I decided to fly shortly after the above-mentioned conversation with the Führer in June 1940.... It took until May 10, 1941, until all necessary preconditions coincided…. [Hess here goes into details about weather conditions, etc.]

"Q.Where did you take off?

"A.I took off from an airfield of the Messerschmitt plant at Augsburg, from where I had made several short training flights previously, as well as several take-offs for England which I had to break off because of bad weather.

"Q.Were you aware in England, or have you since learned, that it was announced officially in Germany that you were demented? How did you react to this?

"A.I wrote in a letter which I left behind for Hitler that I had decided to carry out my intention even at the risk of the Führer's declaring me insane. A news item to that effect was, therefore, no surprise to me…."

Ought to get in a few lines on another German "operation" that begins to creep into the documentation here. It's called "Felix and Isabella" and concerns German military plans for helping Spain blast the British out of the Rock of Gibraltar ("Felix") and for the invasion of Portugal ("Isabella").

(On March 4, 1946, the State Department released a collection of captured German documents which was much more complete than that assembled at Nuremberg. In view of the current pro-Franco propaganda in this country, a brief note on Franco's real role in World War II may be in order here.

The State Department papers prove beyond dispute that in June 1940, directly after the fall of France, Franco promised Hitler that Spain would enter the war on the side of the Axis. He made two conditions: (1) that Spain be given Gibraltar, French Morocco, and a part of Algeria, including Oran, and receive enlargement of Río de Oro and the colonies in the Gulf of Guinea; (2) that Germany furnish certain military and economic assistance required by Spain for carrying on the war.

The promise and many interesting details concerning it are contained in a "Top Secret" memorandum dated August 8, 1940, which the German Ambassador in Madrid, Dr. Eberhard von Stohrer, dispatched to Berlin, and which later fell into American hands.

That Franco did not throw his country into the war on the side of the Axis was due, as the documents make plain, not to the Caudillo's unwillingness, but to the fact that Hitler would not agree at once to his terms, and that by the time the summer of 1941 rolled around, the Führer was too busy with the Balkans and Russia to pursue his negotiations with Franco further.

Franco, like Mussolini, it is clear from the German documents, thought he saw his great chance as soon as the German panzers tore through France in the late spring of 1940. On June 3, shortly before the fall of Paris, the Caudillo, almost beside himself, wrote Hitler: "In the moment when the German armies under your leadership are bringing the greatest battle of history victoriously to an end… I don't need to assure you how great my wish is not to be aloof from your needs and how great will be my satisfaction to perform for you… the services that you esteem most valuable…."

His first service was to seize—on June 14—the international port of Tangier, opposite Gibraltar. All summer he worked feverishly on plans to capture, with German help, Gibraltar and thus doom the British already fighting for their lives in Egypt. In the middle of the summer he sent Serrano Suñer, his most trusted minister, to Berlin to work out the details. Hitler promised him the planes, the guns, and the men to reduce the fortress of Gibraltar, but was a little vague on Franco's territorial demands and on economic help. Serrano Suñer hurried back to Madrid to report.

In the meantime the German Foreign Minister, Ribbentrop, was in Rome. On September 19 he had a long talk with Mussolini. The secret German minutes of the meeting tell how the Spanish situation was shaping up:

"The Reich Foreign Minister," they say, "further announced a statement by the Führer regarding the military part of the Spanish problem, i.e., the conquest of Gibraltar. The Spaniards wanted to conquer Gibraltar by themselves. But so as to prevent any failure, Germany would provide Spain with special troops equipped with special weapons, and a few squadrons of planes….

"On his return to Berlin, he [the Reich Foreign Minister] intended to sign a secret protocol with Serrano Suñer dealing with Spain's entry into the war, as well as the supplying of Spain with the aforementioned materials, recognizing the Spanish ambitions, and providing an attack against Gibraltar as a declaration of war…. It had been orally provided that Spain would come into the war as soon as Franco had completed his preparations, and particularly after the German special weapons and troops as well as planes had arrived at their destinations in Spain."

The German minutes do not touch on what the Duce said, if anything. Didn't he ask that Italy be permitted to get in on the Spanish operation as she had—at the last minute—on the attack on France? It would seem most likely. But it is also evident that the Germans had no intention of letting their Italian ally participate in Spain. Hitler's famous Directive 18 for "Felix and Isabella," which would be issued on November 12, would say tartly: "An Italian participation is not envisaged."

Three days after the Ribbentrop-Mussolini meeting in Rome, on September 22, Franco wrote a long letter to Hitler discussing in detail joint plans for the attack on Gibraltar. "For our part," he said, "we have been preparing the operation in secret for a long time…." He closed with the assurance "of my unchangeable and sincere adherence to you personally and to the German people and the cause for which you fight."

A month later, on October 23, Franco and Hitler met at Hendaye, on the Spanish-French frontier. We have the German notes on the conversation. "Spain has always been allied with the German people spiritually… and in complete loyalty. In the same sense Spain has in every moment felt herself at one with the Axis," Franco began, and added: "In the present war Spain will gladly fight at Germany's side."

On November 11 Ambassador von Stohrer wired Berlin from Madrid that the Spanish "Foreign Minister has signed." Spain had formally agreed, then, to enter the war on Germany's side.

The next day, therefore, November 12, Hitler issued his "Top Secret War Directive Number 18." It is a fascinating document, but too long to include here. "The aim of German intervention in the Iberian Peninsula," it says, "will be to drive the British out of the western Mediterranean. For this purpose Gibraltar will be taken and the Straits closed.... The attack for the seizure of Gibraltar is to be carried out by German[45] troops. Troops should be mobilized to march into Portugal should the British gain a foothold there.... Support from the Spaniards in closing the Strait after[46] the seizure of the Rock... should be enlisted if required."

If required! Franco is hardly to be allowed to shine in his own part of the war! But the Germans fix the date for his joining it. "Felix and Isabella," we learn from other documents, is to begin on January 10, 1941.

By December 1940 the little Spanish dictator begins to get cold feet. The fortunes of war—through the ages so fickle!—have not been going so well for the Axis. England has not been invaded. In Albania the Italians are in retreat before the valiant Greeks. Marshal Badoglio has been forced to resign as Italian Chief of Staff. On the western border of Egypt, Marshal Graziani's much vaunted invasion has been stalled for three months by a pitifully small and weak British force. Franco hesitates.

On December 12 the dismayed German Ambassador in Madrid has to write Berlin that Franco has informed him "It is impossible for Spain to enter the war on the suggested date." There is, Franco reminds the Germans, "the continued menace of the British fleet, the incompleteness of Spain's own military preparations, and the absolute inadequacy of Spain's provisioning." Franco complains that not only has Berlin not supplied him with the promised reserves of food and oil, but that Hitler has never quite come across on Fascist Spain's territorial demands.

The planned D-Day passes with no action. On February 6, 1941, Hitler writes Franco that "time is running short," that "two months have been lost," that the Axis has missed a great opportunity because of "Franco's refusal to enter the war on January 10." He closes with a warning: "A nationalist Spain will never exist if we do not win."

Replying on February 26, Franco agrees, though today, with the backing he has had from Great Britain and the United States, he must feel that both he and Hitler were wrong on this point. "I want to dispel all shadow of doubt," he tells the Führer in this epistle, "and declare that I stand today ready at your side, entirely and decidedly at your disposal, united in a common historical destiny, desertion from which would mean my suicide and that of the cause that I represent in Spain."

Actually, Hitler has already given up his Spanish friend—for the time being, anyway—though Franco probably is not aware of it. On February 3, three days before his letter of complaint to the Spanish chief, the Führer holds a great operational conference with his top generals on the plan for "Barbarossa." Everyone's mind is concentrated on the grandiose project to conquer Russia. Already planes, guns, and troops earmarked for the Gibraltar operation are being shunted off to the east "for the new undertaking," as General von Brauchitsch, commander-in-chief of the army, notes on February 8. Spain, obviously, can wait. Gibraltar will be a picnic after the Soviet Union has been destroyed.

There is a two-year interval so far as the documents on German-Spanish relations are concerned. On February 10, 1943, however, Spain and Germany sign a secret protocol. Hitler is now on the defensive—in Russia, in Africa, in the air over western Europe. He cannot help Franco wrest Gibraltar from the British, and Morocco and Algeria from the French. He can only offer aid if the Allies attack Spain. And he wants to be sure Franco will resist such an attack. By the February 10 secret treaty the Caudillo promises he will resist should the American and British armies in North Africa invade Spanish territory. Throughout the rest of our difficult North African operation the Spanish fascist dictator then renders his last service to Hitler. By mobilizing strong forces in Spanish Morocco in the rear of the Allied expeditionary army, which is girding to throw the Germans and Italians out of Tunisia, Franco causes a certain worry to General Eisenhower.

This is his final gesture to his fascist friends. The tide of war was turning. The Axis no longer looked like the winner. The vain little Spaniard withdrew his "Blue Division" from Russia, ceased refueling German U-boats in Spanish ports, and began to cultivate his British and American friends. The amazing thing is that Britain and America welcomed the overtures of this vapid turncoat. They alone have kept him in power to this day, unmindful, it would seem, of what he did, of what we fought the war for, and blind to the awful butcheries and dreadful terror of Europe's only surviving fascist regime.)

Worked late on my notes, on the *Digest* piece, and on tomorrow's broadcast, my last from Nuremberg and from Germany. Paul White of CBS thinks it's time I came home. As long as he insists, I might as well try to make it by Christmas. Maybe I can—as I did last year.

Nuremberg, *Sunday, December* 9 (after midnight)
Exhausted from writing the broadcast, giving it twice (recording and "live") and then finishing the last take of the long cable for the *Digest*, which went off at midnight. Must pack my junk now and be up at six to catch the courier plane to Paris.

In one's utter weariness, though, is a strange feeling of relief to be leaving this tortuous, tragic land again—perhaps for the last time. Its fate, its spirit, its character, its culture, its people and their barbaric excesses (and now their excessive self-pity), and finally their ghastly war have absorbed my own little life for nearly fifteen years. I seek a release from it all now. There are, of course, a few things that one can take with one from the German land: the love and appreciation of German music—of Bach and Beethoven and the Austrians, Haydn, Mozart and Schubert—and the beautiful things that a few Germans wrote: Schiller and Goethe and Heine and Thomas Mann and the wonderful lyric poet Rilke, who was born in Prague, and Kafka, who was a Czech but wrote in German. Theirs was a German spirit, if you will, that I can live with for the rest of my days in my own Anglo-Saxon native land.

It is almost five years to a day since my last going-away from Germany. It seemed then that the evil in the German not only had triumphed over himself but was about to triumph over the world. One's soul turned sick and black at the prospect. Man finally had come to this. The bleakness, the loneliness, the injustices of life one could always support. But not this. Not this outrageous cruelty, this lust to destroy, this monstrous tyranny over a man's life and—worst of all—over his spirit.

What seemed like such a certain doom when last I left did not come off. Those who sought to destroy the world are themselves destroyed. One does not rejoice at that either. But it is better than the other way round. The realization of it makes this last departure a different experience. The heart is less hurt, and a man's hope for man begins to rise again.

POSTSCRIPT

Spring, **1947**

I flew home that Christmas of 1945, and there was the wondrous day with the children around the lighted tree and the fine, warm feeling that everyone, all over Christendom, got at observing this first Yuletide of the Peace.

Yet a returning reporter remembered so many things. A thousand and one impressions hammered at the mind. How to fit them together, so that they made sense and were true as a picture of the whole? There was so much that was true that did not make sense: the monumental apathy of the German people and their deep regret, not that they had started the war, but merely that they had lost it; their whining complaints at the lack of food and fuel and their total lack of sympathy or even interest in the worse plight of the occupied peoples, for which they bore so much responsibility; their boredom at the very mention of the Nuremberg trial, which they were convinced was only an Allied propaganda stunt; their striking unreadiness for, or interest in, democracy, which we, with typical Anglo-Saxon fervor and blindness, were trying to shove down their throats.

Can you forget the things Germans said: Paul Lobe, the aging Social-Democrat and former President of the Reichstag, warning—yes, warning!—the Allies that they must not hold the German people responsible for Germany's crimes, but only the Nazis? The poet Johannes R. Becher having the guts to go to the microphone in Berlin and tell his fellow Germans that they all bore a share of guilt for Hitler's crimes and begging them to wake up and face the fact that "the greater part of our people have fallen into an inferno of immorality…. In the immensity of our guilt and the depth of our disgrace our defeat has no parallel in world history…. Let us face the bitter fact that we are despised and hated in the whole world."

Brave words, and Becher meant them, but did they not fall on barren ground and did not the Berliners note that this courageous poet, whose voice cried out in the German wilderness, was booted out of his house and deprived of his library by an American army officer who fancied them for himself and who perhaps did not know a poet—and an anti-Nazi one at that—when he saw one?

Of course, we did not always recognize a Nazi when we saw one, or a German who had served the Nazis. Was not one of my former censors in Berlin during the war recently named program-director of the Austrian radio by the American Military Government? Was not a leading German banker whom the Americans wanted to add to the twenty-two bankers they had already arrested for fraud and robbery in the occupied lands still free because the British had made him one of their chief financial advisers in their zone? Was not that amiable fellow whom all the American correspondents in Berlin knew as "Fatty" and who, we were sure, informed for the Gestapo entrusted with important work by one of the Allied governments in the west? Were not American army officers going around Germany sneering at General Eisenhower's denazification decree and sabotaging it, and was not powerful support gathering for them at home?

Ah, yes. True. But what could you expect, with the Americans pulling out pell-mell, and the army gone to hell, and everyone at home yearning and yapping to get back to "normalcy"? Already what the Germans had done was being rapidly forgotten. A new enemy and a new war was beginning to be talked about. Russia! The Bolsheviks! Gotta fight them bastards next.

I had paused briefly in Paris and London on my way home from Germany that year. The good folk there, shivering and hungering though they were, seemed glad just to have survived the holocaust. Peace would be sweet, they thought. But the cost of the war? The cost to Europe in ruined cities, destroyed lives (counting the living as well as the dead), corrupted morals, wrecked economies, broken-down communications, shattered nerves, and collapsed cultures staggered the mind of a reporter from a vast, rich, well-fed land untouched by the war.

Like the nature of the war itself, the awful dislocation of Europe could not be adequately described. Some, with a glance at history, would say, of course, that Europe had had its vicissitudes before, and that it had survived them all. The Thirty Years' War had turned Germany and most of central Europe into an utter wasteland. But the rest of Europe had been spared this blight. World War I had toppled empires and slaughtered fifteen to twenty million human beings. But its destruction and indeed its savagery had been nothing compared to its successor.

Surveying the demolished cities, the cold and underfed millions upon millions, and the utter breakdown of society, one asked during that winter of 1945: Could Europe survive? Could it come back? Or had it lost its domination of the world for good? To Russia in the east, to America in the west? It would be hasty, I concluded, to say that Europe was finished and could never come back. One could only report that the Europe we had known was gone and that no man could yet foresee in what form its recovery, if there was one, would take place. One felt a great stamina still in the French and British peoples. Unlike most Americans, they did not want to set the clock back to the prewar era. Unfettered "free enterprise," so sacred a thing at home, had lost its attraction for most of them. They were turning hopefully toward a democratic socialism. If in space they were caught between the United States and the Soviet Union, so were they in their ideas. They wanted neither our unbridled capitalism nor Russia's total-itarian communism. They sought something in between.

And so the year 1945 came to its appointed end. It had been, beyond doubt, the most memorable year any of us had ever lived. It was the year of Allied victory, the year that brought an end to the Japanese-German dream of world conquest and the cessation of the most terrible war in the history of the world.

It was the year, too, that saw the birth of the United Nations organization and therewith the second attempt within our lifetime to organize the world's peace. It had brought one other thing—the greatest of all—the era of atomic energy. Some thought a long phase in the history of the human race had ended during the year of 1945. It had ended, they said, when the first atomic bomb exploded in July in New Mexico.

What, then, would the new atomic age be like? And could mankind survive in it for long?

I cannot find much in my own rough notes of 1946 and the beginning of 1947 that provides encouraging answers to the questions. The first two years of the peace were far from propitious.

The United Nations settled on American soil in 1946, but its growth seemed stunted from the beginning. Because of the awesome gulf between the Russian world and our own, the U.N. could not come to grips with any of the earth's major problems, beginning with international control of atomic energy. It did not help much to conclude, as most of us Americans did, that the fault was exclusively Russia's. That still left the problem of world peace unsolved. It still left us in fear of an atomic war that might demolish the planet regardless of who "won."

Indeed, stark *fear* seemed to be at the bottom of most of our troubles. We feared Russia. Russia feared us. And here at home we seemed to be doing our devilish best to conjure up domestic fears of our own. Some feared labor; others management. Everyone feared the Communists, though they were but a miserable handful so out of touch with American life (however closely they might be in touch with the Russian) that they could not even elect a dog-catcher, let alone an alderman, a lieutenant governor, or a congressman. In France, where the Communist Party was the largest and best organized in the country, there was a Communist problem. But we had been spared that, if we only had the sense to know it.

Did we have the sense? One could not be sure. We had, in 1946 and 1947, a "Red" scare and a "Red spy" scare that engendered a rather silly hysteria, at least in the Congress, the press, and the radio, and that resulted in, among other things, too many of us calling a man a "Red" or a "Communist" if he dared to disagree with us or if he mildly protested against dragging America back to the days of McKinley.

There was something unworthy of us in the intolerance that spread over the land. It brought the shocking attack on David E. Lilienthal and the snide remarks of mediocre politicians on those magnificent American scientists whose genius had unlocked the last secret of the atom and who pleaded honestly and sincerely with the politicians not to misuse what they had discovered. It brought the President's executive order prescribing ridiculous "loyalty" tests for the federal government's own employees, an act that smacked to me of the detestable German

Gestapo and the dreaded Russian G.P.U., and that, according to some of the most eminent jurists in the land, denied our civil servants the most elementary rights of Anglo-Saxon justice and relegated them to a category of second-class citizens, which they were not.

The intolerance in the nation spread even to radio and brought the sudden ouster of several of us whose views could no longer be tolerated by those who ran broadcasting in our free land. The airwaves, of course, belonged by law to the American people, who ultimately paid all of radio's bills, but an advertiser, who paid its immediate bills, or a network official who was sensitive to the advertiser's dollar, alone determined whom the free citizens of our Republic could or could not hear on the air.

The exercise of thought-control was proving tempting to a few of our misguided zealots, but surely it was only a temporary phenomenon in our great democracy, a rather silly thing that would be laughed at for the joke it was (though in Europe, where I had long experienced it, it was decidedly no joke) as soon as we returned to our senses and to our true—as opposed to the phony—tradition of American life.

Our fears, our uncertainty about ourselves, now that our nation had emerged from the war the most powerful on earth, brought, in 1947, the so-called "Truman Doctrine," an ill-conceived and hastily concocted plan that aimed to stem Russian expansion and the spread of Communism by shelling out American dollars, American arms, and American military "personnel" in support of democracy everywhere. It was a fine and noble thing to support democracy around the world, and if we had had the gumption to do so in 1939, when Hitler set out to destroy the democratic world, we could have saved ourselves and indeed the world the most destructive war of all time.... There were great democracies to help then—Britain, France, the Lowlands, and Scandinavia—and our aid to them would have been really effective. But now? How could you support democracy in Turkey, which had never experienced it; or in Greece, from which our conception of democracy originally had come, but where now the ruling power was in the hands of a corrupt and most undemocratic group? Would such hypocrisy really save democracy in the world? Was that the way to stem the growth of Communism and halt the Soviet expansion?

Another way obviously did not appeal very much to the Congress. All through the late spring of 1947 our federal legislators threatened to doom the nation's entire program for carrying the American view into sixty-seven foreign countries. Our broadcasts to the world, including those beamed to Russia, as well as other informational and cultural activities that were doing so much to help combat Soviet propaganda and encourage democratic elements everywhere to make a stand, were considered so unimportant by a subcommittee of the House Appropriations Committee that it voted to kill the entire project.

Ah! the sublime shortsightedness of our statesmen and lawmakers in the

Congress! The very week the House subcommittee decided to silence the Voice of America in the world, ostensibly to save the taxpayers twenty-one million dollars a year, the Senate was voting three to one to shell out nearly half a *billion* dollars to implement Mr. Truman's program of saving democracy in undemocratic Turkey and Greece. It was highly likely that the twenty-one million dollars we were spending on telling the American story abroad—through broadcasts, movies, magazines (including one in Russian with a circulation of 50,000 copies a month in the Soviet Union), libraries, and other means—would do infinitely more to buttress democracy in the world and stem the spread of Communism and Russian influence than a half billion dollars, most of which the President wanted to spend for arms for the dictatorial regimes of Turkey and Greece. But America in 1947 was in no mood for common sense in carrying out its foreign policy.

And was resurrecting the strength of Germany and Japan the way to build the peace? Some in America a scant two years after the end of the German and Japanese war seemed to toy with the idea. Early in 1947 former President Herbert Hoover returned from an official mission in Germany and boldly proposed to President Truman that the Potsdam Agreement be scrapped and German industry revived. His recommendations, it seemed to me, would restore Germany as Europe's greatest industrial power. And was not a great industrial power in our time *ipso facto* a great military power? To be sure, Mr. Hoover assumed that the Allies would "stick together" and prohibit Germany from having an army, a navy, and an air force. But was it a very valid assumption, seeing what had happened to the Allies (and to Germany) after the first World War, and seeing how rapidly the victorious Allies were falling out after this one? If we wanted relief from a third German war, would it not be wise to disarm the Reich economically and industrially as well as militarily, as Leo T. Crowley, the Foreign Economic Administrator, had proposed to the Congress in 1945?

He had warned then, with the German war just over: "If we were to leave Germany to its own devices and not to institute a program of economic and industrial disarmament, Germany could be far better prepared for war within five years than she was in 1939."

Did we want to take such a risk so soon?

You had to take into consideration, it seemed to me, the German spirit. Surely you had to consider what the Germans, given their mentality, would do with their economic power if, as Mr. Hoover urged, it was now restored. The disastrous experience of two German wars in a man's lifetime was not very reassuring on this point.

Mr. Hoover argued in his report to the President on Germany that "no industry (except direct arms manufacture) is a war potential if the energies of a people are confined to the paths of peace."

True. But we are dealing with a people who since the days of Bismarck have concentrated their energies and used their heavy-industry production for purposes of war. Since the turn of the century the Germans had not used their surplus iron and steel production merely as exports in exchange for needed food and raw materials—as Mr. Hoover believes they will henceforth do. They had used their enormous surplus production of iron and steel to build up an aggressive navy and army—and, after 1935, an air force.

I cannot think of any compelling reason to believe they will not do it again—at the first opportunity.

This reference to the German spirit reminds me that I have failed to put into this book the material I gathered in Nuremberg on German atrocities. This is not because I was told—as indeed I was—the other day by a British and an American publisher that the people in Britain and America are sick to death of books about German atrocities. It is because the subject is so vast, the material so extensive, the tale so terrible, that an entire book would have to be devoted to this aspect of the world's recent misery. I must leave that to others. This book is already too long.

However, I want to get in here one lone document on the subject that illustrates the awful story. It has to do with a new word that crept into modern languages at Nuremberg: GENOCIDE. You can define it as meaning the planned and deliberate destruction of nations, races, or groups by cold-blooded mass murder. Let a certain Rudolf Franz Ferdinand Hoess illustrate.

I, Rudolf Franz Ferdinand Hoess, being first duly sworn, depose and say as follows:

I am forty-six years old, and have been a member of the NSDAP [Nazi Party] since 1922; a member of the SS since 1934; a member of the Waffen-SS since 1939. I was a member from December 1, 1934, of the SS Guard Unit, the so-called Deathshead Formation *(Totenkopf Verband)*.

I have been constantly associated with the administration of concentration camps since 1934, serving at Dachau until 1938; then as Adjutant in Sachsenhausen from 1938 to May 1, 1940, when I was appointed Commandant of Auschwitz. I commanded Auschwitz until December 1, 1943, and estimate that at least 2,500,000 victims were executed and exterminated there by gassing and burning, and at least another half million succumbed to starvation and disease making a total of dead of about 3,000,000.

This figure represents about 70% or 80% of all persons sent to Auschwitz as prisoners, the remainder having been selected and used for slave labor in the concentration camp industries. Included among the executed and burnt were approximately 20,000 Russian prisoners of war (previously screened out of Prisoner of War cages by the Gestapo) who were delivered at Auschwitz in Wehrmacht (army) transports operated by regular

Wehrmacht officers and men. The remainder of the total number of victims included about 100,000 German Jews, and great numbers of citizens, mostly Jewish, from Holland, France, Belgium, Poland, Hungary, Czechoslovakia, Greece, and other countries. We executed about 400,000 Hungarian Jews alone at Auschwitz in the summer of 1944....

Mass executions by gassing commenced during the summer of 1941 and continued until the fall of 1944. I personally supervised executions at Auschwitz until the first of December 1943 and know by reason of my continued duties in the Inspectorate of Concentration Camps that these mass executions continued as stated above....

The "final solution" of the Jewish question meant the complete extermination of all Jews in Europe. I was ordered to establish extermination facilities at Auschwitz in June 1941. At that time, there were already in the General Government [of Poland] three other extermination camps: Belzek, Treblinka and Wolzek. I visited Treblinka to find out how they carried out their extermination. The Camp Commandant at Treblinka told me that he had liquidated 80,000 in the course of one-half year. He was principally concerned with liquidating all the Jews from the Warsaw ghetto. He used monoxide gas and I did not think that his methods were very efficient. So when I set up the extermination building at Auschwitz, I used Cyclon B, which was a crystallized prussic acid which we dropped into the death chamber from a small opening. It took from 3 to 15 minutes to kill the people in the death chamber, depending upon climatic conditions. *We knew when the people were dead because their screaming stopped. We usually waited about one-half hour before we opened the doors and removed the bodies. After the bodies were removed our special commandos took off the rings and extracted the gold from the teeth of the corpses.*

Another improvement we made over Treblinka was that we built our gas chambers to accommodate 2,000 people at one time, whereas at Treblinka their 10 gas chambers only accommodated 200 people each. The way we selected our victims was as follows: we had two SS doctors on duty at Auschwitz to examine the incoming transports of prisoners. The prisoners would be marched by one of the doctors who would make spot decisions as they walked by. Those who were fit to work were sent into the camp. Others were sent immediately to the extermination plants. *Children of tender years were invariably exterminated, since by reason of their youth they were unable to work.*[46]Still another improvement we made over Treblinka was that at Treblinka the victims almost always knew that they were to be exterminated and at Auschwitz we endeavored to fool the victims into thinking that they were to go through a delousing process.

Of course, frequently they realized our true intentions and we sometimes had riots and difficulties due to that fact. Very frequently women would hide their children under their clothes but of course when we found them we would send the children in to be exterminated. We were required to carry out these exterminations in secrecy but of course the foul and nauseating stench from the continuous burning of bodies permeated the entire area and all of the people living in the surrounding communities knew that exterminations were going on in Auschwitz....

I understand English as it is written above. The above statements are true; this declaration is made by me voluntarily and without compulsion; after reading over the statement, I have signed and executed the same at Nuremberg, Germany, on the fifth day of April, 1946.

(signed) Rudolf Hoess
RUDOLF FRANZ FERDINAND HOESS

There is a great deal I have had to leave out of this book, but I did not feel that I could leave out Herr Hoess. He had to speak in this place. What he said and what he did will haunt me to the day I die.

I come now to the end of a book I think I shall call the *End of a Berlin* Diary. My own days in Berlin are now, happily, over. And though I shall always be restless to travel up and down this sorry earth seeking out what little truth a man can find in distant places among his erring fellow men, I shall try to center what life remains in the land where I was born. The rest of the world will always fascinate me and I shall go on trying to find out what I can of its riddles. But I can only be at home here at home.

The days and years in Berlin among the Germans were not, on the whole, very pleasant. But they were not dull either, and I have no regrets that my own particular and unimportant fate was spun out for so long in the great and convulsive Teutonic capital beyond the Elbe. The suffering and glory of my time stemmed largely from the evil that came out of Berlin and from the success of the non-Germanic world in finally conquering that evil. For a reporter, Berlin, an ugly city with pleasant lake-studded, wooded environs, was decidedly the capital to have worked in.

It is a relief, though, in glancing through my notes for 1946 and the beginning of 1947 to find the Berlin story fading out of one's life. I did jot down an item now and then from Germany—second-hand, of course. On October 1, 1946, came the news from Nuremberg that Göring, Ribbentrop, Keitel, Kaltenbrunner, Rosenberg, Frank, Frick, Streicher, Seyss-Inquart, Sauckel, Jodl, and Martin Bormann—the last tried *in absentia*—had been sentenced by the International Military Tribunal to die on the gallows. Hess, curiously enough, escaped with a life sentence, which was also given to Funk and Raeder. Speer and von Schirach got twenty years in prison, von Neurath fifteen, and Doenitz ten. Surprisingly,

Schacht and von Papen, who had served their Nazi masters so well, were acquitted, as was Fritzsche![47]

Surprisingly too, Senator Taft, who may be our next president, spoke out against the Nuremberg verdicts. On October 5 he called them an "outrage against justice." Bertie McCormick's *Chicago Tribune*, as might have been expected, was even angrier than the Senator from Ohio. "Russia, Britain, France and the U.S.A.," it said on October 3, "…were all guilty of crimes against the peace…. The U.S. under Roosevelt plotted, planned, prepared and initiated aggressive war." But the rest of humanity, I had a feeling, was relieved and grateful at the news from Nuremberg. There was, after all, some sort of rough justice in our world.

Its sword fell on the eleven faded survivors of the Nazi plot to enslave the world in the early morning hours of October 16. Göring, crafty and defiant to the very end, cheated the gallows in Nuremberg by swallowing poison less than three hours before he would have been executed. The ten others were hanged.

There was one other hanging of a character I had known in Berlin during the Nazi time which I noted down in the epilogue to the German story. On the morning of January 3, 1946, William Joyce (Lord Haw-Haw) died on the gallows in Wandsworth Prison in London after having been convicted of high treason. He had been the war's outstanding radio traitor.

The United States had also had its full share of radio traitors—a peculiar phenomenon of the Nazi war—but our government's attitude seemed to be, in their case, to forget and forgive. Some of the most notorious of them (like Donald Day, the veteran former *Chicago Tribune* correspondent) were released outright, and there did not seem to be an undue determination in Washington to bring the rest to trial.

The British, perhaps because they had experienced war at first hand, had been more stern. On the cold, gray December day I had left England in 1945, I had read in a London newspaper on my way to the airport of the hanging of Britain's other distinguished radio traitor, John Amery, the son of a very eminent Tory cabinet minister.

So these were dead now and could do no more harm. The terrible Nazi chapter was over. One could turn one's thoughts to other things. God! there were other things in life. Music, for instance. The great symphony orchestras in New York and elsewhere in America. The Metropolitan Opera. The flowering of ballet in our land. I find a little note for Saturday, November 1, 1946: "To hear Fritz Kreisler. Aged (72), but still wonderful. No one else has quite his mastery, his magic."

There was even time to read again. Notes on reading creep into my diary once more. Ah, this is living again. The entry: "New York, September 20, 1946," for instance:

"Despite the unseemly heat, sat up last night reading Plutarch's *Lives*—an old edition of my father's with the John Dryden translation…. I finished the part on Demosthenes and Cicero about one a.m., flushed with the realization that however troublesome and chaotic and desperate our times may seem to us, they have ever been so among civilized (if that is the word) men. I had forgotten too easily—and Plutarch suddenly caught me up—that even in the great civilizations of Greece and Rome there was constant war, strife, bloodshed, assassination, corruption, treason, double-crossing, intolerance, tyranny, rabble-rousing, and all the other unpleasant practices that make beasts of men most of the time and ruin or prevent the good life to which mankind, apparently, aspires.

"Though both Demosthenes and Cicero attained the highest honors in their lifetime, both were, for a time, driven out of their lands by their ungrateful countrymen. Both their lives were filled with continual struggle—often for very survival. On each was heaped, at times, such abuse as seems to make our own times comparatively mild and decent and mannerly. In the end Cicero was murdered while fleeing his own country by men who had once been his friends. Demosthenes was in frightened flight too when he ended his life by suicide to escape capture and almost certain murder. Maybe if we had today a sense of history we could see our own troubled times in some perspective....

"What a wonderfully wise and urbane writer Plutarch was! In his essay on Demosthenes he pauses to discuss whether it makes much difference from what city or place you come—a matter that has often been argued by my own generation. It was probably Euripides, Plutarch says, who 'tells us that to a man's being happy it is in the first place requisite he should be born in some famous city.' Plutarch is not so sure.

"'For him that would attain to true happiness, which for the most part is placed in the qualities and disposition of the mind, it is, in my opinion, of no other disadvantage to be of a mean, obscure country than to be born of a small or plain-looking woman.' He concedes that for a writer, or at least for a writer of history, the metropolis does offer advantages. '...For him, undoubtedly, it is above all necessary to reside in some city of good note, addicted to liberal arts and populous, where he may have plenty of all sorts of books, and upon inquiry may hear and inform himself of such particulars as, having escaped the pens of writers, are more faithfully preserved in the memories of men.... But for me, I live in a little town, where I am willing to continue, lest it should grow less.'

"...On the subject of man's quest for glory, Plutarch is almost overwhelming. 'The desire for glory,' he says, 'has great power in washing the tinctures of philosophy out of the souls of men.' Between the two great orators of the Greek and Latin worlds, Plutarch holds that Demosthenes was much more modest than Cicero.

"'Demosthenes never touched upon his own praises but decently and without offense... modestly and sparingly. But Cicero's immeasurable boasting of himself in his orations argues him guilty of an uncontrollable appetite for distinction.... At last we find him extolling not only his deeds and actions, but his orations also, as well those that were only spoken as those that were published.... He was always lauding and magnifying himself.... Indeed he also filled his books and writing with his own praises… this ungrateful humor, like a disease, always cleaving to him. Nevertheless, though he was intemperately fond of his own glory, he was very free from envying others.'

"One more wise remark from Plutarch that seems deadly timely today. Of the machinations of Cæsar, Antony, and Lepidus, which finally brought Cicero to his doom, he remarks: 'Thus they let their anger and fury take from them the sense of humanity and demonstrated that no beast is more savage than man, when possessed with power answerable to his rage.'

"No one that I have read has ever said this better."

Yes, books, ancient and modern, helped to make life seem good again.

When I had come home from Germany that Christmas and shed my war correspondent's uniform for the last time, Eileen, who was seven, had said:

"Is the war over?"
    "Yes."
    "Will there be another?"
    "I hope not."
    "At school they say the next one will be with Russia."
    "They're insane."
    "But are they right?"
    "Maybe. Lunatics sometimes are."
    "What are lunatics?"
    "People in America and Russia who want a war."
    She paused a moment. So did I.
    "But that German war is finished?"
    "Definitely."
    "You going to stay home now?"
    "Yes."
    "What you going to do?"
    I wondered a little myself. It was so good just to be home and no war to have to go back to and no Nazis and not even a job overseas any more. It was just twenty years since I had gone abroad to work.

"I guess I'll just stay home, like Candide," I said, "and cultivate my garden."

ENDNOTES

1   Elected President of France in 1947.

2   Copyright 1942 by Stephen Vincent Benét from *We Stand United*, published by Rinehart & Co.

3   Months later in Berlin I would come across the diary of Hitler's Finance Minister, Count Schwerin-Krosigk, and learn indeed how the Nazi chieftains believed this night that God had removed their greatest enemy and that it surely meant a favorable turn for them in the fortunes of war.

4   For the last time, but neither of us knew it.

5   This was a lie. From what I could learn in Berlin later, Hitler was wacky all right (but then, he had always been), but he was not suffering from a brain hemorrhage. I would also learn that just before he killed himself Hitler learned of Himmler's efforts to negotiate a surrender. This, coming on top of what he considered to be Göring's "treason"—Göring had radioed him from Bavaria that he was taking over his job, for which the Führer ordered him immediately shot—was just about the last straw. Eyewitnesses say Hitler went into a fearful rampage, broke down and wept, crying that his most trusted men were "betraying" him in his last hour. Probably he had never trusted Göring very far, but I think his trust in Himmler had been great— hence the special shock. Actually—as I learned from the diary of Count Schwerin-Krosigk, Nazi Finance Minister, Himmler for months had joined a group of top Nazi officials who realized the jig was up, but that Hitler would never admit it; they were therefore seeking some way of surrendering to the western Allies. Idiots that they were, they hoped to the very last that they could persuade the western Allies to join them in turning on Russia. Krosigk, a staunch Catholic, thought the Vatican would help in this.

6   And an eloquent one it turned out to be, with its opening words:

"We, the peoples of the United Nations,

"Determined to save succeeding generations from the scourge of war, which twice in our lifetime has brought untold sorrow to mankind, and

"To reaffirm faith in fundamental human rights, in the dignity and worth of the human person, in the equal rights of men and women and of nations large and small," and so forth.

7 So unlike him, in fact, that later on the Allies *did* find a "final testament," which I believe to be genuine. See note 13.

8 A little farther on in this book you will see in a captured secret German document what Hitler really thought about Britain.

9 Von Greim committed suicide on May 24 at Salzburg, using the poison capsule Hitler had given him in the Chancellery.

10 Security Service.

11 Italics in this report are mine.—W. L. S.

12 There can be no doubt of the marriage. Later Allied authorities discovered the marriage document, a rather curious paper, which reads as follows:
DER OBERBÜRGERMEISTER DER REICHSHAUPTSTADT:
[The first phrase of the following was typewritten and then scratched out with ink.]
Before the Oberbürgermeister of the Reichshauptstadt Berlin as the competent official of Berlin *[then in handwriting]* Municipal Councilor Walter N. Wagner *[typing resumed]*, as a competent official of the Reichshauptstadt, empowered by the Oberbürgermeister, have appeared for immediate conclusion of marriage:

1. ADOLF HITLER
Born: 20 April, 1889, Braunau.
Residence: Berlin, Reichs Chancellery.
Father: *[Blank]*
Mother: *[Blank]*

Marriage date of parents: [*Scratched out in ink*]
Identification: Publicly known.

2. EVA BRAUN
Born: 2 February, 1910, in Munich, Wassenburgerstrasse.
Residence: [*Ditto marks*]
Father: Friedrich Braun.
Mother: Franziska Braun, born Kronburger.
Marriage date of parents: [*Scratched out in ink*]
Identification: Special pass issued by chief of German police.

3. AS WITNESS: REICHSMINISTER DR. GOEBBELS, JOSEPH
Born: 26 October, 1887, Rheydt.
Residence: Berlin, Hermann Goeringstrasse 20.
Identification: Publicly known.

4. AS WITNESS: REICHSLEITER MARTIN BORMANN
Born: 17 June, 1900, in Halberstadt.
Residence: Obersalzberg.
Identification: Publicly known.

The persons of 1 and 2 declared that they are of complete Aryan descent and have no hereditary disease to exclude the marriage. They requested, in view of war developments, a war marriage under exceptional circumstances and requested further that the publications of the banns be done orally and all delays be avoided.

The requests were granted. The orally given bann has been proved and found in order.

I come now to the ceremonial act of marriage. In the presence of the above named witnesses of 3 and 4, I ask you, my Führer Adolf Hitler, whether you wish to enter marriage with Fräulein Eva Braun. In such case I ask you to answer with "Yes."

[*The next line of the document was obliterated by folding and ink smearing*] whether you wish to enter marriage with our Führer Adolf Hitler. In such case I ask you to answer with "Yes."

After both of the engaged gave the declaration to enter into marriage, I declared the marriage concluded legally before the law.

Berlin on the [*date smeared by inkblot*] April, 1945.

Read and signed:

1. Bridegroom, A. Hitler.
2. Bride, Eva B. Hitler, born Braun.
3. Witness 1, Dr. Joseph Goebbels.
4. Witness 2, M.B. [*initials*].
5. W. Wagner, as competent official.

The text of Hitler's personal will, drawn up and signed less than twenty-four hours before he and Eva Braun killed themselves, explains why he decided to marry her at the very end. It reads as follows:

HITLER'S PERSONAL WILL

Although during the years of struggle I believed that I could not undertake the responsibility of marriage, now, before the end of my life, I have decided to take as my wife the woman who, after many years of true friendship, came to this city, almost already besieged, of her own free will in order to share my fate.

She will go to her death with me at her own wish as my wife. This will compensate us both for what we both lost through my work in the service of my people.

My possessions, in so far as they are worth anything, belong to the party, or, if this no longer exists, to the state. If the state, too, is destroyed, there is no need for any further instructions on my part. The paintings in the collections bought by me during the years were never assembled for private purposes but solely for the establishment of a picture gallery in my home town of Linz on the Danube.

It is my most heartfelt wish that this will should duly be executed. As executor I appoint my most faithful party comrade, Martin Bormann. He receives full legal authority to make all decisions. He is permitted to hand over to my relatives everything that is of value as a personal memento or is necessary for maintaining a petit-bourgeois standard of living, especially to my wife's mother and my faithful fellow workers of both sexes who are all well known to him.

The chief of these are my former secretaries, Frau Winter, etc., who helped me for many years by their work.

My wife and I choose to die in order to escape the shame of overthrow or capitulation. It is our wish for our bodies to be cremated immediately on the place where I have performed the greater part of my daily work during twelve years of service to my people.

Berlin, 29 April, 1400 hours.

A. HITLER

Witnesses: Martin Bormann, Dr. Joseph Goebbels, Nicolaus von Buelow.

13   It reads as follows:

MY POLITICAL TESTAMENT

More than thirty years have passed since I made my modest contribution as a volunteer in the First World War, which was forced upon the Reich.

In these three decades, love and loyalty to my people alone have guided me in all my thoughts, actions, and life. They gave me power to make the most difficult decisions which have ever confronted mortal man. I have spent all my time, my powers and my health in these three decades.

It is untrue that I or anybody else in Germany wanted war in 1939. It was wanted and provoked exclusively by those international statesmen who either were of Jewish origin or worked for Jewish interests.

I have made too many offers of limitation and control of armaments that posterity will not for all time be able to disregard for responsibility for the outbreak of this war to be placed on me. Further, I have never wished that after the appalling First World War there should be a second one against either England or America. Centuries will go by, but from the ruins of our towns and monuments the hatred of those ultimately responsible will always grow anew. They are the people whom we have to thank for all this: international Jewry and its helpers.

Three days before the outbreak of the German-Polish war, I suggested to the British Ambassador in Berlin a solution of the German-Polish questions, similar to that in the case of the Saar, under international control. This offer, too, cannot be denied. It was rejected only because the ruling political clique in England wanted war, partly for commercial reasons, partly because it was influenced by propaganda put out by the international Jewry.

I also made it quite plain that, if the peoples of Europe were again to be regarded merely as pawns in a game played by the international conspiracy of money and finance, they, the Jews, the race that is the real guilty party in this murderous struggle, would be saddled with the responsibility for it.

I left no one in doubt that this time not only would millions of grown men meet their death and not only would hundreds of thousands of women and children be burned and bombed to death in cities, but this time the real culprits would have to pay for their guilt even though by more humane means than war.

After six years of war, which, in spite of all setbacks, will one day go down in history as the most glorious and heroic manifestation of the struggle for existence of a nation, I cannot forsake the city that is the capital of this state. As our forces are too small to withstand an enemy attack on this place any longer, and our own resistance will gradually be worn down by men who are merely blind automatons, I wish to share my fate with that which millions of others have also taken upon themselves by staying in this town. Further, I shall not fall in the hands of the enemy, who requires a new spectacle, presented by the Jews, to divert their hysterical masses.

I have therefore decided to remain in Berlin and there to choose death voluntarily at that moment when I believe that the position of the Führer and the Chancellery itself can no longer be maintained. I die with a joyful heart in my knowledge of the immeasurable deeds and achievements of our peasants and workers and of a contribution unique in history, of our youth that bears my name.

That I express to them all the thanks that come from the bottom of my heart is as clear as my wish that they should therefore not give up the struggle under any circumstances but carry it on wherever they may be against the enemies of the Fatherland, true to the principles of the great Clausewitz.

From the sacrifice of our soldiers and from my own comradeship with them to death itself, the seed has been sown that will grow one day in the history of Germany to the glorious rebirth of the National Socialist movement of a truly united nation.

Many brave men and women have decided to link their lives with mine to the last. I have asked and finally ordered them not to do this, but to continue to take part in the nation's struggle. I ask the commanders of the armies, of the navy, and of the air force to strengthen with all possible means the spirit of resistance of our soldiers in the National Socialist belief, with special emphasis on the fact that I myself, as the founder and creator of this movement, prefer death to cowardly resignation or even to capitulation.

May it be in the future a point of honor with the German army officers as it already is in our navy, that the surrender of a district or town is out of the question and that, above everything else, the commanders must set a shining example of faithful devotion to duty until death.

Before my death, I expel the former Reich Marshal Hermann Göring from the party and withdraw from him all the rights that were conferred on him by the decree of 29 June 1941, and by my Reichstag speech of the 1st of September 1939. In his place I appoint Admiral Doenitz as President of the Reich and supreme commander of the armed forces.

Before my death I expel the former Reichsführer of the SS and the Minister of the Interior Heinrich Himmler from the party and from all his state offices. In his place I appoint Gauleiter Karl Hanke as Reichsführer of the SS and chief of the German police and Gauleiter Paul Giesler as Minister of the Interior.

Apart altogether from their disloyalty to me, Göring and Himmler have brought irreparable shame on the country and the whole nation by secretly negotiating with the enemy without my knowledge and against my will, and also by illegally attempting to seize control of the state.

In order to give the German people a government composed of honorable men who will fulfill the task of continuing the war with all means, as the leader of the nation I appoint the following members of the new Cabinet:

President, Doenitz; Chancellor, Dr. Goebbels; Party Minister, Bormann; Foreign Minister, Seyss-Inquart; Minister of the Interior, Gauleiter Giesler; Minister of War, Doenitz; Supreme Commander of the Army, Schoerner; Supreme Commander of the Navy, Doenitz; Supreme Commander of the Air Force, Greim; Reichsführer of the SS and Chief of the German Police, Gauleiter Hanke; Industry, Funk; Agriculture, Backe; Justice, Theirack; Culture, Dr. Scheel; Propaganda, Dr. Naumann; Finance, Schwerin-Krosigk; Labor, Dr. Hupfauer; Armaments, Sauer; Leader of German Labor Front and member of the Cabinet, Reichsminister Dr. Ley.

Although a number of these men, such as Martin Bormann, Goebbels, etc., as well as their wives, have come to me of their own free will, wishing under no circumstances to leave the Reich capital, but instead to fall with me here, I must nevertheless ask them to obey my request and, in this case, put the interests of the nation above their own feelings. They will stand as near to me through their work and their loyalty as comrades after death, as I hope that my spirit will remain among them and always be with them. May they be severe but never unjust, may they above all never allow fear to influence their actions, and may they place the honor of the nation above everything on earth.

May they finally be conscious that our task, the establishment of a National Socialist state, represents the work of centuries to come and obliges each individual person always to serve the common interest before his own advantage. I ask all Germans, all National Socialists, men, women, and all soldiers of the army, to be loyal and obedient to the new government and its President until death.

Above all, I enjoin the government of the nation and the people to uphold the racial laws to the limit and to resist mercilessly the poisoner of all nations, international Jewry.

Berlin, 29 April 1945, 0400 hours.

A. HITLER

Witnesses: Dr. Joseph Goebbels, Wilhelm Burgdorf, Martin Bormann, Hans Krebs.

APPENDIX BY GOEBBELS

The Führer has ordered me to leave Berlin if the defense of the Reich's capital collapses and take part as a leading member in the government appointed by him.

For the first time in my life I must categorically refuse. Apart from the fact that on the grounds of fellow-feeling and personal loyalty we could never bring ourselves to leave the Führer alone in his hour of greatest need, I would otherwise appear for the rest of my life a dishonorable traitor and a common scoundrel and would lose my own self-respect as well as the respect of my fellow citizens, a respect that I should need in any further service in the future rebuilding of the German nation and the German state.

In the nightmare of treason that surrounds the Führer in these most critical days of the war, there must be at least some people to stay with him unconditionally until death, even if this contradicts the formal and, from a material point of view, entirely justifiable order that he gives in his political testament.

I believe I am thereby doing the best service to the future of the German people. In the hard times to come, examples will be more important than men. Men will always be found to show the nation the way out of its tribulations, but a reconstruction of the national life would be impossible if it were not inspired by examples that are clear and easily understandable.

For this reason, together with my wife and on behalf of my children, who are too young to be able to speak for themselves, and who if they were sufficiently old would agree with this decision without reservation, I express my unalterable decision not to leave the Reich capital even if it falls, and at the side of the Führer to end a life that for me personally will have no further value if I cannot spend it at the service of the Führer and at his side.

14   Italics in this document are mine.—W. L. S.

15   Question mark is Schwerin-Krosigk's.—W. L. S.

16   Italics are Schwerin-Krosigk's.—W. L. S.

17   In a speech at Stuttgart, Germany, on September 6, 1946, James F. Byrnes, then Secretary of State, declared that the United States favored giving the control of the Ruhr and Rhineland back to the Germans. His reasoning, it seems to me, bordered on the ridiculous. He said: "So far as the United States is aware, the people of the Ruhr and the Rhineland desire to remain united with the rest of Germany. And the United States will not oppose their desire." To allow the inhabitants of the Ruhr and the Rhineland to decide this all-important problem of European and world peace is sheer lunacy.

18   Schacht's italics.

19 Italics in the text of this report, unless otherwise noted, are mine.—W. L. S.

20 These italics are Hitler's.—W. L. S.

21 In the text of this document the italics unless otherwise noted, are mine.—W. L. S.

22 This time italics are Hitler's.—W. L. S.

23 Italics mine in this document.—W. L. S.

24 Italics in this document are mine.—W. L. S.

25 The official translator speaks here between the parentheses, but with some awkwardness. The word *Schweinehund*, a great favorite with the Nazis, simply means "damned pig."

26 Italics in this document are mine.—W. L. S.

27 Italics in this document are mine.—W. L. S.

28 This is a reference to the "bomb attempt" against Hitler in a Munich beer-cellar two weeks earlier. As we shall see, it was arranged by the Gestapo to stir up the people. There can be no doubt that Hitler knew this.

29 Italics in this document are mine.—W. L. S.

30 Italics in the text of this document are mine.—W. L. S.

31 Here, as in the last paragraph of page 254, Jodl is repeating the Hitler-Goebbels propaganda line that, had Germany not attacked Russia, Russia would have attacked Germany. I found in Germany that most Germans still believed it.

32 This, of course, is the fundamental reason why Britain was not invaded in the fall of 1940.—W. L. S.

33 For—says Clausewitz—every attack that does not lead either to an armistice or to peace must of necessity end in defense. [This is Jodl's footnote.]

34 Italics mine.—W. L. S.

35 The general, later executed at Nuremberg, was certainly not a bad prophet, considering that he spoke in 1943 and considering our own headlines in 1947.

36 Vlasov was a Soviet general who, after capture, attempted to raise an army from Russian prisoners of war to fight for the Germans.—W. L. S.

37 General Jodl seems—conveniently—to have forgotten Coventry and even London.—W. L. S.

38 Italics are mine.—W. L. S.

39 Italics mine.—W. L. S.

40 One also learned at Nuremberg that the Nazi-Soviet pact signed at Moscow on August 23, 1939, a week before Germany attacked Poland, contained a secret appendix providing for the division of eastern Europe into Russian and German spheres of influence. The State Department, which has a copy of this interesting document, declined to release it for publication in this book. But we know from the testimony of Baron Ernst von Weizsäcker,

former Secretary of the German Foreign Office, its main provisions. On May 21, 1946, Weizsäcker made the following statement to the tribunal in Nuremberg: "I know this document well. It was a comprehensive, extensive secret appendix to the non-aggression pact and partitioned spheres of influence and put in lines between areas that would come under the control of Russia and Germany. To the Soviet sphere went Finland, Estonia, Latvia, the eastern part of Poland and certain areas of Rumania, while anything west of the area belonged to the German sphere. In September or October [1939] a vital amendment gave Lithuania to the Soviet sphere and moved the demarcation line in Poland westward."

41   Italics mine.—W. L. S.

42   Italics mine.—W. L. S.

43   Italics mine.—W. L. S.

44   Italics mine.—W. L. S.

45   Italics mine.—W. L. S.

46   Later all three were convicted by German denazification courts, Schacht and von Papen receiving sentences of eight years at hard labor, and Fritzsche nine years.

Italics mine.—W. L. S.

Printed in Great Britain
by Amazon

44030235R00172